ACROSS GENERATIONS

RECIPES OF CARLENE BANKS & FRIENDS

ART FROM THE WICHITA ART MUSEUM

Artfully Done

FOOD, FLOWERS & JOY ACROSS GENERATIONS

BROUGHT TO YOU BY THE FRIENDS OF THE WICHITA ART MUSEUM

THE WICHITA ART MUSEUM

was established in 1915 when Louise Murdock's will created a trust for the acquisition of works by "American painters, potters, sculptors, and textile weavers." Her foresight made the Wichita Art Museum one of the earliest in the country to concentrate on American art.

Now the largest art museum in Kansas, the Wichita Art Museum is a major cultural center serving the state's largest city, the surrounding rural region and the Great Plains. Its mission is to collect, preserve and exhibit American art, and educate the public about America's artistic heritage and evolving cultural identity.

The Friends of the Wichita Art Museum, Inc.— affectionately known as "The Friends"— supports the Museum by raising funds for art acquisitions, exhibitions, and education as well as providing events and programs to promote participation in the Museum.

CURRENT ACTIVITIES AND MEMBERSHIP AT
WWW.WICHITAARTMUSEUM.ORG

Proceeds from the sale of this book benefit the

WICHITA*art*MUSEUM

Published by the
Friends of the Wichita Art Museum, Inc. (FWAM)
1400 W. Museum Blvd.; Wichita, Kansas 67203;
(316) 268-4936
For ordering information visit
www.artfullydonecookbook.com

Editor: RoxAnn Banks Dicker, Ph.D.
Curator: Stephen Gleissner, Ph.D.
Book Design: SaraBeth Dicker
Photographer: Kirk Eck
Assistant Editor: Analee Etheredge
Cookbook Development and Recipe Team:
Cindy Banks   Lee Banks, Chief Taster
Michele Banks   SaraBeth Dicker
Linda Ade Brand   Analee Etheredge
FWAM Chairperson: Mary Ellen Joyner
FWAM Sales Co-Chairs: Patty Bennett and Joan Seaton

First Edition
This cookbook is a collection of favorite recipes,
which are not necessarily original recipes.
Manufactured by
McCormick-Armstrong Co.; Wichita, Kansas
Printed in China

ISBN 10: 0-939324-53-9
ISBN 13: 978-0-939324-53-8

Cover and page 4: Russian goldsmiths, retailed by Tiffany & Co., *Demitasse Spoons*, 1908-1917, silver gilt and enamel, WAM 1964.24.

Page 1: Steuben Glass (Frederick Carder, designer), *Red Decorated Aurene Vase*, ca. 1910, lead glass, WAM, F. Price Cossman Memorial Trust, Intrust Bank, Trustee. 2007.6

Page 2: Donald Roller Wilson, *Cookie Had Seen One Before ... In Church During An Evening Service ... (About Seven Hours Past)*, 1992, oil on board, WAM, gift of the family of Elton I. "Buddy" Greenberg. 2007.2.9, © Donald Roller Wilson, 1992

Page 3: Severin Roesen, *Nature's Bounty*, ca. 1860, oil on canvas, WAM, gift of George E. Vollmer, 1995.15

Contents

DEDICATION

This cookbook represents not only many hours of hard work by various Friends of the Wichita Art Museum, but, more importantly, deep commitment by many to the art museum as institution and to the concept of volunteerism. Volunteers are the backbone of any art museum. Few museums can afford to pay the number of staff that they require. Besides, to be an effective cultural vehicle, an art museum must reflect the tastes and interests of its community.

No one exemplified the ideal museum volunteer more than my friend and colleague-- the late Carlene Banks. Carlene was at once a Trustee of the Museum, a Board member of the Friends, a chairwoman of various events from galas to ladies' luncheons, worker bee, and cheerleader. During her lifetime, the Wichita Art Museum worked as efficiently as a machine because Carlene saw to it that every aspect of its program was a success. Whether she had to make and bring in 100 tea sandwiches or hang holiday decorations, Carlene was indispensable to our Wichita Art Museum. Her legacy will be remembered for years to come, and immortalized with this cookbook. Thanks to all who contributed to this publication and my sincerest thanks to the underwriters who so generously made it possible.

Charles K. Steiner
Executive Director

Artfully Done

Gastronomy: the oldest of the arts and the one
that has done the most to advance civilization.
Jean Anthelme Brillat-Savarin, *The Physiology of Taste*

Could such a claim be an overstatement? Not when we recall that one of the shrewdest statesmen of modern Europe, the Prince Talleyrand-Périgord, won many of his diplomatic victories not through arms, but through the arts of his personal chef, the maestro Antonin Carême.

Indeed, it is entirely appropriate that the Wichita Art Museum associate itself with a cookbook, for food, when it is orchestrated beyond mere nourishment, enters the realm of art. There are numerous ties between the fine arts and fine food. The above-mentioned Carême himself wrote, "The fine arts are five in number, namely: painting, sculpture, poetry, music, and architecture, the principal branch of the latter being pastry."

The myriad connections between fine art and food include art created to enhance the experience of food, the artful presentation of food, and artist-historians who are equally at home in both worlds. Among the latter are the novelist Alexandre Dumas, père, who considered his magnum opus to be a history of food (*The Great Dictionary of Cuisine*, 1873); Baron Karl Frederick von Rumohr,

pioneer scholar of Italian Renaissance painting, who also wrote *The Essence of Cooking* (1826), praised by Hegel and still considered a masterpiece of culinary literature; and more recently, Professor Phyllis Bober, co-author of the great *Census of Classical Works of Art Known to the Renaissance*, and author of *Art, Culture, and Cuisine: Ancient and Medieval Gastronomy* (1999).

A considerable portion of the art of the world's major museums was created to enhance the experience of fine food. Augustus the Strong of Saxony demanded of Böttger that he invent a European porcelain (which he did in 1708) so that his table could rival those of the Chinese emperors. During the late 19th century in America, silversmiths and jewelers such as Tiffany and Gorham designed the most refined tools for food consumption ever known. One could buy special spoons for eating peas, mixed berries, strawberries, jelly, ice cream, or for stirring coffee (see the jacket of this book). This is remarkable, considering that the simple fork wasn't common at European courts until the late 17th century!

That Wichita, Kansas is home to a museum with a collection that includes objects like those mentioned above is due largely to the generosity and dedication of three generations of women. The leader of the first generation is the Museum's founder: Louise Caldwell Murdock (1856-1915), whose Will stipulated that her estate be used for the purchase of an art collection for the community. The pivotal figure of the second generation was Elizabeth Stubblefield Navas (died 1979), who formed the Roland P. Murdock Collection. The third generation was led not by a single figure, but by a group: The Friends of the Wichita Art Museum, of which the dedicatee of this cookbook was a long-standing and loyal member.

Parallel with the development of the Wichita Art Museum by three generations of patrons are three major phases of the history of cookery in the United States. Mrs. Murdock's time was that of the widest gap between the cuisine of the most privileged and that of average Americans. Mrs. Navas witnessed the fluorescence of cookery in the Anglo-Saxon world. Mrs. Banks and the Friends are part of the current phase of advancement of the achievements of the Navas era.

Louise Caldwell Murdock regarded art as she did food: as an essential component of a life lived well. Art was thought to be as much a part of a good life as was knowledge (her husband was the co-founder of the *Wichita Eagle* newspaper), literature, nature, and food. One imagines her dishes as savory as those in Fannie Farmer's book (1st edition 1896). In reality, judging from the recipe of hers reprinted on page 20 of this book and others exchanged among her friends, the best words one could use to describe her cooking are "simple" and "uncomplicated." They are recipes that do not inspire recreation. Yet her more privileged urban contemporaries were enjoying haute cuisine at the pinnacle of its development in the Western world. August Escoffier had brought to the height of refinement the canon of gastronomy as codified by Carême in the early 19th century. Nor were Escoffier's wonders appreciated only in Europe. Charles Ranhofer at Delmonico's in New York served cuisine of comparable perfection. His Baked Alaska and Lobster Newberg are still considered notable American contributions to the repertoire of haute cuisine (his book, *The Epicurean*, 1894, is available in reprint).

The enormous disparity between the food served in most American kitchens and that served at Delmonico's was considerably narrowed during Mrs. Navas' generation. From the 1930s through the '70s, the writing and proselytizing of Irma Rombauer, James Beard, Craig Claiborne, Julia Child, and Richard Olney, among others, changed the way Americans ate and appreciated food; following the lead of Elizabeth David in England and the masters of haute cuisine in France, they taught us to respect the seasons, proper technique, experimentation, and the cuisine of other cultures.

The Wichita Art Museum moved from a concept to a reality at the same time as Americans learned to see food as an art. Parallel events in the development of the Art Museum and of 20th-century gastronomy include the following:

1935: The Art Museum building, designed by Clarence Stein, opened in Riverside. The following year saw the publication of the first commercial edition of *The Joy of Cooking*, which remains one of America's most loved and used cookbooks.

1949: Mrs. Navas purchased Kuniyoshi's *Revelation* the same year that M. F. K. Fisher's magisterial translation of Brillat-Savarin's *The Physiology of Taste* of 1826 was published.

1950-51: Significant paintings are added to the collection, including Prendergast's *Boat Landing, Dinard* and Demuth's *African Daisies*; Elizabeth David published, first, *Mediterranean Food*, then *French Country Cooking*. Her books introduced to the pale Anglo-Saxon world the ingredients, smells, tastes, and sensations of a sunnier world.

1961: Sadly, this is the last year for additions to the Murdock Collection, but it is a landmark year for American art, for Jackie Kennedy appointed Henry Francis DuPont to refurnish the White House with period American fine and decorative arts. She also appointed Rene Verdon chef at the White House. (His *White House Chef Cookbook* appeared in 1967, after he had been fired by Lyndon Johnson for refusing to grill steaks on the White House lawn.)

The generation of Carlene Banks and the Friends expanded upon the achievements of the previous generation, both at the Museum and in their kitchens. The year 1971 saw both the beginning of discussion of a major Museum expansion (realized in 1977) and the opening of Alice Waters' Chez Panisse restaurant in Berkley. The development of the Art Museum collection and the advancement of American cuisine continue. In 2007 the Museum added 255 glass objects to its already strong collections of historic American pressed glass and Steuben of both the Carder and Houghton eras. The same year saw the publication of Alice Waters' *The Art of Simple Food*.

A measure of the health of a culture is the vitality of its cuisine. Key to that vitality is a balance between tradition and experimentation—having core ingredients and techniques that don't become atrophied, but are constantly enlivened by experiment. And key to experiment is exchange, which is what we hope this book inspires: exchange not only of meals and recipes, but also of ideas about what constitutes good food and the good life.

In the future, when historians examine *Artfully Done* for what it says about the Wichita of its time, we might imagine them admiring not only the joy-de-vivre expressed in the recipes, stories, and exchanges, but also how markedly the local culture of cuisine had developed since the time of Mrs. Murdock. *Bon appetite!*

Stephen Gleissner, Ph.D
Chief Curator

ACROSS GENERATIONS

A great museum is not built within a generation, but grows through the work of more than one. Works of art in a museum, like recipes in a kitchen, are material objects of the human touch: made, treasured, gifted, sold and traded. As they move among people they develop histories that traverse generational time, connecting human genealogies as they move through differing regimes of significance and value. As a participant in this process, Carlene enjoyed reading community cookbooks, glimpsing into the lives of the authors and hometown history, gathering that which would enrich her own life and those around her. Author Marian Cunningham notes in *Lost Recipes*: "There is something communal about having shared recipes, about passing tastes and flavors from friend to friend and from generation to generation." As Cunningham's, this book brings forward the best of the past: those recipes which should not be forgotten or lost. It also celebrates the joy of the exchange, the dynamic conditions under which they exist and the resulting warm connections.

Home cooks have power with ingenuity and creativity to encourage and nourish that which is good by gathering others to the table.

Among virtually every culture on Earth, anything worth doing is best done over dinner. Bring out a nicely braised roast, a hot loaf of bread, and a slice of lemon pie, and rifts can be healed, pacts sealed, love revealed.
— Natalie Angier, New York Times, *November 2000*

Art in museums, like a savory meal, provides a focal point for individuals and families to coalesce, have a common experience and discuss events and perceptions. Art, like food, provides a portal for learning more about each other, connecting. This book is about that which is universally enjoyed in food and art, but more importantly about enjoyment and connecting.

Carlene kept chairs in the kitchen. If you could swivel fast enough, you'd see her kicking up a dust cloud, blazing the proverbial culinary trail, throwing down wholesome and inventive plates, and documenting each twist and turn in her notebooks stuffed with recipes. These notebooks held recipes of her own, and those of her friends and mentors. Warm and generous, but ever the fundraiser, her recipes for community events were often rolled up in a scroll and sold at the event; here you will find the complete volume. Proudly, the profits from this book will provide support for the Wichita Art Museum (WAM).

She was passionate about bringing art into Wichita's greater community and would be immeasurably pleased about the way this book provides an enlarged audience for works of art from the WAM collection. While she worked on many events to bring us to the museum, here some of the collection comes to you, replete with engaging commentary and creatively disguised as a cookbook. *Artfully Done* is an outcome of an imaginative museum environment that transcends mere presentation by engaging our community so that we may be nourished in a deeper, richer way by the collection. The Museum and the artists whose work is represented in these pages have been incredibly openhanded. Every artist, or their heirs, generously waived significant fees for reproduction rights. I have enjoyed lively correspondence with a number of the artists and have been greatly enriched by the opportunity to learn more about the collection.

Had it not been for the enthusiasm of the staff and administration of the Museum and the Board of the Friends of the Wichita Art Museum (Friends), this project could easily have been relegated to the back burner (pun intended). It is with sincerest appreciation that I acknowledge the steadfast encouragement of Mary Ellen Joyner, Friends Chairperson, and open door access to Charles Steiner, WAM Executive Director. I am beholden to the talents of Dr. Stephen Gleissner, WAM Chief Curator, for ongoing inspiration and providing insightful narration in this book about the works of art and the artists. (You will enjoy these comments in the margin notes, marked by 'SG'.) Artist and WAM photographer, Kirk Eck, has provided outstanding images of the selected works of art. Both Stephen and Kirk deserve community gratitude for their roles in advancing this book beyond any initial expectation. Thanks too to the Friends board, Patty Bennett and Joan Seaton for carrying things forward now. You have been friends as much as Friends. Much of the enthusiasm for this stunning, original book is owed to the bounty of the team effort from these talented individuals. Thank you.

Thanks also to the extended circle of Carlene's family and friends, who, while hunting errant commas, dangling participles and ingredient measurements, demonstrated our mutual commitment to provide this book. Carlene, at the request of her good friend Paula Varner, began compiling this cookbook in the month before she died in December 2006. Actually though, she had been at work on it for years at her computer, having typed many recipes at the request of those enjoying her cooking. Sitting by my mother's bedside in her final weeks, I recorded comments as we went through recipes, and scribbled quickly as she dictated those not previously written down. Stories brought good laughs and her many comments of "don't forget to …."

Since that time the cooks in the family have come together to compile the recipes. Thank you to the extended Banks family, Carlene's family, for making this book possible: some by active work, others for meal gathering while the cooks toiled on the manuscript. Thank you to her daughters-in-law, Michele and Cindy, as well as her niece Linda for their many contributions to this book; to my father for helping the dream grow; and to my daughters, Analee who served as assistant editor while sharing her grandmother's passion for cooking (and often her sous-chef) and SaraBeth, for her design of this book through which she continues to share her grandmother's interest in art as a professional graphic designer.

We have been greatly enriched by the recipe contributors (p. 281), who have been generous in sharing their heirloom, treasured recipes to accompany Carlene's collection. From everyone that helped, we bring to press this lavishly illustrated book which delivers glimpses of the museum collection to your kitchen table.

Completing this book was a family labor of love but you will find the notes through the book written in first person from Carlene. Her voice has been heard in my head as I have finished putting words on paper and describing her methods; I think more of her context in culinary history, admiring how she transformed her experience – from pioneer to technophile. There was much she could have complained about, but didn't. There was little said about the hardship of living through the Depression, although her values were shaped by that time. Reconstructing the time period of her recipes has helped me understand the vast changes in food and food preparation over the past 75 years. One generation is skilled in making a meal out of seemingly little, the next honors the advent of the electric icebox with gelatin molds, and the next is atwitter about balsamic vinegar and goat cheese. The common thread through the course of time is not ingredients or technique per se, but rather the act of cooking, the act of caring, the portal for connection and nourishment.

Boldly beautiful, *Artfully Done* is packed full of art, good food and stories; the pages are awash with creamy emulsions of creativity, the joy of living and often, butter. Both art and food can nourish one's soul and rejuvenate the spirit. May you find such here.

A grateful daughter,
RoxAnn Banks Dicker, Ph.D.

About the Recipes

Some recipes, which are not cooked use raw eggs, so make sure that your eggs are safe before trying that recipe or if appropriate, use dehydrated egg whites.

When an herb or spice is mentioned, unless otherwise stated, the dried herb is intended. To get the most flavor from dried herbs in leaf form, remember to crush them between your fingers before adding to the dish and to use fresh dried spices and herbs.

For brevity the recipes have been edited for the following:
- unbleached all-purpose flour is used measured without sifting;
- the preference is to use large AA eggs and whole milk, unless you would like to make a lighter version of a particular recipe (in which case, try 2 or 1 percent, avoid fat free milk);
- for sautéing and frying, pure olive oil is fine, but for salad dressings and uncooked dishes use extra virgin;
- when stocks are called for, if you are using canned stocks, try to use low-sodium when available;
- recipes assume use of a medium pan and medium heat, unless noted.

Appetizers

Annie's Famous Caviar Mousse 12
Chèvre with Sun-Dried Tomatoes 13
Chile Relleno Tart 13
Goat Cheese, Pesto and Sun-Dried Tomato Torta 14
Southwest Cheesecake 14
Spicy Shrimp with Capers 15
Thai Style Chicken in Won Ton Cups 15
Chutney and Cheese 15
Phyllo Wrapped Brie with Raspberries 16
Wild Mushroom Torte 16
Bulgarian Bonitzas 17
Chicken Boursin Bundles 17
Spinach Artichoke High Rollers 18
Carmelized Onion and Gorgonzola Tartlets 18
Roquefort Grapes 18
Pita Chips with Za'atar 19
Roasted Red Pepper Hummus 19
Stuffed Tomato Caps 20
Stuffed Strawberries 20
Beer and Cheese Fondue 20
Classic Blue Cheese Crumble 21
Rum Glazed Spiced Nuts 21
Rosemary Walnuts 21
Mozzarella, Tomato and Artichoke Bruschetta 22
Crostini 22
Tapenades: Sun-dried Tomato, Roasted Garlic ,
    Olive, Artichoke and Roasted Pepper 23
Hot Asiago Artichoke Dip 24
Roasted Artichoke Dip 24
Brie Bread 24
Artichoke Cheese Spread 25
Mushroom Spread 25
Spicy Smoked Salmon Spread 25
Curried Chicken Salad Spread 26
Hot Swiss Bacon Dip 26
Vegetable Curry Dip 26
Queso Blanco 26
Hot Pepper Peach Cheeseball 27
Crispy Wontons with Ahi Tuna and Wasabi Cream 27
Poppyseed Blue Cheese Crackers 28
Crispy Cheese Crackers 28
Cheese Puffs 28
Parmesan Pepper Frico 28
Parmesan Baskets 29
Hot Cheese Canapes 30
Cheese Straws 30
Sesame Cheese Straws 30
Parmesan Cheese Twists 30
Hot Ham Canapes with Raspberry Chipotle Sauce 31
Finger Sandwiches: Chicken Salad, Olive-Nut, Onion,
    Turkey Basil Scallion Raisin, Curried Chicken,
    and Cucumber Sandwiches 32 and 33

PLANNING a wonderful start

More often called "starters" now, appetizers today are a far cry from the shrimp cocktail on the side of a radish-and-olive plate served 30 years ago. They can make a significant contribution to the pleasure of the event, and are a showcase where you can take risks in awakening the appetite. The challenge can be figuring out not only what to serve but also how much to provide for the gathering.

General rules are 4 to 6 appetizer servings per person if preceding a meal, or 4 to 6 appetizers per *hour* per guest if served during the dinner hour. Expand the number of choices with the size of the group. For a dinner party of 6 to 10 people, serve just 2 or 3 appetizer items. For a cocktail party of 30 to 50 guests, provide 5 or 6 choices. For 50 to 70 guests, serve 7 to 8 choices; increasing the number of selections accordingly for larger events.

A pleasing array for a cocktail party will include a cheese item, a fruit and/or vegetable item, a seafood item, and a meat hors d'oeuvre. At least one low-fat appetizer is always a welcome addition. When estimating cheese, plan on one ounce per person. For dinner party appetizers, include at least one vegetarian item. Add bulk to your selections with pre-made items such as nuts, olives, or savory bread sticks to graze on.

ANNIE'S FAMOUS CAVIAR MOUSSE

The following recipe makes a three-layer mousse, which is a pretty and very yummy appetizer. This recipe will create thin layers. Double the amounts of each ingredient if you choose to make thicker layers, or use a smaller spring form pan.

2 envelopes unflavored gelatin
$1/3$ cup cold water
4 hard boiled eggs, chopped
$1/2$ cup mayonnaise
$1/4$ cup finely chopped fresh parsley
1 large green onion, finely chopped
Hot pepper sauce
Salt, freshly ground black pepper and
    white pepper

2 medium ripe avocados
2 tablespoons fresh lemon juice plus more
    for caviar
1 shallot, finely chopped
$1/4$ cup finely chopped red onion
1 cup sour cream
4 ounces caviar
Crackers, bread or biscuits

Previous page:

Donald Roller Wilson
Cookie Had Seen One
Before . . . In Church During
An Evening Service . . .
(About Seven Hours
Past), 1992, oil on board,
WAM, gift of family of
Elton I. "Buddy" Greenberg,
2007.2.9, © Donald
Roller Wilson, 1992

Coat an 8-inch springform pan with cooking spray. If you like, you can line the bottom with wax paper for easier unmolding. Soften gelatin in cold water and heat over very low heat until just dissolved. Combine the eggs, mayonnaise, parsley, green onion and a dash of hot pepper sauce with 2 tablespoons of gelatin. Season to taste with salt and white pepper. Spread in the bottom of the pan and refrigerate. Mash the avocados then stir in the shallots, lemon juice, a dash of hot pepper sauce, and 2 tablespoons gelatin. Season to taste with salt and black pepper. Spread over the first layer and refrigerate. Combine the sour cream, red onion and remaining gelatin and spread carefully over the second layer. Cover with plastic wrap and chill at least 3 hours or overnight.

Just before serving, spread caviar onto a thick layer of paper towels and squeeze with lemon juice; then let drain well. Spread over the mousse. Unmold onto a large serving platter and encircle with crackers, water biscuits, buttered rye toasts or your favorite cracker-type dipper. Serve with knives so that each guest gets the flavors from each layer. Makes 10 to 12 servings. From Ann Garvey.

CHÈVRE with SUN-DRIED TOMATOES

½ cup sun-dried tomatoes, packed in oil, drained, rinsed and minced
1 clove garlic, minced
2 tablespoons olive oil

1 tablespoon chopped fresh rosemary
1 (11-ounce) package goat cheese (log)
Garnish: fresh rosemary and parsley

Reserve oil from the sun-dried tomatoes for use in vinaigrettes — it packs a lot of flavor.

Combine tomatoes with garlic, oil and rosemary. Cover and chill for 1 to 8 hours. Place goat cheese on serving tray. Spoon tomato mixture over top. Garnish with fresh rosemary sprigs and parsley. Serve with crackers or fresh vegetables. Makes 12 servings.

CHILE RELLENO TART

Served in thin wedges, this is a great appetizer; but sliced larger, it is also good as an entrée.

Crust
⅔ cup corn meal
⅓ cup flour
¼ teaspoon salt
¼ cup butter, melted
¼ cup boiling water

Filling
2 eggs, slightly beaten
¾ cup milk
1 tablespoon flour
¼ teaspoon cayenne pepper
¼ teaspoon salt
1 (7-ounce) can chopped green chilies, drained
1¼ cups shredded Cheddar cheese
1¼ cups shredded Monterey Jack cheese

Preheat oven to 350°F. Coat a 9-inch tart pan with cooking spray, or butter lightly. Combine corn meal, flour, and salt in a bowl; stir in butter. Add water, stirring until well mixed. Spread into tart pan, pressing firmly and evenly over bottom and sides. Bake for 10 minutes while preparing the filling. Whisk together eggs, milk, flour, cayenne pepper and salt. Stir in green chilies. Mix cheeses together; sprinkle one-third of cheese on crust. Stir remaining cheese into egg mixture and pour into tart shell. Return to oven and bake in lower third of oven for 45 minutes or until filling is slightly puffed in center and golden. Cool 20 minutes before cutting. To serve, cut into thin wedges. Garnish as desired. Serve warm or room temperature. Makes 16 appetizer servings (or 8 as an entrée). From Bonnie Aeschliman.

Steuben Glass (Frederick Carder, designer)
Rouge Flambé Vase,
ca. 1920, lead glass,
WAM, F. Price Cossman
Memorial Trust, Intrust Bank,
Trustee, 2007.5.

GOAT CHEESE, PESTO AND SUN-DRIED TOMATO TORTA

This torta is not only a beautiful display but also packs great flavor and can be made ahead: a trifecta of winning attributes for a starter. If you happen to have any leftovers, toss the torta with some pasta.

$^1/_2$ to $^3/_4$ cup pesto (recipe below,
   or purchased)
1 (11 ounce) package goat cheese
1 (8-ounce) package cream cheese, softened
4 garlic cloves, minced
$^1/_2$ teaspoon salt

$^1/_4$ teaspoon pepper
$^3/_4$ cup sun-dried tomatoes, packed in oil,
   drained, rinsed, patted dry and minced
$^1/_4$ cup finely chopped pine nuts
Garnishes: fresh basil sprigs, pecans, pine nuts
   French baguette slices

Prepare pesto; set aside. Line a 3-cup bowl with plastic wrap, allowing 4 inches to hang over sides (keeps torta from sticking to the bowl when you are ready to invert and serve), coat lightly with cooking spray. Blend goat cheese, cream cheese, garlic, salt and pepper with a mixer or food processor until smooth. Spread half of cheese mixture into bowl; top evenly with $^1/_2$ to $^3/_4$ cup pesto, half of sun-dried tomatoes and half of pine nuts. Repeat layers with remaining ingredients. Tap bowl lightly to help ingredients settle. Fold plastic wrap overhang over top, and chill at least 8 hours (or up to 3 days). Thirty minutes before serving invert chilled torta onto a serving platter; remove plastic wrap. Garnish with sun-dried tomato slices, fresh basil sprigs, pecans or pine nuts. Serve with baguette slices or crackers. Makes 10 to 12 servings.

Pesto

$^1/_4$ cup chopped pecans
$^1/_4$ cup pine nuts
$2^1/_2$ cups firmly packed fresh basil leaves
$^1/_2$ cup chopped fresh parsley

2 garlic cloves, chopped
$^2/_3$ cup olive oil (divided use)
$^3/_4$ cup shredded Parmesan cheese

Toast pecans and pine nuts at 350°F for 12 to 15 minutes or until toasted, stirring once. Let cool 5 minutes. Process basil, parsley, garlic, and $^1/_3$ cup olive oil in a food processor until coarse paste forms. Add nuts and cheese, and process until blended. Add remaining $^1/_3$ cup oil in a slow, steady stream while processor is running. Cover and chill up to 5 days. Makes $1^1/_2$ cups.

SOUTHWEST CHEESECAKE

This can be easily made a day ahead. Adapted from recipe published in Southern Living *magazine.*

Bringing the eggs to room temperature helps them to incorporate easier.

$1^1/_2$ cups finely crushed blue tortilla chips
$^1/_4$ cup butter, softened
2 (8-ounce) packages cream cheese, softened
2 cups (8 ounces) shredded Monterey
   Jack cheese
$^1/_4$ teaspoon salt
3 (8-ounce) containers sour cream (divided use)

3 eggs, room temperature
1 cup thick and chunky salsa
1 (4-ounce) can chopped green chilies, drained
1 cup fresh or frozen (thawed) guacamole
1 medium-size tomato, seeded and diced
Banana pepper slices (or jalapeno)
Tortilla chips or crackers

Preheat oven to 350°F. Combine crushed tortilla chips and butter, and press into bottom of a 9-inch springform pan coated with cooking spray. Bake for 12 minutes. Cool on a wire rack; leave oven on.

Beat cream cheese, cheese, and salt at medium speed with an electric mixer until fluffy (about 3 minutes). Add one container of sour cream, beating until blended. Add eggs, one at a time, beating until blended; stir in salsa and chilies. Pour over prepared crust. Bake for 40 minutes, or until center is almost set. Remove pan from oven; let stand 10 minutes on wire rack. Run a knife around edge of pan to loosen sides. Remove sides of pan; let cheesecake cool completely. Stir remaining two containers of sour cream together until smooth; spread evenly over top of cooled cheesecake. Cover and chill at least 3 hours, or up to 1 day. Spread evenly with guacamole; sprinkle with diced tomatoes and banana pepper slices before serving. Serve with tortilla chips. Makes 20 to 25 servings.

SPICY SHRIMP with CAPERS

Served at Wichita Symphony Showhouse Patron dinner, this looks beautiful and has just the right amount of spice.

2¹/₂ pounds shrimp, cleaned, cooked
  and deveined
1 large red onion, sliced
8 bay leaves
2 cups white vinegar

1 cup vegetable oil
3 tablespoons capers, undrained
2¹/₂ teaspoons celery seed
1¹/₂ teaspoon salt
2 teaspoons hot pepper sauce

Alternate shrimp and onions (separated into rings) in a container or a large zipper-lock plastic bag. Combine remaining ingredients in a small bowl and mix well. Pour over shrimp. Cover and chill 4 to 8 hours and stir occasionally. Remove bay leaves, and drain liquid before serving. To serve, arrange in a bowl mounded on ice, or better yet, in the lemon ice bowl described in the margin note.

THAI STYLE CHICKEN in WON TON CUPS

¹/₄ cup fresh lime juice
1 teaspoon salt
1 teaspoon Thai fish sauce
¹/₂ teaspoon chili powder
¹/₄ cup finely chopped cilantro
¹/₂ teaspoon sugar
3 cups cooked, finely chopped, chicken breast

¹/₃ cup minced green onions
¹/₄ cup chopped roasted peanuts
¹/₄ cup mayonnaise
24 won ton skins
Melted butter
Garnish: chopped red bell pepper (optional)

Combine lime juice, salt, fish sauce, chili powder, cilantro and sugar. Stir into chicken, add green onions and peanuts. Add enough mayonnaise to just moisten. (May be made 1 day in advance, covered and refrigerated.) To make the won ton cups, preheat oven to 375°F. Brush won ton skins with butter. Press into mini-muffin tins. Bake for 5 to 8 minutes or until crispy and golden. Cool. Store in airtight container. Right before serving, fill and garnish. (Instead of the won ton cups, you may serve in "cups" made of small endive leaves.) Makes 2 dozen appetizers. From Bonnie Aeschliman.

CHUTNEY and CHEESE

Festive and ambrosial! Mary Ellen Barrier describes her recipe as, "a good peppy chutney that I use as an hors d'oeuvre, spread over a round of cheese (I usually use a port wine Cheddar), with chopped green onions sprinkled over the top. The crystallized ginger is the important ingredient and gives the chutney its piquancy. Sometimes I increase the garlic and sometimes I add a little more cayenne, all to your taste."

1 lemon, chopped (seeds removed)
1 clove garlic, minced
5 cups peeled, chopped firm apples
  (I use Jonathan)
2¹/₄ cups brown sugar
1¹/₂ cups raisins

3 ounces crystallized ginger, chopped
1¹/₂ teaspoons salt
¹/₄ teaspoon cayenne pepper
2 cups cider vinegar
Garnish: chopped green onion

Combine ingredients in a small pan and cook until fruit is tender and sauce has thickened. Cool to room temperature. Place cheese block on serving tray, spoon chutney over top of cheese, garnish with chopped green onion. Serve with crisp crackers, sliced French baguette or rye bread. Makes a wonderful appetizer or gift, wrapped in cellophane. From Mary Ellen Barrier.

Nice to serve this in an attractive lemony ice bowl.

Just find two bowls to stack, one slightly smaller than the other. Fill the larger bowl with water and sliced lemon, place the smaller bowl on top and weigh down the center with a heavy can. Freeze.

Remove the can and both bowls. Place ice bowl on a plate and fill with shrimp.

PHYLLO WRAPPED BRIE with RASPBERRIES

This is a beautiful dish: the phyllo is golden browned and when you cut into the brie the cheese oozes out and the pretty raspberries just peek through.

1 pound phyllo pastry sheets (thawed)
1 cup unsalted butter, melted
1 (32 to 36-ounce) wheel of Brie cheese

1/2 cup raspberry preserves or jam (seedless)
1 teaspoon fresh rosemary leaves, finely chopped
1/4 teaspoon freshly ground black pepper

Brush a heavy baking sheet with oil or line with parchment paper. Unroll pastry. Cover with plastic wrap and damp kitchen towel. Transfer 2 stacked phyllo sheets to work surface, arrange the short side parallel to the work surface edge. Place 2 more stacked sheets on work surface, overlapping long side of first sheet by 2 to 3 inches to form a rectangle about 14 x 16 inches. Brush pastry with butter. Place 2 more stacked sheets atop first set of 2 sheets; then 2 more stacked sheets over second set of 2 sheets. Brush with butter. Repeat layering one more time with phyllo and butter. You will use a total of 12 sheets. Using sharp knife or pizza wheel, trim phyllo corners, forming a large oval.

The best way to defrost frozen phyllo is in the refrigerator overnight, or at room temperature for 3 to 4 hours.

Cut top rind off cheese; discard (freezing the Brie for a few minutes will firm it up and make it easier to trim off the rind). Place cheese, rind-less side up, in center of the pastry. Spoon raspberry jam onto cheese. Sprinkle with rosemary and black pepper. Lift one side of phyllo and fold on top of cheese. Brush folded pastry with butter. Continue to lift phyllo in and pleat or gather it neatly over cheese, brushing with butter and pressing each section to adhere until cheese is wrapped. The top center 2 to 3 inches will not be covered. Use hand and large metal spatula to transfer wrapped cheese to prepared baking sheet.

Make sure that the sheets you are using are not badly torn.

My preferred brand of frozen phyllo is 'Athens'.

To make flowers to cover the opening: Place 1 phyllo sheet on work surface. Brush with butter. Starting with the long side, fold pastry in half. Continue to brush with butter and fold until it is 1 inch wide. Fold under 1/4 inch of one end; then gather pastry up around folded end to make a petal; pinch the base to hold in place. Continue gathering and pinching bottom until flower is formed. Brush with butter and place flower atop uncovered center of cheese. Repeat with additional sheets of phyllo, forming more flowers until all the exposed raspberries are covered. Remember to brush all flowers with butter. Chill 3 hours.

Position rack in center of oven and preheat to 400°F. Bake cheese until pastry is deep golden brown, covering flowers loosely with foil if browning too quickly, about 25 minutes. If cheese leaks from pastry during baking, press piece of foil over tears in pastry; continue baking. Cool cheese on sheet 45 minutes, then using a wide spatula, place on serving tray. Garnish as desired. From Bonnie Aeschliman.

WILD MUSHROOM TORTE

No fuss with this phyllo recipe: just spritz the phyllo sheets with cooking spray and then layer.

6 pints assorted mushrooms, finely chopped
1/4 cup minced shallots
1 1/2 teaspoons minced garlic
1 (8-ounce) package cream cheese, softened
2 tablespoons chopped fresh basil

1 tablespoon coarsely ground black pepper
Salt to taste
10 phyllo pastry sheets, thawed
Rye melba toast rounds

Sauté mushrooms, shallots and garlic in a nonstick pan until they are tender and the juices have evaporated. Remove from heat and let cool. Mix cream cheese, basil, pepper and salt in a bowl and then stir in the mushroom mixture. Fit one of the phyllo sheets over the bottom of a 6-inch springform pan and fold into the edge of the pan. Spray lightly with olive oil cooking spray; layer with another phyllo sheet and spray with cooking spray. Repeat process 5 more times, resulting in 5 layers. Spread mushroom mixture over the layers; bring edges of pastry together to the center, enclosing the filling; twist the top to resemble a flower. Decorate the torte with shapes cut from remaining phyllo sheets. Bake for 25 minutes. Serve warm with melba rounds. Makes 12 servings.

BULGARIAN BONITZAS

Marni Vliet shares that "Bonitzas (pronounced bon' itz ahh) are a family tradition for an appetizer or special treat. This very loose 'recipe' was handed down from my father's (Jim Tasheff) family from Bulgaria. We bake these for all special occasions in the Tasheff and Vliet families. Even if your family is not Bulgarian, we promise these treats will be a hit!"

1 package phyllo dough
$^1/_2$ to $^3/_4$ cup butter, melted
16 ounces feta cheese, crumbled

8 ounces Cheddar cheese, grated (optional)
1 egg, beaten (for egg wash)

Preheat oven to 375°F. Remove phyllo dough one sheet at a time and lay on your work surface with the short side toward you. Paint sheet with a quick "Z" of butter across the sheet (not too much). Sprinkle 2 to 3 tablespoons feta over the sheet. Sprinkle with 1 tablespoon of cheddar cheese, if desired, which makes the bonitzas buttery tasting. Fold in the two long sides leaving a 1 to 2 inch gap in the center. Then from the end closest to you, roll into a cigar shape about 2 inches in diameter. Lay seam side down on cookie sheets about $^1/_2$ inch apart. Repeat process for each of the phyllo sheets. Bake for 20 to 25 minutes, then turn over and brush with egg wash. Return for 10 to 15 minutes until golden brown. Remove from cookie sheet and cool on paper towel lined cooling racks. Cut in half or into quarters and serve warm or at room temperature. Freezes well. Makes about 24. From Marni and Rich Vliet.

CHICKEN BOURSIN BUNDLES

These look and taste like a whole lot more work went into them.

8 phyllo sheets
$^1/_4$ to $^1/_2$ cup butter, melted
4 or 5 chicken tenderloins, cut into $^1/_2$-inch
    pieces (about 2 cups)

1 (5-ounce) carton French garlic and herb
    cream cheese (such as Boursin or Alloute),
    room temperature
1 tablespoon chopped or grated onion
Salt and pepper

Allow phyllo to thaw. Carefully unroll sheets on a smooth dry surface. Remove number of sheets needed and return remaining to package (refrigerate or freeze for later use). Cover phyllo completely with plastic wrap then damp towel. Keep covered until needed. Combine French herb cheese with grated onion.

Place 4 phyllo sheets on countertop. Brush each with melted butter (or butter flavored cooking spray). Cut into 4-inch squares. Spoon about $^1/_2$ teaspoon French herb cheese in middle of each piece. Top with a piece of chicken tenderloin. Season generously with salt and pepper. Gather edges of phyllo dough and pinch together right above filling; spread top edges apart (tie with a blanched onion scallion if desired). Brush with melted butter. Repeat process with remaining ingredients.

Preheat oven to 425°F. Place pouches 1 inch apart on ungreased baking sheet. Freeze filled phyllo for 10 minutes before baking to set the shape of the pouch. Bake on lower rack for 10 minutes or until golden. Cool. Serve warm or room temperature. Adapted from recipe by Bonnie Aeschliman.

SPINACH ARTICHOKE HIGH ROLLERS

These make an attractive presentation mounded on a platter or a cake plate.

Appetizers don't have to be difficult, as I hope you can see from some of these recipes. If you are short on time or want to just have something tucked away "in case", you might consider some of the purchased options.

There are a few good commercially-made frozen hors d'oeuvres you can pop in the oven 10 minutes before your guests arrive, although there are also many horrible ones on the market. Be sure to test.

I recommend pre-made party fare from The Perfect Bite (see "Favorite Things" for how to purchase). Handmade by two chefs who have had a catering business, their products are made from scratch. Try their Caramelized Onion and Feta Pastry Kisses, but then also realize that the recipe here for the Carmelized Onion Tartlets is not difficult and is so delicious.

1 (10-ounce) package frozen chopped spinach, thawed
1 (14-ounce) can artichoke hearts, drained
1/2 cup mayonnaise
1/2 cup grated Parmesan cheese
1 teaspoon onion powder
1 teaspoon garlic powder
1/2 teaspoon pepper
1 (17 1/2-ounce) package of frozen puff pastry, thawed

Drain thawed spinach well by pressing between paper towels. Stir artichoke hearts together with next five ingredients, and then add in spinach. Unfold puff pastry and place on a large piece of heavy-duty plastic wrap. Spread a quarter of spinach mixture over the puff pastry sheet, leaving a 1/2-inch border all the way around. Roll up pastry like a jellyroll; press seam to seal, then wrap in the plastic wrap. Repeat this with the remaining pastry and filling mixture. Freeze 30 minutes (or chill in refrigerator until firm, about 3 hours, but can be up to 3 days); cut crosswise with sharp knife into 1/2-inch slices.

Preheat oven to 400°F and lightly grease 2 baking sheets, or use a silicone liner or parchment paper. Arrange pinwheels 1 inch apart on baking sheets. Bake for 16 minutes or until golden brown. Transfer to a rack and serve warm. Makes 4 dozen.

Variation: An alternative filling for the pastry is 1/4 cup finely grated Gruyere cheese (about 3 ounces), 4 teaspoons of chopped fresh sage leaves, topped with 2 ounces of thinly sliced prosciutto.

CARAMELIZED ONION AND GORGONZOLA TARTLETTES

1 recipe basic pie dough
3 tablespoons olive oil
3 large red onions, thinly sliced
1 tablespoon fresh thyme leaves
2 tablespoons balsamic vinegar
Salt and freshly ground black pepper, to taste
2 eggs, lightly beaten
1/4 cup half-and-half
8 ounces gorgonzola cheese, crumbled (or goat cheese or Brie)
Garnish: chopped fresh parsley

Roll out dough to a thickness of 1/8-inch and line individual or miniature tart pans. Place on a baking sheet and chill 20 minutes. In a large skillet or sauté pan, over medium heat, add the oil and onions. Cover and cook until soft and golden, about 30 minutes. Add thyme and balsamic vinegar, simmer 1 minute more; season with salt and pepper, and transfer to a large mixing bowl. Add eggs, half-and-half and combine thoroughly. Place a layer of the onion mixture in the bottom of each tart shell and top with crumbled cheese. Bake in a preheated 375°oven until golden, about 15 minutes. Serve warm, garnished with chopped parsley. Makes 16 servings.

ROQUEFORT GRAPES

1 pound large, seedless red grapes
10 ounces pecans, crushed
4 tablespoons crumbled Roquefort cheese
1 (8-ounce) package cream cheese, room temperature
2 tablespoons heavy cream

Wash the grapes and let thoroughly dry in a wire mesh colander over the sink. Pat dry if needed. Toast the pecans in a 350°F oven on a large roasting sheet to bring out flavor (about 10 minutes) and let cool. Combine cheeses and cream in a bowl with a large spoon, mixing until fully blended. Roll the grapes in the cheese mixture, then in the pecans, coating entire surface. Cover and refrigerate until serving. Makes about 4 dozen.

PITA CHIPS with ZA'ATAR

These hearty chips can be made ahead of time and stored in an airtight container. The chips are great without spices, but with the many great Middle-Eastern restaurants in Wichita, tastes have expanded to also enjoying these chips topped with Za'atar, a spice combination. A dusting of Za'atar is nice to sprinkle too on top of hummus. Za'atar may be stored in an airtight container for up to six months.

Pita Chips
2 packages whole-wheat pitas
Olive oil spray
Garlic salt (nicely made with kosher salt)

Za'atar
2 tablespoons sesame seeds
2 teaspoons ground sumac
2 tablespoons minced fresh thyme

Preheat oven to 350°F. Trim outer edges of each pita bread with kitchen shears, resulting in two thin rounds. Stack rounds, and using a large knife, slice into 6 triangle pieces as if cutting a pie. Spread triangles smooth side down over 2 baking sheets or a pizza stone. Spray lightly with olive oil, then sprinkle with garlic salt. If you wish to also use the Za'atar, prepare it in advance by toasting the sesame seeds at 350°F for 8 minutes, and after cooling adding the sumac and thyme. Sprinkle Za'atar and garlic salt over the pita triangles. Bake for 6 minutes, remove from oven, turn and bake for about another 6 minutes until chips become crispy and lightly browned.

ROASTED RED PEPPER HUMMUS

From Joumana Tobia and Randa Tobia of "The Muse" café at the Wichita Art Museum.

1 (15-ounce) can garbanzo beans
1/2 teaspoon fresh crushed garlic
1/4 cup tahini
1/3 cup lemon juice

1/2 cup fresh or canned roasted red pepper, drained and patted dry
1/2 teaspoon cayenne pepper
Salt to taste

Empty can of garbanzo beans and bring to a boil for 2 to 3 minutes. Drain beans. Mash beans in food processor and add remaining ingredients. Blend well until smooth. Serve as a dip with fresh vegetables such as cucumbers, tomatoes and carrots, as well as olives, fresh and toasted pita bread and Za'atar chips.

Ground sumac is found in specialty food stores, spice stores, or in areas where there are Middle-Eastern food products.

You may also purchase Za'atar readymade from select spice merchants (See "Favorite Things" at back of book).

Severin Roesen
Nature's Bounty (detail), ca. 1860, oil on canvas, WAM, gift of George E. Vollmer, 1995.15

$\mathcal{T}$IMELESS, ABIDING, EXEMPLARS

STUFFED TOMATO CAPS

James Beard provided the inspiration for tomato cups for many of us with his American Cookery, *published in 1972. They provide a nice presentation for an appetizer, and the filling can be changed to fit the current food trend. Tomatoes for stuffing should be small round ones that are unblemished. This is also a nice technique for serving luncheon portions too, using an unblemished beefsteak tomato instead of the cherry tomatoes. Several filling ideas follow. Another way to serve some of these fillings is to scoop them onto endive leafs, letting the leaf be the "cup". Arrange the leaves on a serving platter for effect.*

Tomato cup: Select 36 unblemished cherry tomatoes. Cut $1/4$ inch from the top of each tomato. Using a small measuring spoon or a melon baller, remove the seeds and pulp to form a tomato shell. Spoon the filling into the tomato shells. Chill, covered, until serving time. Makes 3 dozen servings.

Some good fillings:
- chicken salad (page 32), garnished with an olive slice; or
- make it a BLT by filling with some garlic mayo, chopped green onion and cooked bacon slivers, garnished with a bit of romaine lettuce coming from the top of the tomato; or
- sliced mushrooms marinated in vinaigrette, garnished with tarragon or chives; or
- tuna with garlic mayonnaise, garnished with a slice of hard-boiled egg.

Louise Caldwell Murdock, whose estate provided for the establishment of the Wichita Art Museum, also founded the Twentieth Century Club in 1889. Her stuffed tomato recipe was published in the Club's 1922 cookbook:

"Peel tomatoes and put on ice to cool. Add to cream cheese a little oil mayonnaise, then cucumber and onion chopped fine, and stuff into tomatoes. Put oil mayonnaise on top. Serve on lettuce leaf." (from Mrs. Murdock)

STUFFED STRAWBERRIES

Make the stuffing and clean the strawberries a day ahead. Fill strawberries no more than 4 hours before serving.

20 large fresh strawberries (divided use) $1^1/_2$ tablespoons powdered sugar
1 (8-ounce) package cream cheese, softened   1 teaspoon orange liqueur (or vanilla extract)
2 tablespoons finely chopped walnuts or pecans   Garnish: almond slivers, fresh mint

To make a quick and easy piping bag, put filling in a zippertop plastic bag, cut a small hole in one of the lower corners and squeeze as you would a pastry bag.

Dice 2 strawberries and set aside. Cut a thin slice from stem end of each remaining strawberry, forming a base for strawberries to stand on. Cut each strawberry into four wedges, starting at pointed ends and cutting to, but not through, stem ends. Beat cream cheese at medium speed with an electric mixer until fluffy. Stir in diced strawberries, walnuts, powdered sugar, and if desired, liqueur. Spoon or pipe about 1 teaspoon into each strawberry. Garnish with almond slivers and fresh mint leaves. Makes $1^1/_2$ dozen.

BEER AND CHEESE FONDUE

Just when fondue pots from the '60s are no longer found in the back of cupboards, fondue makes a come back. This hearty flavorful cheese fondue will keep guests hanging out around the table. Works well too in a small crock pot. Stir occasionally when serving to keep blended. Sausage may be omitted but bump up the seasonings a bit.

$1/_2$ pound ground pork sausage   1 cup beer (prefer a lager or pilsner)
6 tablespoons butter   1 (4-ounce) can chopped green chilies
1 onion, chopped $1/_2$ teaspoon salt
1 garlic clove, chopped $1/_4$ teaspoon ground red pepper
6 tablespoons flour   Cubed French or pumpernickel bread
2 cups milk   Sliced apples or pears
2 (8-ounce) blocks Cheddar cheese, shredded

Cook sausage in a large saucepan over medium heat, stirring until it crumbles and is no longer pink. Drain and remove sausage from pan. Melt butter in saucepan over medium heat; add onion and garlic, and sauté until tender. Add flour, stirring until smooth. Cook, stirring constantly, for 1 minute. Gradually add milk, stirring until thickened. Add cheese, stirring until melted. Remove from heat; stir in sausage, beer, chilies, salt and ground red pepper. Transfer to a fondue pot or slow cooker; keep warm on low heat. Serve with cubed French bread or pumpernickel bread, apple slices or sliced pears. Makes 6 cups.

CLASSIC BLUE CHEESE CRUMBLE

This recipe won a recipe contest about 25 years ago and was published in an Oregon newspaper; it is a memorable classic that is just as fresh now as then. It is a great hors d'oeuvre or fruit-cheese course served with crackers and Granny Smith apple slices, or delicious as topping for salads or on top of hamburgers or steaks.

8 ounces blue cheese, crumbled

2 cloves garlic, minced

1/3 cup olive oil

2 tablespoons red wine vinegar

1 tablespoon lemon juice

1/2 cup chopped red onions (or green onions)

1/2 cup minced fresh parsley

Black pepper to taste

Sprinkle cheese in a shallow bowl. Mix the garlic and olive oil together and pour over the cheese. Combine remaining ingredients and pour over the cheese. Cover and chill for 1 hour. Season with pepper on top and serve.

RUM GLAZED SPICED NUTS

I like the improved flavor in this method better than the traditional way of using egg whites to carry the spice mixture for flavored roasted nuts. Using kosher salt is important because of its crunch, and these are best if made ahead of time. Recipe adapted from The New Best Recipe, *one of my favorite cookbooks (see Bibliography).*

2 cups (8 ounces) raw pecan halves, or
  mixed nuts

Spice Mix

2 tablespoons sugar

3/4 teaspoon kosher salt

1/2 teaspoon cinnamon

Dash ground allspice

Rum Glaze

1 tablespoon dark rum

2 teaspoons vanilla extract

1 teaspoon brown sugar

1 tablespoon butter

Preheat the oven to 350°F. Line a baking sheet with parchment paper and spread pecans out in an even layer. Toast for 8 minutes, rotate the pan halfway through. Transfer the nuts to a wire rack. Stir together the spice mix. Bring the ingredients for the glaze to a boil in a medium saucepan over medium heat, whisking constantly. Stir in the pecans and cook, stirring constantly until the nuts are shiny and almost all the liquid has evaporated, about 1 1/2 minutes. Transfer to the bowl with the spice mix and toss to coat. Return the pecans to the parchment-lined sheet to cool. Makes 2 cups.

ROSEMARY WALNUTS

These are great for cocktail nuts as well as adding to salads. Cashews, pecans or peanuts also work well in this recipe. If you use walnuts, look for ones that are pale; and to keep them from tasting bitter after the initial roasting, rub them a bit with a towel before adding spices.

2 cups (8 ounces) walnut halves

2 1/2 tablespoons butter, melted

2 teaspoons dried rosemary, crumbled (or 2
  tablespoons chopped fresh rosemary)

1 teaspoon kosher salt

1/2 teaspoon cayenne

1 teaspoon sweet paprika (optional)

Preheat oven to 350°F. Place raw walnuts on heavy baking pan and roast for about 10 minutes; allow to cool completely. Combine all ingredients in a large bowl, stir in nuts and lightly toss until they are well coated. Line baking pan with parchment paper and spread out nuts in a single layer. Bake for about 15 minutes, stirring once and checking often. Remove when they are deeply colored. Serve warm or at room temperature. Makes 2 cups.

"We observed black walnut and oak among the timber; also honeysuckle and the buck's-eye with the nuts on it."

*- Lewis and Clark
July 3, 1804, along the
Kansas River*

MOZZARELLA, TOMATO and ARTICHOKE BRUSCHETTA

The food processor was a '70s invention that moved home cooks from stirring packaged instant soup into sour cream to more complex tastes and textures.

The American inventor of the food processor, Carl Sontheimer, saw an industrial blender at a food show in France, then invented one for home use. Initially named "Robot Coupe", but soon it was licensed as "Cuisinart". After that, chopping, grinding, puréeing all came to us with the flick of switch and cooking changed!

1 (10-ounce) package frozen artichoke hearts, cooked according to directions, or 1 (15-ounce) can, rinsed and drained
2 Roma tomatoes
3 green onions, thinly sliced
¹/₄ cup chopped Kalamata or black olives
1¹/₂ cups shredded mozzarella cheese
¹/₂ cup grated Parmesan cheese
5 tablespoons regular or light mayonnaise
2 to 3 tablespoons chopped fresh basil (or 1 teaspoon dried basil)
¹/₄ teaspoon crushed red pepper
1 (24-inch long) baguette, cut crosswise into ¹/₂-inch slice

Coarsely chop artichokes and tomatoes and place in bowl. Add onions, olives, cheeses, mayonnaise, basil and crushed red pepper; stir to combine. Cover and chill up to 24 hours. Preheat broiler and place rack in top position. Spread baguette slices out on baking sheet and spread about a teaspoon of mixture over bread slices. Run under broiler until bubbly and hot. Serve warm. Makes about 24 appetizers. From Bonnie Aeschliman.

CROSTINI

Start with making the crostini, and then choose a combination of simple toppings or a tapenade. This toast will hold up well to any of the savory tapenades which follow on the next page. You can also try using a crusty country oblong loaf instead of the baguette.

1 baguette cut on bias into ¹/₂-inch-thick slices
3 tablespoons extra virgin olive oil
1 large clove garlic, peeled and halved

Place oven rack about 4 inches from the broiler element and heat the broiler. Broil the bread slices on each side until golden brown. After removing from oven, rub each side with the garlic clove, then drizzle lightly with olive oil and sprinkle with salt and pepper. To serve, place crostini in a circle on a platter, mounding tapenade in the center. Serve room temperature. Makes 18 servings.

Donald Roller Wilson *Cookie Had Seen One Before . . . In Church During An Evening Service . . . (About Seven Hours Past)* (detail), 1992, oil on board, WAM, gift of the family of Elton I. "Buddy" Greenberg, 2007.2.9, © Donald Roller Wilson, 1992

TAPENADES

Quick and easy, tapenades make flavorful toppings for fresh French bread, toasted bread rounds, crostini (see previous page), bruschetta or baguette slices. All from Bonnie Aeschliman.

Sun-dried Tomato Tapenade

3 ounces dried sun-dried tomatoes
2 cloves garlic, peeled
1/4 cup toasted walnuts
1/4 cup packed parsley and/or basil leaves
1/2 cup dry white wine (or chicken stock)

1/2 to 2/3 cups extra-virgin olive oil
2 teaspoons balsamic vinegar
1/2 cup grated Parmesan cheese
1/2 teaspoon salt
1/4 teaspoon crushed red pepper

Cover dried tomatoes in boiling water. Let stand 20 to 30 minutes; drain. In food processor with metal blade, chop tomatoes, garlic, walnuts and fresh herbs. With motor running, add wine, 1/2 cup olive oil and vinegar. Blend in Parmesan cheese, salt and crushed red pepper with a few on and off pulses of the processor. Add additional olive oil to thin, if desired. Serve with fresh or toasted baguette slices.

Roasted Garlic Tapenade

1 head roasted garlic
2 to 3 tablespoons olive oil
1/2 teaspoon grated lemon rind

2 teaspoons fresh lemon juice
1/2 cup unsalted butter, room temperature
1/4 to 1/2 teaspoon salt

Squeeze garlic cloves from roasted garlic into a small dish. Combine garlic, olive oil, lemon rind and juice in blender or food processor. Process until creamy. Add butter and salt; process until smooth. May be made 2 days in advance. Cover and chill. Spread on fresh baguette or country bread.

Olive Tapenade

1 3/4 cup pitted, brine-cured black (Kalamata)
    and/or green olives
1/2 cup walnuts, toasted (divided use)
1/3 cup olive oil
2 teaspoons Dijon mustard

2 large cloves garlic, minced
2 teaspoons chopped fresh thyme
2 teaspoons chopped fresh oregano
2 teaspoons chopped fresh sage
Pinch of cayenne pepper

Finely chop black olives and half the toasted walnuts in processor. Add olive oil, Dijon mustard, garlic, thyme, oregano, sage, and cayenne pepper; process until chopped. Add remaining walnuts and process until coarsely chopped. If over-processed, the tapenade will turn gray.

Artichoke and Roasted Pepper Tapenade

1 clove garlic
3/4 cup loosely packed parsley, rinsed, dried and
    stems removed
1 (6 1/2-ounce) jar marinated artichoke
    hearts, drained, patted dry, chopped
1/3 cup Mediterranean-style olives, drained
1/3 cup canned roasted red peppers, rinsed
    and drained
1/3 cup grated Parmesan cheese

1/3 cup extra virgin olive oil
1/3 cup walnuts or almonds, toasted
1 tablespoon lemon juice
1/4 teaspoon dried thyme
1/4 teaspoon dried oregano
Pinch cayenne
Salt and pepper
Baguette slices

Fit food processor with metal blade and with machine running, drop garlic clove through feed tube. Process until chopped. Add parsley and process until finely chopped. Add all remaining ingredients to food processor. Pulse on/off until mixture is coarsely chopped. Season with salt and pepper if needed. May be made 24 hours in advance, covered and chilled. Serve with baguette slices. Makes 1 3/4 cups.

ROASTED GARLIC

Slice off top of garlic head to show cloves. Place garlic in a small square of aluminum foil (if roasting more than one, garlic heads can be wrapped together). Drizzle a teaspoon or two of olive oil onto cut top of garlic, season with salt and pepper. Wrap foil tightly and bake for 40 to 50 minutes in a 350°F oven until very tender. Set aside to cool.

The quality and taste of jarred roasted red peppers varies a great deal by brand. Top brand choices are "Divina" or "Greek Gourmet".

... first the traditional approach to this classic dip, which maintains the usual 1:1 ratio of mayonnaise to Parmesan cheese, and then the reduced-guilt version.

In recipes like these, where the cheese is one of the main players, it is worth the money to buy real Parmigiano Reggiano. You know it's the real thing by the distinctive stamp on the rind.

HOT ASIAGO and ARTICHOKE DIP

This recipe appears in so many places, but is easy and always disappears quickly.

1 (10-ounce) package frozen chopped spinach, thawed and squeezed dry
1 (14-ounce) can artichoke hearts, drained and chopped
1 clove garlic, pressed

1 cup mayonnaise
1 cup freshly grated Asiago or Parmesan cheese (4 ounces)
8 to 10 ounces shredded Monterey Jack cheese
Dash sesame seeds

Preheat oven to 350°F. Combine spinach, artichoke hearts, garlic, mayonnaise and Parmesan. Reserve $^1/_2$ cup cheese for top; add rest to spinach mixture. Stir until blended. Transfer to a buttered, 1-quart baking dish (shallow such as a pie plate or quiche plate); sprinkle with remaining Monterey Jack cheese and sesame seeds (dip may be prepared to this point, covered and chilled). Bake for 15 minutes, or until cheese is melted and bubbly. Serve warm with crackers, bruschetta or baked pita chips for dipping. Makes about 3 cups.

ROASTED ARTICHOKE DIP

Adapted from a recipe in The Best Light Recipe, *this version is actually my preferred one, much lower in calories and fat grams (8g. vs. 21g. per serving) than the traditional spinach artichoke dip. The roasted artichokes add a nice fresh kick.*

2 (9-ounce) boxes frozen artichokes (unthawed)
2 teaspoons olive oil (divided use)
1 medium onion, minced (about 1 cup)
2 medium cloves garlic, minced
1 cup reduced-fat mayonnaise
$^1/_2$ cup light cream cheese, room temperature

1 ounce ($^1/_2$ cup) Parmesan cheese, grated
1 tablespoon lemon juice
1 tablespoon minced fresh thyme
Dash hot pepper sauce
1 cup fresh bread crumbs
2 tablespoons grated Parmesan cheese

Preheat the oven to 450°F. Line a rimmed baking sheet with foil. Toss the artichokes with 1 teaspoon of the oil, sprinkle with salt and pepper, and spread over the baking sheet. Roast, rotating the baking sheet from front to back halfway through, until the edges of the artichokes are browned, about 20 to 25 minutes. Set aside to cool. Reduce oven to 400°F.

Combine onion, garlic, remaining oil and $^1/_2$ teaspoon salt in a nonstick skillet. Cover and cook over medium heat about 8 to 10 minutes, stirring occasionally. Transfer onion mixture to a large bowl; add mayonnaise, cream cheese, Parmesan, lemon juice, thyme and hot pepper sauce; stir until combined (important to work with room temperature cream cheese, or else it will not fully combine). Coarsely chop the cooled artichokes and add to the mixture. Scrape into an ungreased 8-inch square baking dish. Toss bread crumbs and Parmesan together, sprinkle on top, and spray the bread crumbs with vegetable oil cooking spray. Bake until browned, about 25 minutes. Serve immediately with baked pita chips for dipping. Makes 3 cups.

BRIE BREAD

1 loaf French bread
$^1/_2$ cup butter
$^1/_3$ cup pecan pieces

8 ounces brie cheese
$^1/_3$ cup minced onion

Cut French bread in half horizontally, then cut almost through the width to your desired sized pieces. In a pyrex measuring cup melt the cheese, butter, onion, nuts in the microwave. Spread on bread and put in warm oven for 10 minutes, then broil until golden brown. Makes 14 servings. From Barbara Pearce.

ARTICHOKE CHEESE SPREAD

This layered spread makes a pretty presentation for gatherings.

2 (8-ounce) packages cream cheese, softened
1/4 cup finely chopped green onion tops
1 (14-ounce) can artichoke hearts, drained and finely chopped
1 cup grated Parmesan cheese
2 garlic cloves, pressed
2 tablespoons olive oil

1 tablespoon lemon juice
1/2 teaspoon ground red pepper
3/4 cup roasted red bell peppers, drained and chopped
Garnish: arugula or lettuce, pepper strips (red, yellow, orange) and radish slices

Line a 4-cup bowl with plastic wrap, allowing 4 inches to hang over the side (keeps the spread from sticking to the bowl when you are ready to invert and serve). You are making three easy layers for this spread. Stir cream cheese and green onions together and set aside. Stir the artichoke hearts, Parmesan cheese, garlic, olive oil, lemon juice and ground red pepper together and set aside. Spread one-third of the cream cheese mixture into the bottom the bowl. Then layer with half of the chopped roasted bell peppers, then 3/4 cup of the artichoke mixture. Repeat layers with remaining ingredients. Cover with plastic wrap overhang and chill for at least 2 hours. To serve, invert on a serving plate and remove wrap. Garnish and serve with small hearty bread slices or pita chips. Makes 3 cups.

MUSHROOM SPREAD

Dora Timmerman shares this favorite recipe, describing that it has been served by the Wichita Art Museum restaurant for special parties.

1 pound mushrooms, diced
1/2 cup sliced green onions
1/4 teaspoon dried thyme
1/4 cup butter
1/3 cup dry sherry
1 teaspoon salt

1 (8-ounce) package cream cheese
1 cup finely chopped walnuts, toasted
1/4 cup minced fresh parsley
Dash of hot pepper sauce
Garnish: 1/4 cup snipped fresh chives

Sauté mushrooms, green onions, thyme and butter until onions are tender, about 5 to 8 minutes. Add sherry and salt and continue cooking until liquid is almost evaporated. Remove from heat and cool. Combine mushroom mixture with whipped cream cheese and blend thoroughly. Stir in walnuts, parsley and hot pepper sauce. Spread in serving dish, cover and chill at least 2 hours. Sprinkle with chives and serve with assorted crackers. Makes 8 to 10 servings.

SPICY SMOKED SALMON SPREAD

You can make this attractive spread a day ahead. Serve with crostini, assorted crackers or toasted bread.

1 pound smoked salmon, sliced
2 tablespoons lemon juice
6 dashes hot pepper sauce, or to taste
1 (8-ounce) package cream cheese, softened
3 teaspoons grated onion

1/2 cup sour cream
1/2 cup finely chopped pecans
3 tablespoon chopped fresh parsley
Garnish: capers

Stir together first 6 ingredients; cover and chill 2 hours. Shape mixture into a 7-inch log. Combine pecans and parsley in a shallow dish. Roll log in pecan mixture, and wrap in plastic wrap (it is helpful to spray plastic wrap and hands with cooking spray); chill. Garnish with capers. Makes 20 appetizer servings.

A quick spread to prepare is to simply pour purchased "Pickapeppa Sauce"(found in the condiment section of the grocery) over a block of cream cheese. Serve with crackers.

MENU:
*AN ELEGANT
HORS D'OEURVES
MENU*

*Caramelized Onion &
Goat Cheese Tartlettes 18*

*Spicy Smoked Salmon
Spread on Toast Points 26*

Stuffed Tomato Caps 20

*Annie's Famous
Caviar Mousse 12*

*Rum Glazed
Spiced Nuts 21*

*Thai Style Chicken in
Won Ton Cups 26*

*Hot Ham Canapés
with Raspberry
Chipotle Sauce 31*

CURRIED CHICKEN SALAD SPREAD

DIPS with CRUDITES

Garden vegetables in a beautiful array are a wonderful way to start a party. Place vegetables of same kind together for best visual effect and use creative serving dishes for the dip. Try hollowing out a pretty little pumpkin or other fresh vegetable such as a red cabbage.

Use a sharp paring knife to hollow the middle and pour the dip into this or put the dip in a small bowl that will set in the cavity. Fold back some of the leaves for a beautiful container.

Also, try a red or yellow pepper, but you may need to cut small slices off of the bottoms so they will stand straight.

4 cups finely chopped cooked chicken
3 (8-ounce) packages cream cheese, softened
3/4 cup golden raisins, chopped
1/2 cup flaked coconut, toasted
2 celery stalks, diced
6 green onions, minced

1 (2 1/4-ounce) package slivered almonds, toasted
1 tablespoon curry powder
1/2 teaspoon salt
1/2 teaspoon pepper
1 tablespoon grated ginger

Stir ingredients together. Form into an egg shape on a serving platter. Chill 8 hours and garnish. Possible garnishes: blanched green onion stems, minced green onions, toasted flaked coconut, pistachios, fresh dill sprigs, yellow squash wedges, fresh chives, mixed salad greens, pansies, cucumber slices. It is fun to create a garnish pattern on this shape, sometimes in stripes (think of a decorated easter egg). Serve with crackers. Makes 20 to 25 appetizer servings.

HOT SWISS BACON DIP

1 (8-ounce) package cream cheese, softened
1/2 cup mayonnaise
1 cup shredded Swiss cheese

2 tablespoons chopped green onion
8 slices bacon, cooked and crumbled
1/2 cup crushed buttery crackers (like Ritz)

Preheat oven to 350°F. Combine cream cheese, mayonnaise, Swiss cheese and green onion in a mixing bowl. Transfer to a shallow baking dish and top with bacon and crushed crackers. Bake for 20 minutes. Serve hot with assorted crackers or chips. Makes 8 to 12 servings.

VEGETABLE CURRY DIP

Serve in hollowed-out whole red, green or orange bell pepper, or in a cored red cabbage. Surround with blanched green beans, slices of red and yellow bell peppers, broccoli florets, carrot strips and celery sticks for dipping.

3/4 cup mayonnaise
2 tablespoons Durkee sauce
1 teaspoon horseradish
1 teaspoon celery seeds
1 teaspoon curry powder

1/2 teaspoon salt
1/4 teaspoon Worcestershire sauce
Hot pepper sauce to taste
Pepper to taste

Besides the dips on this page, consider too a

TARRAGON AIOLI
Mix together:
1 cup mayonnaise
2 tablespoons olive oil
1 tablespoon minced fresh tarragon
2 teaspoons white wine vinegar
2 minced garlic cloves
1 teaspoon fresh lemon juice
Salt and pepper to season

Combine the mayonnaise, Durkee sauce, horseradish, celery seeds, pepper, curry powder, salt, Worcestershire sauce, and hot pepper sauce in a bowl; mix well. Chill for 1 hour or longer. Serve with assorted fresh vegetables and crisp crackers. Makes 1 cup.

QUESO BLANCO

2 cups shredded Asadero cheese
1/2 (4 ounces) can jalapenos, drained and chopped
1/4 cup half-and-half

2 tablespoons finely chopped onion
2 teaspoons cumin
1/2 teaspoon salt

Combine ingredients over low heat, stirring constantly until cheese melts. Serve warm with tortilla chips. This may also be made and kept warm in a small crockpot, but coat pot with cooking spray.

HOT PEPPER PEACH CHEESEBALL

2 (8-ounce) packages cream cheese, softened
1/3 (11-ounce) jar of peach jalapeno preserves
1 heaping tablespoon chopped onions

1 level tablespoon chopped jalapenos
1/2 cup shredded Monterey Jack cheese

Cream the cream cheese, preserves, onions and jalapenos together; cover and chill for at least one hour. Form into ball and roll in shredded Monterey Jack cheese. Keep chilled until ready to serve. May be prepared up to 48 hours in advance. Makes 1 large delicious cheese ball.

CRISPY WON TONS with AHI TUNA and WASABI CREAM

6 ounces Ahi tuna steak (2 inches thick and
   4 inches wide)
8 won ton wrappers, cut in half on a diagonal
1 tablespoon plus 2 teaspoons toasted
   sesame oil
Pinch of fine sea salt

2 tablespoons black sesame seeds
2 tablespoons freshly ground black pepper
1/2 cup crème fraîche
2 tablespoons prepared wasabi
Chives for garnishing

Brush each wrapper with oil and place on a baking sheet. Bake in preheated 350°F oven for 5 to 7 minutes, until golden. Remove from baking sheet and set aside. Cut the tuna steak in half, creating two 2 x 2-inch square pieces. Them cut each piece in half, diagonally. Sprinkle tuna with salt and dredge in sesame seeds and pepper, pressing to create a crust. In a small non-stick skillet heat remaining oil and sauté tuna for 3 to 5 minutes per side. Remove and thinly slice the triangular "log" for 16 nice triangular shaped slices to place on the won ton crisps. Arrange slices on fried won ton. In a mixing bowl, whisk crème fraîche and wasabi until soft peaks form. Spoon into a pastry bag with a small plain tip or plastic squeeze bottle and pipe on each hors d'oeuvre. Garnish with a small piece of chive and serve immediately. Makes 16 servings.

POPPYSEED BLUE CHEESE CRACKERS

To keep these crackers light and crispy don't process the dough for too long once you add the flour. Too much mixing will make the crackers tough.

8 ounces blue cheese, crumbled
1/2 cup butter, room temperature
1 1/3 cups flour

1/4 cup poppy seed
1/4 teaspoon cayenne pepper

Place blue cheese and butter in food processor or electric mixer; mix until creamy. Add flour, poppy seed and cayenne pepper; beat (or pulse if using food processor) just until thoroughly combined. Divide dough in half. Place on a sheet of plastic wrap and shape each into a 9-inch log. Seal in plastic wrap and chill for 2 hours or longer. Cut each log into 1/4-inch-thick slices, and place on ungreased baking sheets. Bake at 350°F for 13 to 15 minutes or until golden; cool. Makes 6 dozen. From Bonnie Aeschliman.

CRISPY CHEESE CRACKERS

1 1/4 cup butter, room temperature
12 ounces sharp Cheddar cheese, shredded
 (about 2 1/2 cups)
2 1/4 cups flour (divided use)

1/2 teaspoon cayenne pepper
1/2 teaspoon kosher salt (divided use)
2 cups crispy rice cereal

Preheat oven to 375°F. Mix butter, cheese, 2 cups of flour, cayenne pepper and 1/4 teaspoon of salt together in a large bowl, using hands. Combine remaining 1/4 cup flour and 1/4 teaspoon salt in a bowl. Roll dough into small balls and place on heavy cookie sheet. Dip tines of a fork into flour mixture and press each ball to flatten. Bake for 10 to 12 minutes until light golden and then cool on wire rack.

CHEESE PUFFS

These look like fancy gougères, but easier as they are made without a pastry bag. The chilled savory dough balloons in a hot oven, resulting in a delicious cheesy puff. You can successfully substitute other cheeses (feta, crumbled goat cheese or blue cheese) for the Cheddar.

6 tablespoons butter, cut into small pieces
 and softened
3/4 cup shredded sharp cheddar cheese
2/3 cup flour
1 1/2 cups ricotta cheese

1 teaspoon salt
1/4 teaspoon pepper
2 tablespoons chopped fresh parsley
1 egg

In a large bowl, stir the butter and cheese together; add the flour, ricotta, salt, pepper, parsley and egg and stir until just combined. Drop rounded teaspoonfuls onto a baking sheet, about an inch apart. Place sheet in the freezer and chill until dough is frozen, about 30 minutes. Preheat oven to 450°F. Place baking sheets directly into the hot oven and bake for about 10 minutes, until lightly browned. Transfer to serving platter and sprinkle with salt. Serve hot.

PARMESAN PEPPER FRICO

You can also form Fricos into shapes. Use a spatula to remove the cheese rounds from the sheet while they are still warm, drape over ramekins, muffin cups or a rolling pin and let cool. Fill with baby greens dressed with lemon juice and olive oil. See further technique on next page.

Crisp and delicate, these are great cheese wafers. Use a frico to garnish savory dishes or serve as an appetizer.

1 cup Parmigiano-Reggiano cheese, coarsely grated (use the largest holes on your grater)
1/4 teaspoon freshly ground black pepper

Preheat oven to 350°F. Line a baking sheet with a silicone liner. For each frico, spoon about 2 tablespoons grated Parmigiano-Reggiano cheese onto baking sheet; spread into a 3-inch round. Space rounds 2 inches apart. Sprinkle tops of rounds with freshly ground pepper. Bake until fricos are crisp and golden, about 12 minutes. Transfer pan to wire rack; let cool completely. Using a spatula, remove frico from baking sheet. Repeat with remaining cheese to make more fricos. May keep in airtight container for 3 days.

PARMESAN BASKETS

Baskets made from Parmesan cheese make a great presentation for salads, or made smaller for appetizer-sized salads or a goat cheese filling. They may be made a day ahead and stored in an airtight container. Until you get the hang of it, make one at a time, as they have to be shaped when they come out of the oven.

To make salad-sized baskets, first wrap the outside of an inverted 6-inch terracotta pot, upside-down custard cup, drinking glass, or coffee cup (something with a good flat bottom and sides which slightly flare out) in aluminum foil. Coat foil with cooking spray. Place a 12-inch square of parchment paper on a baking sheet. Spread $^1/_2$ cup shredded Parmesan cheese onto the parchment paper, patting it into an $8^1/_2$-inch circle (don't use grated cheese, only shredded will work). Bake at 375°F for 5 to 7 minutes or until pale gold in color. Remove from oven and let cool 10 seconds. If you make them too thick they will be chewy rather than crispy, and if you brown them too much they will taste bitter.

Carefully lift the parchment paper off the baking sheet. Working quickly, invert the warm crisp over the prepared pot/cup, etc. Carefully remove the parchment from the warm crisp (reserve the parchment to use again) with fingers or a large thin metal spatula. Gently press the cheese over inverted pot into desired bowl shape. (If the cheese is too hot, it will slide down the pot, causing small tears. If this happens, gently press the cheese together to seal any large gaps.) Cool basket completely (about 5 minutes) and remove. Repeat to create as many baskets as you need.

To make appetizer-sized baskets, first prepare (as above) your target for shaping (upturned egg carton, shot glass, wine cork, miniature muffin tins, or any small cup to form tulip shapes). Spoon 6 evenly spaced tablespoon-size mounds of shredded Parmesan cheese on a heavy nonstick baking sheet lined with parchment paper. Pat each mound into a fairly even 3-inch round. Bake for about 4 minutes at 350°F, or until bubbling and golden; remove from oven and let Parmesan crisps cool slightly, approximately 1 minute or until still warm and pliable and you can gently remove with a thin spatula. Working quickly, remove the lacy rounds from the sheet and drape them over your target. They will crisp up as they cool. Repeat with the remaining Parmesan.

HOT CHEESE CANAPES

5 tablespoons mayonnaise
2 tablespoons finely chopped green onions
1/2 cup shredded Cheddar cheese (or freshly grated Parmesan cheese)

30 thin white or wheat bread rounds, cut with top of spice jar
Garnish: Sliced cherry tomatoes, crumbled bacon (optional)

Combine mayonnaise, onions and cheese and mix well. Spread each bread round with 1/2 to 3/4 teaspoon of mixture. Top with a slice of cherry tomato and freshly cooked crumbled bacon, if desired. Place on baking sheet and broil for 5 minutes or until bubbly. Makes 30 canapés. From Martie Walker.

CHEESE STRAWS

1 cup flour
1/2 teaspoon baking powder
1 teaspoon salt
Dash of cayenne pepper

1 cup grated sharp Cheddar cheese
5 1/3 tablespoons butter
2 to 3 teaspoons water

Preheat oven to 400°F. Mix the flour, baking powder, salt, cayenne and cheese. Add butter and cut in with a fork or pastry knife until the mixture is like a coarse meal. Sprinkle in just enough water to make a stiff dough. Roll out to about 1/8-inch thick and use a pizza knife to cut into 2 x 1/4-inch strips. Bake on a heavy cookie sheet with a silicone liner or parchment paper for 10 minutes, or until barely browned. Makes 7 to 8 dozen. Store in an airtight container. Best if made a day ahead, but can also be frozen.

SESAME CHEESE STRAWS

1/2 pound very sharp Cheddar cheese, shredded
1 (2 1/4-ounce) jar sesame seeds
1/2 cup butter, softened

1 1/4 cups flour
1 teaspoon salt
1/8 teaspoon cayenne pepper

Preheat oven to 400°F. Allow shredded cheese to reach room temperature. Toast sesame seeds in a heavy skillet, stirring constantly over low heat, about 2 minutes till golden; cool. Combine cheese, butter, flour, salt, and cayenne. Blend dough; add sesame seeds. Roll dough to 1/8-inch thickness (on pastry cloth); cut into 4 x 1/2-inch strips. Bake for 12 minutes or until golden brown. Cool on wire rack. Place in airtight container. These keep fresh for several weeks, but can be frozen for a month.

PARMESAN CHEESE TWISTS

1 sheet frozen pastry puff pastry, thawed (from a 17 1/4 ounce package)
1 egg beaten with 1 tablespoon of water

3 tablespoons grated Parmesan cheese
Poppy seeds as needed

Preheat oven to 350°F. Roll out puff pastry sheet on a lightly floured surface to a 10 x 14-inch rectangle. It should be very thin. Cut in half lengthwise to make two rectangles. Brush each rectangle with egg mixture; sprinkle one with grated Parmesan cheese, and the other with poppy seeds. Lay one rectangle directly over the other, making sure the egg-brushed sides are touching. Roll gently with a rolling pin to stick the sheets together. Brush with more egg mixture and sprinkle with poppy seeds.

Cut pastry crosswise into 1/2-inch strips (a pizza cutter works well for this). Twist dough like a corkscrew; lay on an ungreased pan, pressing ends firmly against buttered baking sheet. Repeat with 13 more strips, placing them 1 inch apart on baking sheet. Refrigerate to cool before baking. Bake for 15 minutes, or until puffed and golden brown. Shape remaining strips in same manner and place on second baking sheet. Makes about 28 twists.

CHEESE LAVASH

Lavash, a large round cracker-like flat bread, can be made into a quick appetizer. Place lavash on a greased cookie sheet, top with 8 ounces of thinly sliced Havarti cheese, a dash of garlic powder or cloves of roasted garlic. Cook in a 350°F oven for 5 minutes, just until cheese melts.

Steuben Glass (Frederick Carder, designer) *Indian Vase*, ca. 1925, cased acid cut lead glass, WAM, gift of William and Martha L. Connelly, 1999.4

HOT HAM CANAPES with RASPBERRY CHIPOTLE SAUCE

8 ounces good quality ham
1 cup mayonnaise (prefer "Hellmann's Lite" or "Best Foods" on the West coast)
$^1/_2$ cup thinly sliced green onions
$^1/_2$ teaspoon dry mustard
$^1/_4$ teaspoon hot pepper sauce

$^1/_2$ cup shredded sharp Cheddar cheese
$^1/_2$ cup shredded Monterey Jack cheese
Raspberry chipotle sauce (purchased or recipe below)
French baguette, in $^1/_4$-inch slices
Garnish: fresh minced parsley

Ask the bakery to slice the baguette for you so you will have uniform slices.

Place ham in food processor. Pulse on/off until ham is coarsely chopped. Add mayonnaise, green onions, dry mustard, hot pepper sauce and cheeses, and pulse a few times just until mixed. Don't over do this, as a little texture is needed. Shortly before serving, place bread rounds on cookie sheets. Spoon mixture on bread rounds. Place oven rack in the top position, close to the broiler. Broil canapes until golden. Watch carefully, it only takes a couple of minutes. Before serving, drizzle with Raspberry Chipotle Sauce, garnish with a bit of minced parsley. Makes 3 dozen. From Bonnie Aeschliman.

Raspberry Chipotle Sauce
1 cup frozen raspberries, thawed
2 tablespoons sugar

1 tablespoon Hoisin sauce
1 tablespoon chopped chipotle in adobo sauce

Combine ingredients in a bowl and heat in microwave until mixture simmers and sugar is dissolved. Purée in food processor or blender; strain into small bowl and cool before using. May be made 2 or 3 days in advance.

An afternoon tea is a pleasant and elegant way to entertain. Though an elegant tradition, tea does not have to be a formal affair, and is most successful and enjoyable with small tasty bites, beautifully presented in an unhurried manner. It is also a wonderful venue for parties such as baby or bridal showers.

Use fine china, crisp linens, silver and fresh flowers to employ a "Tea Time" ambience. Coffee should be served at one end of the table, and tea at the other. Plates can be stacked with folded napkins between them.

Between the coffee and tea service, the table could include tea sandwiches, fancy cakes, cookies, nuts, mints, and small fingers of breads such as strawberry or banana topped with flavored butters. A helper should assist with the serving of coffee and tea.

FINGER SANDWICHES

Finger sandwiches are simple to prepare and make an elegant presentation as either an appetizer or for a tea. Don't limit your bread choice to white bread, and remember that a thin coating of butter will keep the bread from becoming soggy. Be creative with your fillings, such as ham with a cream cheese-apricot preserve spread, or peanut butter, honey and a slice of peach. Some other filling ideas are:

Chicken Salad Sandwiches

2 1/2 cups minced chicken breast
1/4 cup minced celery
1 tablespoon minced green onion

2/3 cup mayonnaise
2 tablespoons heavy cream
Garnish: finely chopped smoked almonds

Stir ingredients together, adjusting the cream as needed to bind all together. Makes approximately 2 3/4 cups spread. Assemble finger sandwiches. A nice finishing touch is to spread mayonnaise on edges of sandwich and roll in 1/2 cup of finely chopped smoked almonds. Served at many Wichita Art Museum functions over the years; recipe from Betty Minkler.

Olive-Nut Spread Sandwiches

1 (8-ounce) package cream cheese, softened
1/2 cup chopped pimiento-stuffed green olives
1 cup chopped pecans, toasted

1 to 2 tablespoons mayonnaise
Thin pumpernickel bread slices
Garnish: toasted pecan halves

Stir together first 4 ingredients in a large bowl. Cover and chill until ready to serve. Cut crusts from bread slices; cut each slice into 4 squares. Serve spread on bread slices. Garnish with pecans.

Onion Sandwiches with Mustard Mayonnaise

24 thin slices white bread
1 cup mayonnaise
1 tablespoon Dijon mustard

1 large white onion, sliced very thin
  with mandolin
Salt
1 cup minced fresh parsley leaves

With a 3-inch round cutter, cut out a round from each slice of bread. Combine the mayonnaise with the mustard in a small bowl. Spread the mayonnaise mixture generously on one side of each bread round. Arrange onion on half of rounds. Sprinkle with salt to taste. Cover with a round that has been spread with the mayonnaise mixture. Spread a thin layer of mayonnaise mixture around the edges of the sandwiches and roll in chopped parsley leaves. Keep covered with damp tea towel until ready to serve.

Finger sandwiches should be just large enough for two bites.

Cut them into shapes such as stars, flowers or geometric shapes. Cookie cutters can be used to pair the shape with the party theme (such as for a bridal or baby shower).

For a nice ribbon effect, make each sandwich using both a white and dark slice of bread and cut them into ribbons with an electric knife.

Turkey Basil Scallion Raisin Sandwiches

1 loaf dense raisin-nut bread, unsliced
12 ounces cream cheese, room temperature
½ cup minced green onion or scallions (both white and green parts)

8 thin slices fresh or smoked turkey breast
Fresh basil leaves

Ask the store to slice the bread lengthwise on a meat slicer into ¼-inch-thick slices. If that isn't possible, you can slice it crosswise with a very sharp knife into 8 slices.

Combine cream cheese and scallions with an electric mixer, just until blended. Lay out 8 slices of bread and spread with a thin layer of scallion cream cheese. Place a single layer of turkey on half the slices, cutting the edge to fit the bread. Lay basil leaves on top of the turkey. Top with the other 4 slices of bread, cream cheese side down.

Lay the sandwiches on a baking sheet, and wrap the sheet with plastic. Refrigerate until the cream cheese is cold and firm. Place the sandwiches on a cutting board and, with a very sharp knife, cut off the crusts. Cut each large sandwich in half crosswise, and then cut each half diagonally, twice, to make a total of 8 small triangles. (If the bread was cut crosswise, follow the assembly directions, then cut off the crusts and cut diagonally, twice, to make 4 small triangles.) Serve chilled. Makes 48.

Curried Chicken Tea Sandwiches

2 cups cubed cooked chicken
1 medium unpeeled red apple, chopped
¾ cup dried cranberries
½ cup thinly sliced celery
¼ cup chopped pecans
2 tablespoons thinly sliced green onions

¾ cup mayonnaise
2 teaspoons lime juice
½ to ¾ teaspoon curry powder
12 bread slices
Lettuce leaves

In a medium bowl, combine the first six ingredients. Combine mayonnaise, lime juice and curry powder; add to chicken mixture and stir to coat. Cover and refrigerate to allow flavors to develop, at least 3 hours. Cut each slice of bread with a cookie cutter, top with lettuce and chicken salad.

Cucumber Sandwiches

1 medium cucumber
½ cup cider vinegar
1 cup water
1 (8-ounce) package cream cheese, softened
¼ cup mayonnaise or salad dressing
¼ teaspoon garlic powder

¼ teaspoon onion salt
Dash Worcestershire sauce
1 loaf sliced, firm-textured bread
Thinly sliced pimiento-stuffed green olives or paprika for garnish

Score cucumber lengthwise with a fork; slice thin. In a medium bowl combine vinegar and water; add cucumber slices. Let stand at room temperature at least 30 minutes; drain well. Meanwhile combine cream cheese, mayonnaise, garlic powder, onion salt and Worcestershire sauce. Cut bread slices into 2-inch rounds with a cutter; spread lightly with cream cheese mixture. Top with a cucumber slice shortly before serving. Garnish with an olive slice, sprinkling of paprika, or both. Makes about 48.

MENU:
Art on a Monday Event
"A TEA WITH LOUISE MURDOCK"

Finger Sandwiches:
Sweet Onion,
Chicken Salad,
Crab and Olive spread,
and Cucumber cut as ribbons on dark and white bread 32-33

Crispy Cheese Wafers 28

Strawberry Bread with Strawberry butter 102
Banana Bread with Almond butter 103

Pecan Pie Muffins
Shortbread 170
Phyllo cups with Lemon Curd
Bite sized squares of Pumpkin Sheet Cake 238

Fruit Jewels 278
Chocolate Mice 261
Truffles 262
Almond Brittle Bars

Apricot Brandy Tea

BY THE *Pitcherful*

ORANGE PEACH SPRITZERS

Previous page:

William Glackens
Bouquet of Flowers and Vase, 1915, oil on canvas, WAM, The John W. and Mildred L. Graves Collection, 1991.19

5 cups fresh orange juice
²/₃ cup Peach Schnapps

2 ¹/₂ cups club soda, chilled
Grenadine, optional

Combine orange juice and Peach Schnapps in pitcher. Chill. Stir in club soda just before serving. Pour over ice cubes in stemmed glasses. Drizzle ¹/₂ teaspoon grenadine over each drink; don't stir. Makes 8 servings.

SCREWDRIVER TWISTS

3¹/₂ cups fresh orange juice
¹/₂ cup vodka
2 teaspoons fresh lemon juice

2 teaspoons Triple Sec or other orange-flavored liqueur
Garnish: orange slices

Combine all ingredients in a pitcher. Chill. Serve over ice, garnish glasses with orange slices.

PRAIRIE SUNSET MARGARITA

To line glass rims with salt or sugar, pour ¹/4 cup lemon or lime juice onto a rimmed plate. On another rimmed plate, scatter ¹/4 to ¹/2 cup sugar or salt. Dip the rim of the glass first in the juice, then in the sugar or salt. Shake off excess.

Memorable prairie sunsets, "curtains of rose and gold with pearly edges" described by Laura Ingalls Wilder in Little Town on the Prairie, *represented here in a glass, and a lovely way to end the day.*

³/4 cup premium tequila
¹/2 cup Cointreau (or Peach Schnapps or Grand Marnier)
1 (6-ounce) can frozen limeade concentrate

Zest of 1 lime
Ice
³/4 cup cranberry juice
Garnish: salt or sugar rim, with a fresh sage leaf

Place tequila, Cointreau, limeade concentrate and zest into blender. Add ice to fill container and blend well. Pour 1 inch of cranberry juice into margarita glasses, pour in ice mixture. Serve garnished with salt or sugar, and a fresh sage leaf. Makes 6 servings.

BOURBON SLUSH

1 (12-ounce) can frozen lemonade concentrate
1 (6-ounce) can frozen orange juice concentrate
12 ounces of bourbon (blended)

6 ounces water
1 (2-liter) bottle lemon-lime carbonated soda, chilled

Opposite page:

Left: American *goblet in the Russian pattern*, ca. 1880, cut lead glass, WAM, gift of the family of Marjorie Molz, 2007.4.148.

Right: Steuben Glass *Champagne Glass*, 1925-35, engraved two-color lead glass, WAM, gift of the family of Marjorie Molz, 2007.4.185

Use empty can from lemonade as measuring cup for water, and empty can from lemonade as measuring cup for bourbon. Mix all ingredients except for the soda. Freeze in glass jars or a plastic pitcher. Right before serving fill glass or punch bowl one-third frozen slush, two-thirds soda. Garnish with orange slice. Be careful; it doesn't taste "spiked". Makes 10 to 12 servings.

MANDARIN PEAR MIMOSA

This is a reinvigorated approach to the lovely standard Mimosa. If you can't find mandarin orange juice, try tangerine or blood orange juice.

4 cups mandarin orange juice
4 cups pear juice

2 (750-milliliter) bottles dry champagne, chilled
Garnish: orange or strawberry slice, or a sprig of mint

Stir the champagne into the juices and serve over ice. (May also add a dash of chilled grenadine to each serving to make a "Mimosa Sunrise".) Garnish with orange and strawberry slices. Makes 14 to 16 servings.

JACKIE O'S

This cocktail is feminine, classy and easy to make by the pitcherful. Best well-chilled ahead of time and served with a generous amount of ice in a pitcher, ready to be poured into martini glasses or on the rocks in tall glasses.

2 cups unsweetened pineapple juice
1 cup vodka
¼ cup apricot brandy
1 tablespoon grenadine

Mix ingredients in a pitcher and stir well. Chill. Makes 6 lovely cocktails.

ORANGE BLUSH

1 (12-ounce) can frozen orange juice
   concentrate, thawed
2 cups cranberry juice
½ cup granulated sugar
1 (32-ounce) bottle club soda or champagne, chilled

Combine orange juice, cranberry juice and sugar and stir until sugar is dissolved. Chill. Just before serving, stir in soda and pour over crushed ice. Makes 8 to 10 servings.

PEACH BELLINI

3 cups crushed ice
2 cups peeled, chopped peaches, fresh or frozen
1½ cups Peach Schnapps (or peach brandy)
2 cups champagne
1½ cups sugar
Garnish: edible flower (optional)

Fill blender with ice, add remaining ingredients and process until smooth. Pour into pitcher or wine glasses. Garnish with an edible flower, such as a pansy, marigold or nasturtium. Makes 8 servings.

BASIC DRINK *menu template to please any crowd*

Cocktail party
   Plan A: Keep it simple and serve only wine.
   Plan B: Plan A, plus champagne.
   Plan C: Plan A or B, in addition to one specialty cocktail and/or a full bar.

Dinner party
   Water or iced tea on the table; red or white wine; coffee with dessert.
   Optional: add a specialty drink on the table in a pitcher or have it served. If having a theme dinner, make the cocktail relate.

Brunch party
   Water, flat or sparkling; orange juice (fresh squeezed is always the best); grapefruit juice as a possible addition (or a blend with the orange juice); assortment of coffee and tea; one classic brunch cocktail such as a mimosa, champagne punch or a bellini.

BY THE *Punchbowl*

Call it retro chic, but punch is hip once again. An easy way to spread cheer is to mix up a punch and pull out the punch bowl and ladle. Enjoy these updated classics.

PLANTATION PUNCH

This needs to be made the day ahead, but is a traditional welcoming, but potent, punch.

3 cups fresh orange juice
3 cups unsweetened pineapple juice
1 1/2 cups fresh lemon juice
1 1/2 cups fresh lime juice
3/4 cup superfine sugar

3/4 cup grenadine
1 ripe pineapple, pared, cored and cut into
   1-inch cubes
1 1/2 cups golden or dark rum

The day before serving, mix the juices with the sugar and grenadine, and stir to dissolve the sugar. Place half of the pineapple cubes in a round ring mold (may use a tube cake pan). Pour in about 5 cups of the punch, and place in the freezer. Place rest of pineapple cubes in remaining punch and refrigerate until ready to serve. When ready to serve, add rum to the punch, pour into punch bowl. Dip the outside of the frozen ring in slightly warm water to loosen the ring from the mold (about 10 seconds). Unmold and place in the punch. Makes 12 to 16 servings.

WHISKEY SOUR PUNCH

Sigmund Menkes
Red Roses (detail), 1941,
oil on canvas, WAM,
The Roland P. Murdock
Collection, M38.42

1 (12-ounce) can frozen lemonade concentrate
1 (6-ounce) can frozen orange juice concentrate
3 cups water
3 cups orange juice

1 to 2 cups Jack Daniel's whiskey
1/4 to 1/2 cup fresh lemon juice
1/4 cup maraschino cherry juice
1 (12-ounce) can lemon-lime soda, chilled

Mix all, except for the soda, in a small punch bowl or large pitcher. Chill. Just before serving add soda; pour over ice in glasses. Garnish each with a skewer threaded with assorted fun fruit. Makes 12 servings

POMEGRANATE CHAMPAGNE PUNCH

½ cup water
½ cup sugar
2 (750 millimeter) bottles champagne, chilled
   (or a sparkling wine)

1½ cups white rum
1¼ cups pomegranate juice
Garnish: lemon slices, pomegranate seeds,
   cranberries, mint sprigs, frozen ice ring

Make a simple syrup by boiling the water and sugar in a small saucepan and simmer for 5 minutes. Cool. Combine champagne, rum, pomegranate juice in punch bowl and add syrup to sweeten to taste. Garnish and add frozen ice ring, if desired. Serve at once. Makes 20 servings.

KIR CHAMPAGNE PUNCH

2 (10-ounce) packages frozen
   raspberries (one thawed, one frozen)
1 (32-ounce) bottle club soda, chilled

1 cup crème de Cassis, chilled
3 (750 milliliter) bottles champagne, chilled
   (or a fizzy wine such as Blanc de Blanc)

Place thawed package of raspberries in a blender. Process until smooth. Strain. Pour raspberry purée into punch bowl with club soda and Cassis. Stir gently. Break up remaining package of raspberries and add to punch bowl. Pour champagne in slowly, resting bottles on the edge of punch bowl. Stir gently with an up and down motion. Serve at once. Makes 30 (4-ounce) servings.

FRESH FRUIT PUNCH

When grating lemon, lime or orange rind, be careful to remove only the outer, colorful skin. The white "pith" is too bitter.

2 cups sugar
1 cup water
¼ cup light corn syrup
¼ cup grated lemon rind

⅔ cup fresh lemon juice
4 cups unsweetened pineapple juice
2 cups orange juice
1 (1-liter) bottle club soda, chilled

Bring sugar, water and corn syrup to a boil in a saucepan, stirring constantly. Stir in lemon rind; reduce heat and simmer 5 minutes. Cool. Stir in lemon juice, pineapple juice, and orange juice. Cover and chill for 6 to 8 hours. Stir in club soda, and serve immediately. Makes 3 quarts.

ROSE HIP HIBISCUS TEA PUNCH

12 cups water
9 rose hip-hibiscus tea bags
¼ cup sugar
1 cup fresh lemon juice

1 cup fresh orange juice
6 cups ice cubes
Garnish: orange and lemon slices, rose petals
   that are pesticide-free

Boil water in a large saucepan; remove from heat and add tea bags, steeping for 10 minutes. Remove tea bags and stir in sugar. Chill for at least 1 hour. To serve, pour the tea into punch bowl, add lemon and orange juices and stir. Add ice, fruit slices and rose petals and serve. Makes 10 servings.

MOCHACHINO PUNCH

Simple, but so delicious and a nice alternative to fruit-flavored punch at brunch. For a spiked version, substitute 1 cup of Kahlua for 1 cup of the coffee.

1 cup sugar
6 cups strong brewed coffee
4 cups whole milk

1½ teaspoons vanilla extract
⅓ cup chocolate syrup
½ gallon vanilla ice cream, softened

Combine sugar and coffee in a punch bowl. Stir until the sugar is dissolved; let cool. Add milk, vanilla and chocolate syrup; mix well. Chill for 2 hours or until ready to serve. Add ice cream immediately before serving. Ladle into punch cups and serve. Makes 16 servings.

CROWN WITH AN ICE RING

Decorated ice rings add much to the visual appeal, but also serves to keep the punch chilled.

Use one 8-inch ring or two or three 4-inch molds to chill 8 to 12 servings of punch. A ring mold is traditional but you may also enjoy using other shapes and smaller rings, as they move freely and don't clog up the bowl. Improvise with ramekins, soup bowls or even emptied and cleaned sour cream containers as make-shift molds.

Fill the mold(s) halfway with water and add decorative elements such as fruits, flower petals, berries or herbs, arranging in a nice pattern. Freeze for about 30 minutes or until set. Remove from freezer and fill to the top with water. You may want to top it off again with some petals or fruits. Freeze until solid, about 2 or 3 hours.

When ready to use, run briefly under warm water and gently tap on mold to dislodge. Place immediately in the punch bowl.

FOUR FRUIT SLUSH

1 cup sugar
1¼ cups water
3 cups unsweetened pineapple juice
1 (6-ounce) can frozen orange juice
 concentrate, thawed

2 tablespoons fresh lemon juice
3 very ripe bananas, mashed
1 liter lemon-lime soda, chilled

Combine sugar and water; heat to boiling. Remove from heat. Add pineapple juice, orange juice concentrate and lemon juice. Stir in banana. Freeze overnight or until firm. Remove from freezer 45 minutes before serving. Stir in soda. Serve immediately. Makes about 3 quarts. From Bonnie Aeschliman.

OLD FASHIONED LEMONADE

4 cups water
¾ cup sugar

1 cup fresh lemon juice
1 lemon, sliced

To make the fresh lemon juice, first bring lemons to room temperature. Microwave for 10 seconds or roll on countertop with the palm of your hand. Cut in half and squeeze juice, using juicer. Strain to remove seeds.

Bring water to a boil, add sugar and stir until dissolved. Cool. Pour this mixture and lemon juice into a large pitcher, blending well. Chill. Serve over ice, garnish with lemon slices, carry glass to the porch and lay claim to the porch swing. Makes 4 servings.

FRUITY TEA

12 cups water
4 lemon flavored tea bags
4 orange flavored tea bags
½ cup sugar

6 cups ice
1 orange, thinly sliced
1 nectarine, pitted and sliced
1 peach, pitted and sliced

Boil water in a large saucepan; remove from heat and add tea bags, steeping for 10 minutes. Remove tea bags and stir in sugar; refrigerate until chilled, about 1 hour. Pour tea into large glass container for serving, add ice and fruit slices. Makes 10 servings.

CHARLIE LINDBERGH

Wichita's transformation into the "Air Capitol of the World" was powered by more than just ambition and jet fuel. Paradoxically, this potent cocktail, inspired by Charles Lindbergh, was concocted during the time of Prohibition and served by London's Savoy Hotel.

1 ¼ ounce dry London gin
1 ounce Lillet Blanc (a French wine aperitif)

¼ ounce apricot-flavored brandy
1 dash orange bitters

Shake with ice and strain into a stemmed cocktail glass. Makes 1 serving.

WICHITA TUMBLEWEED

The Tumbleweed was invented in Wichita by bartender Everett Bonner in 1958. "I was working at The Prairie Club and a gentleman wanted an after dinner drink. The Tumbleweed is what I came up with." Wichita bars didn't have a lot of liquors at that time and ice cream drinks were uncommon. The drink quickly gained national popularity. The Wichita Candle Club even offers it as their primary "dessert" fare. Everett doesn't give out the recipe, but here is how it is commonly made. You'll have to ask him about the secret ingredient. You can catch up with him tending bar at the Crown Uptown Dinner Theatre, where at age 80 he is indeed a legend. Thanks for the Tumbleweed, Everett.

1 ½ ounces Kahlua
¾ ounce light Crème de Cacao

½ ounce dark Crème de Cacao
2 to 3 scoops vanilla ice cream

Place ingredients in a blender and combine until creamy. Pour into large stemmed glasses to 1 inch from the top. Top with whipped cream, sprinkle with chocolate shavings and serve with a straw. Makes 2 servings.

THE HAYRIDE

In honor of Governor Sebelius' inauguration, this commemorative cocktail was created by PB&J Restaurants.

Cinnamon sugar
2 apple slices
1 orange slice
½ teaspoon brown sugar
½ teaspoon Drambuie

1 ounce brandy
1 ounce dark spiced rum
2 ounces apple cider
Ice cubes

Moisten edge of a martini glass with water and press into cinnamon sugar to create sugared rim. Slit two apple slices in the middle and place on rim of glass. In a martini shaker, muddle the orange, brown sugar and Drambuie. Add brandy, rum, apple cider and ice cubes. Cover and shake; strain into prepared glass. Makes 1 serving.

Charles Lindbergh (left) and Walter Beech pose in front of a Travel Air airplane in 1929 on one of Lindbergh's visits to Wichita. With a bustling new business, Beech turned down a chance in Feb. 1927 to build a plane for Lindbergh, who was at that time planning his New York to Paris flight. Lindbergh ended up using another plane for the historic crossing in May 1927, but often visited Wichita.

JAZZ IT UP : *beverage garnishes*

A fun garnish is an easy way to turn a simple drink into something special. Here are some ideas:
- edible flower garnish (marigold, nasturtium, pansy)   - float fruit kabobs or melon balls or berries in a drink
- frost the glasses in the freezer for a cold beverage   - freeze berries and drop into the glass

For double impact make floral ice cubes by placing an edible flower or petals in each ice cube tray compartment. Fill tray with water, making sure that the petals are submerged, and freeze overnight. This same flower blossom can be used to carry through the theme by decorating the serving platters, or placed between two glass plates.

Vienna Porcelain Factory
Teapot, late 18th century,
painted porcelain, WAM,
the Florence Naftzger Evans
Collection, 1962.46

HOT SCARLET WINE PUNCH

1 (32-ounce) bottle cranberry juice cocktail (4 cups)

$^1/_3$ cup packed brown sugar

2 sticks cinnamon

4 whole cloves

1 (750-milliliter) bottle white Zinfandel

Combine cranberry juice, brown sugar, cinnamon sticks and cloves in a large saucepan. Bring to boil; reduce heat and simmer, uncovered, for 5 minutes. Remove spices, then add wine and heat just until warm. Ladle into mugs or transfer to a warm, heatproof pitcher. Substitute $3^1/_4$ cups white grape juice for the white Zinfandel and omit the brown sugar for a non-alcoholic drink. Makes 14 servings.

FIVE SPICE WASSAIL

One of the nice things about this wassail is that it can be kept hot in a percolator all day and still be delicious. Use a large coffee percolator dedicated to brewing the cider (after using it for this recipe, the spices may permanently flavor the percolator).

1 gallon apple cider

1 (32-ounce) jar cranberry juice cocktail (or 2 cups cranberry juice and 2 cups orange juice)

1 orange, quartered

1 teaspoon whole cloves

6 whole star anise pods

1 teaspoon nutmeg

$1^1/_2$ teaspoons whole allspice

6 to 8 cinnamon sticks

3 peppercorns (optional)

$^1/_4$ cup brown sugar

1 cup of dark rum

Pour the cider and cranberry juice into the percolator. Add the next 8 ingredients to the coffee basket. Let perk. Add rum before serving. Better even the second day: percolate again through the spices, adding another half cup of rum to cider after it has re-brewed. May be prepared and served from the large percolator, or placed in an attractive pot on the stove with spices tied into a bag and simmered for 30 minutes. If serving from stovetop, remove spice bag prior to serving and garnish with floating lemon and orange slices on top.

WHITE CHOCOLATE LATTÉ

If you have an espresso maker with a steamer you are all set. But you can make this café specialty by heating the milk in the microwave for a minute, frothing with a beater and adding to very strong brewed coffee.

2 ounces white chocolate, grated
1/2 cup of espresso (or strong brewed coffee)

1 1/4 cups hot milk, frothed
Whipped cream

Stir white chocolate into the hot espresso or coffee. Add hot milk and pour into mugs. Top with dollop of whipped cream. Makes 2 servings.

SPIRITED DESSERT COFFEES

Café Viennese: To a cup of strong coffee, add 1 ounce of cognac, top with whipped cream and nutmeg.

Café con Canela: To a cup of strong coffee, add 1 ounce of Kahlua and 1 teaspoon of vanilla extract. Top with whipped cream, grated semi-sweet chocolate and cinnamon; add a cinnamon stick as a stir stick.

Irish Coffee: To a cup of strong coffee, add 1 ounce of Bailey's Irish Whiskey and 2 teaspoons of sugar. Top with whipped cream.

COFFEE FOR GROUPS

It is easy to make really bad coffee for groups, but a little care can make it welcoming instead. The main trick is to get the proportions right, use a good (and clean) percolator, and serve it immediately after it is brewed. Flavor deteriorates when it is kept for more than one hour, either in a percolator or in carafes. Do not re-heat coffee. If you have to brew more while guests are there, it is fine: the smell of the brewing will be nice.

You might consider whether you really need to use a large coffee urn, as most of them brew 36 cups or more. Instead, consider using several pump pots (you can even then serve several types of coffee), and just brew several pots in your regular coffee maker.

If using a coffee urn percolator for a larger group, open a fresh supply of coffee for each event, do not use ground coffee from a can which has been opened for more than a week. Use a medium coffee brew (such as "Folger's Columbian") for greatest acceptance. The general proportion is one tablespoon of coffee per cup; the following will help you estimate what you will need:

To serve 25, use 1/2 pound of coffee and 1 1/4 gallons of water
To serve 50, use 1 pound of coffee, and 2 1/2 gallons of water
To serve 75, use 1 1/2 pounds of coffee and 3 3/4 gallons of water
To serve 100, use 2 pounds of coffee, and 5 gallons of water

Simple additions to the coffee serving area can create a very nice touch, allowing guests to make a specialty coffee. Some fun additions to set out, along with the usual cream, sugar/sweetener include: whipped cream, semi-sweet chocolate shavings (bowl or shaker), shaker with vanilla powder, shaker with cinnamon, cinnamon sticks or flavored Italian syrups.

A BEAUTIFUL TABLE, *happy times*

A COMBINATION OF FRUIT WITH FLORAL CENTERPIECES IS A BEAUTIFUL ADDITION.
Try putting the fruit in the base of a large glass vase so that it is a visible accent to cover stems.
Great combinations:

- Strawberries with pink peonies and pink roses
- Green apples with hydrangeas
- Lemons with sunflowers
- Red grapes with sunflowers

A generation or two ago, children absorbed table manners and social graces at Grandma's dinner table, set with fine china and silver. Now everyone may be dressed in jeans and sneakers, and dinners may be eaten on the go. However, the tradition of learning manners can continue at Grandma's table. Etiquette is not stuffy, but rather useful in making other people comfortable and giving one confidence in a strange situation. Learning the basic rules can help you go anywhere with dignity and esteem.

WAIT UNTIL STARTING Don't be the first to start eating. Let the host or hostess, or the eldest person at the table, begin the meal. Don't eat more quickly or slowly than others at the table; pace yourself by watching others.

DON'T FORGET THE BASICS: Ask, don't reach. Mouth closed when chewing. No food in your mouth when speaking. Smaller bites, and chew completely. Elbows at your side and not resting on the table while eating. Participate in polite conversation. Don't kick the table. Don't "park" chewing gum on the side of your plate; remember to remove it before you come to the table. Ask to be excused.

WHERE DO THE KNIVES AND SPOONS GO, and which plate is yours?
Remember BMW: bread, meal, water. Your bread plate is on the left, then your dinner plate and then your water glass.

The tip of the knife should go right below the water glass on the right, with the blade part turned toward the plate. The teaspoon goes on the outside of your knife, and your soup spoon goes next to the teaspoon. Place the larger dinner fork on the left, close to the plate, and the smaller salad fork next to it.

NAPKIN GOES ON YOUR LAP, as long as you are seated at the table.
If you have to leave the table during dinner, place your napkin on your chair seat. When you have finshed eating, place the folded napkin at the left of your plate.

Cut with your fork in your left hand and your knife in your right…but eat from your fork in your right hand (That is, unless you are using the European method where one holds the fork in the left hand, tines facing down, the knife in the right, and then the entrée may be cut. With the fork still in the left hand, the fork is lifted, tines down, and the food is brought to the mouth). And never gesture with a knife or fork, particularly with food on it, as you are most likely not a pirate.

NO BANGING ABOUT THE BOWL OR SLURPING. Scoop away from yourself, toward the center of the bowl. Sip soup from the side of the spoon. It's OK to tip the bowl to get the last bit of soup into your spoon, but tip away from yourself, not toward. Don't put your face too close to the bowl.

IGNORE A RINGING TELEPHONE DURING DINNER. Dinner is best enjoyed without a television on nearby. Wash your hands before dinner, and while you are doing so begin to think about a conversation that you can bring to the table. And for goodness sake, come to the table when called.

OFFER TO ASSIST WITH SERVING AND CLEARING. Remember to serve from the left, remove dishes from the right, and carry no more than two plates at a time. Do not begin clearing the table until the last person has finished eating. ENJOY!

Right: Mary Cassatt, *Mother and Child*, ca. 1890, oil on canvas, WAM, The Roland P. Murdock Collection, M109.53 (*see* Mary Cassatt's *Caramels au Chocolat* on p. 260)

S ETTING THE TABLE *is a fun activity in our home: start early and let creativity reign.*

For large events, start about a week ahead, setting out the serving platters on the buffet table, with labels of what each will hold, and putting the linens and place settings at the dining table. Fun with napkins is just that: fun. It can bring a smile to do something creative with what to use as a napkin ring, or what to use as a napkin (bandana, maps, interesting fabric squares). Another way to make things interesting is to try out some different ways to fold the napkin. There are lots of little booklets out with creative folds.

Beautiful Salads
Goat Cheese and Spiced Peppered Pecan Salad 48
B.L.T. Salad 48
Big Italian Salad 49
Spinach Apple Salad with Curried Viniagrette 50
Strawberry Jicama Salad with Fruity Viniagrette 50
Luscious Salad 50
Pancetta Wrapped Peach Arugula Salad 51

Grand Quick Salads
Parmesan Croutons 52
Toffeed Pecans 52
Classic Snappy Dressing 52
Feta Dressing 52
Sunburst Dressing 53
Spinach Salad Dressing 53
Basic Great Vinaigrette 53
Raspberry Balsamic Vinaigrette 53
Orange Almond Vinaigrette 53

Vegetable Salads
Earth Salad 54
Pesto Antipasto Salad 54
Crunch Pea Salad 55
Three Bean Broccoli Salad 55
Broccoli Salad 56
Sunshine Broccoli Salad 56
Old Fashioned Sweet and Sour Slaw 56
Chipotle Broccoli Slaw 57
Asian Noodle Slaw 57
Genevieve's Salad 57
Garlic Salad 57

Fruit Salads
Grand Marnier Sauce with Fresh Fruit 58
Poppy Seed Fruit Salad Dressing 58
Mr. Mango Goes To Washington 58
Sunray Fruit Platter 59
Fresh Fruit Salad with Citrus Gastrique 59
White Sangria Fruit Ring 59

Icebox Salads
Apricot Salad 60
Cranberry Pineapple Salad 60
Cranberry Banana Salad 60
Strawberry Pretzel Salad 60
Classic Tomato Aspic 61

Salads & Dressings

Severin Roesen
Nature's Bounty, ca. 1860,
oil on canvas, WAM, gift
of George E. Vollmer,
1995.15

GOAT CHEESE and SPICED PEPPERED PECAN SALAD

Spiced Peppered Pecans

3 cups pecan halves
6 tablespoons unsalted butter
1 teaspoon ground cumin (or hot paprika)

$1/2$ teaspoon cayenne pepper
$1/2$ teaspoon salt

Balsamic Vinaigrette

4 cloves garlic, minced
2 teaspoons Dijon mustard
2 tablespoons honey
1 cup balsamic vinegar

$1/2$ cup red wine vinegar
2 tablespoons fresh lemon juice
1 teaspoon salt
1 to 3 cups olive oil

Salad

2 (6-ounce) goat cheese rounds, at
   room temperature
6 cups assorted baby greens, washed and dried

1 small bunch arugula, washed and dried
1 Granny Smith apple, cored and chopped
2 green onions, chopped

If you don't have a centrifugal salad spinner, or don't wish to store one in your cabinets, try using a clean pillow case to dry your greens. After their bath, put the dripping greens into the pillowcase. Grab the pillowcase about half way down to close it tightly and then swing it around and around. Over your head, or at your side, swing away and you can even dance a jig. After a minute or so, check your greens: the pillowcase will be damp and the greens dry.

To make the spiced peppered pecans, preheat oven to 350°F. Melt butter in a small saucepan over medium heat; stir in cumin, cayenne, and salt. Remove from heat and add pecans; toss to coat well. Spread the coated pecans in a single layer on a baking sheet and toast for 7 to 9 minutes, until golden brown. Set aside to cool for at least 15 minutes. (May be stored in airtight container if made ahead of time.)

To make the vinaigrette, blend garlic, mustard, honey, both vinegars, lemon juice and salt for about 15 seconds in a blender or food processor. Pour in about $1/2$ cup of the olive oil, blending until the mixture emulsifies (about 2 to 5 seconds). Taste and add more oil as desired. Traditionally salad dressing recipes call for three parts of oil to one part of vinegar, but experiment to decide how much oil you like.

To make the salad, cut the goat cheese rounds into quarters and gently form each quarter into a disk. Coarsely grind 1 cup of spiced pecans in a food processor. Pour ground pecans into a medium bowl; roll the goat cheese rounds in the ground pecans to cover completely. To serve, toss baby greens, arugula, apple, onion, and remaining 1 cup spiced pecans and balsamic vinaigrette, to taste, in a large bowl. Serve salads on individual plates, top each with disk of pecan-coated goat cheese. Makes 8 servings.

B.L.T. SALAD

"Rita's Salad," named for Wichita Country Club Ladies Card Room attendant Rita Butler, popular over the past two decades and is ordered there by name: Romaine, iceberg and red leaf lettuce, chopped fine (or shredded), tossed lightly with Ranch dressing, chopped smoked bacon, and finely chopped scallions

6 bacon slices
1 cup $3/4$-inch cubed bread
$1/4$ teaspoon minced garlic
1 tablespoon fresh lemon juice
$1/4$ cup mayonnaise

1 tablespoon water
1 small red onion, sliced
Salt and pepper
$1/2$ pound cherry tomatoes (about $3/4$ pint)
1 head Boston lettuce

Cook bacon in a skillet until crisp; reserve 1 tablespoon bacon drippings in skillet, drain bacon on paper towels and crumble. Sauté bread cubes in bacon drippings, with salt to taste, until golden brown; transfer to paper towels to cool. Whisk garlic, lemon juice, mayonnaise and water together in a small bowl; salt and pepper to taste. Slice onion and halve tomatoes. Tear lettuce into bite-size pieces. In a large bowl toss together onion, tomatoes, lettuce, half of bacon and croutons, salt and pepper to taste, and enough dressing to coat. Divide salad between plates and top with remaining croutons and bacon. Makes 4 servings.

BIG ITALIAN SALAD

How often do you hear "just bring a big green salad" and then lack inspiration at the produce counter? Well, here is a very good salad, with lots of color and flavor, texture variety and a nice zingy dressing.

1 large head romaine lettuce, washed, dried and torn into small pieces, (about 8 cups)

3 Roma tomatoes, cut into wedges (or 1 cup cherry tomatoes, halved)

6 green onions, chopped

1 cup fresh mushrooms, sliced

1 cucumber, peeled, cut lengthwise and thinly sliced

$1/2$ small red onion, cut into thin wedges

$1/2$ red or yellow bell pepper, seeds and membrane removed and chopped

$1/2$ cup shredded carrots

$1/2$ cup sliced, pickled pepperoncini peppers

$1/2$ cup pitted and halved Kalamata olives or other brine-cured black olives

1 cup crumbled Feta cheese (about 4 ounces)

Dressing

$1/2$ cup balsamic vinegar

2 garlic cloves, crushed

2 tablespoons fresh lemon juice

$3/4$ teaspoon salt

$1/2$ teaspoon dried red pepper flakes

1 cup olive oil

Combine lettuce, tomatoes, green onions, mushrooms, cucumber, red onion, yellow pepper and carrots in a large bowl. Place vinegar, garlic, lemon juice, salt and pepper flakes in blender. Blend ingredients. With the motor running, gradually add oil in a slow stream. Taste and adjust salt and pepper. Pour over salad mixture. Toss to mix. Add pepperoncini, olives and Feta cheese and serve. Makes 8 servings.

SPINACH APPLE SALAD with CURRIED VINAIGRETTE

Curried Vinaigrette
1 cup white wine vinegar
1 1/3 cups vegetable oil
2 tablespoons chutney, minced
2 teaspoons curry powder
1 1/2 teaspoons salt
2 teaspoons dry mustard
1/2 teaspoon hot pepper sauce

Spinach Apple Salad
4 pounds fresh spinach, stems removed, torn
1 Red Delicious apple, cored and thinly sliced
1 Granny Smith apple, cored and thinly sliced
1 cup toasted slivered almonds
1 cup raisins
2/3 cup thinly sliced green onions
1/4 cup toasted sesame seeds

Whisk dressing ingredients together (or place in bottle and shake). Set aside. Toss salad ingredients together. Just before serving, pour dressing over salad and serve. Makes 10 servings.

Variation: Substitute almonds for 1/2 cup of chopped peanut garnish, and serve this with Oriental Dressing:

1/2 cup cider vinegar
1/2 cup water
1 tablespoon soy sauce

1 teaspoon sesame oil
1/4 cup natural peanut butter
3 tablespoons brown sugar

Combine ingredients in a blender and purée until smooth. Add dressing to salad and toss to coat.

STRAWBERRY JICAMA SALAD with FRUITY VINAIGRETTE

Dressing
1 cup hulled and halved strawberries
2 tablespoons raspberry vinegar
2 tablespoons brown sugar
1/4 cup olive oil
1/4 teaspoon sesame oil
1/2 teaspoon lemon juice
Kosher salt and freshly ground black pepper

Salad
4 cups mixed field greens
1 cup hulled and halved strawberries
1 medium jicama, peeled and julienned

Garnish: 1/4 cup toasted pistachios, chopped

Process dressing ingredients in a food processor or blender until smooth. Set aside. Combine salad ingredients, and just before serving toss with dressing and sprinkle with pistachios. Makes 6 servings.

LUSCIOUS SALAD
Served by the Dairy Hollow House in Eureka Springs, Arkansas, the recipe of this great combination of spinach, avocados and orange still creates great salads although the inn is now a retreat center for writers (The Dairy Hollow House Cookbook can still be found online, however). Prepare to make this luscious salad again and again.

Dressing
1/3 cup fresh orange juice
3 tablespoons red wine vinegar
1 tablespoon lemon juice
1 tablespoon sugar
1/2 teaspoon soy sauce
1/2 teaspoon grated orange rind
Freshly ground black pepper

Salad
6 cups fresh spinach
1 or 2 navel oranges, peeled, sectioned
  and seeded
1 ripe avocado, peeled and diced
4 green onions, sliced, including tops
1 large clove garlic
1/3 cup peanut oil (or canola)

Combine dressing ingredients in a jar and shake. Wash the spinach throughly, dry and wrap in a towel. Prepare oranges, avocado and onions and add to a bowl which has been rubbed with a large clove of garlic. Add spinach and lightly toss with the oil. Shake dressing again and pour over salad just before serving. Makes 6 servings.

PANCETTA WRAPPED PEACH ARUGULA SALAD

2 tablespoons balsamic vinegar
2 teaspoons fresh lemon juice
1/4 teaspoon salt
4 tablespoons olive oil (divided use)
4 firm-ripe peaches (1 1/2 pounds)
24 thin slices pancetta (1 1/4 pound Italian
   unsmoked cured bacon)

6 ounces arugula and lettuce mix (6 cups)
2 1/2 ounces crumbled feta cheese or ricotta
   salata (1/2 cup)
Freshly ground black pepper
Optional: thin slices red onion, dried cranberries

Whisk vinegar, juice, and salt together, add 2 tablespoons olive oil, whisk until emulsified. Immerse peaches in boiling water 15 seconds, then plunge in a bowl of cold water. Peel peaches and cut each into 6 wedges; wrap a pancetta slice around each wedge, overlapping ends of pancetta. Heat remaining oil in a nonstick skillet until hot but not smoking, then cook peaches in 2 batches, placing the side down first which has the loose end of the pancetta. Turn peaches occasionally with tongs, until pancetta is browned on all sides and cooked through, about 5 minutes per batch. Transfer to a plate and cover loosely with foil. Divide arugula and lettuce among 8 plates, top with warm pancetta-wrapped peaches. May also wish to add thin slices of red onion or dried cranberries. Drizzle with dressing and sprinkle with feta or ricotta and pepper. Serve immediately. Makes 8 servings.

Mary Petty
The Conservatory, 1952, watercolor and graphite on paper, WAM, The Roland P. Murdock Collection, M117.54

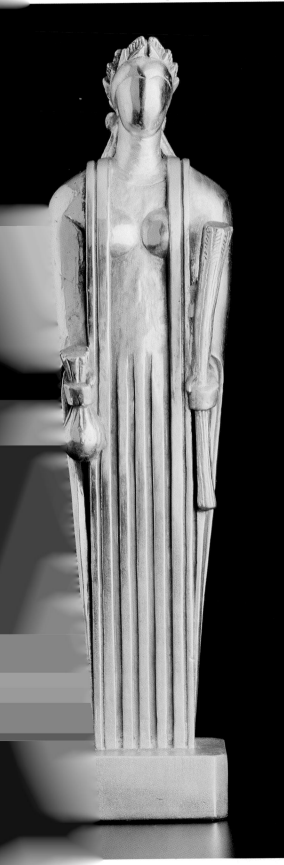

PARMESAN CROUTONS

1 baguette
1/4 cup good olive oil, plain or flavored with basil or garlic
Kosher salt
Freshly ground black pepper
3/4 cup shredded Parmesan cheese (3 ounces)

Preheat oven to 400°F. Slice the baguette diagonally into 1/4-inch thick slices (or simply ask the bakery to do so). Depending on the size of the baguette, you should get about 20 to 25 slices. Lay the slices in one layer on a baking sheet and brush well with olive oil and sprinkle liberally with salt and pepper. Sprinkle with shredded Parmesan (grate the Parmesan as you would carrots, rather than the more traditional "grated" Parmesan, which is actually finely ground). Bake the toasts for 15 to 20 minutes, until browned and crisp. Serve at room temperature.

TOFFEED PECANS

3 tablespoons butter
1/2 cup sugar
1 1/2 cups pecan halves

Line baking sheet with foil; butter foil. Set baking sheet aside. In a heavy 10-inch skillet, melt butter over medium heat; stir in sugar and add pecan halves. Cook over medium-low heat, stirring constantly, for 4 to 5 minutes or until sugar melts and turns rich, golden brown. Spread pecan mixture onto prepared baking sheet. Cool completely. Break into small pieces. Makes about 1 1/2 cups.

DRESSINGS

Classic Snappy Dressing

1/2 cup chopped sweet onion
1 cup sugar
2 teaspoons dry mustard

1/2 cup red wine vinegar
1 cup canola oil

In a blender, combine onion, sugar, mustard, and red wine vinegar. With the motor running, blend and slowly add canola oil until well mixed. Pour on salad and toss. Good with toffeed pecans (above), feta cheese and red onion slices.

Feta Dressing

1/4 cup balsamic vinegar
1 teaspoon Dijon mustard
1 tablespoon honey
1 clove garlic

1/2 teaspoon dried basil
  (1 tablespoon fresh)
1/4 teaspoon dried red pepper flakes
3/4 cup olive oil
1/4 cup Feta cheese

Place vinegar, mustard and honey in food processor or blender. With motor running, drop in garlic, basil and pepper flakes. While still running, add olive oil, then Feta cheese, processing until smooth. Season with salt and freshly ground black pepper. Good over salad of romaine, red bell pepper strips, sliced cucumber and tomatoes with herb croutons.

Sunburst Dressing

2 tablespoons mayonnaise
1 1/2 teaspoons Dijon mustard
1/3 cup white wine or balsamic vinegar
1/2 teaspoon salt

1/4 teaspoon hot pepper sauce
1 teaspoon Worcestershire sauce
1 cup olive oil (or 1/2 olive and 1/2 canola oils)

Place mayonnaise, mustard, vinegar, salt, hot pepper sauce and Worcestershire in a blender. With motor running, add oil in a thin stream until it emulsifies. Good over a salad of mixed greens, cucumber slices, marinated artichoke hearts, green olives, bacon, blue cheese, garnished with red bell pepper strips placed like a sun burst.

Basic Great Vinaigrette

1/4 cup balsamic vinegar
2 cloves garlic
1 teaspoon Worcestershire sauce
1 teaspoon Dijon mustard

1 1/4 teaspoon cayenne pepper
3/4 cup olive oil
3/4 to 1 teaspoon salt

Combine vinegar, garlic, Worcestershire sauce, mustard, and cayenne pepper in blender or food processor. Whirl to combine. With blender on, slowly pour in oil. Season to taste with salt.

Raspberry Balsamic Vinaigrette

3/4 cup thawed frozen unsweetened raspberries
1/2 teaspoon Dijon mustard
1/4 cup white balsamic vinegar (or white
    wine vinegar)

1 clove garlic, peeled
2 tablespoons honey
1/2 teaspoon salt
1 cup canola oil

Purée raspberries in food processor; strain through sieve to remove seeds. You will have about 1/2 cup raspberry purée. Return this to the food processor and add mustard, vinegar, garlic, honey and salt; blend. With motor running, slowly add the oil until mixture thickens. Taste; adjust seasonings. Great over romaine lettuce, red onion slices, dried cranberries, feta cheese crumbles, toasted pecans and bacon crumbles. (Note: Substitute 1 cup of strawberries for the raspberries and omit the mustard to make this into a Strawberry Balsamic Vinaigrette.)

Orange Almond Vinaigrette

1 tablespoon Dijon mustard
1/3 cup orange juice concentrate, undiluted
1/3 cup rice vinegar
1 1/2 teaspoons grated orange rind
3/4 teaspoon salt

Dash cayenne pepper
1 1/2 tablespoons honey
3/4 cup vegetable oil
1/3 cup toasted chopped almonds
1/3 to 1/2 cup chopped fresh chives

Place first 7 ingredients in a bowl of food processor fitted with metal blade or blender. Process until mixed. With motor running, gradually add enough oil to make a thin emulsion. Add chives and almonds. Process only 3 to 4 seconds to mix. Great with well-washed greens and plenty of mandarin oranges, garnished with slivered almonds.

Spinach Salad Dressing

2 tablespoons chopped onion
1/2 cup sugar
1 teaspoon salt
1 teaspoon dry mustard

2 tablespoons plain yogurt
1/3 cup cider vinegar
1 cup vegetable oil

Mix onion, sugar, salt, mustard, yogurt and vinegar in a food processor. With the motor running, slowly add oil. Blend well and refrigerate. Serve over fresh spinach leaves with bacon crumbles, slices of hard boiled egg and Parmesan croutons. From Susan Wilhite and Karen Root.

When dressing a large salad, start with half of the dressing, toss, then add more dressing a few tablespoons at a time until it is dressed to your liking. This will avoid too much dressing on your beautiful salad.

Opposite Page:

John Bradley Storrs
Ceres, ca. 1928,
nickel-plated cast terracotta,
WAM, gift of the Friends
of the Wichita Art Museum,
Inc., 1987.7

Ceres, the Roman goddess of grain and the growth of plants, was worshiped in order to encourage a fertile harvest. The Art Museum's Ceres is a reduced version of the 31-foot-high figure by John Storrs that stands atop Chicago's Board of Trade Building (1928), still the world's leading grain market. - SG

EARTH SALAD

Served at a Wichita Art Museum "Art on a Monday" featuring Stan Herd, this orzo and bulgur salad was named to reflect its hearty, earthy nature, representative of Herd's crop art. Bulgur wheat (kernels which have been steamed, dried and crushed) is often confused with, but is not the same as, cracked wheat. It is used in pilafs and other salads such as tabbouleh, and found in most grocery stores. This is best made a day ahead and served on a bed of greens.

MENU:
Art on a Monday Event
*"STAN HERD:
A PRAIRIE ART STORY"*

*Earth Salad with
Roasted Pork
Tenderloin Medallions
served on a bed
of greens 54*

Wheat Potato Bread 105

*Apple Cake with Hot
Buttered Rum Sauce 230*

1 cup orzo pasta
1 cup bulgur wheat
1/4 to 1/3 cup olive oil
1/4 to 1/2 cup balsamic vinegar
1/2 cup fresh parsley
2 tablespoons chopped shallots
1 teaspoon sugar
1 teaspoon dry mustard
1 cup sliced celery

1 cup shredded carrots
1 cup seeded, diced fine, cucumber
1/2 to 1 cup dried cranberries
1/4 to 1/2 cup chopped green onions
   (including tops)
1/2 cup feta cheese, crumbled
1/4 teaspoon black pepper
1 teaspoon salt

Cook orzo according to package directions. Drain, reserving hot liquid. Put bulgur wheat into 2-cup glass measure. Pour enough orzo liquid into glass measure to make 2 cups. Let stand 45 minutes. Meanwhile whisk together the olive oil, balsamic vinegar, parsley, shallots, sugar and dry mustard in a large bowl (adjust amounts of vinegar and oil to your taste). Add orzo, celery, carrots, cucumber and cranberries and toss to coat. When bulgur is finished, add to orzo and vegetable mixture. Chill at least 4 hours. Toss with green onions and feta cheese before serving. Salt and pepper to taste. Makes 10 to 12 servings. From Susan Wilhite.

Variations: Other vegetables can be added, such as chopped tomatoes or peppers (green, red, yellow). Additions of toasted nuts (pecan or walnuts) or toasted shelled sunflower seeds may also add crunch. You can also top this salad with medallions of roast pork tenderloin or grilled chicken and turn it into an entreé.

PESTO ANTIPASTO SALAD

1 pound rotini or fusilli pasta
1/2 pound sharp provolone cheese, diced into
   1/2-inch cubes
1 (15-ounce) can garbanzo beans, drained
   and rinsed
3 1/2 ounces sliced hard salami, cut into strips
1/2 cup pitted, brine-cured black olives
1/2 small red bell pepper, chopped (seeds and
   membrane removed)
1/2 teaspoon dried hot pepper flakes
3 Roma tomatoes, cut into thin wedges
1/4 cup minced parsley or basil (page 64
   for basil technique)

Dressing

3 garlic cloves
1/3 cup white balsamic vinegar
1 tablespoon water
1 teaspoon salt
2/3 cup olive oil
3 tablespoons grated Parmesan cheese
3 to 4 tablespoons pesto (purchased or recipe,
   page 14)

Cook pasta according to package directions. Do not overcook. Drain; rinse under cold water and drain again, and place in a large bowl. In a food processor or blender, combine garlic, vinegar, water and salt. While machine is running, slowly add olive oil. Blend in Parmesan and pesto. Toss pasta with three-fourths of the dressing (reserve the rest to add right before serving). Stir in cheese, garbanzo beans, salami, olives, bell pepper and pepper flakes. Cover and chill for 1 hour. Before serving add tomatoes, parsley (or basil) and toss with remaining dressing. Makes 10 to 12 servings.

CRUNCH PEA SALAD

Most families have folklore about the inventive ways kids try to hide their uneaten vegetables at the family dinner table. So I had to chuckle when my adult daughter, who had been most inventive in hiding peas as a child, served this salad. Yes, indeed, the crunchy pea salad (not the "squish" of cooked peas she disliked)! Makes a very nice side dish to an elegant dinner or as a plated salad served on a bed of lettuce.

$^1/_3$ cup sour cream

2 tablespoon red wine vinegar

1 tablespoon milk

1$^1/_4$ teaspoon sugar

$^1/_8$ teaspoon garlic powder

1 (10-ounce) package frozen peas, thawed

$^3/_4$ cup sliced water chestnuts

3 tablespoons sliced green onion

2 to 3 slices bacon, crisp cooked, drained and crumbled

Combine sour cream, vinegar, milk, sugar, salt and garlic powder in a small bowl; set aside. In large bowl combine peas, water chestnuts, onions and bacon. Add ingredients from the small bowl, tossing lightly to coat, cover and chill. Makes 4 servings. From RoxAnn Dicker.

BROCCOLI-THREE BEAN SALAD
With Red Cabbage and Orange Vinaigrette

1 (15-ounce) can red kidney beans

1 (15-ounce) can navy beans

1 (15-ounce) can pinto beans

2 cups thinly sliced red cabbage

1 cup small broccoli florets

$^1/_3$ cup raisins

$^1/_3$ cup sliced dried apricots

$^1/_3$ cup walnut pieces

Dressing

$^1/_3$ cup cider vinegar

$^1/_4$ - $^1/_3$ cup honey

2 tablespoons canola oil

3 tablespoons frozen orange juice concentrate, undiluted

2 teaspoons poppy seeds

Rinse and drain kidney beans, navy beans and pinto beans, and combine with red cabbage and broccoli florets in a salad bowl. Add raisins, apricots and walnut pieces. Set aside. Whisk together vinegar, honey, oil, orange juice concentrate and poppy seeds. Drizzle over bean and vegetable mixture and toss. Makes 8 servings. From Carol Jones.

Iva McCullough
Victorian Bouquet (detail), 1953, oil on canvas, WAM, bequest of Mrs. Iva McCullough, 1986.1.1

BROCCOLI SALAD

This deli standard is also favored at home. Easy to make and can keep for several days.

Frugal cooks will find that they can use almost all of the broccoli stem/stalk by simply trimming or peeling the outer skin off of the tougher, lower ends. Chop or slice as indicated in the recipe.

¹/₂ cup mayonnaise
1 ¹/₂ teaspoons sugar
1 tablespoon vinegar
1 bunch broccoli (florets and tender stalks)

¹/₂ sweet onion, chopped
¹/₂ pound bacon, cooked and crumbled
¹/₂ cup grated Cheddar cheese

Combine the mayonnaise, sugar and vinegar and allow to set for 3 or 4 hours in the refrigerator to allow flavors to develop. Chop the broccoli into bite-sized pieces. Add the onion, bacon and cheese. Toss with the mayonnaise mixture. Makes 6 servings.

SUNSHINE BROCCOLI SALAD

This is an improvement over the standard broccoli salad: it transports well, the blanched broccoli makes it easier to eat, and cranberries give it a tangy flavor. Adapted from a recipe in the Wichita Eagle.

8 cups fresh small broccoli florets (1 pound)

Dressing
1 cup mayonnaise (reduced-fat is fine, prefer Hellmann's)
1 tablespoon sugar
3 tablespoons vinegar

8 ounces cooked bacon slices, cut into ¹/₂-inch pieces
1 small purple onion, sliced thinly and quartered
³/₄ cup roasted, salted, shelled sunflower seeds
³/₄ cup dried cranberries
1 cup coarsely shredded Cheddar cheese

Bring a large pot of salted water to a vigorous boil. Add broccoli, and after water returns to a boil, cook for just 30 seconds. Drain immediately and plunge broccoli into a pot of ice water. Drain well in a mesh colander over the sink for at least 15 minutes. May need to be patted dry with paper towels before adding dressing.

While the broccoli cools, combine dressing ingredients in a small bowl. Combine bacon, onion, sunflower seeds and dried cranberries in a very large bowl. When broccoli has drained, add to this mixture and combine gently with a large spoon. Add cheese and dressing, stir just to combine. Cover and refrigerate at least one hour before serving. Makes 10 to 12 servings.

OLD FASHIONED SWEET AND SOUR SLAW

My childhood home was a farm right outside of the small town of Brookville, Kansas. Buffalo Bill slept at the Brookville Hotel, as did many cowboys when Kansas was the end of the line for trail drives up from Texas. The hotel opened in 1870 and has served family-style chicken dinners since 1915, and this coleslaw is part of that dinner. The Brookville Hotel, now located in Abilene, continues with the same delicious menu and is a Kansas tradition.

1 ¹/₂ pounds green cabbage, shredded
1 teaspoon salt
²/₃ cup sugar

¹/₃ cup cider vinegar
1 cup whipping cream (do not whip)

Placed shredded cabbage in covered dish in refrigerator for several hours. Mix ingredients in order given 30 minutes before serving. Chill and serve.

CHIPOTLE BROCCOLI SLAW

Dressing
1 cup mayonnaise
½ cup plain yogurt
2 tablespoons lemon juice
2 cloves garlic
½ teaspoon salt
1 or 2 chipotle chili peppers, canned in
   adobe sauce

Slaw
4 large broccoli stalks (florets removed), peeled
   and julienned
4 large carrots, peeled, julienned or grated
½ head of red cabbage (cored), shredded

Chipotle chili peppers are dried, smoked jalapenos. You can buy them dried, canned in adobo or powdered.

Combine dressing ingredients in food processor blender, adding just 1 chipotle chili pepper. Taste and adjust, adding more chipotle chili pepper if desired. Cover and chill. Combine slaw ingredients in a serving bowl; pour dressing over slaw and toss. Cover and chill until ready to serve. Makes 6 servings.

ASIAN NOODLE SLAW

2 (3-ounce) packages Ramen noodles (Beef or
   Oriental flavor)
¼ cup butter
4 ounces slivered almonds (about ¼ cup)
4 ounces roasted, salted, shelled
   sunflower seeds (about ¼ cup)
1 large head Chinese cabbage, chopped fine
   (or 2 [12-ounce] bags broccoli cole slaw)

6 green onions, sliced including tops

Dressing
½ cup red wine vinegar
½ cup canola oil
¾ cup sugar (brown or white)
2 tablespoons soy sauce (or 1 Ramen Noodle
   seasoning packet)

Break the noodles into small pieces, but do not include the flavoring packets. Sauté noodles in butter. Add almonds and sunflower seeds, sauté and set aside. Add cabbage and green onions. Make dressing in glass jar with lid. Shake to mix. Add to noodle mixture just before serving, toss to coat. Makes 8 to 10 servings. From Melba Webster.

GENEVIEVE'S SALAD

Jeanne Gordon describes a favorite "concoction" made by daughter Genevieve. Mix in proportions to your liking:
Chopped celery
Dried cranberries
Walnuts (or home-made granola)

Crumbled blue cheese (prefer Maytag)
Granny Smith apples, chopped
Wild rice cracker sticks

GARLIC SALAD

Joe Stumpe, Food Editor for The Wichita Eagle, *states Garlic Salad might well be "Wichita's Signature Salad" (2003). A popular menu item for several local restaurants (including Abe's Steakhouse, Doc's Steakhouse, Nu-Way Café and Spear's), Stumpe projects that it may have been "invented" here. While restaurants currently serving it regard it as a secret recipe, the daughter of Ken Hill, founder of Ken's Klub and the likely originator, shared his recipe. Hill describes that the key is to use real mayonnaise, extract as much moisture as possible from the lettuce, and to apply the dressing just prior to serving. Some versions use cabbage and dress it as a slaw, but usually served over shredded lettuce. Keep your breath mints handy.*

1 cup mayonnaise (prefer Hellmann's)
1 to 2 teaspoons garlic salt (prefer McCormick's)
2 tablespoons tomato juice

1 head lettuce, rinsed and dried
1 cup grated carrots and radishes
Garnish: Parsley, radish roses, paprika

Mix mayonnaise, garlic salt and tomato juice. Refrigerate. Remove outer leaves and core from lettuce (outer leaves may be used to line salad plate or bowl). Chop remaining lettuce into dime-size pieces to fill 6 cups. Line a colander with paper towels, add lettuce and top with more paper towels. Press down on lettuce to extract moisture. Remove lettuce and place in plastic bag lined with more paper towels. Refrigerate several hours. Grate carrots and radishes and pat dry. Refrigerate. Just before serving, toss chopped vegetables with dressing. Mound salad in bowl or plate and garnish. Serve with crackers such as Club or Ritz. From Suzy Hill, submitted by Joe Stumpe.

GRAND MARNIER SAUCE with FRESH FRUIT

1 cup cream	6 tablespoons Grand Marnier
1/2 cup sugar	1 teaspoon grated orange rind
1 tablespoon fresh lemon juice	Fresh fruit

Whip cream to soft peaks. Fold in sugar and rest of ingredients. Spoon over any fresh fruit, but this is especially good on strawberries and raspberries. Makes about 2 cups. From Martie Walker.

POPPY SEED FRUIT SALAD DRESSING

MANGO MOVES

Be careful when peeling a mango. It is a slippery little bugger and has an odd shaped flattened pit.

1/2 cup fresh lime juice	1 tablespoon ginger
1/2 cup honey	1 tablespoon dry mustard
1/3 cup distilled white vinegar	2 cups vegetable oil
1 teaspoon salt	1 tablespoon poppy seeds
1 cup sugar	

Hold the mango flat on a cutting board with the stem end in your palm. Use a very sharp knife and slice one half of it into 6 to 7 strips, down to the pit. Pull the peel back to release the strips so they fall into a bowl. Repeat with the second half.

Blend all ingredients except for the oil and poppy seeds in a food processor or blender. While the machine is running, gradually stream in oil and blend until mixture is thick and does not separate. Stir poppy seeds in by hand; refrigerate until ready to use. Serve with fresh fruit. Keeps for up to 2 weeks.

MR. MANGO GOES TO WASHINGTON

Vicki Tiahrt (wife of Rep. Todd Tiahrt) shares her favorite mango salsa, which won an award for ease of preparation at the 2006 Gourmet Gala in Washington, DC. It can be served as a side dish or as a salsa with chips.

3 mangoes, chopped	1 cup cilantro, chopped and loosely packed
Juice of 1 lime	Pinch of salt
1 inch fresh ginger root, peeled and finely chopped	

Combine all ingredients. Let sit at room temperature for 30 to 60 minutes to let flavors meld. Serve with chips as a salsa or as a side to grilled chicken, fish or pork.

SUNRAY FRUIT PLATTER

This works well for a buffet and was often served by Marjorie Merriweather Post at Mar-a-Lago. It can also be served as luncheon dessert instead of as a salad.

Banana Dressing
2 ripe bananas
2 tablespoons lemon juice
1/4 cup packed brown sugar
1/4 cup honey
1 cup heavy cream, whipped

Sunray Fruit
1 cup watermelon balls
8 slices cantaloupe
8 slices honeydew (Crenshaw) melon
8 grapefruit sections
16 orange sections

To make the banana dressing, combine the bananas, lemon juice, brown sugar and honey in a blender or food processor and purée until smooth; fold in the whipped cream. Mound watermelon balls in the center of a serving platter which is covered with dark green leafy lettuce. Arrange the remaining fruit around the center, like rays of the sun. Serve with banana dressing. Makes 8 to 10 servings.

FRESH FRUIT SALAD with CITRUS GASTRIQUE

Citrus Gastrique
1 cup fresh orange juice
1/4 cup sugar
Pinch salt
1 tablespoon lemon juice
1 tablespoon Grand Marnier (optional)

Fruit Salad
4 navel oranges, peeled and sectioned
1 pint fresh strawberries, rinsed, capped and sliced
1 cup fresh blueberries, rinsed and dried
2 cups seedless green grapes, rinsed and dried

In a small saucepan, combine orange juice, sugar and salt; simmer over high heat until syrupy, honey-colored and reduced to 1/4 cup, about 15 minutes. Remove from heat and add lemon juice and Grand Marnier, if desired.

Combine fruit in a trifle bowl (or other glass bowl). Pour warm dressing over fruit and toss to coat. Serve immediately or cover and chill for up to four hours. May serve room temperature or chilled. Makes 8 servings. From Bonnie Aeschliman.

WHITE SANGRIA FRUIT RING

With delightful color, this is a surprise hit and an updated use of gelatin. To make it a blush color, use a rose wine instead. If you wish to make this without the wine, you may substitute 1 1/2 cups white grape juice for the wine, making a total of 3 cups of juice.

2 envelopes unflavored gelatin
1 1/2 cups Riesling or Rose wine (divided use)
1 1/2 cups white grape juice
1/4 cup sugar

1 1/2 cups orange segments (cut from 2 navel oranges, or canned mandarin oranges)
1 cup seedless green grapes, cut in half lengthwise
1/2 pint fresh raspberries or sliced strawberries

Spray decorative mold with cooking spray. Sprinkle the gelatin over 1/2 cup of the wine in a small bowl, let stand for about 5 minutes (the gelatin will soften and swell). In a medium non-reactive saucepan over medium heat, combine 1 cup of wine, grape juice, sugar and bring to a soft boil and remove from heat. Add gelatin mixture and stir constantly until it is dissolved completely (about 2 minutes). Pour mixture into a medium bowl, set inside of a larger bowl of cool water. Let stand until thickened, but not set (about 20 to 30 minutes), then whisk to create tiny bubbles in the mixture. Fold in fruits and spoon into prepared mold. Refrigerate at least 4 hours.

When ready to serve, dip the mold in warm water for about 5 seconds, then run finger around the outer top edge to help break the seal. Place the mold over serving platter and then invert. Serve chilled. Makes 8 to 10 servings.

MICROWAVE JAM

If you have fruit that is just slightly too ripe, or leftover fruit, make it into a quick jam in the microwave. This is great for plums, nectarines, peaches and berries and you don't have to have a large quantity.

Wash and cut up the fruit, removing pits or blemishes. Combine equal amount of sugar to the amount of fruit, spritz with fresh lemon juice and place in a glass dish. Microwave on high for 8 to 15 minutes (depends on amount of fruit), stopping the cooking every minute or so to stir, until jam is thickened to desired consistency (will thicken more as it cools). Store in refrigerator for no more than two weeks.

ICEBOX SALADS

The early esteem of gelatin was closely tied to the development of the electric refrigerator. To be able to serve gelatin meant that one had a refrigerator, which was for a while, a mark of status (first sold in 1916 for $900, exceeding the cost of a car). Gelatin salads were seen as "dainty" and were popularized in the 1920s by recipe pamphlets. Now collectibles, these included beautiful food illustrations created by outstanding artists such as Norman Rockwell, Guy Rowe (Giro), Linn Ball, and Maxfield Parrish.

By the 1930s, refrigerators were found in many homes, and gelled or "congealed" salads of all types rose in celebrity. During the early quarter of the 20th century, immigrants entering Ellis Island in New York City were even served gelatin as a "Welcome to America" treat.

With blithe jocularity, yet reverence for the pervasive cultural phenomenon, the Smithsonian Institute held in a quasi-conference in 1991 on Jell-O brand history, featuring such topics as "American History is Jell-O® History," "The Dialectics of Jell-O® in Peasant Culture," "The Semiotics of Jell-O®," and "Jell-O® Salad or Just Desserts: The Poetics of an American Food".

APRICOT SALAD

Served at Wichita Sedgwick County Historical Museum Wreath Festival luncheon and Holiday Tables Luncheon at the Wichita Center for the Arts.

3/4 cup sugar
1 cup water
1 (17-ounce) can apricots, drained and diced
2 ripe bananas, diced

2 (10-ounce) boxes frozen strawberries
1 (15-ounce) can crushed pineapple
2 tablespoons lemon juice

Mix sugar and water; bring to a boil and let cool. Stir apricots, bananas, strawberries, and pineapple into sugar syrup. Add lemon juice. Spoon mixture into cupcake papers set in muffin tin; freeze. When frozen, store in zipper-lock bag. Remove from freezer 5 minutes before serving. Makes 15 servings.

CRANBERRY PINEAPPLE SALAD

1 (16-ounce) can cranberry sauce
1 (16-ounce) can crushed pineapple
1 (16-ounce) can fruit cocktail
1 (8-ounce) package cream cheese

1 (8-ounce) small container of frozen whipped topping, thawed
3/4 cup chopped pecans

Mix all ingredients together with an electric mixer. Spoon mixture into foil cupcake papers in a muffin tin. Fill almost full and freeze. When frozen put in zipper-lock bag or covered container. Remove from freezer 5 minutes before serving. Makes 12 servings.

CRANBERRY BANANA SALAD

1 (20-ounce) can pineapple tidbits
5 medium firm bananas, halved lengthwise and sliced
1 (16-ounce) can whole berry cranberry sauce

1/2 cup sugar
1 (12-ounce) carton frozen whipped topping, thawed
1/2 cup chopped walnuts

Drain pineapple juice into a medium bowl; set pineapple aside. Add bananas to the juice. In a large bowl, combine cranberry sauce and sugar. Remove bananas, discarding juice and add to cranberry mixture. Stir in pineapple, whipped topping and nuts. Pour into a 9 x 13-inch baking dish. Freeze until solid. Remove from freezer 15 minutes before cutting. Makes 12 to 16 servings.

STRAWBERRY PRETZEL SALAD

2 1/2 cups crushed pretzels
3/4 cup melted butter
2 tablespoons sugar, plus 3/4 cup sugar
1 (8-ounce) package cream cheese

1 (8-ounce) carton frozen whipped topping, thawed
2 (3-ounce) packages strawberry gelatin
1 (8-ounce) can crushed pineapple
2 (10-ounce) packages frozen strawberries

Preheat oven to 400°F. Mix pretzels, butter, and 2 tablespoons of sugar; press into a 9 x 13-inch baking dish and bake for 7 minutes. Set aside to cool. In a mixing bowl, cream together cream cheese and remaining sugar; fold in the whipped topping, and spread over the cooled crust. Chill. Drain the pineapple, reserve juice and add water to equal 2 cups; bring this to a boil in a microwave. In a medium bowl, dissolve the gelatin in the boiling water, and allow to cool slightly. Add the strawberries and pineapple; pour over the cream cheese mixture. Refrigerate until serving. Serve slices with dollop of whipped topping and a sliced strawberry.

CLASSIC TOMATO ASPIC

Tomato aspic is a low fat salad, high in vitamin C, and while it may seem a little "retro" it is a healthy, elegant and pretty classic worth rediscovering. Pamela D. Kingsbury shares this recipe of her mother's, Donna Evans Kingsbury, noting that the aspic is a very attractive salad, like a mosaic, and leaves a delightful aroma in the kitchen.

3 cups tomato juice (preferably Campbell's), divided use

2 envelopes unflavored gelatin

2 tablespoons sugar

2 teaspoons salt

4 tablespoons apple cider vinegar

4 tablespoons Worcestershire sauce

1 teaspoon Dijon mustard

1 cup finely chopped celery

1 cup finely chopped cucumber

1/2 cup finely chopped green pepper

4 tablespoons chopped green onions

Garnish: Lettuce leaves, mayonnaise, ripe sliced avocados

Place 1/2 cup of tomato juice in a small bowl, add the unflavored gelatin and stir. Set aside until firm. In a small saucepan bring the remaining tomato juice to a simmer and stir in the salt and sugar. In a small bowl combine the vinegar with the Worcestershire sauce and mustard and whisk vigorously until the mustard is smooth. Stir into the saucepan. Once the tomato gelatin mixture is firm, add it to the saucepan. Stir until the mixture thickens. Take saucepan off the stove and stir in the celery, cucumber, green peppers and green onions. Pour aspic into a mold or a 8 x 12-inch pyrex dish; place in refrigerator to set. The aspic is usually firm in 2 hours. Cover with plastic wrap. To serve, place each serving on a bed of lettuce, top with small dollop of mayonnaise (preferably "Hellmann's Light") and place avocado slices on each side. From Pamela D. Kingsbury.

French faience
Platter, ca. 1750, WAM, the Florence Naftzger Evans Collection, 1962.49

CREAMY TOMATO BALSAMIC SOUP

Cooking the vegetables at the high temperature caramelizes their natural sugars and deepens their flavor; the liquid poured over them ensures they won't burn. Prepare the soup up to two days ahead; reheat over medium heat.

1 cup beef stock (divided use)
1 tablespoon brown sugar
3 tablespoons balsamic vinegar
1 tablespoon low-sodium soy sauce
1 cup coarsely chopped onion

5 garlic cloves
2 (28-ounce) cans whole tomatoes, drained
$^{3}/_{4}$ cup half-and-half
Freshly ground black pepper

Preheat oven to 500°F. Combine $^{1}/_{2}$ cup stock, sugar, vinegar and soy sauce in a small bowl. Place onion, garlic and tomatoes in a 9 x 13-inch baking dish coated with cooking spray. Pour stock mixture over tomato mixture. Bake for 50 minutes or until vegetables are lightly browned. Place tomato mixture in a blender. Add remaining $^{1}/_{2}$ cup stock, and half-and-half, and process until smooth. Strain mixture through a sieve into a bowl. Discard solids. Garnish with crushed black pepper, if desired. Makes 4 servings.

CREAM OF ROASTED TOMATO BISQUE

Oven roasting the tomatoes adds great flavor to this easy bisque. Good topped with buttered garlic croutons.

2 pounds large ripe tomatoes
1 to 2 tablespoons olive oil
8 shallots, coarsely chopped
2 medium carrots, coarsely chopped
1 small fennel bulb, coarsely chopped
2 cups chicken stock

5 to 6 sprigs fresh tarragon
5 to 6 sprigs fresh parsley
3 tablespoons unsalted butter
1 cup whipping cream
Salt and freshly ground black pepper

Preheat oven to 450°F. Cut tomatoes in half, seed and coat with olive oil. Arrange the seeded tomatoes in a single layer on a foil-lined baking sheet. Bake about 30 minutes, turning every 10 minutes until skins darken and blister. Remove from oven and cool slightly before trying to remove them from the foil. Remove skins and reserve pulp and juices.

In a heavy skillet or Dutch oven, melt butter in a large, and sauté the vegetables until tender. Add stock and herbs and simmer on low for 30 minutes. Add tomato pulp and reserved juices. Remove herb sprigs. Purée, season to taste with salt and pepper. Add cream and warm to serve. Makes 6 to 8 servings. From Cindy Banks.

MOM'S OLD-FASHIONED TOMATO SOUP

Alta DeVore remembers her mother's tomato soup fondly, and was so happy to find the recipe after her passing. Nothing like warm delicious soup to bring back good memories and home comfort. Thank you, Alta.

1 (32-ounce) can diced tomatoes
9 ounces chicken stock
2 tablespoons butter
2 tablespoons sugar

1 teaspoon baking soda
2 cups milk (or 1 cup milk and 1 cup half-and-half)

Combine tomatoes, chicken stock, butter, sugar and soda in a large Dutch oven; simmer over medium-low heat for one hour. Heat milk in double boiler or microwave and add to tomato mixture. Makes 6 servings. From Alta DeVore.

SWISS CHEESE VEGETABLE SOUP

Preferred labels for purchased chicken stock are both Swansons, either the "Natural Goodness" or "Certified Organic Free Range Chicken Stock".

3 tablespoons butter
3 tablespoons flour
1 (32-ounce) carton chicken stock
2 cups coarsely chopped broccoli
3/4 cup chopped carrots
1/2 cup chopped celery
1 small onion, chopped

1/2 teaspoon salt
1/4 teaspoon garlic powder
1/4 teaspoon dried thyme
1 egg yolk
1 cup heavy cream
1 1/2 cups (6 ounces) shredded Swiss cheese

In a heavy 4-quart saucepan melt butter; add flour. Cook and stir until thick and bubbly. Remove from heat. Gradually whisk in stock. Add all vegetables and seasonings; return to heat and bring to a boil. Reduce heat; cover and simmer for 20 minutes until vegetables are tender. In a small bowl, blend egg yolk and cream. Gradually blend in several tablespoons of hot soup; return all to saucepan, stirring until slightly thickened. Simmer for another 15 to 20 minutes. Stir in cheese and heat over medium heat until melted. Makes 8 servings.

CHEDDAR ALE SOUP

2 tablespoons butter
1 large onion, diced
4 large potatoes, peeled and diced
1 bay leaf

3 cups chicken stock
1 cup ale, room temperature
1 cup grated sharp Cheddar cheese
Salt and white pepper

In a stockpot, melt butter and sauté onion until translucent (about 5 minutes). Add potatoes, bay leaf, stock and ale; bring to a boil. Reduce heat and simmer for 45 minutes or until the potatoes are tender. Remove from heat, let cool slightly and then purée in batches in a food processor or blender. Return to stockpot, add cheese and heat on low fire until melted and soup is warm. Season with salt and white pepper. Makes 6 servings.

HAM and CHEESE CHOWDER

2 cups chicken stock (or turkey stock)
2 cups diced peeled potatoes
1/2 cup diced carrot
1/2 cup chopped celery
1/4 cup chopped onion (or leek)
1 1/2 teaspoons salt
1/4 teaspoon freshly ground black pepper

1 cup cubed fully cooked ham (or cooked, crumbled pork sausage)
1/4 cup butter
1 1/4 cups flour
2 cups milk (or half-and-half)
2 cups (8 ounces) shredded Cheddar cheese

In a large saucepan, combine the first seven ingredients; bring to a boil. Reduce heat; cover and simmer until the vegetables are tender. Add ham or sausage. In another saucepan, melt the butter; stir in flour until smooth. Gradually add milk or half-and-half. Bring to a boil. Cook and stir for 2 minutes or until thickened. Stir in cheese until melted; add to soup. Makes 6 to 8 servings.

HEARTY HAM and CORN CHOWDER

3 slices bacon, chopped
1/2 cup chopped onion
1/2 cup chopped carrot
1/2 cup chopped celery
1/2 cup chopped roasted red pepper
2 cups milk
1 (15-ounce) jar alfredo sauce
2 cups frozen corn

2 cups canned creamed corn
1 cup diced cooked ham
1 (4-ounce) can diced green chile
   peppers, undrained
1 teaspoon oregano
1 teaspoon Worcestershire sauce
1 teaspoon salt
1/4 teaspoon black pepper

Cook bacon in a large (4 to 6 quart) pot or Dutch oven over medium heat. Remove when crisp and set aside. Add onion, carrots, celery and roasted red pepper; cook over medium heat until they are tender. Add bacon, milk, alfredo sauce, corn, creamed corn, ham, chile peppers, oregano, Worcestershire sauce, salt and pepper. Gently simmer the chowder, uncovered, for 25 to 30 minutes, stirring frequently to make sure it doesn't scorch. Makes 8 servings.

MR. MONEYBAGS MUSHROOM SOUP

This soup is even more wonderful on the second day. Use any mushrooms you have in this soup.

2 cups red wine
2 cups white wine
1 pound fresh mushrooms, sliced
2 tablespoons butter
2 tablespoons flour
2 cups milk

1/2 cup heavy cream
1 teaspoon white pepper
2 cubes chicken bouillon (or 2 teaspoons
   chicken bouillon paste)
2 cubes beef bouillon (or 2 teaspoons beef
   bouillon paste)

In a large pot bring red and white wine to a rolling boil. Add mushrooms, return to boil, and simmer for 3 minutes. In another pot melt the butter, add flour and stir with a whip constantly over high heat for 2 minutes (this is the roux, the secret to the soup's thickening) until a pale golden color develops. Remove from heat. Add the milk to the butter and flour, and keep stirring constantly for another 4 to 5 minutes. Return to heat and cook over low heat stirring, for 5 minutes until smooth and thickened. Add this hot milk mixture to the hot wine and mushroom mixture and stir until blended and very hot. Don't boil the soup or it will separate. Serve hot with a little paprika sprinkled on top for color. Makes 6 to 8 servings.

CORN and SAUSAGE CHOWDER

Good flavor, and a filling hearty supper soup. Do not use hot sausage.

1 (20-ounce) package refrigerated
   shredded potatoes
1 (14.5-ounce) can chicken stock
1 (10-ounce) package frozen whole kernel corn
2 cups skim milk

1 (12-ounce) package 97 percent fat-free
   cooked link sausage, halved lengthwise
   and sliced
1/3 cup sliced green onions
1/4 teaspoon pepper

In a large Dutch oven combine shredded potatoes, chicken stock and whole kernel corn, bring mixture just to boiling; reduce heat. Simmer, covered, for 10 minutes or until potatoes are just tender, stirring occasionally. Using a potato masher, slightly mash potatoes. Stir in skim milk, sausage, onions and pepper. Heat thoroughly. Makes 5 servings.

Tom Otterness
Dreamers Awake (detail
of "Moneybag Man"),
1995, cast bronze, WAM,
Burnetta Adair Endowment
Fund, 1995.14

PASTE SOUP BASES

Paste soup bases are an excellent alternative to making your own stocks when you are pressed for time. Not only are these pastes less expensive than canned stock, you have much more control over the concentration of flavor. When selecting a paste soup base (available at your local supermarket), be sure to select a brand that has the flavor listed as one of the first main ingredients. These bases come in a variety of meat and vegetable flavors. Look for low or no sodium varieties.

President Dwight Eisenhower, shown below grilling on the balcony of the White House, considered cooking as one of his favorite hobbies. Recipe above is from around 1907, during his more modest childhood in Abilene, KS, made after he would go hunting with his brothers (from the Eisenhower Library).

BAKED POTATO SOUP

4 large baking potatoes
²/₃ cup butter or margarine
1 small onion, diced
²/₃ cup flour
6 cups milk
³/₄ teaspoon salt
¹/₂ teaspoon pepper

4 green onions, thinly sliced (divided use)
12 slices bacon, cooked, crumbled (divided use)
1¹/₂ cups (6 ounces) shredded Cheddar cheese (divided use)
1 (8-ounce) carton sour cream

Wash potatoes and prick several times with a fork; bake at 400°F for 1 hour or until done. Let cool. Cut potatoes in half lengthwise; scoop out pulp, and set aside. Discard skins. Melt butter in a heavy saucepan over low heat; sauté onions until tender, 5 to 8 minutes. Add flour, stirring until smooth. Cook 1 minute, stirring constantly. Gradually add milk; cook over medium heat, stirring constantly, until mixture is thickened and bubbly. Add potato, salt and pepper, 2 tablespoons green onions, ¹/₂ cup bacon and 1 cup cheese. Cook until thoroughly heated; stir in sour cream. Add extra milk, if necessary, for desired thickness. Serve with remaining onion, bacon, and cheese. Makes 8 servings.

POTATO CHOWDER with GREEN CHILIES

1 large red bell pepper
4 large poblano chili peppers
5 cups chicken stock
1 large potato, peeled and cubed
1 large onion, chopped
1 jalapeno pepper, seeded and chopped
1 teaspoon salt
¹/₄ to ¹/₂ teaspoon freshly ground pepper
¹/₄ cup butter or margarine

¹/₃ cup flour
1 teaspoon salt
1 teaspoon dry mustard
¹/₄ to ¹/₂ teaspoon freshly ground pepper
2 cups half-and-half
1 cup milk
1 cup (4 ounces) shredded Cheddar cheese
6 bacon slices, cooked and crumbled
1 bunch green onions chopped

Broil red pepper and chili peppers on an aluminum foil-lined baking sheet 5 inches from heat for about 5 minutes on each side or until peppers look blistered. Place peppers in a heavy-duty zipper-lock plastic bag; seal and let stand 10 minutes to loosen skins. Peel peppers; remove and discard stems and seeds. Coarsely chop peppers. Bring chopped roasted peppers, chicken stock, and next 5 ingredients to a boil in a Dutch oven over medium heat. Reduce heat, and simmer 15 minutes or until potato is tender. Melt butter in a heavy saucepan over low heat; whisk in flour, salt, dry mustard and pepper and stir until smooth. Cook, whisking constantly, 1 minute. Gradually whisk in half-and-half. Stir this white sauce and milk into chicken stock mixture; cook over medium heat 8 to 10 minutes or until thickened and bubbly. Sprinkle each serving evenly with cheese, bacon and green onions. Makes 8 servings.

QUICK POTATO SAUSAGE SOUP

¹/₂ pound ground pork sausage
1 (16-ounce) package frozen hash brown potatoes (4 cups)
1 large onion, chopped
1 (14¹/₂-ounce) can chicken stock
2 cups water

1 (10³/₄-ounce) can cream of celery soup, undiluted
1 (10³/₄-ounce) can cream of chicken soup, undiluted
2 cups milk
Garnish: shredded Cheddar cheese

Brown sausage in a large Dutch oven over medium heat, stirring until it crumbles and is no longer pink. Drain. Return to Dutch oven. Add potatoes, onion, stock and water to sausage; bring to a boil. Cover, reduce heat, and simmer 30 minutes. Stir in soups and milk; cook, stirring often, until thoroughly heated. Garnish, if desired. Makes 8 to 10 servings.

Herschel C. Logan
Squirrel, 1927, block
print, WAM, gift of Samuel
H. and Martha F. Logan,
2005.13.33

CHUNKY PEANUT SOUP with PICKLED CHERRIES and BACON

Peanut soup is a Southern classic and while this combination sounds very strange, the tart pickled cherries next to the creamy soup, topped with bacon are surprisingly delicious. Thanks to Mitchell Davis (Kitchen Sense) *for this inspiration.*

It is important to use a 'natural' peanut butter, containing only ground nuts, in this recipe. Commercial ones tend to contain sugar and stabilizers.

$1/2$ cup butter
1 small onion, chopped fine
1 large carrot, shredded
1 celery stalk, chopped fine
3 tablespoons flour
3 quarts chicken stock
$1/3$ cup dried cherries, chopped
$1/4$ cup balsamic vinegar

2 cups smooth, unsweetened natural
  peanut butter
2 tablespoons fresh lemon juice
$1/4$ teaspoon salt
Kosher salt and freshly ground pepper
Bacon, cooked crisp and crumbled
$1/2$ cup dry-roasted, salted peanuts, chopped

In a large saucepan, melt butter, add onion, carrot and celery and cook until soft (about 5 minutes), add flour and cook for another 2 minutes. Stir in chicken stock, bring to a boil then reduce heat and let simmer for 30 minutes. If a smooth consistency is desired, let this cool slightly and purée in blender and return to pot. Meanwhile, place cherries and vinegar in a small bowl and microwave for 2 minutes and then let cool. After soup has simmered, stir in the peanut butter and bring back to a simmer. Add lemon juice and salt. Adjust seasoning with kosher salt and pepper. Consistency should be pourable, adjust with more stock or water as needed. Strain cherries. Divide bacon and cherries into bowls, ladle in soup and top with peanuts. Makes 10 servings.

QUICK FRENCH ONION SOUP

This very easy recipe originally came from the French's Worcestershire Sauce company, and then had modifications in Bon Appetit *magazine. It is very quick, and tastes like a lot more effort went into it. Good for an "emergency" dish.*

2 tablespoons butter
1 large onion, sliced
$1/2$ teaspoon sugar
1 ($10^{1/2}$-ounce) can condensed beef
  stock, undiluted

$1^{1/4}$ cups water
2 tablespoons Worcestershire sauce
4 slices French or pumpernickel bread
$1/2$ cup shredded Swiss cheese
1 tablespoon grated Parmesan cheese

In a medium saucepan, melt butter over medium heat. Add onion and sugar; cook and stir for 5 to 10 minutes until lightly browned. Add bouillon, water and Worcestershire sauce; simmer 10 to 15 minutes. Preheat oven to 300°F. Arrange bread on baking sheet; bake for 20 to 30 minutes, until crisp and dry. Spoon soup into 4 ovenproof serving dishes; top each with 1 slice bread and sprinkle generously with cheeses. Place under broiler 2 to 3 minutes to melt cheese. Makes 4 servings.

CHICKEN and WILD RICE SOUP

Versions of this wonderful soup are found in several community cookbooks, including our own Women of Great Taste *from the Junior League of Wichita. It is hard to improve upon this great combination of flavor, and the wild rice stays firm as well as adding a nice nutty touch. A shredded rotisserie chicken makes it easy to assemble.*

5 cups chicken stock
1/2 cup wild rice (uncooked)
1/2 cup sliced celery
1/2 cup finely diced onion
1/2 cup diced carrots
3 tablespoons butter
3 tablespoons flour

1/2 teaspoon salt
Fresh ground black pepper
1 cup hot milk
2 cups diced chicken (cooked)
1 1/4 cup sliced almonds, toasted
1/4 teaspoon pepper
1/3 cup dry sherry

In a 3-quart saucepan over medium-high heat, bring chicken stock, wild rice, celery, onion and carrots to a boil. Cover and reduce heat, simmering for 45 minutes or until rice is tender. Melt butter in a saucepan until it foams and stir in flour, salt and pepper and stir with a fork just until thickened to make a roux. Add milk and whisk over medium heat until combined and slightly thickened. Stir milk mixture into rice mixture then add chicken, almonds and pepper. Simmer until soup is thoroughly heated. Stir in sherry, if desired, just before serving. Makes 6 servings.

CHICKEN HOMINY SOUP

Easy and delicious, this is a contemporary version of Posol, made with a pre-cooked rotisserie chicken. Be sure to use a large stock pot as this makes a large quantity. Serve with sides of sour cream and warmed tortillas. Give the "Soft Corn Tortillas" a try. Rolled up with butter they will melt in your mouth: full flavor of hot buttered corn on the cob but without the work.

3 tablespoons olive oil
3 bunches green onions, sliced
4 1/2 teaspoons ground cumin
2 1/2 teaspoons smoked paprika (or puréed adobe pepper in sauce)
8 cups chicken stock
1 (14.5-ounce) can petite tomatoes, undrained

1 purchased roast chicken, meat shredded, skin and bones discarded
4 teaspoons hot pepper sauce
3 (15-ounce) cans golden or white hominy, undrained
1 cup chopped fresh cilantro
Garnish: shredded Mexican cheese or crushed tortilla chips

In a heavy large stock pot over medium-high heat, heat oil and sauté green onions, cumin, and paprika for 5 minutes. Add stock, tomatoes with juice, chicken, and hot pepper sauce. Purée 2 cans of hominy with juice in processor or blender. Mix all hominy into soup and simmer 15 minutes. Stir in cilantro. Ladle into serving bowls and top with shredded Mexican cheese or crushed tortilla chips. Makes 8 to 10 servings.

CHICKEN SAUSAGE GUMBO

This is worth all the effort. Add shredded carrots for more color if desired. Adapted from recipe in Traditions, *by the Junior League of Little Rock, Arkansas.*

3 quarts water
1 (4 to 5 pound) chicken
2 celery stalks, with leaves
1 carrot, cut into fourths
1 onion, cut into fourths
2 bay leaves
1 teaspoon salt
1/3 cup vegetable oil
1/2 cup flour
1 cup chopped onion
3/4 cup chopped celery
1/2 cup chopped green pepper
2 medium carrots, shredded

1/3 cup chopped green onions
2 cloves garlic, chopped
2 bay leaves
1 teaspoon dried thyme
1 teaspoon dried marjoram
1 teaspoon dried basil
1 (14 1/2-ounce) can tomatoes, undrained
1/2 pound ham, cubed
1 pound smoked sausage, sliced
2 tablespoons Worcestershire sauce
1 tablespoon salt
1 teaspoon freshly ground black pepper
Hot pepper sauce to taste

In a stockpot bring water to a boil. Add chicken, celery, carrot, onion, bay leaves and salt; simmer for 25 minutes. Remove chicken and take meat from bones. Set meat aside and return bones to stock, continuing to simmer. In another 4 quart pan, heat oil and flour over medium heat. Cook this roux until a nice brown color (30 minutes) stirring constantly. Add onions, celery, green pepper, shredded carrots and cook about 5 to 10 minutes. Add green onions, garlic, bay leaves, thyme, marjoram, basil, tomatoes, ham and cooked chicken. Strain stock and add to gumbo. Fry sausage, drain well, and add to gumbo. Simmer 1 1/2 hours. Add Worcestershire sauce, salt and pepper. Add hot pepper sauce to taste. Serve over steamed rice or noodles in a bowl. Makes 12 to 16 servings.

SOFT CORN TORTILLAS

Nice by themselves, served hot with a smear of butter, or great to roll up and serve rolled up next to a bowl of Chicken Hominy Soup or any of the vegetable soups. Easy as crêpes!

1 egg
1 cup milk
1/2 cup masa harina
1 heaping tablespoon flour
1/2 teaspoon salt

Blend ingredients in a blender and let stand for 1 hour or overnight. Heat a small skillet or crepe pan over medium heat, spray with cooking spray and then brush with soft butter after skillet is heated. As it sizzles, pour in 2 tablespoons of batter, just enough to cover the pan. Shake pan to evenly distribute the batter and cook for 30 seconds to 1 minute or just until the top is slightly dulled. Flip with a spatula and cook for 20 seconds and place on a wire rack to briefly cool before stacking and covering with foil. Makes about 18.

*Edmund L. Davison
(1877-1944) was a
leading figure in the art
worlds of Wichita and Taos
during the first half of the
20th century. Visitors to the
Art Museum who have never
heard of Davison are always
amazed by the beauty
and sophistication of his
paintings. From his friend
Birger Sandzen he learned
to embrace vibrant color.
Yet his own brushwork and
pictorial structure are very
different from Sandzen's
work. Davison used his
brush like a filter to
dissolve all the components
of color; similarly, he
dissolved supposedly solid
forms, thereby achieving
a magical sense of space.
Davison gained national
recognition through awards
at major competitions across
the country. His relative
obscurity today is due to
his belief that an artist
of independent economic
means should not deprive
other artists of sales. The
copper tray depicted in this
painting was made by his
wife Faye. — SG*

KAREN'S "Flying D" BISON CHILI

Several authors credit this recipe as the one served by Ted's Montana Grill.

¹/₄ cup vegetable oil	1 teaspoon dried oregano
2¹/₂ pounds ground buffalo	¹/₄ teaspoon cayenne pepper
1 cup diced onion	¹/₂ teaspoon freshly ground black pepper
3 cloves garlic, minced	1¹/₂ teaspoon sugar
1 quart water	1¹/₂ teaspoon ground cumin
3 tablespoons beef base	3 tablespoons chili powder
1 cup tomato paste	1 cup ranch-style beans
1¹/₂ teaspoon salt	1 cup stewed tomatoes

In a large Dutch oven heat oil and add the meat, breaking up any large chunks. When the meat is half way cooked, add the onion and garlic. Sauté until soft. Add water, beef base, and tomato paste. Bring to a boil. Add seasonings and simmer for 10 minutes. Add beans and stewed tomatoes. Cook for one additional minute. Makes 10 to 12 servings.

WHITE CHILI with WILD RICE

1 tablespoon olive oil	2 (4-ounce) cans diced green chilies
1 large onion, chopped	1 (14¹/₂-ounce) can chicken (or turkey) stock
2 cloves garlic, pressed	1 teaspoon ground cumin
1¹/₂ pounds boneless, skinless turkey or chicken, diced or shredded (cooked)	2 teaspoons chili powder
2 cups cooked wild rice	1 teaspoon salt
1 (15-ounce) can Great Northern beans, drained	Hot pepper sauce as desired
1 (11-ounce) can white corn, drained	Toppings: shredded Monterey Jack cheese, sour cream
	Garnish: fresh parsley, or chopped green onions

In a large skillet, sauté onions until tender with olive oil. Add garlic, turkey, rice, beans, corn, chilies, stock, cumin, chili powder and salt. Cover and simmer over low heat for 30 minutes, or until the meat is tender. Add hot pepper sauce to taste. Ladle into bowls and top with cheese and sour cream, garnished with fresh parsley or a few chopped green onions. Makes 8 servings.

ITALIAN CHILI

1 pound coarsely ground ground beef	1 (46-ounce) can tomato juice
1 onion, chopped	1 (28-ounce) can tomatoes, undrained, coarsely chopped
¹/₂ green pepper, chopped	
1 clove garlic, minced	1 (3¹/₂ ounce) package sliced pepperoni
¹/₂ large celery stalk, including leaves	1 (15-ounce) can kidney beans
Salt and pepper	1 tablespoon dried oregano
1 (8-ounce) can mushroom stems and pieces, drained	1 tablespoon dried basil
	¹/₄ - ¹/₂ teaspoon red pepper flakes

In a 6-quart kettle sauté ground beef, onion, green pepper and garlic over medium heat until meat is no longer pink. Add chopped celery and leaves and sauté mixture until celery begins to be translucent. Salt and pepper to taste. Add mushrooms, tomato juice, tomatoes, pepperoni slices, kidney beans, oregano, basil and red pepper flakes and simmer, stirring occasionally until everything is tender and tasty (about 20 minutes). May be made in advance, refrigerated and reheated; flavors blend on standing. Makes 8 servings. From Carol Jones.

CHOCOLATE CHILI

3 pounds ground chuck
1 pound pork shoulder or Boston Butt, cubed
2 cans (28 ounces each) peeled and
  diced tomatoes
4 cloves garlic, minced
2 teaspoons coriander
2 tablespoons flour

4 teaspoons cumin
4 teaspoons salt
2 large onions, chopped
1 teaspoon ground oregano
6 tablespoons chili powder
4 bay leaves
2 ounces semi-sweet chocolate, chopped

Chocolate adds a rich depth to this chili.

Buy high quality chocolate (70% cocoa and above); do not use chips as they contain ingredients to help them hold their shape during baking which can make them lumpy in the chili.

In a large skillet over medium heat, cook beef until brown. Add pork and brown; drain. Stir in tomatoes, garlic, coriander, flour, cumin, salt, onions, oregano, and chili powder. Simmer 1 hour. Add bay leaves and cook 10 minutes. Remove bay leaves and add chocolate. Stir to combine. Cook 10 minutes longer to blend flavors.

Edmund Davison
Still Life, Copper Tray, 1943, oil on canvas, The Edmund L. and Faye Davison Collection, 1968.30

HEARTY AUTUMN VEGETABLE SOUP

Served at the Wichita Symphony Showhouse Tea Room, the chickpeas and spinach give an unexpected twist.

2 tablespoons olive oil
1 tablespoon minced garlic
1 1/2 cups chopped onion
1 1/2 cups chopped carrot
1 cup chopped celery
1 (28-ounce) can peeled, crushed
  tomatoes (undrained)
1 (28-ounce) can vegetable stock
  (prefer Swanson)

4 cups water
4 cups frozen vegetables (mixture of peas, corn,
  and green beans)
Salt and freshly ground black pepper
5 ounces frozen chopped spinach (1/2 box),
  thawed and drained
1 (15-ounce) can garbanzo beans
  (chickpeas), drained

In a large Dutch oven, heat oil over medium high heat. Sauté onion, carrot, celery, and garlic for 5 minutes. Add tomatoes, stock, water, frozen vegetables, and salt and pepper. Bring to a simmer. Simmer, partially covered for 15 minutes. Add spinach and garbanzo beans and simmer until vegetables are tender, about 15 more minutes. Adjust seasoning with salt and pepper. Makes 10 servings.

SPICY VEGETABLE SOUP

Simple, yet very good, this soup is easy to assemble and then let it cook while you are out.

1 pound ground beef
1 cup chopped onion
2 garlic cloves, pressed (or 2 tablespoons
  chopped garlic)
1 (30-ounce) jar chunky spaghetti sauce with
  mushrooms and peppers
1 (10 1/2-ounce) can condensed beef
  stock, undiluted

2 cups water
1 teaspoon sugar
1 teaspoon salt
1/2 teaspoon freshly ground pepper
1 (10-ounce) can diced tomatoes and green
  chilies (prefer Rotel)
1 (16-ounce) package frozen mixed vegetables
  (or black-eyed peas)

In a large Dutch oven over medium heat, cook first 3 ingredients stirring until meat is crumbled and no longer pink. Drain and transfer to crockpot. Add rest of the ingredients except frozen vegetables and cook on low for 3 to 4 hours. Add vegetables and cook until done, about 30 minutes. Makes 8 servings.

BLACK-EYED PEA SOUP

This is a fast and tasty way to prepare black-eyed peas, from a recipe published in the Wichita Eagle Beacon *in 1988. Good for making a small quantity, and may be cooked in microwave or in slow cooker.*

4 slices bacon, diced
1 cup chopped onion
1 tablespoon finely chopped jalapeno pepper
  (more if desired)
1 clove garlic, minced

1/2 teaspoon black pepper
1 (18-ounce) package frozen black-eyed peas
3 cups hot tap water
1 (16-ounce) can stewed tomatoes
Garnish: 1 cup shredded sharp Cheddar cheese

Place bacon, onion, peppers, garlic and pepper in a 3-quart casserole. Cover and microwave on high for 5 to 6 minutes. Stir in peas and pour water over ingredients; cover. Stirring midway through cooking, microwave on high for 20 minutes. Stir in tomatoes and microwave on high 4 to 6 minutes. Garnish individual servings with cheese. Makes 4 servings.

SANTA FE SOUP

There are many recipes for soups like this, often called "taco soup". The nice thing is that they are easy and flexible, allowing variation based on what is in your cupboard, and the seasoning mixes will both flavor and thicken the soup.

2 tablespoons vegetable oil
6 corn tortillas, cut into 1-inch pieces
1 1/2 pounds lean ground beef (or turkey)
1 large onion, chopped
1 teaspoon minced fresh garlic
3 (16-ounce) cans ranch-style chili beans undrained (or a combination of cans of black beans [rinsed and drained], small red beans [undrained], or pinto beans [undrained])
1 (15-ounce) can hominy (or whole kernel white corn), undrained

1 (14 1/2-ounce) cans Mexican style diced tomatoes, undrained
2 (14 1/2-ounce) cans water
1 (7-ounce) can chopped green chilies, undrained
1 (1 1/4-ounce) package taco seasoning mix
Optional: 1 (1-ounce) package ranch-style salad dressing mix
Garnish: crushed tortilla chips, shredded cheese, sour cream, chopped avocado, sliced green onions, as desired

Charles M. Russell
The Scouts, 1915,
watercolor on illustration
board, WAM, the M.C.
Naftzger Collection,
1973.9

Heat oil in a large Dutch oven or soup pot. Add tortillas to oil, stir until brown; remove and set aside. Cook meat, onion and garlic together over medium-high heat until meat is browned, stirring until it crumbles; drain. Stir in beans and rest of ingredients. Bring to a boil; reduce heat and simmer 1 hour. Add package of ranch-style salad dressing mix if you prefer a creamy base and flavor of sour cream. If mixture is too thick, add more water. If more spice is desired, add 1 teaspoon chili powder. Ladle into bowls, garnish with desired toppings. Serve with tortilla strips on top, or on the side. Makes 8 servings.

NEW YEAR'S SOUP

This has become my favorite for New Year's Day, easily serving a relaxed group enjoying the game or sitting by the fire. A nice way to serve good luck black-eyed peas and a good use of leftover holiday ham, make this and you are finished cooking for the whole day for whoever drops by.

1 tablespoon butter
1 tablespoon olive oil
1 to 2 cups diced smoked lean ham
2 celery stalks, chopped
1 medium onion, chopped
2 carrots, chopped
4 cloves garlic, minced
2 (15-ounce) cans black-eyed peas, drained

2 (14 1/2-ounce) cans chicken stock
2 (14 1/2-ounce) cans stewed tomatoes, undrained
1 (8-ounce) can tomato sauce
1 1/2 cups chopped fresh spinach
1/2 cup chopped fresh parsley
1/2 teaspoon pepper
Garnish: chopped fresh spinach

In a Dutch oven, sauté ham, celery, onion, carrots and garlic over medium heat in olive oil and butter until vegetables are tender. Stir in black-eyed peas, chicken stock, tomatoes and tomato sauce; bring mixture to a boil. Cover, reduce heat, and simmer 1 hour and 30 minutes. Add spinach, parsley and pepper right before serving. Garnish with chopped fresh spinach. Makes 8 to 10 servings.

CREAM of WATERCRESS SOUP

This has a lovely bright green color, perfect for a spring dinner, and excellent flavor.

1/3 cup butter
1 medium onion, chopped
2 cloves garlic, minced
2 large potatoes (1 pound) peeled and sliced
2 cups water
1/2 teaspoon salt
1/4 teaspoon white pepper

2 bunches (about 8 ounces) watercress, washed and coarse stems removed
2 to 2 1/2 cups chicken stock
2 1/2 cups half-and-half
1/2 cup flour
2 tablespoons fresh lemon juice

Melt butter in a large saucepan over medium heat. Add onion and garlic; sauté until tender. Add potatoes, salt, pepper and water. Bring to a boil; reduce heat and simmer 20 minutes or until potatoes are tender. Set aside a few sprigs of watercress for garnish. Coarsely chop remaining watercress and add to potatoes along with chicken stock. Simmer for 10 minutes. Pour 1 cup half-and-half in a blender; add flour. Blend until smooth. Ladle watercress-potato mixture into a blender. (Do this in batches so blender does not overflow.) Blend until mixture is smooth; repeat process until all has been puréed. Return to saucepan. Bring to a boil over medium heat and simmer until thickened. Stir in remaining half-and-half. Bring back to a simmer. Season with lemon juice, freshly grated nutmeg and additional salt and pepper if desired. Ladle into bowls and garnish with watercress sprigs. Makes 8 servings. From Bonnie Aeschliman.

NEW ENGLAND SEAFOOD CHOWDER WITH DILL

Be careful to not cook the soup too long after adding the clams or they will become tough.

Brands differ greatly for quality of canned clams and bottled clam juice. I like 'Doxsee's' or 'Snow's Minced Clams and Clam Juice'.

3 tablespoons olive oil or vegetable oil
2 leeks (or 1 large onion), chopped
2 celery stalks, chopped
1 teaspoon dried thyme
1/4 teaspoon cayenne pepper (or a few drops of hot pepper sauce)
1/4 cup flour
2 (10-ounce) cans baby clams, drained and juice reserved
2 1/2 cups chicken stock

3 medium red-skinned potatoes (about 1 1/2 pounds), peeled and cut into 1/2-inch dice
1 pound cod fillets or other firm-fleshed white fish, cut into 3/4-inch pieces
1 cup half-and-half
1/2 cup heavy cream
1/4 cup chopped fresh dill
Salt and pepper to taste
Garnish: fresh dill

In a large heavy pan heat oil over medium heat, heat oil and sauté leeks and celery until tender, about 5 minutes. Add thyme, cayenne pepper and flour; cook, stirring for 1 or 2 minutes. Drain clams, reserving juice. Set clams aside. Add reserve clam juice, chicken stock, and potatoes. Bring to a boil, reduce heat and simmer until potatoes are tender, about 15 minutes. Add cod; simmer until fish is cooked through and potatoes are tender, about 5 minutes longer. Add half-and-half, cream and clams. Cook just until heated through, about 5 minutes. Mix in dill, season to taste with salt and pepper. Garnish with dill if desired. Makes 6 to 8 servings. Adapted from a recipe by Bonnie Aeschliman.

CREAMY CLAM CHOWDER

Opposite Page:

Worcester Plate (British), ca. 1765, enameled and gilded porcelain, WAM, the Florence Naftzger Evans collection, 1962.60

6 slices bacon, diced
2 medium carrots, shredded
2 celery stalks, finely diced
1 large onion, diced (or 2 leeks)
2 tablespoons diced green pepper (optional)
1 clove garlic, minced or pressed
1 1/2 pounds red potatoes, 1/2-inch diced
2 (8-ounce) bottles clam juice

8 (6 1/2 ounce) cans chopped clams with juice
1 bay leaf
1/2 teaspoon hot pepper sauce
1/4 teaspoon pepper
1 1/2 teaspoon Worcestershire sauce
3/4 teaspoon dried thyme
4 cups half-and-half

In a medium skillet over medium heat, cook bacon; drain and set aside. Discard bacon drippings except for 2 tablespoons. Add carrots, celery, onion, green pepper and garlic; cook, stirring often for 10 minutes. Add potatoes and clam juice to vegetables, cover and simmer until potatoes are tender. Stir in clams, bay leaf, seasonings, cream and bacon; cook just to heat through. Do not boil; only warm to serve, or clams will get tough. Adjust salt and hot sauce to taste. Garnish with paprika. Makes 8 servings.

SHERRIED CRAB BISQUE

This delicious yet quick version of a classic takes less than 30 minutes from countertop to tabletop.

6 tablespoons butter
1 large onion, finely chopped
1 celery stalk, finely chopped
1/3 cup plus 1 tablespoon flour
2 (13 3/4-ounce) cans chicken stock
2 (8-ounce) bottles clam juice

1/2 cup dry sherry
1 1/2 tablespoons tomato paste
1 pound crabmeat
3/4 cup heavy cream
Hot pepper sauce to taste
Salt to taste

In a large saucepan, melt the butter over medium heat; add the onion and celery and cover. Cook for about 10 minutes, until vegetables are tender (but not browned). Stir in flour, continue cooking for about a minute, without browning the flour. While whisking, gradually add the stock, clam juice, sherry and tomato paste. Turn up heat and bring to a boil, then reduce heat to low, put the lid on halfway and continue to simmer for about 10 minutes, until it is slightly thickened. Add crab and cream and cook until just hot, but do not boil. Season with hot pepper sauce and salt. Makes 8 to 10 servings.

Worcester, the county seat of Worcestershire, was renowned as the place of manufacture of fine English porcelain. It was also home of the company that made its namesake bottled sauce. Ironically, the inspiration for Worcestershire sauce was not traditional English cooking, but England's colonial empire. The mixture of vinegars, molasses, sugar, and "secret" ingredients such as anchovies, garlic, tamarind, and cloves is a British adaptation of Indian cuisine. Since its introduction in 1837, it has traveled full circle, now a staple of the Japanese kitchen, where it enhances the sense of taste known as 'unami'. -SG

SWEET RED PEPPER BISQUE

The '70s and '80s were greatly influenced by Alice Waters and her fresh cuisine from Chez Panisse in California. Chefs on both coasts began making sweet pepper soups (yellow, orange and red), often swirling two colors in a single bowl. Sweet red pepper soup has been my favorite and can be served with equal success either chilled or hot.

3 tablespoons olive oil
6 large red bell peppers, cored, seeded, diced
6 medium leeks (whites only), washed and
  thinly sliced
2 sprigs fresh rosemary

2 sprigs fresh marjoram
2 cloves garlic, minced
2½ cups beef stock
¾ cup crème fraiche (or sour cream)
Salt and freshly ground black pepper

In a large heavy saucepan, heat olive oil over high heat, add red peppers and sauté until just softened (about 2 minutes). Add leeks and sauté for 2 more minutes. Add rosemary and marjoram, dash of pepper and reduce heat to low, cover tight and cook for about 1 hour (vegetables should be very soft and have released a lot of juice). Remove herb sprigs, let cool and purée vegetables in batches in a food processor blender. Strain into saucepan; add stock and cook, uncovered just until hot (about 3 minutes). Stir in crème fraiche, season to taste. Chill well (or serve warm). Ladle into soup plates and garnish each serving with 1 tablespoon of crème fraiche (swirl slightly) and tiny sprig of rosemary. Makes 6 servings.

WHITE GAZPACHO SOUP

If you only know gazpacho as a tomato-based soup, you will be surprised by this delicious soup based on almonds, garlic and olive oil. This makes an elegant savory appetizer before dinner, served with a dry white wine. "Yes, it is work to peel grapes, oh but the flavor is fantastic in this soup," shares Barbara Rensner.

4 ounces (1 cup) blanched almonds,
   lightly toasted
2 cloves garlic, peeled
1/2 teaspoon salt
1/4 cup water
4 slices day-old bread (less crusts)

6 tablespoons olive oil
3 tablespoons white wine vinegar
1 quart cold chicken stock
Garnish: seedless green grapes, peeled
   and croutons

In blender or food processor, mince the almonds, garlic and salt until nuts are ground extra fine. Soak bread in cold water, squeeze dry. Add bread to almond mixture in blender. Pour oil in steady stream. Add vinegar and chicken stock. Strain bread mixture into bowl, squeezing liquid through strainer with back of spatula. Stir to combine and chill several hours or overnight. Before serving, peel grapes with a paring knife and refrigerate. Put 2 or 3 peeled white grapes in bottom of chilled demitasse cup, carefully ladle in soup and garnish with croutons. Makes 4 servings. From Barbara Rensner

STRAWBERRY SOUP

This recipe is adapted from that served at the Victorian Sampler Tea Room, in Eureka Springs, Arkansas. It makes a beautiful first course for a special luncheon.

1 (15-ounce) package frozen strawberries with
   juice, thawed
2 (8-ounce) cartons low fat sour cream
1 ounce vanilla extract
3 ounces powdered sugar

1/2 ounce grenadine syrup (or 2 tablespoons
   light rum)
2 ounces half-and-half
Garnish: mint sprigs and sliced fresh strawberries

Mix strawberries and sour cream. Beat slowly until well mixed. Add vanilla, sugar and grenadine while mixing to a smooth consistency. Add half-and-half last, mixing only until well blended. Chill several hours or overnight. Shake well before serving. Garnish with mint sprig or fresh strawberry slices, if desired. Makes 6 servings.

RASPBERRY SOUP

Served at the Wichita-Sedgwick County Historical Museum event 'Souper Suppers'. Excellent!

1/2 pint fresh raspberries
1 quart vanilla yogurt
1/3 cup sugar

1 teaspoon fresh lemon juice
1 cup heavy cream

Reserve 4 raspberries for garnish. Pour remaining berries into a bowl and gently mash with a fork to release some of the juices. Stir in the yogurt, sugar and lemon juice. Whip cream. Reserve half for garnish and fold the other half into the soup. To serve, place a dollop of whipped cream on each serving and top with a raspberry. Makes 4 servings.

MENU:
LUNCH FOR MOM

Strawberry Soup 81

Baby Spinach Greens
with Classic Spinach
Salad Dressing 53

Cognac Marinated Beef
Tenderloin Sandwiches
with Horseradish
Cream Sauce 96

Classic Cheesecake 244

BLACKENED STEAK SALAD

This recipe originated from the Chicago Chop House and is reportedly one of the most requested items from the lunch menu. Adaptation by Bonnie Aeschliman. Great served with Cheese Herb Bread (page 111).

Spice Mixture
1 tablespoon paprika
2 teaspoons ground black pepper
1 1/2 teaspoons salt
1 teaspoon garlic powder
1 teaspoon cayenne pepper
1/2 teaspoon dried oregano
1/2 teaspoon dried thyme

1/4 cup butter, melted
4 (5 to 6-ounce) beef tenderloin steaks,
  1/2-inch thick

Dressing
1/2 cup olive oil
1/4 cup balsamic vinegar
2 teaspoons Dijon mustard
Kosher salt and freshly ground black pepper

Salad
12 cups mixed greens (baby greens
  and romaine)
1/2 medium green bell pepper, thinly sliced
1/2 medium sweet onion, cut into thin wedges
4 ounces (about 1/2 cup) crumbled blue cheese
2 tomatoes, cut into 8 wedges

Mix all spice mixture ingredients in a small bowl (may be done ahead and stored in air-tight container). Spread spice mixture on a pie plate. Coat both sides of steaks with spice mixture. Dip steaks into melted butter. Heat a heavy skillet over high heat until very hot. Add steaks and cook to desired doneness, about 2 minutes per side for medium rare. Transfer to cutting board, cover and let stand 2 minutes. Whisk oil, vinegar and mustard to blend. Season with salt and pepper. Place greens, bell pepper and onion in a large bowl. Toss with dressing. Divide salad between plates. Thinly slice steaks crosswise. Arrange slices on top of salad. Sprinkle with cheese, garnish with tomato and serve. Makes 4 servings.

WILD RICE, HAM and CHICKPEA SALAD

Adapted from a recipe originally appearing in Food and Wine *magazine, this has gone on to achieve some fame as a light entrée at some spas. It is full of flavor and a delicious light entrée. Just needs a better name!*

1 ¹/₂ cups wild rice (uncooked)
1 tablespoon kosher salt
2 ¹/₂ tablespoons fresh lemon juice
2 tablespoons red wine vinegar
2 tablespoons Dijon mustard
1 tablespoon honey
1 teaspoon curry powder
1 tablespoon ground cumin

Dash of cayenne pepper
¹/₄ cup olive oil
1 (15-ounce) can chickpeas, drained and rinsed
¹/₂ pound smoked ham, diced
8 green onions, thinly sliced
¹/₄ cup golden raisins (or dried cranberries)
Salt and freshly ground black pepper
Hot pepper sauce to taste

Cook wild rice according to package directions until tender but firm. Drain and rinse under cold water. Set aside. In a large bowl, whisk together the lemon juice, vinegar, mustard, honey, curry powder, cumin and cayenne. Add olive oil and continue whisking until all combined. Add the remaining ingredients, season to taste with salt, pepper and hot pepper sauce and serve at room temperature. Makes 6 servings.

ROASTED SALMON SALAD

This impressive salad was served at the Wichita Symphony Showhouse Tea Room 2003, and also at the Wichita Symphony Showhouse Special Event luncheons, 2005.

2 pounds fresh salmon fillets, with skin
Salt and pepper
1 cup finely diced celery
1 cup almonds, toasted and chopped
1 cup petit peas
¹/₂ cup sliced black olives
¹/₂ cup diced red onion

2 tablespoons capers, drained
2 tablespoons minced fresh dill
2 tablespoons raspberry vinegar
3 tablespoons olive oil (divided use)
¹/₂ teaspoon kosher salt
¹/₂ teaspoon freshly ground black pepper

Preheat oven to 375°F. Line a baking sheet with foil. Rub the salmon fillets with 1 tablespoon olive oil and sprinkle with salt and pepper. Bake for 5 to 6 minutes on each side, letting the interior remain rare. Wrap fillets and all juices in the foil and refrigerate until cold and very firm. When chilled, remove any skin and break fillets into large flakes into bowl with all juices left from baking. Add celery, almonds, peas, black olives, red onion, capers and fresh dill. Mix raspberry vinegar, 2 tablespoons olive oil, salt and pepper in jar and shake to mix. Add to the salad ingredients and mix well. Can be served cold or at room temperature. Serve on bed of greens, pretty with a bit of fruit for garnish.

STEAK and MUSHROOM SALAD

A wonderful lunch with wine and French bread.

Dressing
¹/₂ cup olive oil
¹/₄ cup red wine vinegar
2 teaspoons Dijon mustard
1 clove garlic, crushed
1 teaspoon salt
¹/₂ teaspoon freshly ground black pepper
¹/₂ teaspoon sugar

12 small fresh mushrooms, washed or brushed
  clean and sliced
1 to 1 ¹/₂ pounds leftover roast or steak,
  thinly sliced
12 cherry tomatoes, halved
1 can artichoke hearts, drained and halved
1 head of lettuce, shredded
2 tablespoons chopped fresh parsley
3 tablespoons crumbled blue cheese

Combine dressing ingredients in a jar and shake well. In a large bowl, combine the mushrooms, beef, tomatoes, artichokes and half of the dressing (may substitute sliced avocado for the artichoke hearts). Refrigerate several hours or overnight to allow flavors to meld. Line salad bowl or individual chilled plates with lettuce and arrange beef mixture on top. Sprinkle with parsley and blue cheese. Makes 4 to 5 servings. From Becky Middleton.

ASIAN CHICKEN SALAD

Other entrées to consider for a special luncheon include Chicken Supreme on Pastry Shells (p. 120), Cheese Soufflé with Chicken Spinach Mushroom Filling (p. 119), the Primavera Cheese Torte (p. 152) or several offerings in the Salad chapter.

Dressing

1 green onion, coarsely chopped
1 large clove garlic
1/4 cup white wine vinegar
1/4 cup soy sauce
2 tablespoons sugar
1 teaspoon dry mustard
3/4 teaspoon minced fresh ginger
1/2 teaspoon Worcestershire sauce
3/4 cup vegetable oil (or 1/2 cup peanut oil)
2 tablespoons sesame oil
2 tablespoons sesame seeds, toasted (350°F for 7 minutes)

Chicken and Green Salad

3/4 pound cooked chicken breast, cut into thin strips
1/2 small Chinese cabbage, thinly sliced
1/2 small jicama, peeled, cut into matchstick size strips (or 1 can drained water chestnuts)
2 cups sliced romaine lettuce
1/2 red bell pepper, cut into thin strips
6 green onions, thinly sliced
Optional: 1 carrot, peeled and shredded
Garnish: alfalfa sprouts, lettuce leaves

For the dressing: Combine onion, garlic, vinegar, soy sauce, sugar, mustard, ginger and Worcestershire sauce in blender. Process to combine ingredients. With blender running, gradually add oils until emulsified. Then add sesame seeds. (Dressing will keep for one week in refrigerator.) Sprinkle 1 tablespoon dressing over chicken. Set aside.

For salad: Combine cabbage, jicama, lettuce, bell pepper and green onions in a large bowl (and carrots if desired). Toss with enough dressing to coat ingredients. Mound salad onto lettuce lined plates. Arrange chicken strips on top of salad. Garnish with alfalfa sprouts, if desired. Serve, passing remaining dressing separately. From Bonnie Aeschliman.

My favorite variation is to make this into a warm salad: Instead of chicken described above, cut 1 pound uncooked boneless chicken breasts into strips. Marinate in a mixture of 2 tablespoons soy sauce, 2 tablespoons white wine and 1 minced garlic clove for 30 minutes. Prepare salad ingredients as above. Toss with enough dressing to coat. Then stir fry chicken strips in 1 tablespoon oil until done. Arrange hot chicken over salad. Garnish with alfalfa sprouts, and serve with additional dressing if desired.

Another hearty variation, either hot or cold, is the addition of Chinese noodles. Cook 4 ounces of Chinese egg noodles according to package directions, drain and add to the vegetables.

WELSH RAREBIT

For many homecooks this is one of those lost or forgotten recipes and yet it is an easy, delicious dish that should be in every recipe box. It makes for a light dinner or dresses up a brunch. Cook this melted cheese dish gently to keep the cheese from becoming grainy.

1/2 pound sharp Cheddar cheese, grated or cut into small cubes
1 tablespoon butter
1/2 teaspoon dry mustard
Sprinkle of cayenne pepper or 1/4 teaspoon of hot pepper sauce

1 egg, lightly beaten
Salt to taste
1/2 cup beer (or milk, if you must)
4 slices toast or English muffins
Optional: cooked bacon slices or sliced smoked turkey

In a heavy pan or the top of a double boiler, mix cheese, butter, mustard and cayenne. Cook over low heat, constantly stirring, until cheese melts. Add a little of the cheese to the egg and beat briefly, then add egg-cheese mixture to the pot. Add beer and cook until rarebit is hot but not boiling (about 1 or 2 minutes), add salt to taste. Pour at once over warm toast, each slice on it's own plate. (Also good to add bacon or sliced smoked turkey on toast before spooning the rarebit over the toast.) Makes 4 servings.

CURRIED CHICKEN CHEESECAKE with CHUTNEY

This savory cheesecake is a nice change from quiche, and is a favorite. Choose a fruit or vegetable salad to go with it. Adapted from a Southern Living *recipe.*

1 1/3 cups round buttery cracker crumbs
   (like Ritz)
1/4 cup butter
1 1/2 teaspoons chicken bouillon granules
1 tablespoon boiling water
3 (8-ounce) packages cream cheese
3 eggs
1 (8-ounce) carton sour cream
4 tablespoons grated onion

4 tablespoons minced celery
1 tablespoon flour
1 tablespoon plus 1 teaspoon curry powder
1/4 teaspoon salt
3 cups cooked chicken, chopped
1/2 cup almonds, toasted and chopped
1/3 cup raisins
Assorted condiments
Curried Sour Cream Sauce or Chutney

Preheat oven to 300°F. Combine cracker crumbs and butter; press in bottom and 1 inch up the sides of a 9-inch springform pan. Set aside. Combine bouillon granules and boiling water, stir until dissolved. Beat cream cheese at high speed in a mixing bowl until light and fluffy; add eggs, one at a time, beating well after each addition. Add bouillon mixture, sour cream and next 5 ingredients; beat at low speed until blended. Stir in chicken, almonds and raisins. Pour mixture into prepared pan. Bake for 45 minutes, or until set. Turn oven off, and partially open oven door; leave cheesecake in oven 1 hour. Remove from oven and let cool completely on a wire rack. Cover and chill.

Unmold cheesecake onto lettuce-lined platter. Garnish with several of the following: flaked coconut, toasted slivered almonds, chopped green or sweet pepper, raisins, and crumbled bacon. Serve with Curried Sour Cream Sauce or Chutney (recipes below). Makes 8 to 12 servings. Can be served room temperature.

Curried Sour Cream Sauce
1 (8-ounce) carton sour cream, 1 1/2 teaspoons curry powder and 1/8 teaspoon ground ginger
Combine all ingredients, stir well; cover and chill. Makes 1 cup.

Chutney
1 yellow onion, sliced thin
1 1/2 cups currants, raisins, dried cherries
   or apricots (or combination)
3 cups diced and peeled apples
4 cups brown sugar
1 cup balsamic vinegar

1 teaspoon freshly ground black pepper
1 teaspoon salt
2-2 1/2 tablespoons Worcestershire sauce
1 tablespoon fresh minced ginger
2 tablespoons fresh lemon juice

Combine all ingredients in saucepan. Bring to a boil, lower heat and cook until fruit is tender and syrupy. After removing from heat add fresh lemon juice. Makes 3 cups. From Jean Gaunt.

Mennecy (French) *Sauceboat on Stand*, ca. 1760, painted porcelain, WAM, The Florence Naftzger Evans Collection, 1962.51

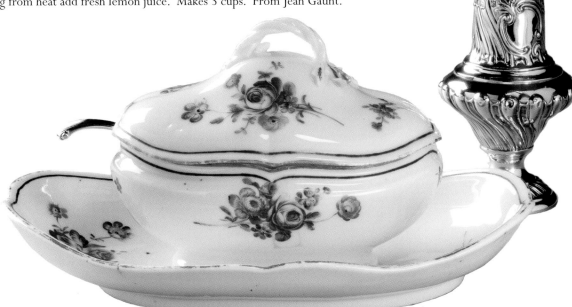

CRANBERRY CHICKEN SALAD

Served at Wichita Art Association 'Holiday Tables.' Recipe easily multiplies.

1 pound (4 cups) cooked chicken, cubed
$\frac{1}{2}$ cup walnuts, toasted and chopped
1 cup sliced water chestnuts
2 cups chopped celery
$\frac{1}{2}$ cup dried cranberries

Dressing

1 cup mayonnaise
1 tablespoon soy sauce
$\frac{1}{2}$ teaspoon curry powder
$\frac{1}{2}$ teaspoon salt
$\frac{1}{4}$ teaspoon black pepper
$\frac{1}{2}$ tablespoon lemon juice

Mix chicken and next four ingredients together. Combine dressing ingredients and toss with chicken mixture. Chill. Good served on whole wheat bread, croissant, warm potato buns or on a bed of lettuce. Makes 8 servings.

HOT CHICKEN SALAD

This tasty and popular hot chicken casserole has lots of crunch and flavor which appeals to all ages. You may be inclined to leave off the potato chip topping but it adds a lot. Easy to make in quantity too. Kathie Molamphy, Jean Trump, Mary O'Brien, Lisa Parcell and I made 480 casserole servings for the Wichita-Sedgwick County Historical Museum Wreath Festival.

6 cups cooked and chopped chicken
6 cups thinly sliced celery
$1\frac{1}{2}$ cups chopped or slivered almonds
3 cups mayonnaise (prefer Hellmann's, may use low-fat)

$1\frac{1}{2}$ teaspoons salt
6 tablespoons grated onion
6 tablespoons fresh lemon juice
$1\frac{1}{2}$ cups grated Parmesan cheese
2 to 3 cups potato chips, crushed

Preheat oven to 450°F. Mix chicken, celery, and almonds together. Mix mayonnaise, salt, onion and lemon juice together and toss with the chicken mixture. Scrape into a 9 x 13-inch casserole dish. (May be frozen, but do not put the topping on until thawed and ready to bake.) Cover with Parmesan cheese and top with crushed potato chips. Bake for 20 minutes. Makes 8 to 10 servings.

CURRIED CHICKEN SALAD

The taste of curry and the chunks of pineapple, water chestnuts and grapes make this is a delicious chicken salad. Great served on leaves of butterhead lettuce or as a sandwich.

4 cups finely diced cooked chicken
2 cups grated coconut
1 ($5\frac{1}{2}$ ounce) can pineapple tidbits (if chunks, cut in half), drained
2 cups green or red seedless grapes, cut in half
1 cup sliced water chestnuts (or may substitute finely sliced celery)

Dressing

$1\frac{1}{2}$ cups mayonnaise
1 tablespoon lemon juice
1 teaspoon curry powder (or more to taste)
1 tablespoon soy sauce

1 small can smoked almonds, cut in half
1 small can cashews (optional)

Combine chicken, coconut, pineapple, grapes and water chestnuts in a large bowl. Mix mayonnaise, lemon juice, curry and soy sauce together in a small bowl, add additional curry if desired. Can be made the day ahead for flavors to blend. Toss chicken mixture with dressing. If it seems too dry, add pineapple juice. Add nuts before serving. Makes 6 servings.

Variation: add either 1 onion diced finely or 6 finely sliced green onions and $\frac{3}{4}$ cup sliced green olives.

Titian Ramsay Peale
*Ruffed Grouse in a
Landscape* (detail), 1873,
oil on canvas, WAM, gift
of the Wichita Art Museum
Members, 1968.78

CHINESE CHICKEN PEANUT SALAD

3 to 4 cups chopped cooked chicken
1 medium head napa cabbage, shredded
2 cups honey-roasted peanuts
5 green onions, thinly sliced
1 cup sliced red pepper (optional)
1/4 cup vegetable oil
3 tablespoons rice vinegar

2 tablespoons sugar
1 tablespoon toasted sesame oil
1 1/2 teaspoons dry mustard
1 teaspoon soy sauce
1 teaspoon grated ginger
2 cups crispy Chinese noodles

Combine chicken, cabbage, peanuts, green onions in a large bowl. Add red pepper strips if desired. Place oil, vinegar, sugar, sesame oil, mustard, soy sauce and ginger in a jar with a tight-fitting lid, cover and shake well. Pour dressing over chicken mixture and toss. Gently stir in 1 cup of the Chinese noodles; portion into serving bowls top with remaining noodles. Makes 6 servings.

TURKEY TARRAGON SALAD

Tarragon serves as an excellent complement to the roasted turkey, and the grapes add great sweetness and texture. Served at the Wichita Symphony Showhouse Tea Room, 2005.

8 cups white turkey (prepared as below)
2 cups diced celery
1/2 cup chopped scallions
1 1/2 cups seedless green grapes, cut in half
1/2 cup sliced almonds, roasted

Dressing
1/2 cup mayonnaise
1/2 cup sour cream
2 teaspoons dried tarragon leaves
1 tablespoon tarragon white vinegar

Preheat oven to 325°F. Brush turkey with olive oil, minced garlic, salt and pepper. Roast until meat thermometer indicates poultry is done. Cool, and cube meat. Chill. Combine dressing ingredients and refrigerate, covered, for at least one hour for flavors to blend. Mix turkey, celery, scallions, and grapes. Stir in dressing mixture. Adjust seasoning with salt and pepper. Serve as a salad on bed of greens garnished with roasted almonds, or as a sandwich on a croissant. Makes 8 servings.

SMOKED TURKEY SALAD

Delicious served on fresh salad greens, in half a cantaloupe, or on good bread as a sandwich filling.

2 1/4 cups diced smoked turkey
1 cup chopped red onion
4 hard-boiled eggs, chopped fine
2 cups mayonnaise
2 tablespoons Dijon mustard

1 teaspoon celery salt
1 jalapeno pepper, diced
1 teaspoon white pepper
1 teaspoon black pepper
1 teaspoon cumin

Combine turkey, onion and eggs. In separate bowl, combine mayonnaise with remaining ingredients. Add mayonnaise mixture to turkey mixture and blend well. Refrigerate until ready to serve. Makes 6 to 8 servings.

CRÊPES

CRÊPE TIPS

Strain any lumps out of the batter.

Fill a big measuring cup with a pour lip full of batter to make pouring tidy and easy.

Slightly undercook the first side of the crêpe, flip, cook the second side, then flip back to the first side and add filling. Let the filling ingredients heat up, then fold. Undercooking the first side a bit buys some time later for the filling to heat up.

Crêpes can be combined with a variety of fillings to create an elegant main course or dessert. Try some of the following fillings or experiment with your own favorites.

1 1/3 cups whole milk, room temperature	3 tablespoons butter, melted
1 cup flour	1 tablespoon sugar
3 eggs, room temperature	1/4 teaspoon salt

Process all ingredients in blender until smooth. Cover and chill at least 1 hour, or up to 1 day. Spray 7-inch nonstick skillet with vegetable oil spray and heat over medium heat. Pour about 2 tablespoons of batter into a crêpe pan and swirl to coat bottom. Cook until edge of crêpe is just barely light brown, about 1 minute. Loosen edges gently with spatula; turn or flip crêpe over. Cook until bottom begins to brown in spots, about 30 seconds, turn back over (see margin note). Add filling, cook until filling is heated; fold. Transfer to plate. Repeat with remaining batter, spraying pan as needed and covering each crêpe with paper towel if not filling them immediately. Makes about 20 crêpes.

Some filling ideas:
- Chicken à la King
- Lobster or crab in a sherried cream sauce
- Scrambled eggs, cheese, and picante sauce
- Creamed spinach
- Broccoli with cheese sauce
- Ice cream and a favorite topping
- Sautéed apples with raisins, brown sugar, and cinnamon, topped with whipped cream
- Chocolate hazelnut spread (like Nutella) and a sprinkle of Grand Marnier liqueur

HARWIG'S SUGAR SNAP-FETA SALAD

American Glass *Goblet*, ca. 1840, apple green pressed lead glass, WAM, gift of the family of Marjorie Molz, 2007.4.149

This can be served as a side dish or as a main entrée by adding grilled chicken.

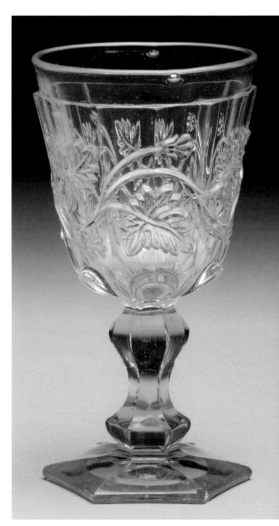

2 cups fresh sugar snap peas
3/4 cup crumbled Feta cheese
2 teaspoons chopped red onion
1/2 tomato, diced
2 tablespoons chopped toasted walnuts
2 tablespoons grated Parmesan cheese

Dressing
1/2 cup chopped fresh mint
1 teaspoon chopped garlic
1/2 cup white wine vinegar
Salt and pepper
1/2 cup olive oil

Blanch and chill sugar snap peas. (If using frozen sugar snaps, thaw but do not blanch.) Combine first 6 ingredients in a bowl. For the dressing, combine mint, garlic, vinegar, salt and pepper in a food processor. With the machine running, slowly add olive oil and blend well. Toss dressing with salad and refrigerate until ready to serve. Makes 3 to 4 servings. For a milder taste, use 1/4 cup white wine vinegar and 1/4 cup rice vinegar. From Anita Jones.

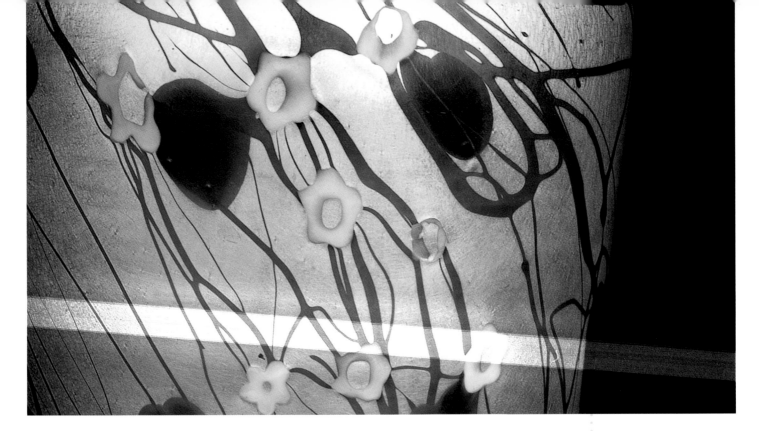

DR. REDBIRD'S SUPREME PRESERVATIVE

Marni Vliet describes the beginning of a popular Wichita eatery, and one of my favorites: "The first Dr. Redbird's opened April 20, 1971 at 124 S. Main in Wichita. The Supreme Preservative sandwich meal was the favorite sandwich at all locations for 14 years."

¹/₄ cup butter	Salt and freshly ground black pepper
1 cup flour	1 pound shaved turkey breast, kept warm
1 cup 1% milk	8 broccoli spears, steamed
8 ounces Swiss cheese, grated	8 wheatberry bread slices, toasted and buttered

Melt the butter over medium heat. Add the flour and whisk to combine. Stir in the milk and bring to a boil. Decrease the heat and simmer until sauce is thick. Remove from heat and stir in the cheese. Season to taste with salt and pepper. Place the warm turkey on the bread slices. Top with the broccoli spears and pour the cheese sauce over each. Season to taste with salt and pepper. Serve immediately. Makes 8 open-faced sandwiches. From Marni and Rich Vliet.

MONTE CRISTO SANDWICHES

Often regarded as irresistible by the men in the family, these are outstanding sandwiches for a casual change of pace. Not deep-fat fried like the restaurant version, so even better.

3 tablespoons mayonnaise	6 Swiss cheese slices
1¹/₂ teaspoons prepared mustard	2 eggs
12 sandwich bread slices, trimmed	1 cup milk
6 cooked turkey slices	1¹/₂ cups pancake mix
6 cooked ham slices	Butter or margarine

Stir together mayonnaise and mustard; spread on 1 side of each bread slice. Place 1 slice each of turkey, ham, and cheese on top of 4 bread slices. Top with remaining bread. Cut each sandwich in half diagonally; secure with wooden picks. Stir together eggs, milk, and pancake mix in a dish until blended. Dip each sandwich into batter. Melt butter in a heavy skillet; add sandwiches, and cook 3 to 4 minutes on each side or until lightly browned and cheese begins to melt. Serve with strawberry or raspberry preserves on the side, if desired. Makes 6 servings.

TURKEY, BACON and HAVARTI LOAF SANDWICH
This stuffed sandwich is great for a picnic. It could also be sliced thinly and served as an hors d'oeuvre.

1 (7-inch) round sourdough bread loaf
4 tablespoons balsamic vinaigrette (divided use)
½ pound thinly sliced smoked turkey

1 (12-ounce) jar roasted red peppers, drained and sliced
6 (1-ounce) slices Havarti cheese
4 to 6 bacon slices, cooked and crisp

Cut top 2 inches off of sourdough loaf, reserving top. Hollow out loaf, leaving a 1-inch thick shell. Drizzle 2 tablespoons vinaigrette in bottom of bread shell. Layer with half of turkey, peppers and cheese. Repeat layers, and top with bacon. Drizzle remaining 2 tablespoons vinaigrette evenly over these layers, and cover with bread top. Press down firmly. Wrap in plastic wrap until ready to slice and serve. Makes 4 servings.

ANTIPASTO CHICKEN PANINI
Surprise your guests with this twist on an old favorite. The red peppers, olive paste and sun-dried tomatoes pack a lot of zing into this loaf sandwich.

1 (10-ounce) loaf round focaccia, cut in half horizontally
2 tablespoons olive paste
2 cups shredded, roasted, skinless, boneless chicken breast (can use a rotisserie chicken)
½ cup coarsely chopped marinated artichoke hearts, drained

½ cup chopped oil-packed sun-dried tomatoes, drained
½ cup bottled roasted red peppers, drained and coarsely chopped
2 ounces thinly sliced prosciutto (or salami)
½ cup (2 ounces) shredded fontina cheese (or mozzarella)

Spread inside bottom half of focaccia with olive paste. Arrange chicken on top of that layer. Then arrange artichokes, tomatoes, peppers, and prosciutto over chicken. Sprinkle with cheese. Top with the top half of the focaccia and press gently. Heat a large skillet over medium heat with just a mist of olive oil. Add sandwich to pan, place a cast iron pan on top of sandwich, pressing gently to flatten. Cook 2 minutes on each side or until bread is lightly toasted (with the cast iron skillet on top of sandwich). Of course, if you have a panini press, use it instead. Cut into 4 wedges. Makes 4 servings.

SMOKED TURKEY, APPLE and CHIPOTLE MAYO SANDWICHES

Chipotle Mayonnaise
1 cup nonfat or low-fat mayonnaise (prefer Hellmann's/Best Foods on West coast)
1 tablespoon Dijon mustard
3 drops liquid smoke
1 lime (juice, zest and pulp with seeds removed)
1 or 2 chipotle chili peppers in adobe sauce plus 1 tablespoon sauce from can of chipotle chili peppers

12 slices whole wheat bread
2 Granny Smith apples, cored and thinly sliced
6 to 8 smoked turkey breast slices
6 to 8 Muenster cheese slices

Combine all mayonnaise ingredients in a food processor or blender; cover and refrigerate for 1 hour. Spread mayonnaise on bread and assemble sandwich with cheese, turkey and apples. Makes 6 servings.

CUBANO SANDWICH WITH RED ONION MARMALADE

1 slightly stale French bread loaf, cut into 4
   portions (Cuban bread if you can get it!)
1 to 2 tablespoons mustard
Long slices of dill pickle ('Sandwich Stackers'
   work well)

1 pound sliced ham
1 pound roasted pork
$1/2$ pound Baby Swiss cheese (or Provolone or
   Monterey Jack)
Butter, softened

Let meat and cheese come to room temperature to avoid burning bread while the cheese melts during grilling. Preheat a pancake griddle or large fry pan. Slice open each of the quartered bread pieces, but not all the way through. Paint the bottom inside with mustard, the top inside with butter, then generously layer the pickle, ham, pork and cheese. Place on a buttered pancake griddle or large fry pan to cook, and place a heavy iron skillet or bacon press on top of the sandwich to flatten the bread to about a third of original size (or use a sandwich press or George Foreman grill if you have one). Cook for 5 to 7 minutes until cheese is melted and sandwich is nicely compacted, flip and cook the other side for about 3 minutes. Cut in half, serve immediately. Makes 4 servings. Great with Red Onion Marmalade.

Red Onion Marmalade

$3/4$ cup red wine
$3/4$ cup red wine vinegar
$3/4$ cup sugar
2 pounds red onions,
   finely sliced

4 ounces butter
$1/2$ teaspoon salt
$1/2$ teaspoon pepper

In a large saucepan, heat wine, vinegar and sugar, then add onions, cover and cook over low heat for 30 minutes until they are very soft. Remove lid and cook until liquid reduces; stir frequently. Cool and store in refrigerator for up to a month.

*Enrique Riveron (1902-
1998) was a dashing and
well-liked member of the
Wichita art community
from the 1930s through
the '60s. Riveron's art
education began in his
native Cuba and was
followed by three years of
study in Paris and Madrid.
His work is marked
formally by interpretations
of European modernism,
such as Cubism, and
psychologically by what
he described as "individual
freedom and intensity
of feeling."*

*In New York he met his
second wife, Noella Wible,
then a student at Columbia
University. They moved to
Wichita because it was
Noella's hometown. Later
Riveron worked frequently
in Los Angeles for the
Disney Studio and in New
York as an illustrator for
The New Yorker and
Vanity Fair. - SG*

Scott Banks recalls his mother's sandwiches: "I was popular at lunchtime at school. Everyone wanted to see what Mom packed for my lunch. She made the best sandwiches - I could trade half of one of them for someone's entire lunch pail."

Wichita has been the founding home for several fast food chains. White Castle was founded here in 1928. (A decade later, the Wichita division was bought by A.J. King, who changed it to Kings-X. The original building is preserved intact on a ranch south of Wichita.) The world's first Pizza Hut was opened in a converted bar on East Kellogg in 1958 by Frank and Dan Carney. (The Carneys sold the company to Pepsico, and the original "Hut" is on the campus of Wichita State University.) Taco Tico was started in Wichita a few years after Pizza Hut.

Wichita is also home to several regional chains: Taco Grande, Big Cheese Pizza, Spangles and NuWay. NuWay Café, a Wichita tradition since 1930, still operates from the original location at 1416 W. Douglas (and 5 other locations), serving their unique "crumbly" sandwich made from a secret recipe in patented cookers.

TARRAGON SHALLOT EGG SALAD SANDWICH

Toasted whole grain bread, thinly sliced, keeps this crunchy. An important technique is how the eggs are boiled: you want them to just set so, and to be yellow (avoiding the green/grey ring). So avoid overcooking (see p. 159).

Basic egg salad

6 eggs, hardboiled and peeled
3 green onions, thinly sliced, or half bunch
   of chives, chopped
2 celery stalks, thinly sliced
1/4 cup mayonnaise

1 tablespoon Dijon mustard
Dash lemon juice
8 slices 13-grain whole wheat bread
Boston lettuce leaves
2 large tomatoes, sliced

Coarsely chop warm eggs with a pastry blender, but don't overdo it, as some texture is desired. Add onions, celery, mayonnaise and mustard. Season with dash of lemon juice, salt and pepper.

To make this into a tarragon-shallot egg salad sandwich substitute 3 tablespoons of finely chopped shallots for the green onions, add 1/2 tablespoon tarragon, 2 teaspoons white wine vinegar. May also use additions of chopped bacon, capers or fresh dill instead of tarragon. Chill. Assemble sandwiches using remaining ingredients. Makes 4 servings.

BLT with BASIL MAYO

The basil mayonnaise makes this a great version of a classic, and is worth the effort.

Basil Mayonnaise

1 egg, room temperature
1 tablespoon fresh lemon juice
1 teaspoon Dijon mustard
1/4 teaspoon salt
1/2 cup vegetable oil (canola or safflower)
1/2 cup olive oil
3/4 cup chopped fresh basil

12 potato bread slices
1 pound bacon, cooked crisp
Boston lettuce leaves
2 large tomatoes, sliced thin

Make the mayonnaise by combining egg, lemon juice, mustard and salt in a food processor or blender until well mixed. While machine is running on low speed, pour oils in a small stream until mayonnaise has thickened. Add chopped basil leaves and pulse a few times. Assemble sandwiches, first spreading Basil Mayonnaise on bread and then stacking ingredients. Makes 6 servings.

OURWAY NUWAYS

NuWay Cafe has been a Wichita destination for decades. If you find yourself with a craving and hours away, give this home version a try. I think you will like it!

3 pounds ground beef
3 (10.5 ounce) cans French onion soup

Salt and pepper, to taste
Dash of chili powder, to taste

Boil beef in 2 quarts of water until done; drain water. Add French onion soup, salt, pepper and chili powder and simmer 3 to 4 hours. Drain and serve on hamburger buns with dill pickle slices and mustard, with hot pepper sauce on the table.

FRANCOISE'S TUNA TOMATO VINAIGRETTE SALAD

Try this easy tuna salad, made with vinaigrette instead of mayonnaise. Served without bread, it is a nice change.

4 large ripe tomatoes
1/2 cup olive oil
2 tablespoons balsamic vinegar

2 cups fresh corn kernels (or canned corn, drained)
1 (6-ounce) can tuna, drained

Cut each tomato in half, scoop out the seed pockets and dice into 1/2-inch cubes. Sprinkle these with salt and allow to set for 30 minutes; drain. Whisk together the vinegar and oil, add tomatoes, corn and tuna and toss to combine. Season with freshly ground pepper; serve immediately. Makes 4 to 6 servings.

CHIPOTLE BURGERS

1 1/2 pounds ground beef (not too lean)
3 chipotle chilies from a can of chipotles in adobo sauce
3 tablespoons adobo sauce
3/4 teaspoon ground oregano

1/4 teaspoon ground cumin
3 green onions, minced
1 1/2 teaspoons salt
6 hamburger buns

Mix all the ingredients together and form into 6 hamburger patties. Heat cast-iron skillet over medium-high heat and cook, turning once. (Alternatively, grill over high heat until cooked through.) Serve on a bun with guacamole, salsa and even a slice of Monterey Jack cheese. Makes 6 servings.

When selecting ground beef for burgers, you want something with a little fat. "Lean" or "extra-lean" ground beef will fall apart and make for dry burgers. Aim for 10 to 20% fat. Also resist the urge to press on the patties while cooking — that liquid squishing out is vital juice.

TURKEY SLOPPY JOES

1 pound lean ground turkey
1/4 teaspoon chopped dried onions
2/3 cup ketchup
1 tablespoon vinegar
1 tablespoon Worcestershire sauce

1/4 teaspoon onion powder
10 drops hot pepper sauce or chili powder to taste
6 hamburger buns, toasted

In a sauce pan over medium heat, cook ground turkey until browned, add onions. Mix all other ingredients together in the pan and heat. Add more ketchup, vinegar or hot pepper sauce as needed. Serve on toasted hamburger buns. Makes 6 servings. From Matt Burch.

If you are making a sandwich that has a soupy filling, like sloppy joes, toast the bread before assembling the sandwich.

WORTH IT GRILLED CHEESE SANDWICH

Combining two cheeses gives the best result. Two other secrets are to butter the bread evenly with softened butter and use a cast iron skillet.

4 white sandwich bread slices
2 ounces Monterey Jack cheese, cut into 1/8-inch thick slices

2 ounces Cheddar cheese, cut into 1/8-inch thick slices
Unsalted butter

Heat large cast iron skillet over medium-low heat. Place two slices of bread on a work surface, and cover each with a layer of Monterey Jack, and then a layer of Cheddar; top with the remaining slices of bread. Generously butter the tops and the bottoms of the sandwiches. Place the sandwiches in the skillet, and using a spatula, press down lightly. Cook until golden brown on each side, 3 to 4 minutes per side, and the cheese has completely melted. Cut sandwiches in half; serve immediately. Makes 2 servings.

COGNAC MARINATED BEEF TENDERLOIN SANDWICHES with HORSERADISH CREAM SAUCE

These may be served as pre-made sandwiches, or have the beef on a platter, the rolls in a basket, and the horseradish cream in a bowl and let your guests make their own. The beef can marinate up to two days in advance, and the sauce made one day ahead.

1 (2¹/₂-pound) center-cut beef
 tenderloin, trimmed
¹/₃ cup finely chopped shallots
¹/₃ cup cognac
¹/₃ cup water
2 tablespoons minced fresh tarragon
2 teaspoons chopped fresh thyme
¹/₂ teaspoon ground black pepper
2 garlic cloves, minced

1 teaspoon kosher salt
30 (1¹/₂-ounce) sandwich rolls, cut in
 half horizontally

Horseradish Cream Sauce
¹/₂ cup reduced-fat sour cream
¹/₃ cup low-fat mayonnaise (prefer Hellmann's)
2 tablespoons minced fresh chives
2 tablespoons prepared horseradish

Loosely bind tenderloin at 1-inch intervals with kitchen twine. Combine shallots, cognac, water, tarragon, thyme, pepper and garlic in a large zipper-lock plastic bag. Add tenderloin and seal. Shake to coat tenderloin evenly. Marinate in refrigerator for at least 2 hours, turning bag occasionally. Prepare Horseradish Cream Sauce by combining ingredients, cover and chill.

Preheat oven to 450°F. Remove tenderloin from bag, discard marinade. Sprinkle tenderloin with salt and place in a shallow roasting pan coated with cooking spray. Bake for 40 minutes or until medium-rare or desired degree of doneness. Let stand 10 minutes before slicing. Cut tenderloin crosswise into thin slices. Spread 1¹/₂ teaspoons horseradish cream on bottom half of each roll, top each roll with about 1 ounce beef and top half of roll. Makes 30 sandwiches.

WOOTTON HAM SANDWICHES

Easy!

¹/₂ cup butter
2 tablespoons poppy seeds
2 teaspoons prepared mustard
2 teaspoons Worcestershire sauce
1 small onion, chopped

1 package small party rolls (such as Pepperidge
 Farms, 20 per package)
4 to 6 slices baked ham (deli-sliced)
4 to 6 slices Swiss cheese

Mix butter, poppy seeds, mustard, Worcestershire and onion in a food processor until well mixed. Cut the rolls in half before separating them. Spread mixture on both sides of the rolls. Lay the ham and cheese across the rolls; cut the rolls into individual sizes. Seal all in aluminum foil. Bake at 300°F for 20 minutes. Makes 20 small sandwiches. From Valerie Edwards.

FRENCH DIP SANDWICHES

This sandwich is a favorite served in the Victorian Sampler Tea Room in Eureka Springs, Arkansas.

6 to 8 pound beef roast
1½ teaspoons salt
1 teaspoon coarse ground black pepper
1 teaspoon dried oregano
1 teaspoon dried basil
1 teaspoon dried rosemary
Beef bouillon cubes (as desired)
Worcestershire sauce (as desired)

Horseradish Sauce
1 cup reduced fat sour cream
3 teaspoons prepared horseradish
2 teaspoons Dijon mustard
Salt

French rolls, cut in half horizontally
Sliced red onion

Cut roast into 4 to 6 pieces, place in large pot. Sprinkle with all seasonings, except bouillon cubes, and barely cover with water. Bring water to a boil, then reduce heat, cover pot and simmer 6 to 8 hours or until meat is very tender. Remove meat and allow juices to cool until fat forms on top. Remove fat from sauce and from the roast. Cut meat into thin strips, cover and refrigerate until ready to serve.

To serve, return meat to juices and heat to serving temperature. Add bouillon cubes and Worcestershire sauce to juices for more flavor. Prepare Horseradish Sauce by combining ingredients. Serve beef on a heated French roll with cup of juices for dipping, and a side of horseradish sauce and sliced red onion. Makes about 16 sandwiches.

Right: Charles Levier (French), *Fleurs*, ca. 1950, oil on canvas, WAM, gift of Mr. and Mrs. Kurt A. Olden, 1979.4. © 2008 Artists Rights Society (ARS), New York/ADAGP, Paris

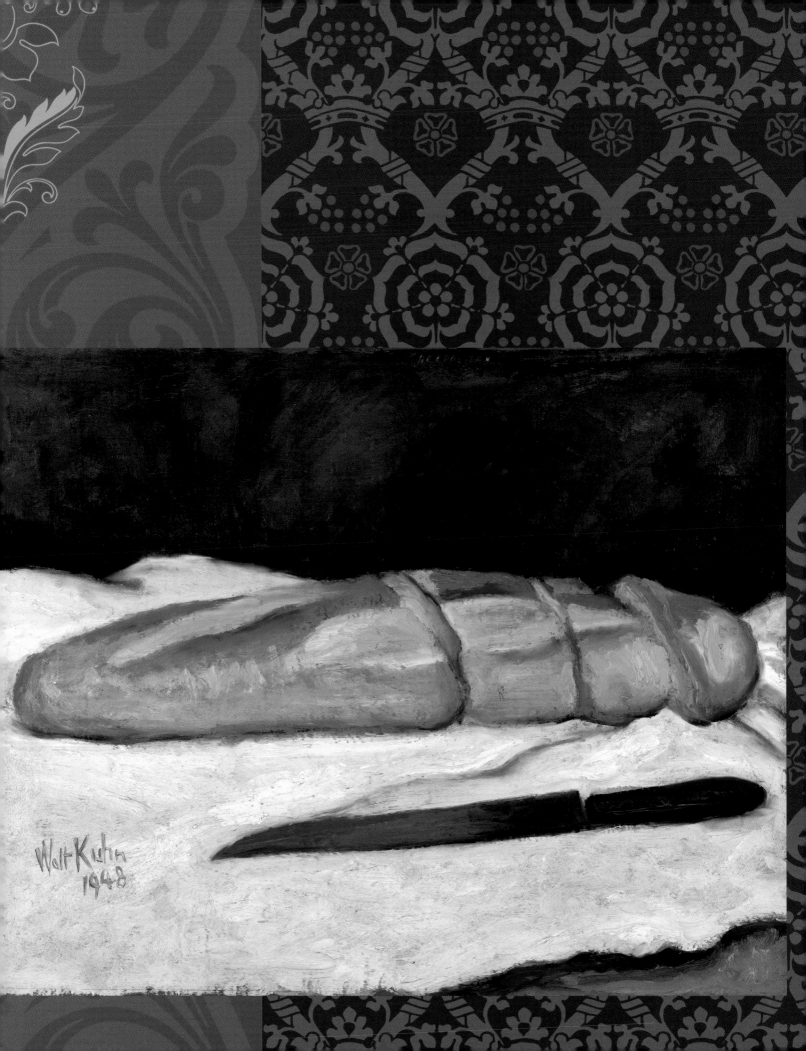

Breads & Rolls

CREAM BISCUITS

Easy and versatile. No need to cut in fat as it is there in the cream. For shortcake, just add 2 tablespoons of sugar.

2 cups self-rising flour
1 cup whipping cream

Preheat oven to 425°F. Lightly grease a baking sheet. Place flour in large bowl; stir in cream, just until dough is blended. Use 2 large serving spoons to drop dough onto a very lightly greased cookie sheet. Bake for 15 minutes, checking bottoms for doneness. Serve immediately.

For rolled biscuits: Melt 5 tablespoons of butter, set aside. Turn dough onto a lightly floured surface and knead for one minute. Then roll or pat dough out to $^1/_2$-inch thickness. Cut dough into 12 squares and dip each into melted butter. Place biscuits 2 inches apart on baking sheet. Bake for 10 to 15 minutes at 425°F, or until lightly browned. Serve hot. Makes 8 to 10 biscuits.

Note: If using regular flour, add $^1/_2$ teaspoon salt, $^1/_2$ teaspoon baking soda and 3 teaspoons baking powder.

ANGEL BISCUITS

1 package dry yeast, or 1 teaspoon instant yeast
$^1/_4$ cup very warm water (110 to 115°F)
1 $^1/_4$ cups stone ground flour
  (prefer 'Wheat Bin')
1 $^1/_4$ cups unbleached flour

$^1/_2$ teaspoon baking soda
1 teaspoon baking powder
2 tablespoons honey
$^1/_2$ cup shortening
1 cup buttermilk

Preheat oven to 400°F. Dissolve yeast in water. Whisk together dry ingredients. Cut shortening into dry ingredients. Add buttermilk and honey, then yeast. Stir until flour is dampened. Knead on floured board for less than a minute. Roll to $^1/_2$-inch thickness; cut with biscuit cutter. Bake for 12 to 15 minutes. No rising is necessary. (Dough can be refrigerated and used as needed for a week)

FLAKY BUTTERMILK BISCUITS

5 cups flour
$^3/_4$ cup shortening, cut into $^1/_2$-inch chunks
1 teaspoon baking soda
1 teaspoon baking powder

1 teaspoon salt
3 tablespoons sugar
1 package dry activated yeast
2 cups cold buttermilk, preferably low fat

Preheat oven to 400°F. Sift dry ingredients. Cut in shortening and add buttermilk and yeast dissolved in water. Mix until all flour is moist. Cover the bowl and put in refrigerate until ready to use. Dough will keep several weeks in the refrigerator. Roll out as much as needed on floured board $^1/_2$ to $^3/_4$-inch thickness; cut out and place on lightly greased baking sheet. Bake for 12 minutes. Makes 2 dozen.

FLOUR TIPS

If you don't bake very often, or tend to keep flour around for a long time, check your flour before using to make sure it doesn't smell rancid.

Measure flour by spooning lightly into a measuring cup until it overflows, then level the top with the edge of a metal spatula or knife. Do not tap the cup to settle the flour.

Store flour in a cool place in an airtight container. Whole wheat flour spoils faster than white flour. The bran contains more oil. which goes rancid quickly. Freeze it to get the most life out of it.

CHEDDAR BISCUITS
What a guilty pleasure these beauties are!

2 1/4 cups flour
2 1/2 teaspoons baking powder
3/4 teaspoon baking soda
2 teaspoons sugar
1 teaspoon salt
6 tablespoons butter, cut in cubes

1 cup shredded extra-sharp Cheddar cheese
3 scallions (whites only) or
   chives, chopped
1 cup buttermilk
Topping: melted butter, dash garlic powder

Preheat oven to 450°F. Whisk flour, baking powder, baking soda, sugar and salt together in a medium bowl. Blend in the butter with pastry blender or fingertips until it is all crumbly. Stir in Cheddar and scallions; add buttermilk and stir until just barely combined. Drop onto buttered baking sheet, about 12 biscuits placed 2 inches apart. Bake for 18 minutes or until lightly golden. Brush warm biscuits with melted butter and sprinkle with garlic powder before serving. Serve warm. Makes 12 biscuits.

BEER BREAD
Beer breads are surprisingly good and easy. Great served with barbeque, and just fantastic served warm.

3 cups self-rising flour (or 3 cups flour, plus 1 tablespoon baking powder and 1 teaspoon salt)
3 tablespoons sugar
1 (12-ounce) bottle lager beer, room temperature
2 tablespoons butter, melted

Preheat oven to 350°F. Mix flour and sugar together. Pour in beer and stir until just incorporated; the dough will be sticky. Grease a 5 x 9-inch loaf pan with butter and spoon in batter. Bake for 50 minutes, and then brush top with butter and return to oven for 10 minutes more until top is golden. Remove from pan and serve immediately. This bread is best when warm, and it cuts most easily with a serrated knife. Makes 10 servings from one loaf.

Variations: For a richer version, melt 1/2 cup of butter. Before placing dough into pan, pour half of the butter into the prepared pan. Spoon in the dough, and pour the remaining half of the butter on the top. This dough also adapts well to additions such as sliced green onions, grated cheese, chilies or chives.

ONION CHEESE BREAD
This savory, moist bread works well as muffins too, and complements a range of entrées. We served 500 of these tasty, memorable muffins at the Wichita-Sedgwick County Historical Museum Wreath Festival Luncheon.

3/4 cup chopped onion
1 tablespoon vegetable oil
1 1/2 cups buttermilk
1 egg, lightly beaten
1 1/2 cups Bisquick baking mix

1 cup shredded sharp Cheddar cheese
   (divided use)
2 teaspoons poppy seeds
4 tablespoons butter, melted

Preheat oven to 400°F. In a small skillet over medium heat, sauté onion in oil about 7 minutes, until golden brown. Set aside to cool. Combine buttermilk and egg in a medium sized bowl. Stir in biscuit mix, onion and 1/2 cup cheese. Pour into a greased 9-inch round baking pan. Sprinkle with poppy seeds and remaining cheese. Drizzle with butter. Bake for 35 minutes or until golden brown. Cool slightly. Cut into wedges. Makes 8 servings.

Variation: my favorite way is to bake this batter as muffins. Reduce baking time to 30 minutes. Remove from muffin tin after cooling for 5 minutes to prevent bottoms from getting soggy. Cool upside down on wire rack. Makes 12 muffins.

GREAT PUMPKIN BREAD

This recipe has been a long-time favorite, first appearing on a Del Monte pumpkin can label in the '60s and then in many community cookbooks. It is very easy and consistently good. This variation notches up the spices and adds a pecan streusel topping.

Ever wonder about the saying "best thing since sliced bread"?

By 1928, the bread slicer was perfected and used in a commercial bakery in Missouri. By 1930, sliced bread along with the introduction of the automatic toaster, toast became popular for breakfast. However, in 1942 during WWII rationing, the sale of sliced bread was banned in an effort to hold down prices.

3¹/₂ cups flour
1¹/₂ teaspoon salt
2 teaspoons baking soda
3 cups sugar
1 teaspoon nutmeg
1 teaspoon cinnamon
1 teaspoon ground allspice
1 teaspoon ground cloves
1 (16-ounce) can solid pack pumpkin

1 cup vegetable oil
1 cup water
4 eggs, beaten
1¹/₂ cups pecan pieces, toasted

Topping
¹/₂ cup golden brown sugar
¹/₄ cup butter, melted and slightly cooled
2 teaspoons cinnamon

Preheat oven to 350°F. Grease six 3 x 5-inch loaf pans. Combine dry ingredients in a large bowl. Add remaining ingredients and mix well. Prepare topping by stiring ingredients together. Fill prepared pans half full, sprinkle topping over top and bake for 1 hour. Cool in pans on a wire rack. This may also be prepared in two 5 x 9-inch loaf pans, or muffins (bake 30-35 minutes or until they test done).

STRAWBERRY BREAD

Served at the first Wichita Art Museum 'Art on a Monday' event, which was a Tea, reminiscent of the times of the Wichita Art Museum founder, Louise Murdock. Can be served with a flavored butter or with a dollop of whipped cream topped with lemon zest. Adapted from the Stephens College Alumnae Cookbook.

STRAWBERRY BUTTER

1 (10-ounce) package frozen strawberries, thawed
1 cup powdered sugar
1 cup butter (or margarine)

Combine and beat with electric mixer 10 minutes. Use spread in place of butter. Good for tea sandwiches. Also good spread on toasted English muffins.

Recipe from Joan Schulz, who recalls how her son used to put this butter on everything possible.

3 cups flour
1 teaspoon baking soda
1 teaspoon salt
1 teaspoon cinnamon
2 cups sugar

4 eggs, well beaten
1¹/₄ cups vegetable oil
2 cups frozen sliced strawberries, thawed
   (or 3 cups chopped fresh strawberries)
Optional: 1 cup pecans, chopped

Preheat oven to 350°F. Combine flour, baking soda, salt, cinnamon and sugar in large bowl. Form a shallow well in center of mixture. Combine remaining ingredients and add to dry ingredients. Stir well. Spoon into two 5 x 9-inch loaf pans that have been greased on the bottom. Bake for 1 hour, or until a wooden pick inserted comes out clean. Allow loaves to cool in the pan for 5 minutes, and then turn out onto a rack. Do not slice until ready to serve. Makes two loaves.

OLD FASHIONED DATE NUT BREAD

This recipe first came from the Dromedary Date company in the '30s. It is good served with a bowl of cream cheese whipped up with a bit of sour cream, and enjoyed with a fresh cup of coffee.

³/₄ cup water
¹/₄ cup shortening
1 (8 ounce) package chopped dates (or pitted
   dates, snipped)
³/₄ cup chopped walnuts
2 eggs, slightly beaten

¹/₂ teaspoon vanilla extract
1¹/₂ cup flour
³/₄ cup sugar
1¹/₂ teaspoons baking soda
¹/₂ teaspoon salt

Preheat oven to 350°F. Grease and flour a 5 x 9-inch loaf pan. Bring water and shortening to boil in a small saucepan; pour over dates in a medium bowl. Allow to stand for 15 minutes; stir to blend. Add nuts, eggs and vanilla. In a small bowl, combine flour, sugar, baking soda and salt. Stir into date mixture until blended. Do not over mix. Pour into pan. Bake 65 to 70 minutes or until it tests done. Cool in pan on wire rack for 10 minutes, then loosen edges with spatula and turn out onto wire rack to cool completely. Makes one loaf.

BANANA BREAD

3 medium ripe or overripe bananas, mashed
1 cup sugar
1 egg
4 tablespoons butter, melted

1 teaspoon vanilla extract
1 1/2 cups flour
1 teaspoon baking soda
1/2 teaspoon salt

To make the basic banana bread, follow this process. Preheat the oven to 325°F. Use cooking spray to prepare an 8-inch loaf pan. Combine the bananas, sugar, egg, butter and vanilla in a large bowl. Beat until mixed. In a separate bowl, whisk together the flour, baking soda and salt. Add the flour mixture into the banana mixture just until blended. Pour the batter into the prepared pan. Bake for 60 to 65 minutes or until inserted toothpick comes out clean. Allow the bread to cool in the pan for 10 minutes before turning out onto a rack. Makes one loaf. Good with Honey Almond Butter.

Banana Coconut Macadamia Bread
To make this into a very rich bread, add 2 tablespoons of sour cream and 1/2 cup sweetened flaked coconut to the batter. After placing batter in loaf pan, sprinkle 3 ounces (1/2 cup) of chopped salted macadamia nuts on top, gently pressing them in. Bake as specified above.

COCONUT BREAD

3 cups flour
2 teaspoons baking powder
1/2 teaspoon baking soda
1/2 teaspoon salt
2 cups sugar
1 cup vegetable oil

4 eggs, beaten
2 teaspoons vanilla
1 cup buttermilk
1 cup shredded unsweetened coconut
1 cup chopped walnuts

Preheat oven to 300°F. Combine flour, baking powder, soda and salt; set aside. In a large bowl combine sugar, oil, eggs and vanilla. Add dry ingredients alternately with buttermilk. Stir just until moistened. Fold in coconut and walnuts. Pour into three small loaf pans coated with cooking spray. Bake for 30 to 35 minutes or until wooden pick inserted in middle comes out clean. Makes three loaves. From Debbie Deuser.

HONEY ALMOND BUTTER

*1 stick butter
1/3 cup almonds, finely chopped
2 teaspoons honey
1 teaspoon cinnamon*

*Mix well together.
From Joan Schulz*

Copper Lusterware (British), 1830-50, glazed ceramic, WAM, bequest of Mrs. Walter Innes, Jr., 1988.5.10 - 13

PREFERMENT BREAD STARTER

Preferment (meaning "to ferment before") bread doughs differ from yeast breads. This category includes most sourdough breads and the popular potato bread (or sometimes called Amish bread) starters that have circulated in the community.

Doughs made with preferments are prepared in stages. The yeast and some flour and water are mixed together first and allowed to ferment for several days, and then this mixture is used as a foundation with which to build dough. These preferment "starters" give the fermentation process a big boost and prove great flavor and leavening to the bread.

Just like a good wine, bread with a long slow fermentation time gets better with time. They have been used for centuries and were used exclusively before commercial yeast became available.

The easiest way to get going with making this kind of bread it to receive a gift of a "starter" from a friend. This is best because older starters only get better with time. Breads made with a new starter will not be quite as wonderful as bread made with an older, more mature starter.

Only a portion of a starter is used at any one time. This leaves plenty that can be fed and maintained indefinitely.

If you can't find someone with one to be divided, you can also purchase a mix for starter (see "Favorite Things"), or make one from scratch. The advantage of purchasing one is that you will be able to take advantage of proven wild yeast cultures.

MY FAVORITE POTATO BREAD

All of these doughs are so very easy and make it worth keeping a starter fed. If you don't have a starter, see directions below on how to start a starter or see "Few Favorite Things" to purchase. Feed the starter every 5 to 7 days and keep it in the refrigerator. You can then have fresh bread in a jiffy whenever you want. Here is how I do it, making a loaf once a week:

In morning, the day before you plan to bake bread, add to starter, and set out all day:

3 tablespoons potato flakes
$^3/_4$ cup sugar
1 cup warm water

In evening, make bread dough by adding:

1$^1/_2$ to 1$^3/_4$ cup starter (keep remaining 1 cup + for next time)
1$^1/_2$ cups warm water
$^1/_2$ cup oil
$^1/_4$ cup sugar
1 teaspoon salt
6 cups bread flour

Mix together and cover with plastic wrap. Let stand overnight. (I put it on a heating pad on low. It helps to make it rise if your kitchen isn't warm.) In the morning, punch down and shape into bread loaves or cinnamon rolls. Let rise 1$^1/_2$ hours. Makes 2 medium loaves or 1 sheet cake size pan of cinnamon rolls.

Potato Bread Loaf

Place loaf in cold oven set at 300°F for 20 minutes. Increase temperature to 350°F for 20 minutes.

Cinnamon Rolls

Roll dough out to a large rectangle, spread with softened butter. Sprinkle with sugar and cinnamon. Roll up along long side. Cut with serrated knife into 1-inch pieces. Place on a sheet cake pan that has been sprayed with nonstick cooking spray. Three round cake pans will work. Bake cinnamon rolls 350°F for 20 to 25 minutes.

Dilly Bread

Add 3 tablespoons dill weed to flour as you mix for dough. Bake into 3 round cake pans or 2 regular loaves. Place loaf in cold oven set at 300°F for 20 minutes. Increase temperature to 350°F for 20 minutes.

STARTING A POTATO BREAD STARTER

Starter (first time)

1 cup warm water   1 package (2-$^1/_4$ teaspoons) dry yeast
$^1/_2$ cup sugar   3 level tablespoons instant potato flakes

Mix and let ferment on counter for two days. Then feed with starter feeder. (If you get a starter from someone else, you can omit this step.)

Starter Feeder

1 cup warm water   3 tablespoons potato flakes
$^1/_2$ cup sugar

Add to starter. Let stand on countertop eight hours. Refrigerate 3 to 5 days, then make bread dough.

Maintenance of the starter
Match the volume of the starter with the volume of flour and water. Can be stored in the refrigerator for several weeks without any feedings. When storing label it with the amount of the starter and the date it was fed. To bring back to a state for baking, bring it to room temperature for approximately 2 hours.

GRANDPA'S SWEDISH RYE BREAD

When Grandpa Olson boarded the ship to emigrate from Sweden, he didn't bring any written recipes with him to homestead in Kansas. However, the family carried forth the tradition of this pleasing, aromatic bread. Fantastic when served warm, with lots of butter.

Niece Linda Ade Brand finds her Great Grandpa's Swedish Rye Bread pretty grand and suggests grilling a slice lightly in a panini press, then topping it with a slice of brie and an accent of ginger preserves or orange marmalade.

3 1/2 cups lukewarm water (divided use)
1/4 cup butter
1 cup brown sugar
1 1/2 cups molasses (divided use)
2 teaspoons salt

Pinch orange rind
3 cups rye flour, sifted
4 1/2 to 5 cups flour
2 packages dry yeast (or 4 1/2 teaspoons dry yeast)

Boil butter, 3 cups of water, brown sugar, 1 cup molasses, salt and orange rind. Cool to lukewarm. Dissolve yeast in 1/2 cup water. Add 3 cups sifted rye flour and yeast mixture. Add white flour to make dough easy to handle.

Transfer the dough to a large buttered bowl, grease the top, cover with a towel and let rise in a warm place until doubled, about 2 hours. Punch the dough down and let rise again until doubled. Punch down again and turn out onto a lightly floured surface. Either makes one large loaf (baked in a springform pan), or two smaller loaves (baked on a baking sheet), so divide accordingly. Let rise again for about another 1 1/2 hours, until nearly doubled. Brush with 1/2 cup molasses and 1/2 cup water, mixed together.

Bake 1 hour in a preheated 325°F oven. Put foil over loaves during the last 30 minutes if browning too quickly. Brush with butter immediately from oven, or if you wish instead to have a little glaze, dissolve 2 teaspoons of sugar in a little hot water and brush over the tops of the loaves while the bread is still hot. Makes 1 large spring pan loaf or 2 to 3 smaller loaves.

Robert T. Aitchison Threshing, *1921, woodcut on paper, WAM, purchased with funds from the sale of a painting donated by Arthur Kincade, 2003.20.6 (See curator note on p.190 for information on the artist.)*

DILLY BREAD

Delicious with stews or any savory meal, this moist savory bread adds a nice kick. Modified from a Pillsbury's Bake-Off Recipe winner from 1969, this has been a consistent hit over the years.

2 packages active dry yeast (or 4 1/2 teaspoons
   dry yeast)
1/2 cup very warm water (110 to 115°F)
1/2 teaspoon sugar
2 tablespoons butter
2 teaspoons salt
4 tablespoons sugar
3 teaspoons dill seed

1 teaspoon dried dill weed
1 tablespoon minced onion
2 cups small curd cottage cheese
5 cups bread flour, or as needed
2 eggs
3/4 cup Cheddar cheese, grated
1/2 teaspoon baking soda

In a small bowl, sprinkle the yeast over 1/2 cup warm water mixed with 1/2 teaspoon sugar. Let stand until foamy. Melt butter in saucepan and add the butter, salt, sugar, dill seed, dill weed, onion and cottage cheese, heat to lukewarm. Put into a warm bowl and add cheese, eggs, soda, yeast and 1 cup of the flour; stir with a wooden spoon or mixer until well blended. Stir in as much of the remaining flour as possible with a large wooden spoon, and then turn the dough out onto a floured surface. Knead in enough additional flour to make moderately stiff dough. Continue kneading until the dough is smooth and elastic, about 8 minutes. Place in a large greased bowl, cover and let rise until doubled in bulk (about 1 to 1 1/2 hours).

To make small loaves:
Punch down and divide into 6 to 8 equal parts. Form into balls and place on greased cookie sheets. Butter tops; cover and let rise until double in size. Bake at 350°F for 25 to 30 minutes. Butter tops again when taken from the oven.

Or to make two large round loaves:
Generously grease two 8-inch round 1 1/2 or 2-quart casserole dishes. Stir down dough; turn into the casserole dishes. Let rise in warm place until light and doubles in size, 30 to 40 minutes. Bake at 350°F for 40 to 45 minutes until golden brown, switching positions of loaves on the racks halfway through. Immediately remove from pan; brush with butter and sprinkle lightly with salt. Makes 2 loaves.

OATMEAL BATTER BREAD

I like to make 4 loaves at a time of this bread, freezing half. However, the recipe is easy to cut in half for 2 loaves.

1 1/3 cups old-fashioned rolled oats
2 1/2 cups boiling water
1/2 cup mild molasses (I like to use Grandma's
   Molasses as it is milder)
4 tablespoons butter
2 teaspoons salt

2 teaspoons sugar
1/2 cup warm water
2 packages dry yeast (or 4 1/2 teaspoons
   dry yeast)
2 eggs
6 cups flour

Measure oatmeal into large bowl. Pour boiling water over oats, stir. Add molasses, butter and salt. Stir well. Cool to lukewarm. Stir sugar in warm water in small bowl. Sprinkle yeast over top. Let stand 10 minutes. Stir to dissolve yeast. Add to oat mixture. Beat in eggs. Beat in flour. Cover with greased waxed paper and tea towel. Let stand in oven with light on and door closed for about 1 hour until doubled in bulk. Stir batter down. Spoon into 4 greased 8 x 4-inch loaf pans. Cover with greased waxed paper and tea towel. Cover and let rise in a warm place, free from drafts, 35 to 45 minutes or until doubled in bulk. (I like to have it stand in oven with light on and door closed for this.) Bake in 375°F oven for 30 to 35 minutes or until lightly golden. Turn out onto racks to cool. Brush warm tops with butter. Makes 4 loaves.

"All parts of Kansas grow good corn but in wheat Kansas can beat the world."
Topeka Daily Capital, 1888

Recognized worldwide for superb quality wheat, Kansas ranks first in the US for wheat production and flour milled. This wheat, planted in the fall and harvested in early summer, was not always the state's dominant crop. Early settlers after the Civil War planted corn familiar to them from the humid eastern areas they previously called home. However, in an effort to bolster shipping business and to sell land, railroads mounted advertising campaigns to recruit emigrants among the Germans living in Russia. Experienced wheat growers (no corn in Russia) they quickly settled into what would become Kansas' major wheat producing areas. Legend has it that the strains of hard red winter wheat so successful in the Great Plains were first brought to Kansas in 1872 by Russian Mennonites. Their success convinced other farmers to switch to wheat.

CROISSANTS

3/4 cup margarine, frozen
2 1/2 to 3 cups flour
3 tablespoons sugar
1 teaspoon salt

2 packages dry yeast (4 1/2 teaspoons)
3/4 cup milk, scalded
1/4 cup water
1 egg, room temperature

Heat milk on high in microwave for 1 to 2 minutes and let cool until just lukewarm. In a large bowl, mix yeast with lukewarm milk, water and sugar and salt. Stir to dissolve the yeast and sugar. Add aabout 1 1/2 cups flour and beat with mixer. After mixing in the flour, add the egg and beat again. If needed, beat in some additional flour with the mixer: you want a soft, sticky dough, not a runny batter.

Place about 1 cup flour on the counter and scrape out the dough onto this. Knead in this additional flour until you can handle the dough with your hands. It should no longer be sticky, but will be soft and supple. With a rolling pin, roll out the dough to a 5 x 13-inch rectangle.

With a medium size grater, grate all the frozen margarine onto the center part of this rectangle. Fold over the outer two portions of the rectangle onto the margarine. Give the dough a quarter turn and roll again into a rectangle. Fold into thirds, turn a quarter and roll again. Repeat this two to three times. If dough is sticky, dust with a little flour. If there are lumps of margarine showing, pinch the dough over them or fold and roll again. Do not handle the dough with your hands any more than necessary to fold and turn. Wrap the dough in a plastic bag and chill at least two hours (Can make this at night and let it stay in the refrigerator until morning, but do not to wait too long the next morning to finish the rolls).

With a knife, cut the dough in thirds. Working with one third at a time, roll quite thin into a circle. Cut into 8 pie shaped pieces. Starting at the outside edge (wide end), roll with your fingers to the point. Place this roll on your baking sheet with the point on the bottom (no need to grease the baking sheets). Repeat with other pieces of dough. Put baking sheets into a large plastic bag (13 gallon trash bags work well!), "fluffing" the bag so it does not rest on the rolls. Do not touch for 70 minutes.

Preheat oven to 400°F. Carefully remove baking sheets from plastic bags and bake for about 12 minutes, until just golden brown. (Light golden brown is fine as they will brown more when reheated; to do so put into a 250 to 300°F oven for 5 to 10 minutes.) Makes 2 dozen. From LeahDean (Dean) Ross, submitted by Pat Thiessen.

REFRIGERATED YEAST ROLLS

1 cup shortening
1 cup sugar
2 teaspoons salt
1 cup boiling water
2 eggs, lightly beaten

2 envelopes active dry yeast (4 1/2 teaspoons)
1 cup warm water (105 to 115°F)
6 cups flour
1/4 cup butter or margarine, melted

Combine shortening, sugar and salt in a large bowl; stir in boiling water. Cool. Stir in eggs. Combine yeast and 1 cup warm water in a 1-cup glass measuring cup; let stand 5 minutes. Stir into egg mixture. Gradually add flour, stirring until blended. Cover and chill at least 4 hours.

Preheat oven to 375°F. Pinch off one-third of dough. Cover and chill remaining dough up to 5 days, if desired. Roll dough to 1/4-inch thickness on a floured surface. Cut with a 2-inch round cutter. Place 2 inches apart on lightly greased baking sheets. Brush with melted butter. Let rise at room temperature 1 hour or until doubled in bulk. Bake for 10 to 12 minutes or until golden.

OVERNIGHT CINNAMON ROLLS

Served at the Wichita-Sedgwick County Historical Museum Wreath Festival 1999-2002; made 500 rolls each time.

2 3/4 cups boiling water
1 cup plus 1 teaspoon sugar (divided use)
1/2 cup butter
1 tablespoon salt
1/4 cup warm water
1 envelope instant dry yeast (2 1/4 teaspoons)
8 cups unbleached flour

Filling
3 cups packed light brown sugar
1 1/2 cups butter
6 tablespoon cinnamon

Icing
8 ounces cream cheese, softened
2 tablespoons corn syrup
2 tablespoons heavy cream
1 cup powdered sugar, sifted to remove lumps
1 teaspoon vanilla extract
Pinch salt

Chinese export porcelain teapot, late 18th century, painted porcelain, WAM, the Florence Naftzger Evans Collection, 1962.24

Begin at 5:00 p.m. Pour boiling water into large mixing bowl. Stir in 1 cup sugar, butter and salt until sugar is dissolved and butter is melted. Cool to lukewarm. Stir 1 teaspoon sugar in warm water in small bowl. Sprinkle yeast over top. Let stand 10 minutes. Stir to dissolve yeast and add to first mixture when cooled to lukewarm.

Beat in about 2 cups of the flour. Work in enough remaining flour until dough pulls away from sides of bowl. Place in greased bowl, turning once to grease top. Cover with tea towel. Let stand on counter until 7:00 p.m. Punch down dough. Cover with tea towel. Let stand on counter until 10:00 p.m. Punch dough down and divide into thirds. Roll dough into a 12 x 14-inch rectangle. Combine filling ingredients. Spread each square with filling, leaving a 1/2-inch border on far long edge. Roll up from long side closest to you. Moisten the top border with water and seal the roll. Lightly dust the roll with flour and press if necessary to make a uniform cylinder. Repeat with each dough third. Cut each cylinder into 12 even segments (dental floss works well). Arrange on greased baking sheets. Cover with tea towel. Let stand on counter until morning. Bake in 375°F oven for 15 to 20 minutes. Makes 36 rolls.

These are delicious plain, but if icing is desired, prepare while the dough is rising. Combine all icing ingredients in the bowl of a standing mixer, blend together at low speed for about 1 minute to incorporate. Then turn on high for another 2 minutes until icing is smooth. Transfer to small bowl, cover and refrigerate until ready to use. Let rolls cool for 10 minutes before frosting with a rubber spatula.

DANISH ALMOND CREAM ROLLS

2 (3-ounce) packages cream cheese, softened
1/2 to 1 teaspoon almond extract
1/2 cup powdered sugar
1/2 cup finely chopped almonds
2 (8-ounce) cans crescent dinner rolls
1 egg white
1 teaspoon water
1/4 cup sliced almonds

Glaze
2/3 cup powdered sugar
1/4 to 1/2 teaspoon almond extract
3 to 4 teaspoons milk

Preheat oven to 350°F. Combine cream cheese, almond extract and powdered sugar in a small bowl; beat with an electric mixer until fluffy. Stir in almonds by hand. Separate 1 can of dough into 4 rectangles; firmly press perforations to seal. Press or roll each dough piece to form a 4 x 7-inch rectangle; spread each with about 2 tablespoons of the cream cheese filling to within 1/4 inch of edges. Starting at longer side, roll up each rectangle, firmly pinching edges and ends to seal. Gently stretch each roll to a 10-inch cylinder. Coil each roll into a spiral with the seam on the inside, tucking end under. Place on ungreased cookie sheets. Repeat with remaining can of dough. In small bowl, combine egg white and water; brush over rolls. Sprinkle with sliced almonds. Bake for 17 to 23 minutes or until deep golden brown. In small bowl, blend all glaze ingredients, adding enough milk for desired drizzling consistency; drizzle over warm rolls.

PEACHES and CREAM CINNAMON ROLLS

1 (26.4-ounce) package frozen biscuits
1 (6-ounce) package dried peaches
1/2 (8 ounce) package cream cheese, softened
3/4 cup brown sugar
1 teaspoon cinnamon

1/2 cup chopped pecans, toasted
1 cup powdered sugar
3 tablespoons milk
1/2 teaspoon vanilla extract

Preheat oven to 375°F. Place frozen biscuits on a lightly floured surface, with sides touching, 3 rows of 4 biscuits; let stand 30 to 45 minutes just until they are thawed but still cool. Pour boiling water to cover dried peaches and let stand 10 minutes; drain well; chop. Sprinkle thawed biscuits very lightly with flour; press edges together, patting to form a 10 x 12-inch rectangle; spread evenly with cream cheese. Stir together brown sugar and cinnamon, and sprinkle over cream cheese. Sprinkle peaches and pecans over brown sugar mixture. Roll up, starting at one long end; cut into 12 slices (about an inch each). Place into a 10-inch round baking pan, cut sides up. Bake for 35 to 40 minutes or until golden brown. Cool slightly and glaze with mixture of 1 cup powdered sugar, 3 tablespoons milk and 1/2 teaspoon vanilla. Makes 12 rolls.

HONEY BUNNIES

Frozen dinner roll dough (prefer Mrs. Butterworth's)
Raisins

Thaw dough overnight in refrigerator. Place 1 thawed roll on greased cookie sheet (dough should be cold). Gently press to form a 2 1/2-inch circle, about 1/2 thick. Form nose from small part of second roll. Divide remaining roll into 2 parts to make ears. Make whiskers with knife tip and press raisins in dough to form eyes. Let dough rise according to directions. Bake in preheated 350°F oven for 15 minutes, or until golden brown. Makes 6 bunny rolls. If desired, decorate with colored egg whites and sugar.

SESAME ONION TWISTS

2 tablespoons butter
1 1/2 cup finely chopped onions
1/4 teaspoon paprika

1 (16-ounce) loaf frozen bread dough, thawed
1 large egg, beaten
1 tablespoon sesame seeds

Grease large baking sheet; set aside. Melt butter in a medium skillet over medium heat until foamy. Add chopped onion and paprika; cook until onion is tender, stirring occasionally. Remove skillet from heat.

Spray work surface with nonstick cooking spray. Roll thawed dough into a 12 x 14-inch rectangle. Spread onion mixture on one side of dough. Fold dough over onion mixture to make a 6 x 14-inch rectangle. Pinch long edge of dough to seal over onion mixture. Using a pastry wheel, cut dough into 14 lengthwise dough strips. Gently twist one dough strip 2 times and place on prepared baking sheet. Press down both ends of dough strip on baking sheet to prevent curling. Repeat with remaining dough strips.

Cover twists with towel and let rise in warm place until doubled in size, about 40 minutes. Brush with beaten egg; sprinkle with sesame seeds. Preheat oven to 375°F. Bake twists until golden, about 15 to 18 minutes. Serve immediately. Makes 14 twists.

CHEESE HERB BREAD

1 1/2 cup mayonnaise
1/3 cup chopped fresh parsley
1 cup shredded Cheddar cheese

3 cloves garlic, pressed
1 cup chopped green onion (include some stem)
2 loaves French bread

Preheat oven to 450°F. Mix above ingredients together. Slice 2 large French bread loaves in half horizontally. Spread generously on each half and sprinkle paprika on top. Bake (or broil) for 10 minutes or until toasted.

CRUSTY GARLIC HERB BREAD

1 loaf French bread (or artisan loaf with some
   good width to it)
1/2 cup butter
1 head garlic, minced or pressed

1/4 cup grated Parmesan cheese
2 tablespoons minced fresh herbs (parsley,
   basil, snipped chives, marjoram, etc.)
Lemon zest or chives (optional)

Preheat oven to 350°F. Split loaf of bread horizontally so you have two long halves. Melt butter; add garlic, cheese and herbs. Slather on surface of bread halves and let it soak in. Place bread buttered side up on baking sheet and bake for about 10 minutes to heat up the bread. Then to finish it off, turn on the broiler and broil for 1 to 2 minutes or until edges are golden. Sprinkle with lemon zest and chives, if desired, after removing from oven. Cut bread into serving size pieces. Serve warm.

Ethel Magafan
Wheat Threshing, 1937,
egg tempera on panel,
WAM, gift of the Friends
of the Wichita Art Museum,
Inc., 1981.19

Seafood and Fish
Grilled Salmon With Red Pepper Sauce 114
Broiled Hoisin Honey Glazed Salmon 114
Cedar Planked Salmon 114
Broiled Salmon with Crisp Potato Crust 115
Sautéed Salmon with Martini Sauce 115
Grilling and Compound Butters 115
Spice-Rubbed Grilled Salmon 116
Trout Almondine with Toasted Almond Dressing 116
Simple Shrimp Scampi 116
Shrimp a'la Grecque 117
Hot Mama Shrimp 117
Grand Leeky Tuna with Chèvre 117
Roasted Sea Bass with Fresh Tomato Basil Sauce 118
Crispy Catfish with Pecan Tartar Sauce 118

Chicken
Cheese Soufflé with Sautéed Mushroom Spinach
  Chicken Filling 119
Chicken Supreme in Pastry Shells 120
Chicken Marbella 120
Sautéed Chicken Breasts with Pan Sauces (Tarragon Cream,
  Lemon Caper, 40 Clove Garlic Sauce or Warm Cherry
  Tomato Sauce) 121
Pecan Chicken with Dijon Sauce 122
Mrs. William A. White's Chicken in Cream 122
Grilled Spice Rubbed Moroccan Chicken 122
Buttermilk Fried Chicken 123
Chicken Cacciatore 123

Seafood or Chicken Pasta
Favorite Pasta 123

Turkey
Herb Roasted Brined Turkey with Rosemary Gravy 124
Spiced Cranberry Sauce 125
Sausage and Cornbread Dressing 125
Sausage Pecan Stuffing 125

Poultry & Seafood

GRILLED SALMON with RED PEPPER SAUCE

Salmon grills beautifully: firm enough to hold together and doesn't dry out.

8 salmon fillets, 1 to 1 1/2 inch-thick, pin bones removed
Kosher salt and freshly ground black pepper
Vegetable oil

Prepare charcoal grill and lightly oil the grate with a wad of paper towels soaked with vegetable oil to remove any residue but to also lightly oil the grate so the fish won't stick. Light charcoal fire, set the grill in place, and cover the grill with the lid to heat up. The grill is ready when the coals are medium-hot. Generously sprinkle each side of the salmon with salt and pepper. Place the fillets skin-side down on the grill. Grill, uncovered, over medium coals (or broil) until skin shrinks and turns black (2 to 3 minutes). Turn with metal spatula. Continue to grill, uncovered until meat is opaque, about 3 to 4 minutes. Serve immediately. Serve with prepared Red Pepper Butter Sauce, if desired.

Red Pepper Butter Sauce

1/4 cup plus 2 tablespoons butter
2 tablespoons olive oil
3 shallots, chopped
1 teaspoon honey

1/2 cup chopped, roasted, peeled, and seeded
   red bell pepper
Dash salt
Freshly ground black pepper to taste

Melt butter over low heat, add olive oil and sauté shallots until softened, but not browned. Remove from heat, stir in honey until dissolved and set aside. Purée peppers in a blender, and while machine is running, slowly add the butter mixture; process until smooth. Season to taste.

BROILED HOISIN HONEY GLAZED SALMON

This glaze can be used for either broiling or grilling salmon fillets. Also good with chicken.

1/4 cup honey
1/4 cup chopped fresh cilantro
1/2 cup hoisin sauce
1 tablespoon grated fresh ginger
1 tablespoon brown sugar

1 scant tablespoon chopped canned chipotle
   chilies in adobo sauce
Salt and freshly ground black pepper
4 (8-ounce) skinless salmon fillets
Vegetable oil

Preheat oven to broil. Combine honey, cilantro, hoisin sauce, fresh ginger, brown sugar and chilies in a small bowl. Brush salmon steaks with oil; season with salt and pepper. Brush with hoisin honey glaze. Place salmon fillets on a heavy baking sheet, lined with foil. Broil 4 minutes, turn, and baste with remaining glaze. Broil 3 to 4 minutes or until fish flakes and appears opaque on the inside. From Bonnie Aeschliman.

CEDAR PLANKED SALMON

Son Todd makes this on the outdoor grill, or indoors in their oven. It is wonderful! Be sure to use a plank of untreated Western red cedar that is specifically made for cooking, available from cooking specialty stores.

Salmon fillet
Cedar plank, untreated and specifically for cooking
Salt and freshly ground black pepper

Season salmon with salt and pepper. Use any size fillet or plank, depending on oven/grill size. *To cook on a grill*, soak plank in water for 2 hours. Place salmon skin side down on plank, place on the grill and put the lid down. There should be lots of smoke, but monitor the cooking as the plank may catch on fire. Cook for about 10 minutes until desired doneness. *To cook in an oven*, preheat oven to 450°F. Place the plank directly on the oven rack and bake for 8 to 10 minutes to lightly toast the wood (soak only for grilling, not for oven use). Remove the plank from the oven and rub with a thin coating of olive oil while plank is still hot. Place salmon skin side down on the hot plank and roast for about ten minutes. Use caution and monitor for fire.

BROILED SALMON with CRISP POTATO CRUST

Salmon is delicious, but difficult to make for a large group. The best way is to cook a whole side of salmon in the oven, which can then serve 8 or more. This recipe, adapted from my favorite cookbook, The New Best Recipe uses the surprising ingredient of potato chips, but it is delicious, crisps well and no one will guess the secret.

1 whole side of boneless salmon fillet
   (about 3 1/2 pounds)
Olive oil
Salt and freshly ground black pepper
3 tablespoons Dijon mustard

Potato/crumb Crust
4 ounces plain potato chips, (about 1 cup)
6 tablespoons chopped fresh dill
3 slices of bread, crusts removed, toasted
   and processed to make bread crumbs

Preheat oven to broil. Prepare a foil sling for the fish by cutting a piece of heavy duty foil about six inches longer than the fillet; fold over in thirds lengthwise. On rimmed baking sheet, place salmon on top of the foil. Check and remove any bones with kitchen tweezers. Rub with a drizzle of olive oil and season fish with salt and pepper. Broil the salmon on the upper rack until it has some spots which are browning, about 9 to 11 minutes. Prepare crust mixture. Remove salmon from the oven, spread evenly with mustard and press crumb and chip mixture into fish. Return to lower oven rack and continue broiling until crust is deep golden brown, about 1 minute. Using the foil sling, transfer the fillet by grasping the foil and setting the fish on a serving board. Makes 8 servings.

SAUTÉED SALMON with MARTINI SAUCE

Look for juniper berries in the spice section of a large supermarket, a health food store or spice vendor.

Martini Sauce
2 cups dry vermouth
1/4 cup minced shallots
2 teaspoons coarsely crushed juniper berries
1 teaspoon coarsely crushed green peppercorns
1 8-ounce bottle clam juice
3/4 cup whipping cream
3 tablespoons butter
1/4 cup sliced pimento-stuffed green olives

2 tablespoons dry gin
2 tablespoons fresh lemon juice

2 teaspoons olive oil
4 (6-ounce) skinless boneless salmon fillets
1 tablespoon chopped fresh parsley
Salt and freshly ground black pepper
1 tablespoon chopped fresh chives

Combine vermouth, shallots, juniper berries, and peppercorns in heavy small saucepan. Boil until liquid is reduced to 1/4 cup, about 12 minutes. Add clam juice and boil until reduced by half, about 8 minutes. Add cream and boil until mixture is reduced to 3/4 cup, about 8 minutes. Add butter 1 tablespoon at a time, whisking until melted before adding more. Strain sauce through fine-meshed strainer. Return to saucepan. (Can be made 2 hours ahead. Keep at room temperature.)

Heat oil in heavy large skillet over medium-high heat. Sprinkle salmon with parsley, then salt and pepper. Add salmon to skillet and sauté until just cooked through, about 4 minutes per side. Meanwhile, re-warm sauce. Stir in olives, gin, and lemon juice. Season sauce to taste with salt and pepper. Place salmon on plates, drizzle with sauce over the top, garnish with chives and serve. Makes 4 servings.

GRILLING and COMPOUND BUTTERS

Flavored butters excite simple dishes, freeze well, and are perfect for grilled meat or fish, corn on the cob or fresh breads. To prepare, place on plastic wrap, shape into a cylinder with your hands, and freeze. Cut diagonally into rounds for serving.

Chili Butter: In the food processor, blend garlic, cilantro, green onion and chili powder. Add softened butter and a little olive oil and blend. Try on grilled chicken.

Maitre d' Butter (Garlic Parsley Butter): Blend garlic, chives, parsley, black pepper, lemon juice, paprika and butter. Great on grilled meat, fish or chicken.

Shallot Thyme Butter: Blend shallots, fresh thyme, butter, pepper and lemon juice. Serve with grilled fish.

SPICE-RUBBED GRILLED SALMON

Toasting the spices before grinding brings out their aromatic flavors.

1 tablespoon whole coriander
1 tablespoon cumin
1 tablespoon yellow mustard seeds
2 tablespoons whole fennel seeds
1 tablespoon salt
1 tablespoon dried dill

1/2 teaspoon freshly ground pepper
2 tablespoons sugar
8 (6-ounce) fillets of salmon, skin on, small
  bones and excess fat removed
Olive oil for grilling

Combine the coriander, cumin, mustard and fennel seeds in a skillet over medium heat. Toast spices while shaking pan; cook until aromatic, 4 to 6 minutes. Grind spice mixture in a coffee grinder until coarse. Transfer to a bowl; add salt, dill, pepper and sugar. Rub spice mixture into flesh sides of salmon. Let stand 30 minutes; if not grilling right away, refrigerate, wrapped in plastic, for up to 2 days. Bring to room temperature before grilling. Brush a ridged cast iron grill pan with olive oil; heat to medium hot. Spray both sides of salmon and pan with oil. Grill salmon, flesh-side down, until firm and slightly charred, about 6 minutes. Carefully turn salmon. Cook until mostly opaque and cooked through, about 4 minutes. Makes 8 servings.

TROUT ALMONDINE with TOASTED ALMOND DRESSING

3/4 cup dry seasoned or Italian-style
  bread crumbs
3/4 cup toasted whole almonds, chopped
  coarsely in food processor
1/2 cup chopped fresh Italian parsley
  (divided use)
Salt and freshly ground black pepper

8 trout fillets
4 tablespoons vegetable oil
1/2 cup butter
3 tablespoons sliced almonds
1/4 cup fresh lemon juice
2 teaspoons grated lemon rind (divided use)

Preheat oven to 350°F. Line a large baking sheet with foil or parchment paper for easy clean up. Combine bread crumbs, almonds and 2 tablespoons parsley in medium bowl. Season trout with salt and pepper. Press almond mixture into flesh side of fish. In a heavy nonstick skillet, heat 1 tablespoon oil over high heat. Add trout, almond side down (you will do this in 2 or 3 batches depending on your skillet). Sauté until golden, about 2 minutes. Transfer trout, almond-crumb side up to prepared baking sheet. Repeat with remaining oil and trout. Place trout in oven and roast until opaque in center, about 5 minutes.

Meanwhile, melt butter in same skillet over medium heat and allow to brown. Add sliced almonds, 1/3 cup chopped parsley, lemon juice and 1 teaspoon lemon rind. Stir until sauce is hot. Season with salt and pepper and pour over fish. Sprinkle with remaining teaspoon lemon rind, serve immediately. Makes 4 servings. From Bonnie Aeschliman.

SIMPLE SHRIMP SCAMPI

2 pounds unpeeled, jumbo shrimp
  (21 count per pound)
1/2 cup finely chopped onion
4 cloves garlic, minced
1/2 cup butter or margarine, melted
1/2 teaspoon dried tarragon

2 tablespoons fresh lemon juice
1/2 teaspoon Worcestershire sauce
1/4 teaspoon hot pepper sauce (or dash of
  cayenne pepper)
2 tablespoons chopped fresh parsley
Hot cooked fettuccine (or white rice)

Peel and devein shrimp; set aside. In a large skillet cook onion and garlic in butter over medium heat, stirring constantly, 3 to 4 minutes. Add shrimp, and cook over medium heat, stirring constantly, 5 to 6 minutes or just until shrimp turns pink. Do not overcook or the shrimp will become tough. Off heat, add tarragon, lemon juice, Worcestershire and hot pepper sauce. Sprinkle with parsley. Serve immediately over fettuccine. Makes 4 to 6 servings.

SHRIMP A LA GRECQUE

This dish consists of quickly sautéed shrimp in olive oil tossed with fresh garden tomatoes, artichoke hearts and feta cheese and served on pasta. Recipe from Chef Linda Hager who says that it is the most requested dinner at the Cottage Inn (Eureka Springs, Arkansas).

1 pound peeled and deveined shrimp
1 tablespoon chopped garlic
2 tablespoons olive oil
¹/₄ cup chopped fresh tomatoes
¹/₂ cup chopped canned artichoke hearts

1 tablespoon chopped fresh parsley
¹/₂ cup crumbled feta cheese
Lemon to squeeze for juice
¹/₂ pound capellini pasta, cooked
Garnish: Lemon and oregano, fresh or dried

In a large skillet heat olive oil; add garlic, and then shrimp. Cook quickly. Add tomatoes, artichokes, parsley and feta, stir to warm. Squeeze lemon over pan. Divide pasta on warm plates and spoon shrimp over pasta. Sprinkle oregano on dish and serve with lemon garnish. Makes 4 servings.

HOT MAMA SHRIMP

Instead of ordering carryout Thai food, try this easy dish.

1 tablespoon red curry paste
1 (13¹/₂-ounce) can unsweetened coconut milk
1 (8-ounce) bottle clam juice
1¹/₄ pounds uncooked large shrimp, peeled, deveined

¹/₃ cup fresh cilantro
Salt and pepper
1 lime, cut into 8 wedges

Stir red curry paste in large skillet over medium-high heat until fragrant, about 1 minute. Add coconut milk and clam juice and bring to boil, whisking until paste dissolves. Boil until sauce is thick enough to coat the back of a spoon, stirring occasionally, about 7 minutes. Add shrimp to sauce. Cook until shrimp turns pink and are just opaque in center, turning occasionally, about 4 minutes. Stir in cilantro. Season to taste with salt and pepper. Divide shrimp and sauce among 4 shallow bowls. Garnish with lime wedges and serve with steamed jasmine (or other white) rice. Makes 4 servings. From Tom Otterness.

GRAND LEEKEY TUNA with CHÈVRE

This luxurious combination tastes like a wish beyond a dream. Developed by Granddaughter Analee.

2 (6 to 8 ounce) tuna steaks
  (³/₄ to 1-inch thick)
¹/₂ cup seasoned flour for dredging
2 tablespoons butter and/or oil
2 cups leeks, washed and julienned
  (about 1 bulb)

1 cup chopped red onions
1 teaspoon capers
2 tablespoons chopped green olives
1 to 2 ounces chèvre
2 tablespoons balsamic vinegar

Heat a large skillet over medium heat until a drop of water beads and evaporates. Turn up heat to medium-high and add the butter/oil to the pan. Dredge the tuna steaks in the seasoned flour and shake off excess. When the butter is no longer foaming or the oil begins to shimmer, add fillets. For fillets that are ³/₄-inch thick, cook on the first side for 3 to 4 minutes and after turning fish carefully with a spatula, cook the second side for 2 to 3 minutes for medium rare. For fillets that are 1-inch thick, increase cooking time on the first side to 5 to 6 minutes and increase cooking time on the second side to 4 to 5 minutes for medium rare. Remove fish from heat and set aside. Sauté leeks and onions in olive oil until tender, about 4 minutes. Add capers and chopped green olives, cook just until warmed through and remove from heat. Assemble the dish by layering the leeks and onions atop the tuna steaks, topping with the capers and olives. Place chèvre on top of the fish and drizzle with balsamic vinegar. Makes 2 servings.

Tom Otterness
Dreamers Awake (detail of "Cigar Woman"), 1995, cast bronze, WAM, Burneta Adair Endowment Fund 1995.14

Native Wichitan Tom Otterness is recognized by both the art world and the general public as one of the most significant contemporary sculptors. His work brings delight to countless youth (and the young at heart) in major urban centers and prompts debate among adults about politics, economics, and the function of public art. Tom is far too engaged in life to make art that is about pure or abstract form; rather, he is part of the great tradition of modeling (even refashioning) the human figure in order to stimulate dialogue about our assumed structures of life and society. That Tom addresses his dialogue from the comic point of view only adds charm to the exchange and enigma to his intent. - SG

ROASTED SEA BASS with FRESH TOMATO BASIL SAUCE

MENU:
*ITALIAN SEA
BASS DINNER*

*Mozzarella, Tomato and
Artichoke Bruschetta 22*

Big Italian Salad 49

*Roasted Sea Bass with Fresh
Tomato Basil Sauce 118*

Couscous Risotto 160

*Zabaglione with Fresh
Strawberries 267*

2 tablespoons olive oil
1 teaspoon balsamic vinegar
6 (6-ounce) sea bass fillets
Salt and freshly ground black pepper
2 to 3 tablespoons flour
Garnish: fresh basil

Tomato Basil Sauce
3 Roma or garden-ripe tomatoes, seeded
   and chopped
$1/2$ medium cucumber, peeled and diced
   (about $1/2$ cup)
1 green onion, thinly sliced
2 tablespoons pitted, chopped black olives
$1/4$ cup chopped fresh basil
1 tablespoon olive oil
1 tablespoon drained capers
1 teaspoon balsamic vinegar
Salt and pepper

Stir olive oil and balsamic vinegar together; pour into a 9 x 13-inch glass baking dish. Season fish with salt and pepper. Place in oil-vinegar mixture, turning each piece to coat. Cover and chill for 1 to 2 hours. Meanwhile prepare the Tomato Basil Sauce. Place all the sauce ingredients in a bowl; stir to combine. Cover and refrigerate for an hour or two for flavors to blend.

Preheat oven to 400°F. Position oven rack in middle of oven. (If desired, line a large baking sheet with foil for easy clean up.) Preheat pan in oven for 5 to 10 minutes. Remove pan and brush generously with oil. Remove Tomato Basil Sauce from refrigerator. Dredge each fish fillet in flour and place floured side down on hot pan. Return to oven and roast for 12 minutes or until fish turns opaque in center. If more browning is desired, run fish under broiler for a minute or two until golden. Plate fish and spoon Tomato Basil Sauce over and around fish and garnish with fresh basil if desired. Makes 6 servings. From Bonnie Aeschliman.

CRISPY CATFISH with PECAN TARTAR SAUCE

CATFISH FRY TIP

*When the oil reaches the
temperature, gently add
just a few of the fillets. The
fish will fall to the bottom
of the pan and then float
up to the top of the hot oil
when done on that side and
turn themselves. If they
don't, help them along
with tongs.*

4 (6-ounce) catfish fillets
Milk
2 teaspoons hot pepper sauce
2 teaspoons salt (divided use)
1 large egg
$3/4$ cup flour
1 teaspoon ground red pepper
1 teaspoon freshly ground black pepper
1 cup finely chopped pecans
Vegetable oil

Pecan Tartar Sauce
$1/2$ cup sour cream
$1/2$ cup mayonnaise
2 tablespoons roasted, chopped pecans
$1/4$ teaspoon grated lemon rind
1 tablespoon lemon juice
1 teaspoon paprika
2 teaspoons capers, drained and chopped

Garnish: lemon wedges

Rinse and dry catfish with paper towels, place in shallow dish and cover with milk; sprinkle with hot pepper sauce. Cover and chill for 8 hours, turn once or twice. Stir Pecan Tartar Sauce ingredients together, chill for at least 1 hour. Remove catfish from milk mixture (reserve milk) and sprinkle evenly with $1/2$ teaspoon salt and set aside. Whisk egg into milk. Combine flour, red pepper, black pepper and $1 1/2$ teaspoons salt. Dredge catfish in flour mixture, shake off excess, dip in egg/milk mixture and then coat with chopped pecans. Pour 2 inches of oil into a Dutch oven or cast-iron skillet; heat to 360 to 370 degrees. Fry catfish for 3 minutes on each side, or until fish flakes on a fork. Drain on paper towels. Serve with Pecan Tartar Sauce and lemon wedges. Makes 4 servings.

American, *Cheese Dish*, ca. 1900, pressed glass, WAM, gift of the family of Marjorie Molz, 2007.4.186

CHEESE SOUFFLÉ
with Sautéed Mushroom Spinach Chicken Filling

¹/₄ cup plus 2 tablespoons flour	¹/₄ cup (1 ounce) Parmesan cheese
¹/₄ teaspoon salt	7 eggs, separated
Dash red pepper	¹/₄ teaspoon cream of tartar
¹/₃ cup butter	¹/₄ teaspoon salt
1¹/₄ cups milk	Additional grated Parmesan cheese
³/₄ cup (3 ounces) shredded Cheddar cheese	Spinach, mushroom, chicken filling

Preheat oven to 350°F. Grease bottom and sides of a 10 x 15-inch jellyroll pan with cooking spray. Line with parchment paper allowing paper to extend beyond ends of pan; spray with cooking spray. Combine flour, salt, and red pepper; stir well. Melt butter in a large heavy saucepan over low heat; add flour mixture, stirring with whisk until smooth. Cook 1 minute stirring constantly with whisk. Gradually add milk; cook over medium heat, stirring constantly until very thick and mixture leaves sides of pan. Remove from heat; stir in Cheddar and Parmesan cheese. Place egg yolks in a large bowl; beat until thick and lemon colored. To this, gradually stir in a quarter of the hot cheese mixture; add remaining cheese mixture, beating well. Combine egg whites (at room temperature) and cream of tartar; beat on high until foamy. Add a quarter of the egg whites into cheese mixture; then carefully fold in remaining egg whites.

Pour cheese mixture into jellyroll pan spreading evenly. Bake on center rack of oven for 15 minutes, or until puffed and firm to the touch (do not overcook). Loosen edges of soufflé with metal spatula, but do not remove from pan; place pan on wire rack. Let cool 15 minutes. Prepare filling (below).

Place 2 lengths of waxed paper (longer than the jellyroll pan) on a smooth, slightly damp surface; overlap edge of paper nearest you over second sheet. Sprinkle additional Parmesan cheese over the waxed paper. Quickly invert jellyroll pan onto waxed paper, with long side nearest you; remove pan, and carefully peel waxed paper from soufflé. Spoon prepared filling over surface, spreading to edges. Starting at long side, carefully roll the soufflé in a jellyroll fashion; use the waxed paper to help support the soufflé as you roll. Using your hands, gently smooth and shape the roll. The soufflé is very fragile and may crack or break during rolling. Carefully slide the roll, seam side down, onto a large ovenproof platter or cookie sheet. Garnish with fresh spinach if desired.

Mushroom Spinach Chicken Filling

2 (10-ounce) packages frozen chopped spinach	³/₄ cup (3 ounces) shredded Cheddar cheese
¹/₄ cup finely chopped onion	¹/₄ cup (1 ounce) grated Parmesan cheese
¹/₄ cup butter, melted	¹/₂ cup sour cream
¹/₂ cup finely diced mushrooms	¹/₄ teaspoon salt
1¹/₂ cups finely diced cooked chicken	¹/₄ teaspoon nutmeg

Cook spinach according to package directions; drain and press dry. You may wish to press spinach between sheets of paper towels to get it very dry. Sauté onion in butter over medium heat until transparent. Add mushrooms, and sauté 3 minutes. Stir in chicken and remaining ingredients. Makes about 2 cups.

CHICKEN SUPREME in PASTRY SHELLS

This dish combines a wonderful creamy chicken filling for pastry shells, enriched by a delicious white sauce.

Buxton Inn White Sauce

1/4 cup butter
1/3 cup flour
3 cups half-and-half
1 tablespoon chicken bouillon granules

1/2 teaspoon onion powder
1/2 teaspoon garlic powder
1/8 teaspoon crushed dried thyme
Dash of white pepper

In a heavy saucepan, cook and stir butter and flour over medium-low heat for about 2 minutes, stirring constantly to prepare a roux. Remove from heat. Heat half-and-half in microwave for 30 seconds on high heat. Carefully stir half-and-half into the roux, gradually adding the rest of the sauce ingredients. Cook and stir until thickened and bubbly. Cook and stir for 1 minute more. Set aside.

Chicken Supreme Filling

3 cups sliced fresh mushrooms (8 ounces)
1 medium green pepper, coarsely chopped
1/4 cup butter
4 cups cooked and diced chicken breast
   (3/4-inch cubes) (about 2 pounds)

1 (2-ounce) jar pimentos, drained and chopped
1/4 cup cooking sherry or dry sherry
1/2 teaspoon fresh lemon juice
6 puff pastry shells, baked (or hot rice)

In a large skillet, cook the mushrooms and green pepper in butter over medium-high heat until tender but not brown. Stir in chicken and pimento. Stir until the chicken is heated through. Stir warm white sauce, cooking sherry and lemon juice into chicken mixture. Heat through. Serve the warm chicken filling in hot puff pastry shells or over hot cooked rice. Makes 6 servings.

CHICKEN MARBELLA

When a version of this classic dish was published in 1979 in The Silver Palette Cookbook, *we thought it was most exotic with prunes, olives, and large amounts of oregano and garlic. Now it's bold sweet-savory flavor is a mainstream, delicious no-fuss dish for a dinner buffet or large family gathering.*

2 cups pitted prunes
1 cup pitted Spanish green olives (or a mix of
   pitted olives such as French and Greek)
1/2 cup capers, partially drained
1/2 cup red wine vinegar
1/2 cup olive oil
1/4 cup dried oregano
3 large cloves garlic, minced or puréed

4 bay leaves
Coarse salt and freshly ground black pepper
10 boneless chicken breasts (or chicken
   quarters), rinsed and dried
1 cup brown sugar
1 cup white wine
Garnish: 1/4 cup fresh flat-leaf parsley

Combine prunes, olives, capers, vinegar, olive oil, oregano, garlic, bay leaves, salt and pepper in a large zipper-lock plastic bag and mix well. Add chicken breasts to the bag and place in refrigerator. Turn bag every couple of hours, marinating for 4 to 12 hours.

Preheat oven to 350°F. Place chicken and marinade mixture in a large baking dish. Sprinkle the brown sugar over the chicken, pour the wine around but not on the chicken. Bake for 45 minutes until cooked through, basting every 10 minutes. Remove bay leaves before serving. Transfer to serving platter, reserving most of the juices in serving bowl for passing separately. Garnish chicken with parsley. Makes 10 servings.

HONORABLE MENTION

BOYS & GIRLS CHICKEN PROJECT · 1942

SPONSORED BY SALINA, KANSAS CHAMBER OF COMMERCE

To fuel the enormous military effort of WW II, food conservation was mandatory. Beginning in 1942 every American received two ration books monthly: 48 blue coupons (for canned goods) and 64 red coupons (for meat, fish, and dairy). M.F.K. Fisher's How to Cook a Wolf, *published in 1942, helped guide homemakers through rations and short budgets. Increased production was also encouraged: with victory gardens and youth raising livestock given civic recognition for "Chicken Clubs".*

[Editor's note: Ribbon (above) was given to 13-year-old Carlene in 1942. Her award letter conveys congratulations for having raised chickens "classed among the best" and encouraged that , "our government needs food products now as never before . . . Develop your flock and you will be doing a bit to help feed our Army and win the war."]

SAUTÈED CHICKEN with TARRAGON CREAM SAUCE
or other great pan sauces

Sautéing boneless chicken breasts is easy, but the technique to keep it flavorful with a nice juicy interior is important. You can serve them without a pan sauce, but even nicer with one. Tarragon Cream is a favorite, but other pan sauces can be made with what you have on hand to take advantage of the wonderful bits of caramelized bits left in the pan from browning. Some variations for delicious pan sauces are described, all favorites from daughter RoxAnn.

Chicken Breast Cutlets
4 to 6 boneless chicken breasts, rinsed
  and dried
Salt and ground black pepper
$1/2$ cup flour (as needed to coat chicken)
2 tablespoons butter
2 tablespoons vegetable or olive oil

Tarragon Cream
4 tablespoons butter
2 to 3 shallots (or scallions), chopped
1 cup dry white wine
2 cups chicken stock
2 tablespoons fresh chopped tarragon
$1/2$ cup whipping cream

Sprinkle salt and pepper on both sides of the cutlets. Place flour on a plate and press each side into flour. Shake cutlet gently to remove excess flour. In a heavy bottomed skillet over medium-high heat, add butter and oil. When butter begins to color and has stopped foaming, lay cutlets in the skillet, with the large smooth side down. The oil should sizzle but not smoke. Sauté until browned on one side, about 4 minutes. Turn with tongs (a fork would pierce meat) and cook other side for 3 to 4 minutes (should feel firm and clotted juices around edges). Serve or transfer to a 200°F oven and continue with the pan sauce.

Melt butter in same pan, reduce to medium heat. Add shallots, cook until tender. Add wine and cook, scraping brown bits from bottom of pan. Simmer until about half of the liquid remains. Add stock and tarragon. Bring to boil for 3 to 4 minutes, and then simmer 10 to 15 minutes before returning chicken (and any juices) to pan with sauce to heat. Add cream to sauce, stir well. Simmer, but do not boil. Serve over pilaf or rice, drizzled with sauce. Makes 4 to 6 servings. From daughter RoxAnn.

OTHER PAN SAUCES

Lemon-Caper Pan Sauce
After sautéing and transferring the chicken, add 1 tablespoon of butter and 1 minced shallot to the skillet, lower heat and sauté until softened. Add 1 cup chicken stock and increase heat to high, and scrape the brown bits from the bottom of the pan. Add $1/4$ cup of freshly squeezed lemon juice and 3 tablespoons drained capers. Boil until reduced to about $1/3$ cup, about 3 to 4 minutes. Add any juices from the chicken and reduce again. Remove from heat and add 2 tablespoons butter until it melts. Spoon sauce over sautéed chicken and serve immediately.

40 Clove Garlic Sauce
Separate 40 cloves of garlic (about 3 whole heads of garlic) and drop in boiling water for 60 seconds; drain and peel. Sauté chicken cutlets as above and set aside. Add peeled garlic to the skillet. Lower heat and sauté for 5 to 10 minutes, stirring often, until evenly browned. Add 2 tablespoons of cognac and $1^1/2$ cups of dry white wine, return to a boil, and scrape the brown bits from the bottom of the pan. Return chicken (and juices) to the pan and 1 tablespoon fresh thyme leaves. Cover and simmer over low heat for 25 minutes. Remove chicken to a platter and keep warm. In a small bowl, whisk $1/2$ cup of the sauce and 2 tablespoons of flour and then whisk it back into the sauce in the skillet. Raise heat, add 1 tablespoon of cognac and 2 tablespoons cream; boil for 3 minutes. Add salt and pepper to taste. Pour sauce and garlic over chicken and serve.

Warm Cherry Tomato Sauce
Cut 1 pint of cherry tomatoes in half. After sautéing and transferring the chicken, add 1 teaspoon lemon zest, 2 minced garlic cloves and $1/2$ teaspoon fresh rosemary leaves to skillet; sauté for 30 seconds. Add tomatoes and $1/4$ cup pitted, chopped Kalamata olives and cook, scraping up browned bits, until tomatoes are hot and slightly wilted (about 4 minutes). Stir in juices from chicken and 2 tablespoons of olive oil. Season with salt and pepper and serve over chicken.

PECAN CHICKEN with DIJON SAUCE

4 boneless chicken breasts
³/₄ cup butter (divided use)
4 tablespoons Dijon mustard
   (divided use)
6 ounces pecans, chopped finely

2 tablespoons canola oil
²/₃ cup sour cream
1 teaspoon kosher salt
¹/₄ teaspoon freshly ground black
   pepper

Preheat oven to 350°F. Pound chicken to an even thickness between
sheets of waxed paper. Combine ¹/₂ cup melted butter and 3 tablespoons
Dijon mustard in a shallow dish and mix; dip each chicken breast into
this mixture. Coat with pecans, set aside. Heat ¹/₄ cup butter and oil in
a skillet. Add chicken breasts, cooking until just lightly browned on each
side; remove to a baking pan. Bake for 30 minutes or until cooked through.
Drain the remaining oil and butter from the skillet, add sour cream and
scrape up any browned bits; stir in 1 tablespoon Dijon mustard, salt and
pepper. Spoon the Dijon sauce onto serving plates; top with the chicken.
Makes 4 servings.

GRILLED SPICE RUBBED MOROCCAN CHICKEN

1 (3¹/₂-4 lb) chicken, cut up,
   or 4 bone-in chicken breasts
4 garlic cloves, peeled
   and pressed
1 teaspoon ground cumin

¹/₄ teaspoon ground allspice
1 tablespoon paprika
1¹/₂ teaspoons salt
1¹/₂ teaspoons turmeric
3 tablespoons vegetable oil

Prepare the chicken by washing it and patting it dry (whole or cut up).
Make a spice paste by combining remaining ingredients together in a small
bowl. Place chicken in a large bowl or zipper-lock bag and pour paste over
them, mixing until all pieces are coated. Chill for one hour, or up to eight
hours. Grill slowly over medium-low heat until done. Makes 4 to
6 servings.

MRS. WILLIAM A. WHITE'S CHICKEN IN CREAM

*William Allen White's great granddaughter, Kathrine Schlageck, writes that
this was served to many visiting dignitaries by Sallie White. This recipe has been
passed down from Sallie White (Mrs. William A.) White to Kathrine K. White
(Mrs. W.L.) to Barbara White Walker to Kathrine Walker Schlageck (See opposite
page for story about William A. and Sallie White).*

1 chicken (fryer), cut in pieces
Salt and pepper
Flour
¹/₂ cup butter

8 strips bacon
1 cup water
1 cup heavy cream

Wash and dry chicken. Season with salt and pepper. Roll in flour and
brown in butter. Place in baking dish and lay a strip of bacon over each
piece of chicken. Add water, cover and bake in 350°F oven for about 40 to
45 minutes, basting frequently when chicken is almost tender. Add cream
and finish baking. Serve chicken and sauce over rice.

BUTTERMILK FRIED CHICKEN

The buttermilk and salt act as a brine, tenderizing and infusing the chicken with flavor and resulting in a crispy crust.

1 quart buttermilk
1 cup kosher salt
1/4 cup sugar
2 cups ice cubes
2 (3 to 4 pound each) frying chickens, each cut into 8 pieces

5 cups flour
1 teaspoon paprika
1/2 teaspoon freshly ground black pepper
1/2 teaspoons baking soda
1 quart canola or non-fragrant peanut oil, for frying

Bring buttermilk, salt and sugar to a simmer and stir until sugar dissolves. Remove from heat and cool to room temperature; add ice and stir until mixture cools to about 40°F. Place chicken in 2 or 3 large zipper-lock bags and divide buttermilk mixture between the bags. Place these in a large shallow dish or a large bowl (in case there are leaks) and refrigerate 6 to 12 hours, turning the bags occasionally.

Heat the oil in 2 large, deep skillets until shimmering. (Surface of the heated oil will look like a pebble has been dropped in a still pond at 350 to 370°F. If the oil isn't hot enough the chicken will be greasy.) On a rimmed cookie sheet, combine flour, paprika, pepper and baking soda. Remove the chicken from the marinade, do not rinse or pat dry; drop chicken into flour mixture, turning to coat. The marinade combined with the flour will create a thick coating. Working in batches, add chicken to the skillets in a single layer, without crowding, and fry over moderate heat. Cover for the first five minutes. Uncover and cook turning occasionally, until deep golden and cooked through, 18 to 20 minutes (internal temperature of 165°F). Drain chicken on wire racks over rimmed cookie sheets and if you wish to serve it hot, put on cookie sheets in a 300°F oven while you cook the rest. Serve hot or refrigerate and pack for picnics. Makes 6 to 8 servings.

CHICKEN CACCIATORE

2 tablespoons olive oil
1/4 pound pancetta, diced
3 tablespoons all-purpose flour
1 teaspoon salt
1/8 teaspoon freshly ground black pepper
1/2 teaspoon paprika
4 pounds skinless chicken thighs
2 onions, chopped

2 cloves garlic, finely chopped
2 tablespoons finely chopped parsley
1 teaspoon chopped fresh oregano
2 carrots, chopped
1 stalk celery, chopped
3 cups peeled, seeded and chopped tomatoes
1 cup white wine
3 tablespoons tomato paste

Preheat oven to 350°F. In a large Dutch oven, heat the oil. Sauté pancetta until crisp, about 3 to 5 minutes. Remove from pan and set aside. Combine flour, salt, pepper and paprika on a plate. Dredge chicken pieces in the flour mixture and add to pan, browning on all sides. Transfer to a plate. Pour off all but 2 tablespoons of oil from the pan. Add onions and sauté until translucent, about 5 minutes. Stir in garlic, parsley, and oregano and sauté another minute. Add carrots, celery, tomatoes, and white wine. Scrape the bottom of the pan to loosen any brown bits. Return the chicken and pancetta to the pot, and stir to cover chicken with the sauce. Bake in oven for 45 to 50 minutes, until chicken is tender. Transfer chicken to a warm platter. Stir tomato paste into the sauce and simmer until thickened. Season with salt and pepper and pour over chicken. Makes 6 to 8 servings.

FAVORITE PASTA

4 ounces spinach linguine, uncooked
1 cup whipping cream
1 cup chicken stock

1/2 cup freshly grated Parmesan cheese
1/2 cup frozen English peas
3 slices bacon, cooked and crumbled

Cook linguine according to package directions; drain and keep warm. Combine whipping cream and chicken stock in a saucepan; bring to a boil. Reduce heat, and simmer 25 minutes or until reduced to about 1 cup. (Whipping cream and chicken stock may be simmered longer if a thicker sauce is desired.) Remove from heat. Add cheese, peas, and bacon, stirring until cheese melts. (For a heartier dish, add peeled, cooked shrimp or chopped, cooked chicken at this time.) Toss with linguine, serve immediately. Makes 2 servings.

HERB ROASTED BRINED TURKEY with ROSEMARY GRAVY and SPICED CRANBERRY SAUCE

This is the requisite Thanksgiving trifecta, and one of my all-time favorite dishes to serve.

SALT TIPS

There are many great salts to use now.

For brining use coarse-grained kosher salt.

For baking use fine-grained table salt because it sifts easily with flour and dissolves easily.

Sea salt is great to keep in a small bowl in your kitchen. Use it to sprinkle on top of salad and foods ready to be served.

1 (20-pound) fresh or thawed turkey
3 gallons cold water
2 cups kosher salt or ½ cup regular salt
½ cup packed brown sugar
½ cup butter, room temperature
2 tablespoons chopped fresh sage (or 1 teaspoon dried)
2 teaspoons chopped fresh thyme (or ½ teaspoon dried)

1 teaspoon chopped fresh rosemary (or ½ teaspoon dried)
1 clove garlic, minced
Salt and freshly ground black pepper
1 onion, quartered
2 celery stalks
1 carrot, quartered
2 cups chicken stock (divided use)
Garnish: Fresh sage or parsley, crabapple or grape clusters

Rinse turkey inside and out and reserve giblets, neck and liver for another use. In a large container, stir salt and brown sugar into water. Soak turkey in this brine, covered and chilled for 10 to 24 hours. Remove turkey from brine; rinse and pat dry inside and out. Preheat oven to 325°F. Combine butter, sage, thyme, rosemary and garlic together in small container. Place turkey on rack in a roasting pan breast side up. Season cavity with salt and pepper. Place onion, celery and carrot in cavity. Tie legs together loosely just to hold shape. Loosen skin on breast of turkey and rub 3 tablespoons butter mixture over turkey breast under the skin. Pour 1 cup water or chicken stock in roasting pan. Place turkey in preheated oven, on bottom rack, and roast 3½ hours or until the thickest part of the thigh registers 175°F, basting every half hour with chicken stock and brushing with herb butter. Transfer cooked turkey to platter, cover with foil and keep warm. Let rest at least 30 minutes for easier carving. Makes 12 servings. From Bonnie Aeschliman.

Rosemary Gravy

Pan juice from roasting pan
½ cup dry white wine
1 to 2 cups turkey (or chicken) stock
¾ cup flour
1 tablespoon chopped fresh rosemary
Salt and freshly ground black pepper

Pour pan juice from roasting pan into a large glass measuring cup. Add wine to the roasting pan, scraping up all the brown bits along the sides. Pour into the glass measure with pan drippings. Spoon fat from surface. Add enough stock to drippings to equal 3 cups. Place 1 cup water and ¾ cup flour in a jar with a screw-top lid. Shake to mix. Place turkey stock in a saucepan over medium heat, add rosemary. Bring to boil. Whisk in enough of flour-water mixture to thicken gravy to desired consistency, whisking vigorously as mixture returns to a boil. Simmer 1 to 2 minutes. Season with salt and pepper.

Spiced Cranberry Sauce

Serve as a side dish, or as a spread later with turkey sandwiches.

1 (12-ounce) bag cranberries
2 cups sugar
2 cups port
½ teaspoon cinnamon
½ teaspoon nutmeg
½ teaspoon ground cloves

Rinse cranberries and pick through them. Heat cranberries, sugar and port over medium heat, stirring until sugar dissolves. Boil, uncovered, for about 5 minutes or just until cranberries pop and the liquid is a good red color. Remove from heat, stir in spices; cool and serve.

SAUSAGE AND CORNBREAD DRESSING

4 cups crumbled corn bread
8 ounces French or other white bread, broken into small pieces
2 to 3 teaspoons dried sage
1 teaspoon dried thyme
½ teaspoon dried rosemary
2 teaspoons salt
1 teaspoon freshly ground black pepper
1 pound mildly spiced pork sausage (prefer Jimmie Dean's or Rice's), cooked and drained
¾ cup butter
2 cups chopped onions
1½ cups chopped celery
4 to 5 cups chicken stock
4 eggs, slightly beaten

Preheat oven to 350°F. Combine cornbread and bread; bake on a large baking sheet until slightly dry and toasted. Mix breads, sage, thyme, rosemary, salt and pepper in a large bowl. Add cooked sausage. Melt butter in heavy skillet over high heat. Add onions and celery; sauté about 10 minutes until tender Pour contents of skillet over bread crumbs and mix well. (May be made to this stage one day ahead and refrigerated). Mix 4 cups chicken stock and eggs into dressing. Add additional stock if mixture appears dry; it should be quite moist. Transfer to a buttered 9 x 13 dish. Bake 1 hour until cooked throughout and top is brown and crispy, covering lightly with aluminum foil if browning too quickly. Makes 12 servings. From Bonnie Aeschliman.

SAUSAGE PECAN STUFFING

1 pound mildly spiced pork sausage
4 tablespoons butter
2 medium onions, chopped
6 medium celery stalks with leaves, chopped
1 teaspoon dried thyme
1 teaspoon dried sage
1 teaspoon dried marjoram
1 teaspoon dried rosemary
½ teaspoon freshly ground black pepper
1 (16-ounce) package herb seasoned bread cubes for stuffing
⅓ cup chopped fresh parsley
1 cup chopped pecans
2 cups turkey or chicken stock, as needed

Add butter to skillet you have used to cook the sausage, add onions and celery, cover and cook 10 minutes, stirring occasionally, until tender. Remove from heat, stir in all herbs, add sausage and mix well. Place stuffing cubes, pecans, sausage mixture and parsley all into a large bowl. Gradually add in stock to moisten stuffing evenly. Either stuff into turkey or serve as a side dish by placing in a buttered baking dish, cover with aluminum foil and heating in a 350°F oven for 30 minutes or until brown on top. Makes 12 servings. From Linda Boerger.

Opposite page:

Titian Ramsay Peale
*Ruffed Grouse in a
Landscape*, 1873, oil on
canvas, WAM, gift of
the Wichita Art Museum
Members, 1968.78

Beef, Pork & Lamb

BEEF MEDALLIONS with COGNAC CREAM SAUCE

1 cup beef stock
1 cup chicken stock
2 pounds beef tenderloin, cut into
    $^3/_4$-inch medallions
2 to 3 tablespoons oil for frying
3 tablespoons minced shallots
$^1/_4$ cup red wine vinegar

1 tablespoon bottled green
    peppercorns, drained
3 tablespoons cognac
2 cups cream
3 tablespoons prepared horseradish
Salt and freshly ground black pepper

In a small saucepan over high heat, bring the beef and chicken stocks to a boil. Cook until reduced by half and set aside. Place oil in hot skillet and quickly brown the medallions, removing each as it browns. Set aside to rest, uncovered. Lower the heat and add the shallots to the pan. Cook until softened. Add vinegar and peppercorns and reduce by half, scraping up the browned bits. Add cognac away from fire, then ignite and cook away by half. Add the stock reduction and cream. Bring to a slow boil, allowing mixture to thicken. Check seasonings and adjust. When desired sauce consistency has been achieved, stir in the horseradish and remove from heat.

To serve, arrange medallions on serving plate, and drizzle with sauce, passing remainder on the side. Makes 6 to 8 servings. From Anna Anderson

STEAKS with CARAMEL BRANDY SAUCE

This rich sauce is a decadent partner for the inevitably delicious fillet. Very good!

Russell Cowles's County
Fair *with proud owners
parading Brown Swiss
cattle past judges in the
livestock pavilion provides
a nostalgic view of grand
white exhibition buildings
smelling of hay and youth
vying for ruffled blue
ribbons. As in Iowa, the
source of Cowles' study, this
scene is repeated in county
fairs as well as the Kansas
State Fair, since in 1873
in Hutchinson, KS. Cattle
is big business in Kansas.
In 2007 there were 6.4
million cattle on ranches
and feedyards, nearly two
and one-third times the
state's human population of
over 2.7 million people.*

4 (6-ounce) beef tenderloin fillets
1 teaspoon salt
1 teaspoon freshly ground black pepper
3 tablespoons butter (divided use)

3 tablespoons brandy
1 tablespoon light brown sugar
$^1/_4$ cup whipping cream
Garnish: fresh chives

Sprinkle steaks evenly with salt and pepper. In a medium skillet melt 1 tablespoon butter over medium-high heat. Add steaks, and cook 3 minutes on each side or to desired degree of doneness. Remove steaks from skillet, and keep warm. Add brandy to skillet, stirring to loosen particles from bottom of skillet. Add remaining 2 tablespoons butter and sugar; cook, stirring constantly, until sugar dissolves and browns. Remove skillet from heat; whisk in cream until blended. Return to heat, and bring to a boil; cook, stirring constantly, 1 minute or until thickened. Serve immediately over steaks. Garnish, if desired. Makes 4 servings.

GOVERNOR'S FILLET OF BEEF BOURGUIGNON

Governor Kathleen Sebelius says she always was a beef fan but didn't know how great it could taste until she came to Kansas. "My first Kansas meal was when I met Gary's family in Norton, and we enjoyed juicy steaks, cooked on the grill," she says. Her family's celebration dinners often include a fancy beef recipe, and their favorite comfort food starts with pot roast. Here, Governor Sebelius shares a variation on a traditional Beef Bourguignon, using the best beef and cooked for far less time than similar recipes. She last served it at a Valentine Party at Cedar Crest.

1 (3-pound) fillet of beef, trimmed
Salt
Freshly ground black pepper
3 to 4 tablespoons good olive oil (divided use)
4 ounces bacon, cut into $^1/_4$-inch pieces
2 garlic cloves, minced
1$^1/_2$ cups good dry red wine, such as Burgundy or Chianti
2 cups beef stock
1 tablespoon tomato paste
1 sprig fresh thyme
8 ounces pearl onions, peeled
8 to 10 carrots, cut diagonally into 1-inch slices
3 tablespoons butter, room temperature (divided use)
2 tablespoons flour
8 ounces mushrooms, sliced $^1/_4$-inch thick

With a sharp knife, cut the filet crosswise into 1-inch-thick slices. Season both sides of slices with salt and pepper. Heat oil in a large, heavy-bottomed pan on medium-high heat. Sauté the slices of beef in batches, cooking 2 to 3 minutes on each side. Remove from pan and set aside on a platter. In the same pan, cook the bacon on medium-low heat 5 minutes, until browned and crisp. Remove the bacon and set it aside. Drain all but 2 tablespoons fat from the pan. Add the garlic and cook 30 seconds. Add red wine to the pan and cook on high heat 1 minute to deglaze, scraping the bottom of the pan. Add the beef stock, tomato paste, thyme, 1 teaspoon salt and $^1/_2$ teaspoon pepper. Bring it to a boil and cook uncovered on medium-high heat 10 minutes. Strain the sauce and return it to the pan. Add the onions and carrots and simmer uncovered 20 to 30 minutes, until the sauce is reduced and vegetables are tender.

With a fork, mash 2 tablespoons butter and the flour into a paste and whisk it gently into the sauce. Simmer 2 minutes to thicken. Meanwhile, cook the mushrooms separately in 1 tablespoon butter and 1 tablespoon oil about 10 minutes until browned and tender.

Add the beef slices, mushrooms, and bacon to the pan with the vegetables and sauce. Cover and heat gently 5 to 10 minutes. Do not overcook. Season to taste with salt and pepper and serve immediately. Makes 6 to 8 servings.

Right: Louis Comfort Tiffany, *Favrile Vase*, 1892-1920, iridescent lead glass, WAM, gift of Mr. Phil Buck in memory of Elsie Fitch Buck, 1965.5

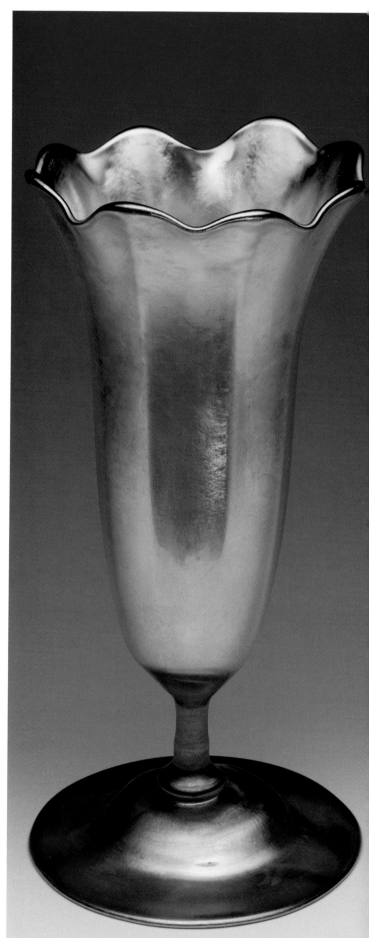

GRILLED TRIANGLE TIP ROAST

This classic marinade is also great for chicken or other cuts of beef.

2 pounds (more or less) triangle tip(tri-tip) roast

The triangle tip (or more commonly called 'tri-tip') is not a familiar cut of beef for many, but it is worth asking for at the butcher counter as it is very tender and delicious. It shouldn't be grilled more than medium rare and be sure to cut against the grain in thin slices.

Marinade

1/3 cup barbecue sauce	2 to 3 teaspoons garlic powder
1/2 cup soy sauce	1/2 teaspoon seasoned flavor enhancer
1/4 cup vegetable oil	(like Accent)
1/4 cup white wine	

Combine all marinade ingredients in a large zipper-lock bag. Prick roast all over with fork. Add roast to the bag, turning to coat well, and marinate in refrigerator for 8 hours or more. If you can, after 4 hours, prick meat with fork again all over and marinate for 4 hours or more. Allow roast to stand at room temperature for 20 to 30 minutes before grilling. Grill over direct heat until well marked on both sides, turning once. Move to indirect heat on grill and continue cooking until desired doneness is reached, about 20 minutes. Brush the meat with the marinade and turn it about every 5 minutes or so. Remove from grill and let rest 5 to 10 minutes. Slice against the grain and serve. Makes 6 to 8 servings. Marinade recipe from Carl Bell's Meat Market, 1970.

ADOBO MARINADE FOR BEEF OR PORK

3 tablespoons fresh lime juice	1 teaspoon cumin
1 tablespoon chipotle peppers in adobo sauce	1/2 teaspoon salt
4 teaspoons brown sugar	1/4 cup chopped cilantro leaves
2 tablespoons minced garlic	3/4 cup olive oil

Combine all ingredients, use as marinade for beef tenderloin (served as sliced medallions) or as marinade for other cuts to be grilled. Reserve some unused marinade to spoon over beef when served.

CELEBRATION ROAST

This tender rib-eye roast is easy to slice and serve.

2 tablespoons cream-style prepared horseradish	1/2 teaspoon salt
4 cloves garlic, chopped finely	1 (4 to 6-pound) boneless beef ribeye roast
4 to 5 teaspoons cracked black peppercorns (divided use)	Horseradish Sauce

Preheat oven to 350°F. Combine horseradish, garlic, rest of the peppercorns and the salt. Rub this mixture onto the meat. Place the roast, fat side up, on a rack in a shallow roasting pan. Do not cover or add liquid. Insert a meat thermometer into the center. Roast, uncovered, 1 1/2 to 2 hours until thermometer registers 135°F for medium rare and up to 2 1/2 hours, or until thermometer reaches 150°F, for medium. The meat will rise about 10° F in temperature while standing after removing from the oven. Makes 8 to 10 servings.

TIPS *for a great pot roast*

All you need to prepare a pot roast are a heavy, non-reactive pot, such as a Dutch oven with a tight-fitting lid and select the proper cut of meat. Pot-roasting works well to tenderize tougher cuts of meat from the shoulder, arm, or leg sections. Season the meat before cooking. Salt and pepper are essential; but you may include spice blends or chopped fresh herbs. Brown meat before braising to build flavor and add an appealing golden-brown appearance. A flavorful stock mixture yields tasty results. The cooking liquid usually consists of stock, wine, and seasonings, such as garlic, fresh herbs, bay leaves, or other aromatic ingredients. Most vegetables cook more quickly than the large cuts of meat so add the vegetables to the pan partway through cooking. Carrots, mushrooms and potatoes are traditional. Use two forks to shred the tender meat before serving.

ELIZABETHAN BISON ROAST

Stephen Gleissner describes "When I returned to Kansas from England in 1995, I was pleasantly surprised to learn of the appearance of local ranchers and vendors of bison (North American buffalo). Enticing was the promise of meat that was slightly sweeter and richer than beef, yet lower in fat and higher in protein, iron, and omega-3 fatty acids. It sounded ideal for preparation the way English country cooks had done game since Elizabethan times. The following recipe evolved from that first experiment."

Marinade

$^1/_2$ bottle of good red wine, preferably
   cabernet sauvignon
$^1/_3$ to $^1/_2$ cup orange juice
$^1/_4$ cup olive oil (plus extra for coating pot)
4 carrots, chopped
4 cloves of garlic, crushed
6 whole cloves
1 tablespoon whole juniper berries
4 to 5 sprigs of fresh thyme (or 2
   teaspoons dried)
2 sprigs of rosemary (or 1 teaspoon dried)
$^1/_2$ teaspoon ground allspice
2 tablespoons light molasses
1 teaspoon or more sea salt, preferably
   "Fleur de Sel"

Roast

1 large onion, sliced
5 to 7 pound bison roast
1 teaspoon salt
1 teaspoon ground pepper
3 whole bay leaves
1 orange, sliced
Seeds of one pomegranate
1 tablespoon balsamic vinegar
Arrowroot or another thickening agent

Whisk together all marinade ingredients. Coat a heavy, covered roasting pan (Dutch oven) with olive oil. Spread onion across bottom of pan, place roast (salted and peppered, and even perhaps seared on all sides in oil and butter) on the onions, top the roast with bay leaves and orange slices, and pour marinade over meat. Refrigerate at least 8 hours.

Preheat oven to 275°F. Place pan on stove and bring marinade to simmer, then transfer to oven. Roast (covered) for 5 to 7 hours, depending on your wellness preference. The internal temperature should be 135 to 150°F. Since bison is so low in fat, it must be cooked at a low temperature or it will be tough. When the meat has reached your desired wellness, transfer to cutting board or platter, strain the liquid, add the balsamic vinegar, reduce to one or two cups, and thicken. Slice the meat and decorate it with the pomegranate seeds, which play on the deeper red color of bison than beef. Serve the sauce with your accompanying vegetable or starch—puréed cauliflower is especially good. From Stephen Gleissner.

MUSHROOM STUFFED BEEF TENDERLOIN

3/4 cup Marsala wine
1/4 cup minced onion
1/4 cup olive oil
2 tablespoons red wine vinegar
1/2 teaspoon salt
1/2 teaspoon freshly ground black pepper
1 (5 to 6 pound) beef tenderloin, trimmed
1 pound fresh mushrooms, sliced
1/3 cup sliced green onions

2 cloves garlic, crushed
3 tablespoons butter or margarine, melted
1/2 cup Marsala wine
1 1/2 cups soft whole-wheat bread crumbs
Garlic salt
Freshly ground black pepper
8 slices bacon
Garnish: tomato roses and fresh parsley sprigs

Combine the first 6 ingredients in a small bowl; stir well. Place tenderloin in a large shallow dish; pour wine mixture over tenderloin. Cover and marinate in refrigerator 8 hours, turning occasionally. Preheat oven to 425°F. In a large skillet sauté mushrooms, green onions and garlic in butter over medium heat until tender. Add 1/2 cup Marsala, and simmer until liquid evaporates. Remove from heat. Add bread crumbs; toss gently, and set aside. Remove tenderloin from marinade; discard marinade. Slice tenderloin lengthwise to, but not through, the center, leaving one long side connected. Spoon stuffing mixture into opening of tenderloin. Fold top side over stuffing, and tie securely with heavy string at 2-inch intervals. Sprinkle with garlic salt and pepper. Place tenderloin, seam side down, on a rack in a roasting pan. Insert an oven-safe meat thermometer into thickest portion of tenderloin.

Roast, uncovered, for 30 minutes. Cut strings and remove from tenderloin. Arrange bacon strips in a crisscross pattern over tenderloin; secure at ends with wooden picks. Bake an additional 15 to 20 minutes or until bacon is crisp and thermometer registers 140° (rare), 150° (medium-rare) or 160° (for medium). Remove wooden picks. If desired, garnish with tomato roses and parsley. Makes 10 to 12 servings.

NEVER FAIL BEEF TENDERLOIN

Beef tenderloin is such a simple but elegant way to dress up a dinner. While impressive it is actually easy to make because it bakes unattended while you tend to the rest of the meal.

1 (5 to 6 pound) beef tenderloin, trimmed
1/4 cup Dijon mustard
2 garlic cloves, pressed
1 teaspoon garlic salt

1/2 teaspoon onion salt
3/4 teaspoon freshly ground black pepper
3/4 cup brown sugar
1 cup beef stock

Preheat oven to 375°F. Combine mustard, garlic, salts and pepper. Coat tenderloin with even layer of mustard mixture. Cover with brown sugar. Bake unovered for 50 minutes, or until desired doneness by checking with thermometer: 140° (rare), 150° (medium-rare) or 160° (for medium). After removing from oven, let the tenderloin rest for 10 minutes before slicing. Meanwhile, add stock to pan drippings, stirring to loosen browned bits; heat through. Serve with sliced beef. Makes 12 servings.

NO PEEKIE ROAST BEEFIE

1 (5-pound) standing rib roast (preferably one well marbleized and aged)
Salt, garlic salt and pepper

Allow chilled rib roast to stand at room temperature for 1 hour. Preheat oven to 375°F. About 3 to 4 hours before serving, place room temperature roast in a shallow roasting pan, fat side up with bones resting on a rack. Season with salt, garlic salt, and pepper. Do not cover or add water. Cook in preheated oven for 45 minutes. Do not open oven; do not baste. After 45 minutes turn oven off, but do not open the door at any time (you might put a note on the oven door or even tape shut). Let roast rest in sealed oven no more than 2 hours. About 45 minutes before serving, turn the oven back on to 350°F and finish cooking. Remove from oven and let stand 15 minutes before carving; transfer to serving platter and garnish. Meat will be crisp and brown on the outside and pink all the way through: medium rare and very juicy. (For a roast that is 10 to 12 pounds, leave in heated oven for 60 minutes in the beginning and 60 to 90 minutes in the end for medium rare.)

EASY BEEF WELLINGTON

Preheat oven to 400°F. Sear fillet mignon and paint, with modest coverage, with Dijon mustard. Wrap in puff pastry. Bake for 15 minutes. Serve with a sauce made by poaching mushrooms in red wine and reducing slightly.

SPECIAL BEEF WELLINGTON

1 (3 to 4 pound) beef tenderloin, trimmed
Salt and freshly ground black pepper
5 tablespoons olive oil (divided use)
1 cup minced onions
2 tablespoons minced shallots
4 cups assorted mushrooms, finely chopped
2 teaspoons chopped garlic
3/4 cup red wine

1/2 cup chopped fresh parsley
1/2 pound foie gras, sliced into 1-ounce slices
1 cup port wine syrup
2 pieces of frozen puff pastry (from a 17-ounce package), thawed
1 egg, beaten with 1 tablespoon water
1 tablespoon finely chopped mushrooms, sautéed in butter

Preheat oven to 350°F. Season tenderloin with salt and pepper. Heat 3 tablespoons oil in a large saucepan over medium-high heat; when hot, sear the tenderloin on all sides, for about 2 minutes per side; remove the tenderloin and set aside. Reduce heat to medium and add remaining olive oil; add onions and sauté for 2 minutes; season with salt and pepper. Add shallots and sauté for another minute; add mushrooms and garlic and sauté for another 2 minutes. Add red wine; increase heat to a simmer; cook until mixture is dry, about 4 minutes. Remove from heat and add parsley; adjust with salt and pepper. Let mixture cool. Season the foie gras slices with salt and pepper. Sear the foie gras in a hot sauté pan for 30 seconds on each side; remove and drain on a paper lined plate. Remove to a clean plate and pour the port wine syrup over; set aside.

To assemble the tenderloin, join 2 sheets of puff pastry together along the vertical edge, sealing the ends to form one big piece. Place tenderloin in the center; smear the mushroom mixture over the top of the tenderloin; top with the foie gras slices. Wrap the tenderloin in the puff pastry, tuck in the sides; brush with the egg wash and place on a baking sheet. Bake for about 30 to 35 minutes (medium rare) or until pastry is golden brown. Remove from oven and allow to rest for 5 minutes before serving. Serve with a drizzle of port wine sauce and sprinkle of sautéed mushrooms. From Cindy Banks, adapted from a recipe on 'Food Network'. Makes about 8 servings.

Phillip Reisman
Basement Kitchen, 1933, tempera on masonite, WAM, gift of the Friends of the Wichita Art Museum, Inc., 1988.39

Foie gras is a savory preparation containing goose or duck liver, wine and seasonings. You may find it at large grocery stores in cans, jars or vacuum pack blocks (usually with the specialty cheeses) or purchase online through vendors such as www.dartagnan.com.

THESE HEARTY DISHES *are easy to prepare*

...can even be made in a slow cooker, and leftovers are even better the second day after the flavors mellow.

BOEUF BOURGUIGNON STEW

This dish has a rich aroma, tender meat and a sauce that is great to mop up with crusty bread.

Kitchen Bouquet can be seen as a culinary cop-out, but there are some recipes, like this one and others with a deep gravy, where it is just the right thing, so don't be afraid to bring it out of the closet when needed. It is a dark syrup made from vegetable protein and it deepens the flavor and color of sauces.

3 pounds beef stew meat, cut into 1-inch cubes (prefer boneless beef chuck, well trimmed)
1/2 cup vegetable oil
2 large yellow onions, chopped
1 pound mushrooms
1/4 to 1/3 cup firmly packed light brown sugar
1/2 cup Worcestershire Sauce
2 bay leaves
1 teaspoon dried oregano
1/2 teaspoon garlic powder
1/2 teaspoon celery salt
1 (10 1/2-ounce) can beef consommé or stock
1 (10 1/2-ounce) can onion soup
1 cup spicy tomato juice (like V-8)
1 cup dry burgundy wine
3 tablespoons cornstarch
1/3 cup water
1/2 bottle Kitchen Bouquet seasoning, as desired

Brown meat in oil until brown; may need to do in several batches. Slightly sauté onions and mushrooms in the drippings. Deglaze pan with a bit of wine. Combine drippings, meat, onions, mushrooms, brown sugar, Worcestershire, bay leaves, oregano, garlic powder, celery salt, consommé, onion soup, V-8 juice and wine in a Dutch oven. (Works well too to use a crockpot slow cooker.) Cover and simmer slowly (1 to 2 hours) until meat is tender (or about 4 hours on low in crockpot). Remove bay leaves. Add Kitchen Bouquet seasoning to taste. Combine cornstarch and water. Stir into meat mixture and cook until sauce thickens. Serve over rice or noodles or orzo with frozen peas. Nice to also serve the same wine for drinking as used in the stew. Best if made the day before serving. Makes 8 servings.

HEARTY NEW ENGLAND DINNER

Very good, and is even better the second day. Make in a slow-cooker.

4 medium carrots, sliced
1 medium onion, sliced
1 celery stalk, sliced
1 boneless chuck roast (about 3 pounds)
1 teaspoon salt (divided use)
1/4 teaspoon pepper
1 envelope onion soup mix
2 cups water
1 tablespoon vinegar
1 bay leaf
1 medium head cabbage, cut into wedges
3 tablespoons butter
2 tablespoons flour
1 tablespoon dried minced onion
2 tablespoons prepared horseradish

Place carrots, onion and celery in 5-quart slow cooker. Place the roast on top; sprinkle with 1/2 teaspoon salt and pepper. Add soup mix, water, vinegar and bay leaf. Cover and cook on low for 7 to 9 hours or until beef is tender. Remove beef and keep warm; discard bay leaf. Add cabbage. Cover and cook on high for 30 to 40 minutes until cabbage is tender.

Shortly before serving, melt butter in a small saucepan; stir in flour and onion. Add 1 1/2 cups cooking liquid from the slow cooker. Stir in horseradish and remaining salt; bring to a boil. Cook and stir over low heat until thick and smooth, about 2 minutes. Serve with roast and vegetables. Makes 6 to 8 servings.

BEEF STROGANOFF with PILAF

Tender beef in a mushroom flavored sauce makes this a delicious simple meal. This recipe is easy to scale up for larger groups. We served 80 at Wichita-Sedgwick County Historical Museum, Sunday Supper at the Schwab's.

3 pounds triangle tip steak
1 cup sliced onions
³/₄ cup vermouth
1 tablespoon Kitchen Bouquet

2 cans condensed cream of mushroom soup, undiluted
8 ounces sliced mushrooms
1 envelope dried onion soup mix
1 (8-ounce) carton sour cream

Cut steak into small bite-size pieces. Brown steak in vegetable oil over medium-high heat, move to crock pot. Brown onions in meat juice; add to meat in pot. Add vermouth, Kitchen Bouquet, soup, sliced mushrooms and soup mix; cook for 4 hours. (Alternatively, bake, covered in a 325°F oven for 3 hours.) Stir in sour cream when ready to serve. Serve over pilaf. Makes 8 to 10 servings. Adapted from recipe by Becky Ritchey.

Pilaf

2 cups white rice
¹/₂ cup butter
1 cup crushed vermicelli noodles

3 cups chicken stock
Salt

Rinse and soak the rice in water for 15 minutes. Drain well. Brown the vermicelli noodles in butter, add rice as vermicelli begins to turn golden and sauté for another 2 minutes. Add stock and salt; bring to a boil, cover, reduce to simmer and cook for about 20 minutes or until liquid is absorbed. Stir with fork and serve. Makes 8 to 10 servings. A nice addition is to add 2 cups thawed peas in the last 5 minutes, heat just until warm but still crunchy.

MENU:
*SUNDAY SUPPER
FOR 80*

*Smoked Salmon on
Rye toasts with Herbed
Cheese Sun-dried Tomato
Tapenade on Crostini 23
Parmesan Pepper Frico 28*

*Strawberry Jicama
Salad 50*

*Beef Stroganoff
over Pilaf 134*

Cheese Croissants

*Coconut Cupcakes 235
Macadamia Nut Fudge 260*

Henry Varnum Poor *Family Tea Set* (detail), 1940, tin-glazed earthenware, WAM, Burneta Adair Endowment Fund, 2006.15

CHILIES en NOGADA
Chilies in Walnut Sauce

This festive but labor intensive dish is traditionally served on September 16 in honor of Mexican Independence day, since the colors of the dish are the colors of the Mexican Flag: red, white, and green. Choose nice large unblemished chiles with nice looking stems for this dish.

Nogada (nut sauce)

1 cup chopped walnuts (washed and dark skins removed)
1/2 cup blanched almonds, chopped fine
1/2 cup cream cheese
1 cup Mexican cream (available in the refrigerator section of most grocery stores)
1 tablespoon sugar
1/4 teaspoon cinnamon

Picadillo (ground meat stuffing)

4 tablespoons olive oil
2 pounds ground beef
2 onions, chopped
2 garlic cloves, chopped
1 to 2 teaspoons finely chopped jalapeno
3 medium tomatoes, peeled, seeded, and chopped
3 (4-ounce) cans of chopped green chilies, drained
1/2 cup raisins
1/4 cup pimiento-stuffed olives, drained and chopped
1 cup chopped pineapple (preferably fresh)
1 to 2 pears, seeded and chopped
1/2 teaspoon cinnamon
1/2 teaspoon ground cloves
1/2 cup slivered almonds
Freshly ground black pepper
6 to 8 large poblano chilies, stems intact
Garnish: Freshly chopped cilantro, pomegranate seeds

Nogada: In a food processor or blender, combine the walnuts and almonds with the cream cheese. Add Mexican cream, sugar, and cinnamon. If needed, add a little milk to create a spreadable creamy mixture. Season to taste with salt and white pepper. Set aside.

Picadillo: In a large skillet, heat the olive oil over medium heat and sauté the ground beef for 5 to 8 minutes until it is no longer pink. Add the onions and cook 2 minutes more then add the garlic and jalapenos and cook for 1 minute. Add the tomatoes, green chiles, raisins, olives, pineapple, pears, cinnamon, cloves and almonds. Cook about 10 minutes, until the mixture is thick and bubbly. Set aside to cool.

Wash and dry the chiles (When cleaning or handling the chilies, it is advisable to wear rubber gloves). Using a grill, barbecue or gas burner, roast until the skins are blackened and blistered. Place in a plastic bag for at least 15 or 20 minutes while they cool. Using a paring knife, remove the outer blackened skins. Carefully slit the chili from the top to the point of the pepper. Remove the seeds and veins, being careful to keep the chiles and stems intact. Stuff each chili with the picadillo. Place the peppers on an oven-proof dish and place in the oven for ten minutes to warm them. Cover the warmed chilies with the walnut sauce. Sprinkle chopped cilantro at one end of the chili and pomegranate seeds at the other. Serve immediately. From Teresa Covacevich Grana.

Sue Jean Covacevich in Mexico, ca. 1935

Sue Jean Covacevich (1905-1998) loved life as much as art. At the opening of a 2006-07 retrospective of her work at the Wichita Art Museum, former students came in from all over the country to share stories of how Sue Jean had made them not only painters, but artists of life. Her enjoyment of the people and places around her are apparent both in the bright colors and bravura brushwork of Flowers *and in her pose and costume captured in the photo of her taken in Mexico, where she lived from 1932-43. It should be no surprise that Sue Jean relished cooking and entertaining! - SG*

SUE JEAN COVACEVICH'S TAMALE PIE

Teresa Covacevich Grana writes that her mother, Kansas artist Sue Jean Covacevich, "served this casserole to legions of students and friends."

1¹/₂ pounds ground beef
1 cup chopped onion
1 cup chopped green bell pepper
2 garlic cloves, chopped
1 (14¹/₂-ounce) can Mexican style
    stewed tomatoes
2 (4-ounce) cans chopped green
    chilies, drained
¹/₄ teaspoon dried oregano
¹/₄ teaspoon dried thyme

¹/₄ teaspoon cumin
¹/₂ to 1 teaspoon chili powder
2 cups fresh or frozen yellow corn
³/₄ cup black pitted olives, drained and chopped
2 cups yellow cornmeal
2 cups chicken stock (divided use)
2 tablespoons butter
Optional: 1 cup Cheddar cheese, grated (or
    Parmesan or Mexican blend)
Garnish: Sliced black olives

Preheat oven to 350°F. Brown ground beef until it crumbles, add onion, green peppers, garlic, tomatoes, chilies and spices and cook for 10 to 15 minutes, until the mixture is thick. Add corn and olives during the last five minutes. Set aside.

Mix 2 cups of corn meal with ¹/₂ cup of chicken stock. Bring the remaining stock to a boil and stir in butter and the cornmeal mixture. Cook mixture until thickens. Spread three-quarters of the mixture in a casserole dish; spread meat mixture on top of cornmeal mixture. Cover with remaining cornmeal mixture then top with cheese, if desired. Decorate with olives and bake for 35 to 40 minutes. Makes 6 to 8 servings.

Variation: chicken that has been cooked and boned can be substituted for the beef and is equally delicious.

PRIZEWINNING MEATLOAF

2 pounds "meatloaf mix" of ground chuck,
  pork, and veal
1 cup milk
1 cup firm fresh white bread crumbs or
  uncooked quick oats
1/2 cup minced fresh flat-leaf parsley
1/3 cup finely chopped onion
1 egg
2 tablespoons prepared chili sauce or ketchup

1 tablespoon prepared horseradish
1 1/4 teaspoons salt
1/2 teaspoon freshly ground black pepper

Glaze
1/2 cup prepared chili sauce
1/4 cup apple cider vinegar
3 tablespoons light brown sugar

Preheat oven to 375°F, adjust rack to middle. Prepare baking sheet by folding heavy-duty aluminum foil into a 10 x 16-inch square, center it on a wire baking rack and set it on a rimmed baking sheet. Poke holes in foil so juices will drip off. Spray foil with cooking spray. Gently mix all of the ingredients together, with hands, in a large mixing bowl. Transfer meat to foil rectangle and shape into a 6 x 10-inch oval, about 2 inches high. Bake about 1 hour until the meatloaf is firm, the top is richly browned, and a meat thermometer inserted into the center registers 155°F. Remove from oven and turn on broiler. Prepare glaze by combining ingredients in a small saucepan; simmer for about 5 minutes. Spread half of glaze over meatloaf, broil for about 5 minutes. Remove from oven, add remaining glaze. Place back under for another 5 minutes until glaze is bubbling and begins to brown. Let the meatloaf stand for 10 minutes, then cut into slices to serve. Makes 6 to 8 servings.

MAN CASSEROLE

Variations of this have been called "happy husband casserole" or "heavenly spaghetti" in other cookbooks, but it has come to be called Man Casserole by our family as it satisfies a hefty appetite. Can be easily doubled and freezes well.

1 package (8-ounce) skinny egg noodles
1 1/2 pounds lean ground beef
4 cloves garlic, minced
2 (8-ounce) cans tomato sauce
1 (6-ounce) can tomato paste
Salt and pepper to taste
1 (8-ounce) package cream cheese

1 cup cottage cheese
1/4 cup sour cream
1 1/4 teaspoon garlic salt
1 teaspoon black pepper
3 to 4 green onions chopped, including tops
1 cup Cheddar cheese, grated

Cook noodles according to package directions, drain well. Preheat oven to 350°F. Brown ground beef and garlic in a medium saucepan; drain. Add tomato sauce and paste, salt and pepper. Blend the cream cheese and cottage cheese together; add sour cream, garlic salt, pepper and onions. In a greased 9 x 13-inch casserole put half of cooked noodles, then layer of cheese mixture, and then rest of noodles. Cover with ground beef mixture, another layer of the cheese mixture and top with Cheddar cheese. Bake for 30 minutes. Makes 8 servings, or 4 if he has been bailing hay.

Ethel Magafan
Wheat Threshing (detail),
1937, egg tempera on
panel, WAM, gift of the
Friends of the Wichita Art
Museum, Inc., 1981.19

BRAISED BONELESS BEEF SHORT RIBS with PARSNIP MASHED POTATOES and ROASTED VEGETABLES

Tender boneless beef short ribs cooked in beef stock and red wine, served with its own juices and a creamy blend of parsnips and mashed potatoes make this is a hearty savory dinner.

2 pounds boneless beef short ribs, trimmed of external fat (cut into 4 8-ounce portions)
Salt and freshly ground black pepper
2 tablespoons vegetable oil
1 cup Burgundy wine
6 cups beef stock, simmered until reduced to 3 cups, or 1/2 tablespoons beef demi-glace, reconstituted with 3 cups water

1 cup peeled, cooked, and mashed parnips
2 cups mashed potatoes
2 cups vegetables (carrots, mushrooms, leeks, cut into 1/2-inch dice)

Season short ribs with salt and pepper. In a heavy bottom roasting pan or Dutch oven, heat the vegetable oil over medium-high heat. When oil is smoking hot, brown the short ribs on both sides. Discard excess fat, remove short ribs from the pan. Add wine to the pan, bring to a boil and stir with a wooden spoon to loosen any browned bits from the bottom of the pan. Add the beef stock and short ribs. Bring to a simmer, cover, and cook in a 325°F oven for 2 to 2 1/2 hours, until fork tender.

In the last hour of cooking the short ribs, prepare the roasted vegetables, mashed parsnips and mashed potatoes. To roast the vegetables, line a large, rimmed heavy baking sheet with foil for easy clean up. Spray with vegetable oil or drizzle a little olive oil in pan. Arrange vegetables in pan in a single layer. Drizzle with a little olive oil, garlic, salt and pepper. Roast vegetables in preheated 375°F oven, turning once or twice, until tender and browned, about 30 to 45 minutes. Blend the mashed parsnips and potatoes together; set aside and keep warm.

Remove short ribs from oven and remove any additional fat from the surface of the braised short rib liquid. Season to taste. Spoon Parsnip Mashed Potatoes into individual serving bowls (or plates with a raised rim). Top each serving with a short rib and spoon over some of the braising liquid. Spoon the roasted vegetables over the short ribs. Makes 4 servings. From Chef Stephen Giunta.

Chef Giunta, one of only 61 certified master chefs in the US, serves as the Culinary Director of Cargill Meat Solutions' Culinary Innovation Center in Wichita. He has served as associate professor at the Culinary Institute of America and also as personal chef to former President and Mrs. Reagan at the White House. He is a winner of the Gold Medal at Salon Culinaire, a member of the Gold Medal US Culinary Olympic teams (1984 and 1988) and received the Pioneer Award from the Research Chefs Association (2008).

DEEP DISH SPAGHETTI PIE

This is a great make-ahead recipe for a hungry group of friends.

6 ounces spaghetti, cooked according to package and drained
1 large onion, chopped
1 pound ground beef or ground Italian pork sausage
1 teaspoon sugar
1 tablespoon oregano
1 tablespoon basil
1/2 to 3/4 teaspoon garlic salt

1 (8-ounce) can whole tomatoes with juice, chopped
1 (6-ounce) can tomato paste
2 tablespoons butter
1/2 cup freshly grated Parmesan cheese
2 eggs, well beaten
8 ounces grated Parmesan cheese
1 cup ricotta cheese
16 ounces shredded mozzarella cheese (divided use)

Preheat oven to 350°F. Butter a 10-inch deep-dish pie plate or round casserole. Start cooking the spaghetti in salted boiling water. In a large skillet coated with cooking spray, cook onion until translucent, add ground beef and cook until browned. Drain meat. Put mixture back into skillet, add sugar, oregano, basil, garlic salt, tomatoes and tomato paste, and heat through. Let cook while draining spaghetti. Place hot spaghetti in a large bowl and gently toss with butter to coat, add Parmesan cheese, eggs and half of the mozzarella cheese; toss just to incorporate. Form mixture into the bottom and sides of a deep dish 10-inch pie plate and set aside. Spread ricotta cheese evenly over spaghetti. Fill pie with tomato-meat mixture. Bake uncovered for 20 minutes. Remove from oven and top with remaining mozzarella cheese. Bake for an additional 5 minutes to melt cheese. Cool 10 minutes before serving. Freezes well. Adapted from recipe by Susan Wilhite and Karen Root. Makes 6 servings.

MEATY CHEESE MANICOTTI

This is a fantastic manicotti recipe. It is also easy to make in multiples. Served at University Congregational Church Fellowship dinner with Big Italian salad (p. 49), fresh mixed vegetables, and Crusty Garlic Herb Bread (p. 111).

Bonnie Aeschliman, CCP, whose recipes you will find throughout this book, is a dear friend and seasoned culinary teacher who makes cooking fun. A member of the International Association of Cooking Professionals, she attained the highest level of certification of that group. Author of two cookbooks, she has taught on many levels, won several national competitions for recipe development, and has served as a free-lance food consultant. Her cooking school located in east Wichita, "Cooking at Bonnie's Place", is a beautifully designed teaching kitchen with all of the cozy warmth of being in someone's home. For class schedule: 316.425.5224 or www.cookingatbonniesplace.com

1 (8-ounce) package uncooked manicotti shells
1/2 pound hot Italian sausage
1/2 pound ground round
1 medium onion, chopped
1/2 cups dry white wine
2 cups whipping cream
1 teaspoon dried Italian seasoning
1/2 teaspoon salt
1/2 teaspoon pepper
1 (14 1/2-ounce) can diced tomatoes with basil, garlic, and oregano, drained
2 cups (8 ounces) shredded mozzarella cheese
3/4 cup shredded Parmesan cheese

Cook pasta according to package directions; rinse in cold water. Drain. Place in a single layer on a wire rack; set aside. (An 8-ounce package of manicotti shells has 14 shells; a couple may break so count on using 12 shells in this recipe.)

Remove casings from sausage, and discard. In a large skillet cook sausage, ground round and onion over medium-high heat, stirring until meat crumbles and is no longer pink. Drain and set aside. Add wine to skillet, stirring to loosen browned bits; bring to a boil. Add whipping cream and next 3 ingredients; reduce heat, and simmer, stirring often for about 15 minutes or until thickened. Remove from heat; cover and set aside. Combine meat mixture, tomatoes, and mozzarella cheese. Spoon mixture evenly into 12 manicotti shells; arrange shells in a lightly greased 9 x 13-inch baking dish.

Bake, covered, at 350°F for 20 minutes. Uncover and pour cream mixture evenly over shells; sprinkle with Parmesan cheese. Bake, uncovered, for 10 more minutes. Broil, 5 inches from heat, 2 to 3 minutes or until cheese is lightly browned. Makes 6 servings.

ITALIAN SAUSAGE PENNE with TOMATO CREAM SAUCE

1 pound penne pasta
2 tablespoons olive oil
1 medium onion, thinly sliced
3 cloves garlic, minced
8 ounces mushrooms, sliced
1 pound hot Italian sausage, cooked and drained (prefer Owen's with red pepper)
2/3 cup dry white wine
2 (14 1/2-ounce) cans diced peeled tomatoes, undrained
2 teaspoons dried basil
1/2 teaspoon dried oregano
1 cup heavy cream
6 tablespoons chopped fresh parsley (divided use)
Salt and freshly ground black pepper
1 cup freshly grated Parmesan or Asiago cheese (or a mixture of the two)

Bring 3 quarts of water to a boil in a large pot; cook pasta according to package directions; drain and keep warm (do not rinse).

Meanwhile, heat oil in large skillet over medium high heat. Add onion and garlic; sauté until tender. Add mushrooms; cook until wilted and juices evaporate. Stir in cooked sausage. Add wine to sausage mixture and boil until almost all liquid evaporated. Add tomatoes with juice, basil and oregano; simmer 5 minutes. Add cream and simmer until sauce thickens slightly.

Stir in 1/4 cup chopped parsley. Season to taste with salt and pepper. Pour sauce over hot, cooked pasta. Add 3/4 cup cheese; toss to coat. Sprinkle with remaining cheese and parsley. Makes 8 servings. From Bonnie Aeschliman.

SKILLET PASTA CARBONARA

The discovery that spaghetti can be cooked right in the same skillet makes this a quick version of a tasty dish.

6 slices bacon, cut into $^1/_2$ inch pieces
5 cloves garlic, pressed
Salt and freshly ground black pepper
$^3/_4$ cup dry white wine
3 cups water
3 cups chicken stock (low-sodium preferred)

12 ounces spaghettini (or angel hair),
   broken in half
2 eggs
$^1/_3$ cup heavy cream
$^2/_3$ cup grated Romano cheese

Cook bacon in a large skillet over medium heat until crisp. Transfer bacon to small bowl and set aside. Pour off all but 1 tablespoon bacon fat. Add garlic and $^1/_2$ teaspoon pepper to skillet and cook for about 30 seconds, just to warm. Stir wine into skillet and simmer until almost all evaporated, about 2 minutes. Add water, stock and spaghetti to skillet; increase heat to high. Stir often, cook until spaghetti is tender and liquid has thickened, about 14 minutes. Whisk eggs, cream and cheese together in a small bowl. Remove skillet from heat, add egg mixture and toss to combine. Add bacon and season with salt and pepper to taste. Serve immediately. Makes 6 servings.

Variation: add $^1/_2$ cup of frozen peas into the spaghetti during the last 5 minutes of cooking.

Lino Tagliapietra (Italian) *Pilchuck III*, 1996, blown and cut glass, WAM, gift of Marian Beren and the F. Price Cossman Memorial Trust, Intrust Bank, Trustee, 2004.22

PORK TENDERLOIN in CREAMY MUSTARD SAUCE

4 pounds pork tenderloin (about 5 tenderloins)

Marinade
$^1/_2$ cup bourbon
$^1/_2$ cup soy sauce
3 tablespoons brown sugar

Mustard Sauce
$^2/_3$ cup sour cream
$^2/_3$ cup mayonnaise (prefer Hellmann's)
1 tablespoon Dijon mustard
2 tablespoons dry mustard
3 green onions, finely chopped

In a zipper-lock plastic bag, combine marinade ingredients; reserve $^1/_3$ cup marinade. Add tenderloins; marinate overnight in refrigerator, turning twice. Bake in a 350°F oven for 30 minutes in a large shallow roasting pan, basting frequently with reserved marinade. Combine mustard sauce ingredients. Remove tenderloin from oven and cover loosely with foil; let stand 5 to 10 minutes before slicing. To serve, cut pork diagonally into thin slices, serve with sauce. Makes 12 servings.

BBQ PULLED PORK

A crockpot can do the work for you while you are at work, shopping or doing errands, returning to a great dinner. Serve on soft rolls with coleslaw and chips. Great for a game day party.

Sauce
1 (28-ounce) can crushed Italian tomatoes
   with juice
$^1/_2$ cup molasses
$^1/_4$ cup honey
2 tablespoons tomato paste
2 tablespoons chopped garlic
2 bay leaves

1 tablespoon cumin
$^1/_2$ teaspoon cracked black pepper
$^1/_2$ teaspoon crushed red pepper flakes
3 cups water
$1^1/_3$ cups cider vinegar
Salt to taste (about 2 teaspoons)

1 (5 to 6 pounds) pork butt roast (or sometimes called Boston butt), room temperature

Prepare sauce at least a day before you plan to cook the meat. Place the tomatoes, molasses, honey, tomato paste, garlic, bay leaves, cumin, black pepper and red pepper flakes in a large heavy pot. Bring the mixture to a boil. Reduce the heat to medium-low and simmer gently, uncovered until the mixture is very thick, stirring occasionally. Add the water and vinegar, and then return the mixture to a boil. Reduce the heat and simmer the sauce gently, uncovered, over medium-low heat for $1^1/_2$ hours or more. Remove and discard the bay leaves; season with salt and set the sauce aside to cool. Cover and refrigerate overnight. Makes 3 cups of sauce. Bring to room temperature before adding to the crockpot.

Place the pork in the crockpot. Pour sauce over the pork and turn the meat to cover all over with the sauce. Cover the pot and cook on high heat for 6 hours. Remove the meat from the sauce and set aside to cool.

When the meat is cool enough to handle, trim off and discard the fat or any other parts that are not desirable. Chop or pull the meat coarsely with two knives or forks. Place the shredded meat in a large bowl. Pour the sauce through a strainer, discarding the fat. Pour a small amount of the sauce over the shredded meat. Serve on rolls with coleslaw on top and pickles along side. Serve the defatted sauce on the side. Makes 8 to 10 servings.

HONEY GINGERED PORK TENDERLOIN
Excellent

2 (³/₄ pound) pork tenderloins
¹/₄ cup honey
¹/₄ cup soy sauce
¹/₄ cup oyster sauce
2 tablespoons brown sugar
1 tablespoon plus 1 teaspoon minced
   fresh ginger

1 tablespoon minced garlic
1 tablespoon catsup
¹/₄ teaspoon onion powder
¹/₄ teaspoon ground red pepper
¹/₄ teaspoon cinnamon
Garnish: fresh parsley sprigs (optional)

Place tenderloins in a 7 x 11-inch baking dish. Combine remaining ingredients, stirring well; pour over tenderloins. Cover and marinate in refrigerator 8 hours, turning occasionally. Remove tenderloins from marinade, reserving marinade. Grill tenderloins over medium-hot coals 25 to 35 minutes, turning often and basting with reserved marinade. Pork is done when meat thermometer inserted into the thickest portion of tenderloin registers 160°F. To serve, slice tenderloins thinly, and arrange on a serving platter. Garnish with fresh parsley, if desired. Makes 6 servings.

PORK CHOPS with CARMELIZED ONIONS, MASHED POTATOES and GRAVY
A hearty meal. Adapted from an award winning recipe in Southern Living.

¹/₄ cup olive oil (divided use)
2 medium-sized sweet onions, (about 1¹/₄
   pounds), cut in half and thinly sliced
7 tablespoons butter or margarine (divided use)
1 teaspoon brown sugar
4 medium baking potatoes (about 1¹/₂ pounds),
   peeled and cubed
¹/₃ cup half-and-half
Salt and pepper

1 teaspoon salt (divided use)
³/₄ teaspoon freshly ground black pepper
   (divided use)
4 (10-ounce) boneless pork loin chops, (1 to
   1¹/₄ inches thick)
6 ounces maple-flavored ground sausage
1 cup chicken stock
¹/₂ cup half-and-half
2 tablespoons flour

Heat 2 tablespoons olive oil in a large skillet over medium heat. Add onions; cover and cook, stirring occasionally, 10 minutes or until tender. Add 1 tablespoon butter and brown sugar; cook, uncovered, stirring occasionally, 20 minutes or until onions are caramelized. Meanwhile cook potatoes in boiling salted water, just enough to cover, for 15 minutes or until tender; drain and return to pot. Add 4 tablespoons butter, ¹/₃ cup half-and-half, ¹/₂ teaspoon salt, and ¹/₄ teaspoon pepper. Mash well with a potato masher or electric mixer; set aside and keep warm.

While potatoes cook, sprinkle pork chops evenly with ¹/₄ teaspoon salt and ¹/₄ teaspoon pepper. Heat 2 tablespoons oil in a large skillet over medium heat. Add pork chops, and cook 8 to 10 minutes on each side or until a meat thermometer inserted into the thickest portions registers 155°F. Remove chops, cover and let stand 5 minutes.

Remove 2 tablespoons pan drippings from skillet; set aside. Discard remaining pan drippings. Add sausage to skillet, and cook over medium-heat, stirring until it crumbles and it is no longer pink. Reduce heat to medium. Add reserved pan drippings, 2 tablespoons butter, and chicken stock; bring to a simmer. Whisk together ¹/₄ teaspoon pepper, ¹/₂ cup half-and-half, and flour mixture to sausage mixture, whisking until blended. Simmer, stirring often, 4 to 5 minutes or until thickened. Spoon mashed potatoes onto individual serving plates. Top each serving on one side with caramelized onions, on the other side with a pork chop, and top with gravy drizzled over top. Makes 4 servings.

CHUTNEY GLAZED BAKED HAM

Be sure to use a good quality ham. The label should read "Ham and natural juices". Those marked "Ham and Water Product" may look like a bargain, but they contain up to 23% water, and the texture and flavor are not as good.

1 (14 - 16 pound) smoked, fully cooked, bone-in, half ham (such as Hillshire or Hormel 81)

Glaze

6 garlic cloves
1 (8½-ounce) jar mango chutney
½ cup Dijon mustard
1 cup brown sugar
Grated rind from one orange

¼ cup fresh orange juice
Garnish: Fresh lemon leaves or parsley
Orange slices

Position rack in center of oven and preheat to 325°F. Mince garlic in a food processor, add chutney, mustard, brown sugar, orange rind and juice and process until smooth. Pour glaze over the ham and bake for 1 hour, until ham is fully heated and glaze is well browned.

Let ham stand 30 minutes before slicing. Garnish with lemon leaves and orange slices. Serve with extra mustard and chutney for dinner. Also makes for a nice buffet presentation served with small corn muffins. Makes 10 to 12 servings.

FRENCH HAM

3 pounds ham, boned and cooked
2 tablespoons butter
1½ tablespoons oil
2 tablespoons chopped onions
⅔ cup Maderia or Port wine

3 tablespoons Cognac
2 tablespoons Dijon mustard
1 tablespoon tomato paste
2 cups heavy cream
Freshly ground black pepper

Trim fat from ham and cut into serving pieces. Brown lightly on each side in butter and oil and set aside. Pour off all but 1 tablespoon of oil in pan. Sauté onions slowly until tender, add wine and Cognac and scrape up drippings in pan, stirring until well mixed. Boil rapidly until liquid is reduced to about ¼ cup. Mix in mustard, tomato paste and cream together in a small bowl; add to mustard mixture in saucepan. Simmer until thickened and reduced; add pepper. Return ham to sauce and simmer until ham is heated through. Serve with rice or noodles. Best if made day ahead and reheated. Makes 6 servings.

HAM LOAF

[Editor's note: This was a household favorite, and Carlene's son Todd became a connoisseur of the tangy topping. The following abridged comments are from stories he spins about ham loaf (HL). Ask him about the youtube.com video.] Todd asserts, "the HL is one of the most versatile dishes you can make, and has many twists to keep things lively." In Monty Pythonesque fashion he describes many ways to serve it, including a 'Hamcmuffin', an HLT (variant of the BLT) and the HHL (Hawaiian Ham Loaf). "Even though the HL has a portfolio of exciting presentations, it has a humble background. Popularized in the Depression to stretch resources, brightly glazed and served with a tangy sauce, it was an eye filling and tummy-satisfying dish." We liked this version best.

2 pounds ground pork
2 pounds ground fully cooked ham
4 cups dry bread crumbs
4 eggs, lightly beaten
¾ cup water

1 cup milk
1½ cups packed brown sugar
¾ cup water
½ cup vinegar
1 teaspoon dry mustard

Preheat oven to 350°F. Combine pork, ham, crumbs, eggs, water and milk in a bowl. Shape into 12 ovals, using 1 cup of mixture for each. (Alternatively the mixture may be placed in an ungreased 5 x 10-inch loaf baking pan instead of dividing into loaves.) Combine brown sugar, water, vinegar and mustard; pour over the loaves. Bake uncovered for 1 hour and 15 minutes, basting every 15 to 20 minutes. Place the loaves on a platter and spoon some of the sauce over them. Makes 12 servings.

Herschel C. Logan
Who-o-o-ee-, 1930, block
print, WAM, gift of Samuel
H. and Martha F. Logan,
2005.13.50

LAMB CURRY

Choose tart, crisp apples like Granny Smith. They will hold up during long cooking.

2 cooking apples, cored, pared and sliced
1 green pepper, chopped
2 onions, sliced
1 clove garlic, crushed
2 tablespoons olive oil
2 tablespoons flour
1 tablespoon curry powder
1/2 teaspoon salt
1/2 teaspoon dried marjoram
1/2 teaspoon dried thyme

1 cup chicken consommé
1/2 cup dry red wine
Juice of 1 lemon
Grated rind from 1 lemon
1/2 cup seedless raisins
2 whole cloves
2 cups lamb, cooked and diced
1/4 cup shredded coconut
1 tablespoon sour cream

Sauté apples, green pepper, onions and garlic in olive oil over medium-high heat until onions are limp. Add flour, curry powder, salt, marjoram and thyme. Mix well and cook for 5 minutes, stirring constantly. Add consommé, wine, lemon juice, lemon rind, raisins and cloves. Simmer for 20 to 30 minutes. Add lamb and coconut and heat for 15 minutes. Just before serving, add sour cream and mix. Serve over hot rice with your choice of condiments: mango chutney (purchased or see page 87), chopped egg yolks, chopped egg whites, chopped crisp bacon, chopped green onions, raisins, cashews, pine nuts or peanuts.

ROGAN JOSH

This was originally selected because of it's low-fat approach to lamb curry. It is delicious however, and the spices add a nice red hue and complexity. It is a nice alternative and I have even served it over pilaf for Easter Dinner.

1 1/2 teaspoons cumin
1 1/2 teaspoons ground coriander
1 teaspoon ground ginger
1 teaspoon chili powder
1 teaspoon cinnamon
1/2 teaspoon salt
1/2 teaspoon turmeric
1/4 teaspoon saffron threads

1/4 teaspoon ground cloves
1 1/2 pounds boneless leg of lamb, trimmed and
    cut into 1/2 inch cubes
1 teaspoon canola oil
2 cups beef stock
3/4 cup low-fat yogurt
1/2 cup chopped fresh cilantro (optional)

Combine cumin, coriander, ginger, chili powder, cinnamon, salt, turmeric, saffron, cloves in a zipper-lock plastic bag. Add lamb, seal and shake. Refrigerate 8 hours or overnight. Heat oil in a large saucepan over medium heat. Add lamb and cook 4 minutes, stirring constantly. Add stock, using some of it to rinse out the bag used for the spice marinade. Scrape pan to loosen brown bits, bring the stock to a boil. Cover, reduce the heat and simmer for one hour. Increase heat to medium high and crack the lid for another hour, or until lamb is tender. Uncover and cook 5 minutes until sauce thickens. Remove from heat, and stir in yogurt, add cilantro if desired. Serve as an entrée over rice, in a pita pocket, or with toasted pita chips. Makes 4 servings.

Vegetables & Sides

STEAMED ASPARAGUS with TOMATO HERB SALSA

Asparagus spears may be peeled, but my preference is to simply snap off the tough ends and proceed with cooking. Steaming asparagus, as in this recipe, leaves the tips crisper than boiling. The salsa adds good flavor and color.

Tomato Herb Salsa
2 cups diced, seeded tomatoes
¹/₂ cup thinly sliced green onion
¹/₄ cup chopped fresh basil
3 tablespoons olive oil
1 tablespoon white wine (or white
   balsamic vinegar)
Salt and freshly ground black pepper

Steamed Asparagus
2 pounds fresh asparagus, tough ends
   snapped off
¹/₄ cup butter or margarine
1 tablespoon fresh lemon juice
2 tablespoons chopped fresh parsley
Salt and freshly ground black pepper

To make the Tomato Herb Salsa, combine all ingredients together in a bowl. Season with salt and pepper. Cover and set aside for flavors to blend while asparagus cooks. Can be made ahead.

Place 1 cup water and ¹/₂ teaspoon salt in a deep pan. Insert steamer basket. Place asparagus in basket, stem ends down. Bring to a boil; reduce heat to a simmer. Cover and steam for 7 to 10 minutes until tender. Remove from steamer basket. Drain and arrange on large platter. Melt butter; stir in lemon juice and parsley. Drizzle over asparagus. Sprinkle with salt and freshly ground black pepper. Spoon a ribbon of Tomato Herb Salsa over asparagus and serve. Makes 6 to 8 servings. From Bonnie Aeschliman.

If advance preparation is desired, steam asparagus then immediately plunge in ice water to stop the cooking and to set the color. Drain. Place in covered container and refrigerate up to 24 hours. Before serving, place on microwave platter and reheat, or dip in boiling water for 30 seconds. Drain and proceed with recipe.

ROASTED PARMESAN ASPARAGUS with BALSAMIC GLAZE

The intense heat of broiling brings out good flavor in the asparagus, also resulting in caramelizing the exterior for a bit of sweetness. The result is delicious. Thicker asparagus stalks (³/₄-inch to 1-inch) tend to char before the interior is tender, therefore select thin stalks. This is delicious topped with a Balsamic Glaze.

BALSAMIC GLAZE

Start the glaze before the asparagus is roasted. In a small skillet over medium heat, bring ³/₄ cup balsamic vinegar to a boil; reduce heat and simmer slowly until vinegar is syrupy (about 15 to 20 minutes).

Drizzle glaze and olive oil over the roasted asparagus after arranged on the serving platter.

2 pounds asparagus, tough ends snapped off
1 tablespoon olive oil
Salt and freshly ground black pepper

¹/₂ cup Balsamic Glaze (see margin)
¹/₄ cup olive oil
¹/₄ cup Parmesan cheese shavings

Adjust oven rack so that it is 4 inches from the broiler element. Lay asparagus stalks in a single layer on a sheet pan and drizzle with olive oil. Sprinkle with salt and pepper. Broil, shaking the pan halfway through to turn the spears. Broil 8 to 10 minutes until asparagus is lightly browned and tender. Arrange on serving platter; drizzle with Balsamic Glaze (purchase or see margin note) and olive oil. Scatter cheese shavings on top and serve immediately. Makes 6 to 8 servings

Steuben Glass (Frederick Carder, designer) *Indian Vase* (detail), ca. 1925, acid cut lead glass, WAM, gift of William and Martha L. Connelly, 1999.4

SAUTÉED GREEN BEANS with BACON, SHALLOTS and MUSHROOMS

The green beans may be blanched the day before. This dish has become a favored tradition for special family meals.

3 pounds fresh green beans, ends snipped off
6 tablespoons butter
4 shallots, peeled and thinly sliced
1 pound mushrooms, sliced

2 tablespoons honey (or molasses or brown sugar)
1 tablespoon soy sauce
8 slices bacon, cooked crisp and crumbled
Salt and freshly ground black pepper

Bring a large pot of salted water to a boil; add green beans. Cook until beans are just tender, about 6 to 7 minutes. Drain and plunge immediately into a bowl of ice water; drain when cooled. Melt butter in a large heavy skillet over medium high heat. Add shallots and cook for 1 minute; add mushrooms and cook until tender. Stir in honey, soy sauce, green beans and bacon; toss and cook until heated through. Season to taste with salt and pepper. Mound green beans on heated platter and serve. Makes 12 servings. From Bonnie Aeschliman.

GARLIC BROCCOLI with PANCETTA and RAISINS

The golden raisins in this dish add a delicate sweet counternote to the savory flavors of the pancetta and bacon. To turn this into a main dish, toss with a pound of cooked pasta like penne.

2 pounds broccoli florets
4 ounces pancetta (or bacon), cut in
   1/4-inch strips
1 garlic clove, finely chopped

1/3 cup golden raisins
1/4 cup white wine vinegar
2 tablespoons olive oil
Salt and freshly ground black pepper

Pancetta is an Italian cured, but unsmoked, bacon. You can find it at specialty markets. If you cannot find pancetta, bacon is a good substitute, although try to find one that is not too smoky.

Bring a large pot of salted water to a boil and add broccoli. Cook for 3 minutes, or to desired tenderness. Remove from the water and immediately plunge into a bowl of ice water to stop the cooking. Drain well and set aside. In a very large skillet, cook the pancetta over medium heat for 5 minutes, until crisp. Remove with a slotted spoon and drain on several layers of paper towels. Do not drain the fat from the skillet. Add garlic and raisins to the pan and sauté about 1 minute, until garlic is pale golden, then stir in vinegar and oil. Bring to a simmer, add broccoli to the pan and toss to combine. Cook until the broccoli is heated through. Season to taste with salt and pepper. Makes 4 servings.

SPICY SESAME BROCCOLI

2 tablespoons toasted sesame oil
3 tablespoons sesame seeds
2 teaspoons freshly grated ginger

1 teaspoon dried crushed red pepper
2 pounds broccoli florets
Salt

In a small heavy skillet, heat the oil over medium heat, then add the sesame seeds and cook about 3 minutes until the seeds are golden. Add the ginger and red pepper and cook one minute more. Bring a large pot of salted water to a boil and add the broccoli. Cook for 3 minutes, or to desired tenderness. Drain well and place in a large bowl. Add the sesame oil mixture and toss to combine. Season with salt. Makes 4 servings.

GARLIC SAUTÉED SPINACH

Granddaughter Analee spent a summer in France while in college, and came back with lots of new acquired tastes and ways of cooking. It was a delight to sit at the kitchen island and watch her stir up this dish. It only takes about 5 minutes but needs to be done right before it is served.

1 1/2 pounds fresh spinach leaves
2 tablespoons olive oil
6 cloves garlic, chopped
2 teaspoons kosher salt

3/4 teaspoon freshly ground black pepper
1 tablespoon butter
Fresh lemon juice

Rinse the spinach twice to make sure it is clean, and then dry in a salad spinner. Heat olive oil in a large pot and sauté the garlic over medium heat for about a minute (but not so long as to brown it). Add the spinach, salt, and pepper; toss with the garlic and oil. Cover the pot and cook for 2 minutes. Uncover the pot; turn the heat on high for another 2 minutes, stirring until the spinach is all wilted. Lift out of the pot with a slotted spoon and place into a serving dish, top with butter, a squeeze of lemon and a dash of salt. Serve immediately while piping hot. Makes 6 servings.

SPINACH SOUFFLÉ ROLL with SAUTÉED MUSHROOMS and HOLLANDAISE

This spinach soufflé is baked in a jellyroll pan so that it is thin enough to roll up with the sautéed mushrooms tucked inside. Beautiful resulting slices provide a side dish that adjusts well to the special plated dinner or buffet.

3 (10-ounce) packages frozen chopped spinach
1/4 cup bread crumbs
2 teaspoons salt
1 teaspoon freshly ground black pepper
1/4 teaspoon nutmeg
6 tablespoons butter, melted
4 eggs, separated

1/3 teaspoon cream of tartar
4 tablespoons grated Parmesan cheese
1 1/2 pounds mushrooms, sliced
1/4 cup butter
1 1/2 tablespoons flour
3/4 to 1 1/2 cups Hollandaise Sauce
   (recipe below)

Thaw spinach and squeeze out all excess moisture. Preheat oven to 350°F. Butter a jellyroll pan and line with parchment paper. Spread bread crumbs over parchment paper. Add 1 1/2 teaspoon salt, 1/2 teaspoon pepper, nutmeg and melted butter to the uncooked spinach. In a separate, clean bowl beat egg yolks into the spinach one at a time. Beat whites with cream of tartar to foamy stage. Fold into spinach. Spoon spinach mixture into jellyroll pan. Sprinkle with Parmesan cheese. Bake until center is very firm (about 15 minutes). While baking spinach, sauté mushrooms in butter. Add flour and remaining salt and pepper. After spinach is baked, place a sheet of buttered waxed paper, buttered side down, on spinach. Invert on cookie sheet. Remove bottom paper, spread mushroom mixture on top and roll up jellyroll fashion. Serve immediately or wrap in foil and reheat when ready to serve. Pour Hollandaise Sauce over roll, or serve slices with sauce spooned in a ribbon over the top. Makes 8 to 10 servings.

Hollandaise Sauce

3 egg yolks (reserve whites for another use)
3 tablespoons fresh lemon juice

1/2 cup butter
Salt

In a small heavy saucepan, gently beat the yolks then add lemon juice and combine. Cut butter in half, and add first half to saucepan. Cook over low heat, stirring constantly so as not to curdle the eggs until first half of butter melts. Repeat with second half of butter. Season with salt to taste. Remove from heat. Sauce may sit off the heat on the stove for a short while until ready to use. If it gets too thick, add drops of lemon juice and stir with small whisk. Taste carefully for seasoning. If sauce tastes slightly metallic, add more salt until the correct balance is achieved. Makes approximately 3/4 cup. From Robert Brand.

TRICOLOR VEGETABLE CHEESE TERRINE

While it takes time to prepare the layers, the flavor combination of cheesy broccoli, red peppered rice and carrots will delight most everyone. The colors look great on a plate too, making for a very special presentation. Serve with either a cheese sauce (my favorite) or a cream sauce, depending on the rest of your menu.

First Layer
2 eggs
1 cup cooked, drained
  and finely chopped
  broccoli florets
1 tablespoon butter or
  margarine, softened
¼ teaspoon onion salt
½ cup grated Cheddar cheese

Second Layer
2 eggs
1 cup cooked rice
¼ cup chopped red pepper
1 tablespoon butter or
  margarine, softened
½ cup grated
  mozzarella cheese
¼ teaspoon onion salt

Third Layer
2 eggs
1 cup cooked mashed carrots
1 tablespoon butter, softened
½ grated Cheddar cheese
¼ teaspoon onion salt

Cheese or Cream Sauce
  (recipes below)

Preheat oven to 325°F. *For the first layer*: in a bowl, beat the eggs with spoon. Stir in the broccoli, butter, onion salt and cheese. Pack into a well greased 4 x 8-inch loaf pan. Rinse and dry bowl. *Second layer*: in the bowl, beat eggs with a spoon. Stir in the rice, pepper, butter, cheese and onion salt. Spread over broccoli layer. Rinse and dry bowl. *Third layer*: in the bowl, beat the eggs with a spoon. Stir in the carrots, butter, cheese and onion salt. Depending on the moisture of the carrots, this layer may need to be thickened with 1 tablespoon of flour. Spread over rice layer.

Bake in oven for about 1 hour or until an inserted knife comes out clean. Do not under bake. Let set before unmolding. Unmold onto a serving platter. Top with cheese sauce or a cream sauce, whichever complements the rest of your meal. Garnish with cooked broccoli, carrot, and onion at base of loaf and a few thin slices of red pepper on top. Makes 10 to 12 servings.

Cheese Sauce
1 tablespoon butter
1 tablespoon flour
1 cup whole milk

1 tablespoon heavy cream
½ cup coarsely grated Gruyère or Swiss cheese
  (about 2 ounces)

In a small saucepan heat butter over medium heat until foam subsides; stir in flour. Stirring constantly, cook for 2 minutes until golden in color. Add milk and cream, whisk and simmer until sauce thickens slightly (about 2 minutes). Turn off heat and stir in cheese, salt and pepper to taste; stir until cheese is melted. Keep sauce warm, covered, over very low heat. Makes about 1 cup.

CREAM SAUCE

2 tablespoons butter
2 tablespoons flour
¼ teaspoon salt
Freshly ground black pepper
1 cup milk

Melt butter in saucepan. Mix in flour, salt and pepper. Add milk. Stir until it boils and thickens. Makes about 1 cup

PRIMAVERA CHEESE TORTE

This Gouda cheese torte can be served as a side dish or as an entrée, depending on the portion size. As a luncheon entrée this was a hit at the Wichita Symphony Showhouse Tea Room 2003, outselling all others. We were making them so fast we discovered that while the layered torte presentation described here is beautiful, this may also be made by mixing the cream cheese with the next 13 ingredients and baking as a cheesecake. In fact it is not only simpler, but the flavors also blend very well together. Either way, you will rake in compliments.

1 (10-ounce) package frozen chopped spinach, thawed
1 cup fine dry bread crumbs
$1/4$ cup plus 2 tablespoon butter, melted
$1/3$ cup grated Parmesan cheese
1 teaspoon ground red pepper (divided use)
3 (8-ounce) packages cream cheese, softened
$1/2$ cup whipping cream
$3/8$ teaspoon salt (divided use)
4 eggs

1 cup (4 ounces) shredded smoked Gouda cheese
8 slices bacon, cooked and crumbled
1 (4-ounce) jar sliced pimento, drained
8 ounces fresh mushrooms, chopped
$1/4$ cup chopped green onions
2 tablespoons butter, melted
$1/4$ teaspoon pepper
$1/8$ teaspoon salt
Garnish: fresh spinach leaves, 2 green onion tops

Preheat oven to 325°F. Drain thawed spinach well, pressing between paper towels to remove excess moisture. Set aside. Combine bread crumbs, butter, Parmesan cheese and $1/2$ teaspoon ground red pepper; stir well. Press the crumb mixture into the bottom of a lightly greased 9-inch springform pan. Bake at 350°F for 10 minutes; let cool completely.

Combine cream cheese, whipping cream, $1/4$ teaspoon salt, and $1/4$ teaspoon ground red pepper. Beat at medium speed with an electric mixer until smooth. Add eggs, one at a time, beating at low speed just until blended. Divide cream cheese mixture in half. Add Gouda cheese and bacon to one half, stirring well. Stir reserved spinach and pimento into remaining half. Set aside. Sauté mushrooms and chopped green onions in 2 tablespoons butter until tender and liquid evaporates. Stir in pepper and salt. Pour spinach-cream cheese mixture into prepared crust. Top with mushroom mixture. Pour bacon-cream cheese mixture over mushrooms. Bake for 50 to 55 minutes or just until set (45 to 50 minutes if you use a 10-inch springform pan.) Turn oven off and partially open oven door; leave cheesecake in oven for 1 hour. Let cool to room temperature on a wire rack.

Remove sides of pan. Place cheesecake on a bed of fresh spinach leaves. Remove and discard white portion of 2 green onions, cut tops into long strands. Wilt green onions strands by placing them in boiling water for 5 to 8 seconds. Drain well, and arrange on top of cheesecake in a pattern of choice. Makes one 9-inch cheesecake serving 12 to 15. Can be frozen and thawed in refrigerator at least 24 hours. Best served warm.

FRIED GREEN TOMATOES with ROASTED RED PEPPER REMOULADE and CHÈVRE

Once you try these you will understand why they are a Southern favorite. Best to make these with garden tomatoes. I have combined two recipes here. The tomato recipe is one from a pamphlet put out by the Pet Milk Company during the Great Depression and results in crisp, luscious fried tomatoes. The excellent sauce recipe is adapted from a Southern Living recipe, and doubles easily.

4 medium tomatoes, half ripe from the garden
1/2 cup flour
2 1/2 teaspoons salt
2 1/2 teaspoons sugar
1/4 teaspoon freshly ground black pepper

3/4 cup evaporated milk
Vegetable oil for frying
Roasted Red Pepper Remoulade (recipe below)
4 ounces goat cheese, crumbled
1/4 cup chopped fresh parsley

Wash tomatoes, but do not peel. Cut into 1/2-inch slices; discard end pieces (should have about 12 slices). Place on paper towel to drain. Combine flour, salt, sugar and pepper; dust slices on both sides. Add evaporated milk to remaining flour mixture to make a thick batter. Dip floured tomatoes in batter. Fry in hot oil 1/2-inch deep until golden brown on both sides. Place tomatoes on individual serving plates; drizzle with Roasted Red Pepper Remoulade, sprinkle with goat cheese and parsley. Serve immediately with remaining remoulade. Makes 6 servings.

Roasted Red Pepper Remoulade

1/4 cup egg substitute
1/2 cup vegetable oil
1/2 (12 ounce) jar roasted red bell
  peppers, drained
1/4 cup minced onions
1 tablespoon Creole mustard

1 teaspoon lemon juice
1 clove garlic, minced
1/2 teaspoon sugar
1/2 teaspoon salt
1/2 teaspoon cumin
1/4 teaspoon ground red pepper

Place egg substitute in bowl of food processor or blender. With processor running, pour oil in a slow steady stream, processing until thickened. Pour into small bowl and set aside. Process roasted red bell peppers and remaining ingredients, pulsing until smooth. Stir roasted pepper mixture into egg mixture. Cover and chill until ready to serve. Makes 1 cup.

SNAPPY SUGAR SNAPS with RED PEPPERS

1 pound sugar snap peas, rinsed
2 cloves garlic
6 tablespoons olive oil (divided use)

2 tablespoons balsamic vinegar
2 red bell peppers, julienned
Salt and freshly ground black pepper

Bring water to boil in a small saucepan; blanch sugar snap peas for 1 to 2 minutes. Drain and plunge into ice water for a few minutes so that their bright green color is preserved. Drain peas and allow to dry. Combine garlic, 4 tablespoons of olive oil, salt and vinegar in blender or food processor and blend until chopped and blended; pour over peas and toss. Heat remaining olive oil in a medium skillet and sauté red peppers over medium heat just until soft. Toss them in with the peas and heat. Season to taste with salt and pepper. Serve in a shallow bowl. Makes 4 to 6 servings.

OVEN ROASTED ROSEMARY POTATOES

These are easy and delicious. Be sure to use a heavy baking pan to achieve even roasting.

3 pounds small red potatoes, scrubbed and quartered

3 to 4 tablespoons olive oil

2 large cloves garlic, thinly sliced

1 tablespoon chopped fresh rosemary (or 1 teaspoon dried)

Kosher salt and freshly ground black pepper

Preheat oven to 400°F. Toss potatoes with oil, garlic and rosemary. Season to taste with salt and pepper. Place them on a large shallow heavy baking pan, and roast in the middle of the oven for 45 minutes or until tender and browned. Stir once or twice for even browning. Makes 6 to 8 servings.

CREAMED NEW POTATOES AND PEAS

Grant Wood
Seed Time and Harvest,
1937, lithograph, WAM,
gift of George E. Vollmer,
the Clarence E. Vollmer
Collection, 1977.22,
©Estate of Grant Wood/
Licensed by VAGA, New
York, NY

2 pounds small, new red potatoes

1/2 teaspoon salt

1 (16-ounce) bag frozen baby peas

1 teaspoon sugar (optional)

3/4 to 1 cup heavy cream

Salt and freshly ground black pepper

Scrub new potatoes. Peel a strip from around the equator of each potato. Place potatoes, 1 cup water and 1/2 teaspoon salt in a large saucepan. Bring to a boil. Reduce heat, cover and simmer until tender, about 20 minutes. Add frozen peas and sugar to potatoes; cover and cook for 3 or 4 minutes. There will not be much liquid left in the pan. Remove lid and cook a few minutes to evaporate most of liquid. Add cream. Simmer uncovered a few minutes until cream is thickened to sauce consistency. Season to taste with salt and pepper. Makes 8 servings. From Bonnie Aeschliman.

CREAMY MASHED POTATOES with ROASTED GARLIC

2 heads roasted garlic (page 23)
6 bacon slices
1 bunch green onions, chopped
4 pounds red potatoes, scrubbed
1 (16-ounce) container sour cream
1 1/2 cups (6 ounces) shredded Cheddar cheese
    (divided use)

1/3 cup butter or margarine, softened
1/4 cup milk
1/2 teaspoon salt
1/4 teaspoon freshly ground black pepper
Garnish: chopped fresh chives

Squeeze pulp from roasted garlic; set aside. Cook bacon in a large skillet until crisp; remove bacon, and drain on paper towels, reserving 2 tablespoons drippings in skillet. Crumble bacon, and return to skillet; add green onions. Cook 1 minute or until green onions are tender. Set aside. Peel half of potatoes; cut into 1/4-inch pieces. Cut remaining unpeeled potatoes into 1/4-inch pieces. Cook potatoes in a Dutch oven in boiling salted water to cover 20 to 25 minutes or until tender; drain and place in a large bowl. Add squeezed pulp from roasted garlic into potatoes; add bacon mixture, sour cream, 1 cup cheese, and next 4 ingredients; mash with a potato masher until blended. Spoon potato mixture into a lightly greased 9 x 13-inch baking dish; top with remaining 1/2 cup cheese. Bake at 350°F for 10 minutes or until cheese melts. Garnish, if desired. Makes 8 to 10 servings.

Mashed potatoes are best served right away. On holidays or other times when there are a lot of last minute preparations I put the mashed potatoes in a crockpot on low (but for no more than 30 minutes) while serving or other dishes are being prepared.

FAST CREAMY MASHED POTATOES
To even further shortcut this recipe, substitute frozen mashed potatoes for the boiled potatoes.

5 pounds red potatoes, peeled and cut in
    1-inch pieces
1/4 teaspoon salt
1 (10-ounce) container refrigerated
    alfredo sauce

1/2 cup butter or margarine
1/2 teaspoon salt
1/4 teaspoon freshly ground black pepper

Boil potatoes in enough water to cover (with 1/4 teaspoon salt added) for 15 to 20 minutes or until potato is tender; drain. Stir in remaining ingredients; use a potato masher or mixer until smooth. Makes 6 servings.

BLUE CHEESE POTATO SALAD

5 pounds small red-skinned new potatoes,
    scrubbed, quartered and cooked
1/2 cup wine vinegar
Salt and pepper
8 ounces crumbled blue cheese
1 1/4 cups mayonnaise

1 1/4 cups sour cream
2 1/2 tablespoons cider vinegar
5 green onions, minced
1/2 cup chopped parsley
2 1/2 tablespoons Dijon mustard
Garnish: 8 bacon slices, cooked crisp, crumbled

Cut potatoes into 1-inch pieces. Add wine vinegar. Season with salt and pepper. Toss to coat. Combine remaining ingredients and mix with potatoes. Adjust seasonings. Let stand at room temperature for 30 minutes before serving. Garnish with bacon crumbles. (Can be made 1 day ahead. Cover and refrigerate.) Makes 12 servings.

MENU:
*FATHER'S DAY
AT WILLOW
BANKS FARM*

Fruity Tea 41

*Old Fashioned Sweet
and Sour Slaw 56*

*Grilled Triangle Tip
Roast 130*

*Sweet Summer Corn
with Pesto Butter 156*

Deviled Eggs 159

*Picnic Chocolate
Sheet Cake 252*

ALMOST FARMHOUSE CREAMED CORN

Creamed corn was a favorite on the farm when fresh corn was in the field. This version provides a similar taste, using a simple process to turn frozen corn into something wonderful. Adapted from a Brookville Hotel recipe (Abilene, KS).

2 (12-ounce) bags frozen corn (or 4 cups fresh corn cut from the cob)
3/4 cup water
1 1/2 cups half-and-half (or 3/4 cup heavy cream and 3/4 cup milk) (divided use)

3 teaspoons cornstarch (or flour)
1 teaspoon salt
2 tablespoons sugar
1 tablespoon butter
Salt and freshly ground black pepper

Place frozen corn in 2-quart saucepan with salted water and bring to a boil quickly; reduce heat; cover and simmer for 3 to 4 minutes. Stir in 1 cup of half-and-half. Combine cornstarch, salt and sugar and combine it with remaining 1/2 cup half-and-half. Add to pan. Cook over medium heat, stirring constantly until mixture comes to a boil and is thickened. Remove 1 cup of corn; briefly purée in blender or processor. Pour back into pan and bring to a boil. Season with butter and additional salt and pepper if desired. Makes 8 servings.

SWEET SUMMER CORN with PESTO BUTTER

4 cloves of garlic
1 cup fresh basil
1/2 cup grated Parmesan cheese

1/2 cup butter, cut into pieces
12 ears sweet corn

Pulse garlic and basil in a food processor, then add the Parmesan cheese and butter and process until just blended. Husk corn just before cooking and place in a large pot of boiling water with dash of salt. Simmer for no more than 5 minutes. Remove from pot and coat corn with pesto butter. Serve immediately! Makes 12 servings.

CORN and CHEESE GRITS

This simple dish is well liked and good to serve with steaks or barbeque. It is easy to prepare early in the day and then pop into the oven while the meat is cooking.

Yellow grits are made from coarsely ground dried corn. White grits are made from hominy.

1 (16-ounce) can whole kernel corn
1/2 cup quick-cooking white grits
1/2 teaspoon salt

4 ounces sharp Cheddar cheese, shredded
1 (4-ounce) can diced green chilies, drained
2 tablespoons butter

Preheat oven to 350°F. Drain corn but save the liquid. Add enough water to the corn liquid to make 2 cups, and then bring to a boil. Add grits and salt and simmer until thick, about 5 minutes. Take off heat and stir in corn, chilies, cheese and butter. Place into a buttered 1 1/2-quart casserole dish. Bake for 15 to 20 minutes. Makes 6 servings, and doubles easily.

For a real treat try one of the new "artisanal" or heirloom varieties which are stone ground from native varieties of corn. These grits pack a real whollop of corn flavor and are worth ordering (see "Favorite Things") if you can't find them in the grocery.

BAKED CHEESE GRITS

6 cups water
1 teaspoon salt
1 1/2 cups regular grits, preferably stone-ground
1 (6-ounce) roll of garlic cheese
1 1/2 cups grated Cheddar cheese

1 clove garlic, mashed
1/2 cup butter
1 to 2 tablespoons Worcestershire sauce
1/2 teaspoon hot pepper sauce
2 eggs, beaten

Preheat oven to 350°F. Boil water and salt; add grits while stirring. Reduce heat and simmer for 10 minutes. Add cheeses, garlic and butter and stir. Stir in Worcestershire sauce, hot pepper sauce and eggs, stirring to mix well. Pour into greased 2 1/2 quart baking dish (9 x 13-inch). Bake for 45 minutes. Garnish with cooked bacon crumbles and tomato slices. Makes 8 servings.

CHEESE SPINACH GRITS SOUFFLÉ

Served at a Wichita-Sedgwick County Historical Museum Sunday Supper, this is a delicious side dish.

6 cups water
1 1/2 cups regular grits, preferably stone-ground
1 1/2 teaspoons salt
2 tablespoons chopped garlic
1/2 cup butter
1 1/2 tablespoons Worcestershire sauce
1/2 teaspoon hot pepper sauce
1/2 teaspoon white pepper

1/4 cup cornmeal mix
6 eggs, beaten
1 (12-ounce) package Colby/Monterey Jack Cheese shredded
1 (10-ounce) package frozen spinach, thawed and thoroughly drained between paper towels
Paprika

Preheat oven to 350°F. Boil water, add grits and salt. Cook for 1 minute; reduce heat; cover and cook stirring occasionally with wire whisk for 6 minutes. Remove from heat. In a large bowl combine the grits, garlic, butter, Worcestershire, hot pepper sauce, white pepper, cornmeal, eggs and cheese. Stir well to blend. Add spinach (be sure it is thoroughly drained), and stir to break up before adding to grits mixture. Transfer all into a 9 x 13-inch pan that has been coated with cooking spray. Sprinkle with paprika and bake for 45 minutes. Individual servings may be served topped with Sour Cream Onion Gravy. Makes 8 servings.

Sour Cream Onion Gravy

1/2 cup chopped onions
1/2 cup butter
2 tablespoons flour
1 cup half-and-half

1 teaspoon salt
1/2 teaspoon white pepper
3/4 cup sour cream

Sauté onion in butter over medium-high heat until soft but not browned. Stir in the flour, cream, salt and pepper. Bring to a boil, stirring constantly until blended. Cool slightly and put through blender to break up onions. Stir in sour cream and warm, but do not boil as the sour cream may curdle. Makes 3 cups.

HOMINY and CHILIES

This dish always disappears quickly and is easy to scale up for a large crowd. White or yellow hominy, or a combination, work equally well. I prefer the white, but choose based upon color balance needed for your menu.

1 (14-ounce) can white hominy corn, drained
1 (4-ounce) can chopped green chilies, drained
1 cup sour cream
1/2 teaspoon salt

1/3 teaspoon freshly ground black pepper
1 cup grated Monterey Jack cheese

Preheat oven to 350°F. Mix all ingredients except for the cheese in a 1-quart casserole. Sprinkle cheese over top. Bake uncovered for 20 to 30 minutes until hot and cheese is melted. Makes 4 to 6 servings.

BAKED BEANS

2 (15-ounce) cans pork and beans, drained
3/4 cup barbeque sauce (prefer 'KC Masterpiece BBQ')
1/4 cup golden raisins
1/2 cup brown sugar

1 tart apple, cored, peeled and chopped
1 medium onion, chopped
4 strips uncooked bacon (cut in half)
1 teaspoon ground cumin
1/2 teaspoon ground red pepper

Mix all ingredients, except for one strip of bacon in thirds, in a 9 x 13-inch baking dish. Lay bacon on top of beans and bake at 350°F for 1 hour. Makes 8 servings. Adapted from recipe by Rich Davis.

Dr. Rich Davis, a Kansas City child psychiatrist, is the founder of KC Masterpiece BBQ Sauce - a name that isn't just hype. While a practicing physician and a faculty member at the KU School of Medicine, he concocted sauce from just 5 ingredients in his home kitchen as a secret weapon in the BBQ contests he regularly won. In 1978 Davis began bottling and selling the sauce in Kansas City, as well as various culinary concepts including Muschup *(a combination of ketchup and mustard) and Dilled Muschup. While Muschup sold well, the BBQ sauce was the most popular. The brand was sold in 1986 to the Kingsford division of Clorox corporation who took it nationwide. Now in 8 flavors it is proclaimed to be the top selling premium BBQ sauce in the nation.*

ROASTED HERBED ITALIAN VEGETABLES

*Grilling or roasting is a
no-fuss delicious way to
prepare most vegetables.
Intense heat brings out good
flavor in most vegetables.*

*Grilled vegetables are
wonderful. Vegetables can be
marinated or just grilled
with a brushing of olive oil
and a few seasonings.*

*Oven roasting works easily
too for most vegetables. Just
wash, pat dry and place
vegetables on a cookie
sheet. Drizzle a little olive
oil, sprinkle with kosher
salt and roast at 425° F
or higher until they are
sizzling and begin to
brown. Serve immediately.*

*Try a little cauliflower and
red onion slices prepared
this way, you will be
surprised at the ease and
the great bold flavor.*

1 red or orange bell pepper, seeds removed and cut into strips
1 green pepper, seeded and cut into strips
1 yellow onion, cut into eighths and layers separated
1 small eggplant, peeled and cut into 1-inch pieces
2 medium-sized yellow squash, trimmed and cut into $^1/_2$-inch slices
2 medium-sized zucchini, trimmed and cut into $^1/_2$ slices
1 butternut squash (microwave for 5 minute then cut into $^1/_2$ inch slices or cubes)
8 ounces fresh white mushrooms, trimmed and halved
$^1/_3$ cup olive oil
3 cloves garlic, sliced
1 teaspoon minced fresh rosemary
1 teaspoon kosher salt
$^1/_2$ teaspoon freshly ground black pepper
Garnish: chopped fresh basil or thyme, grated Parmesan cheese

Preheat oven to 425°F. Line a large, rimmed heavy baking sheet with foil for easy clean up. Spray with vegetable spray or drizzle a little olive oil in pan. Arrange vegetables in pan in a single layer. Combine olive oil, garlic, rosemary, salt and pepper; drizzle over vegetables, turning to coat. Roast vegetables in preheated oven, turning once or twice, occasionally, until tender and browned. This will take 30 to 45 minutes. Before serving, sprinkle with chopped basil or parsley. Serve with a Balsamic Glaze (see page 148). From Bonnie Aeschliman. Makes 6 to 8 servings.

MARINATED GRILLED VEGETABLES
This version of roasted vegetables is nicely done outside on the grill.

$^1/_2$ cup balsamic vinegar
$^1/_4$ cup olive oil
2 tablespoons dry white wine
1 tablespoon finely chopped shallots
$^1/_2$ tablespoon minced garlic
$^1/_2$ tablespoon freshly ground black pepper
1 teaspoon kosher salt
4 new potatoes, scrubbed
4 Roma tomatoes, cut in half lengthwise
3 small zucchini, cut in half lengthwise
2 ears yellow corn, cut into 3-inch cobs
2 red onions, cut into $^3/_4$-inch slices
2 Portobello mushrooms, quartered
1 pound fresh asparagus, ends broken off
1 small eggplant, cut lengthwise into 1-inch slices
1 red bell pepper, quartered and seeds and membrane removed
1 yellow bell pepper, quartered and seeds and membrane removed
1 tablespoon chopped fresh chives
1 tablespoon chopped fresh rosemary
1 tablespoon chopped fresh parsley

Combine balsamic vinegar, oil, wine, shallots, garlic, pepper and salt in an extra-large bowl, or divide in half and place in two extra large zipper-lock bags. Cook potatoes in boiling water 4 minutes; drain. Cut potatoes in half. Add potato halves, tomato halves and rest of vegetable ingredients to the vinegar mixture. Toss gently to coat thoroughly. Let stand at room temperature for about 1 hour, tossing occasionally.

Prepare medium hot coals in charcoal grill. Spray grill with no-stick cooking spray. Remove vegetables from marinade; reserve marinade. Cook vegetables, covered with grill lid, for about 12 to 14 minutes, turning once. Remove individual vegetables as they are done to a serving platter. Drizzle remaining marinade over cooked vegetables. Combine chives, rosemary and parsley and sprinkle over vegetables. Makes 8 to 10 servings.

GRILLED PORTABELLOS

My favorite way to serve portabellos is grilled; served as a side, an appetizer, or even as a portabello burger.

4 portabello mushroom caps
2 tablespoons olive oil
Salt and pepper

Vinaigrette
6 tablespoons olive oil

2 tablespoons balsamic vinegar
1 teaspoon chopped garlic
1 tablespoon chopped capers
6 basil leaves, coarsely chopped
1/2 teaspoon dried rosemary
1/2 teaspoon salt

Prepare hot grill (or indoor broiler). Rinse mushroom caps and pat dry; brush with oil on both sides; salt and pepper. When the grill is very hot, cook mushrooms about 10 minutes on each side until they are soft. While they are cooking, whisk together the oil and vinegar to emusify, then add all of the vinaigrette ingredients. When mushrooms are grilled, place on serving platter and pour vinaigrette over them. May serve at room temperature several hours later, or serve immediately. Makes 4 servings.

ROASTED ACORN SQUASH with CRANBERRY RELISH

3 medium acorn squash
1 tablespoon butter
1/2 tablespoon honey
1/4 teaspoon salt
1/4 teaspoon pepper

Cranberry Relish
1/3 cup apple cider

1/3 cup maple syrup
2 tablespoons butter
1/4 teaspoon cinnamon
1/4 teaspoon ginger
1/4 teaspoon nutmeg
1 cup fresh cranberries
1/4 cup chopped pecans, toasted

Preheat oven to 450°F. Remove stem from squash. Cut squash in half lengthwise; remove and discard seeds. Cut each half into 4 wedges, and place on an aluminum foil-lined jellyroll pan. Stir together butter and honey until blended. Brush squash evenly with butter mixture; sprinkle evenly with salt and pepper. Bake for 30 to 35 minutes or until tender, turning once.

To prepare relish bring cider, syrup, butter, cinnamon, ginger and nutmeg to a boil in a small saucepan over medium heat. Reduce heat and simmer 5 minutes. Stir in cranberries and simmer until skins split. Remove from heat, add pecans and spoon over warm squash wedges. Makes 6 servings.

DEVILED EGGS

You can use a pastry bag to fill the eggs or improvise with a zipper-lock plastic bag by filling the bag and snipping one corner then squeezing the filling into the egg white half. Best prepared at the last minute for good flavor. If made in advance, cool the eggs a day ahead, store the whites in a sealed container, and filling in a zipper-lock bag.

12 eggs
1 1/2 teaspoons whole-grain mustard
6 tablespoons mayonnaise (prefer Hellmann's)
3 teaspoons cider vinegar (or Hendrickson's salad dressing, purchased)

1/4 teaspoon Worcestershire sauce
Salt and white pepper
Optional garnish: capers, olive slice, or slivers of cooked bacon

Boil eggs and peel. Slice each in half lengthwise with a sharp paring knife. Remove yolks and place in a small bowl. Arrange the whites on the serving platter. Discard the three or four halves that look least desirable. Mash the yolks with a fork or pastry blender; add mustard, mayonnaise, vinegar, and Worcestershire until process until just blended. Add salt and pepper to taste. Fill a pastry bag or zipper-lock plastic bag with the mixture and pipe into the egg white halves. Garnish with a thin olive slice, capers or a sliver of a cooked bacon slice. Serve immediately. Makes 16 to 18 deviled eggs.

*TIPS for
BOILING EGGS*

Place eggs in a pot and cover with cold water by about a 1/2 inch. Bring water to a gentle boil and then turn off the heat, cover and let sit for 7 minutes. Remove and plunge into an ice bath to stop the cooking.

CARMELIZED ONION RISOTTO with ROASTED CORN and BACON

Adapted from a 1995 recipe in Food & Wine, *this is a dish with great autumn harvest additions to a classic risotto. Pull up a chair to the stove as you will need to do a lot of stirring, but will be rewarded. Try to use very fresh sweet corn.*

3 ears sweet corn, in husks but desilked
7 tablespoons butter, divided use
3 vidalia onions, thinly sliced
1/4 pound bacon, 1/4-inch diced
8 cups chicken stock, as needed
1 yellow onion, finely chopped

1 small carrot, peeled and chopped fine
1 small celery stlk, chopped fine
2 cups arborio rice
1 cup dry white wine
1/4 cup fresh grated Parmesan cheese

Roast corn on a grill until tender, about 15 minutes. Cool, remove husks and cut kernels off cobs. Reserve cobs. Melt 3 tablespoons butter in a large saucepan; sauté vidalia onions until carmelized, about 25 minutes; add to corn. Fry bacon in same pan until crisp, about 3 minutes; drain on paper towels. Pour off drippings except for 2 tablespoons. In a separate large saucepan, bring stock and corn cobs to a boil, reduce heat to a slow simmer and let cook while you sauté the yellow onion, carrot and celery in the saucepan with the bacon drippings, for about 3 minutes. Add rice to the vegetables; stir to evenly coat with fat; add wine and cook, stirring constantly until it is almost all absorbed (about 2 minutes). Add in the corn, carmelized onions and bacon. Decant one cup of the hot chicken stock, add to the rice mixture and stir until all absorbed. Add remaining stock, 1/2 cup at a time, stirring until each addition is absorbed. Continue cooking just until rice is creamy and tender (the entire process will take about 45 minutes). Stir in 4 tablespoons butter, Parmesan, salt and pepper to taste. If it seems sticky or thick, add a bit of stock. Serve immediately. Makes 6 servings.

COUSCOUS "RISOTTO"

Excellent!

1 1/2 cups chicken stock
1 1/2 cups couscous (1 10-ounce box)
3 tablespoons olive oil (divided use)
Salt and freshly ground black pepper
1/3 cup finely chopped onion
2 cloves garlic

3/4 cup chicken stock
1/4 teaspoon crushed red pepper flakes
6 cups baby spinach leaves
3/4 cup heavy cream
1/2 cup grated Romano or Parmesan cheese
1 1/2 tablespoons fresh lemon juice

Bring 1 1/2 cups of chicken stock to boil in heavy saucepan. Mix in couscous. Cover pan and remove from heat. Let stand 5 minutes. Fluff with a fork. Drizzle with 2 tablespoons olive oil; season to taste with salt and pepper. Set aside. Heat 1 tablespoon olive oil in a large heavy pan over medium high heat. Add onion and garlic; sauté 1 minute. Add stock and pepper flakes; bring to a boil. Add spinach and stir. Cover and cook until wilted and tender, stirring frequently. Mix in couscous, cream, cheese and lemon juice. Simmer one to two minutes, or just until hot. Season to taste with salt and pepper. If mixture is too thick, thin with a little hot water, stock or cream until desired consistency. Makes 6 servings. From Bonnie Aeschliman.

KICKY VEGETABLE COUSCOUS

2 tablespoons olive oil
1/2 cup diced yellow summer squash
1/2 cup diced zucchini
1/2 cup diced red onion
1 clove garlic, minced
1 cup cooked chickpeas
1/2 teaspoon cumin

1/2 teaspoon curry powder
1/2 teaspoon dried red pepper flakes
1/2 teaspoon salt
Freshly ground black pepper to taste
3 cups cooked couscous, cooked in chicken
    stock according to package
Garnish: 1/4 cup chopped parsley

In a large skillet over medium-high heat, sauté vegetables in olive oil until fragrant and tender. Add minced garlic, chickpeas and spices and cook for another 5 minutes to warm and blend. Add cooked couscous, stir to heat, then mound on platter and garnish with chopped parsley. Makes 6 servings. From Barbara Keiffer.

Variation: May also add 2 diced carrots or 1 cup of raisins at time of sautéing vegetables.

While dishes like couscous and risotto have become part of our pantry, there was a time not too distant when something fancy called "piccalili" was in the farm cook's repertoire. This version from Alfrida (Mrs. Birger) Sandzén (Lindsborg, Kansas) is particularly memorable with the use of half gallon pails for measuring.

*Mamma's Piccalili
(ca. 1902)*

3 half gallon tin pails
green tomatoes
3 half gallon tin pails
cabbage chopped
3 quarts vinegar
1 3/4 half gallon tin pail sugar
10 onions
3 teaspoons cinnamon
2 teaspoons allspice
2 grated nutmegs
4 green peppers
2 teaspoons white mustard
1/2 cup salt
A little horseradish

Squeeze all the juice out of the tomatoes after chopping them. Mix all ingredients together and boil until tender.

SWEET POTATO SOUFFLÉ

I have served sweet potatoes topped with marshmellows for years, but this recipe will convince you to try pecans instead. You will hope that there are leftovers, so be sure to make plenty.

3 1/2 pounds sweet potatoes, peeled and sliced (about 3 large potatoes)
1/2 cup sugar
1/3 cup cream
2 eggs
1 1/2 teaspoons vanilla
1 cup butter
1/8 teaspoon cinnamon

1/16 teaspoon ground allspice
1/4 teaspoon salt

Topping
1/3 cup butter, melted
1 cup brown sugar
1/3 cup flour
1 cup chopped pecans

In a large pot, bring sweet potatoes and water to a boil over medium heat, cover and cook 20 minutes or until tender; drain. Mash or process with electric mixer; you should have about 3 cups of cooked and mashed sweet potatoes. Preheat oven to 350°F. Beat sweet potatoes, sugar, cream, eggs, vanilla, butter, cinnamon, allspice and salt at medium speed with an electric mixer until smooth. (Optional: stir in 1/2 cup raisins, if desired.) Pour mixture into a lightly greased 9 x 13-inch baking dish. Mix topping ingredients together and sprinkle on top of sweet potatoes. Bake uncovered, for 30 minutes or until bubbly. Makes 6 to 8 servings. Recipe doubles easily. From Beth Boerger.

PRALINE SWEET POTATOES

Here is a nice way to make sweet potatoes for just two servings.

1 cup cooked, mashed sweet potatoes
2 tablespoons milk
1 egg yolk
1/4 teaspoon salt
Dash of black pepper

1/4 cup packed brown sugar
2 tablespoons butter, melted
2 tablespoons corn syrup
2 tablespoons chopped pecans

Preheat oven to 350°F. In a small mixing bowl, combine the sweet potatoes, milk, egg yolk, salt and pepper. Transfer to a greased shallow 2-cup baking dish. In a small microwave-safe bowl, combine the brown sugar, butter and corn syrup until blended. Cover and microwave on high for 1 minute or until sugar is dissolved. Spoon over sweet potatoes. Sprinkle with pecans. Bake, uncovered, for 20 to 22 minutes or until a knife comes out clean. Makes 2 servings.

SUCCOTASH

Succotash is one of those dishes you can vary endlessly without fail according to the tone you want to set with whatever else you are serving.

4 ounces sliced bacon, cut into 1/4-inch pieces
1 small onion, chopped
Sugar
2 garlic cloves, minced
4 ears of corn, kernels removed
1 large fresh jalapeno chili, seeded and
  finely chopped

1 (10-ounce) package frozen baby lima beans
8 ounces okra, cut into 1/3-inch slices
12 ounces cherry tomatoes, halved
1 to 2 teaspoons salt
2 tablespoons cider vinegar
1/4 cup chopped fresh basil
Salt and freshly ground black pepper

In a large skillet cook the bacon over moderate heat until crisp. Drain on paper towels, leaving a good coating of bacon fat in the skillet. Add onion and 1 to 2 teaspoons sugar to skillet and cook until slightly golden. With the skillet still on moderate heat, add the garlic and cook one minute, then stir in all the vegetables, salt and cook until tender, about 15 minutes. Stir in the vinegar, basil and bacon. Season to taste with salt and pepper. Makes 6 to 8 servings. From Kathryn Gleissner.

THE BEST MACARONI AND CHEESE

Granddaughter Analee finds that one of the ways to create a dialogue with the foreign researchers in her laboratory is to have "cooking contests," alternating between American staples and foreign dishes. This recipe takes the prize with its silke béchamel cheese sauce and crowning crunch of melted cheese and bread crumbs. A laboratory winner and my favorite too!

7 tablespoons butter (divided use)
1 cup fresh bread crumbs
1/4 cup grated cheese
1 pound elbow macaroni or shells
Salt
6 tablespoons flour

1 1/2 teaspoons dry mustard
1/4 teaspoon cayenne pepper
5 cups milk
16 ounces shredded Cheddar/Monterey Jack cheese blend (4 cups)

To make the topping heat 2 tablespoons of butter in a skillet over medium-high heat, adding bread crumbs after the foam subsides; cook, stirring crumbs, until golden. Remove from heat. Once cool, add 1/4 cup of cheese. To 4 quarts of boiling water, add macaroni and salt; cook until pasta is tender, just past the al-dente stage and drain in a colander and set aside. In same pot, heat the remaining butter over medium-high heat until foaming. Add flour, mustard, and cayenne, whisking until the mixture turns light golden. Slowly add milk while continuing to whisk. Bring to a full boil and reduce heat to simmer for about 5 minutes, or until thickened. Remove from heat and add cheeses and 1 teaspoon of salt; stir until melted. Turn on oven broiler. Add drained pasta to the sauce and return to medium heat; stir constantly until piping hot (about 5 minutes). Transfer to a 9 x 13-inch casserole dish and sprinkle with topping. Broil until crumbs are golden brown and cheese is melted, about 3 minutes. Let rest for 5 minutes before serving. Makes 8 servings.

PASTA PRIMAVERA with PESTO CREAM SAUCE

Not only is this creamy pasta dish delicious, but it is also very pretty with all of the colors and textures.

12 ounces bow-tie pasta
8 ounces fresh sugar snap peas, with ends and any strings removed
1 large red bell pepper, seeded and cut into thin strips
1 cup heavy cream
1 cup chicken stock

1/4 teaspoon crushed red pepper
3/4 cup grated Parmesan or Asiago cheese
3 to 6 tablespoons pesto sauce
1/4 cup sliced black olives, well drained
1/2 cup thinly sliced green onion
Salt and freshly ground black pepper
Garnish: 1/4 cup Parmesan cheese

Cook pasta in a large pot of boiling, salted water for 7 minutes. Add sugar snap peas and cook for 3 minutes. Add red bell pepper, return water to a boil for 30 to 60 seconds, or until pepper strips are slightly softened. Drain well. Meanwhile combine cream, chicken stock and crushed red pepper in a saucepan. Boil 3 minutes or until it is reduced to half. Remove from heat. Stir in Parmesan cheese and pesto sauce. Pour sauce over pasta; add green onions and black olives. Toss until sauce coats pasta; season to taste with salt and pepper. Garnish with additional Parmesan cheese. Makes 6 servings. From Bonnie Aeschliman.

HEAVENLY GARLIC SPAGHETTI

Oh, the way the warm spaghetti melts the cheese, cooking the egg and turning this into something heavenly ... mmm.

8 ounces spinach linguine (or regular spaghetti)
1 egg
5 to 7 cloves garlic, peeled and pressed
4 tablespoons butter
1/2 cup grated Parmesan cheese

1 teaspoon dried sweet basil
1/4 cup finely chopped parsley
Freshly ground black pepper
Garnish: Red pepper flakes, Parmesan cheese

Cook spaghetti in boiling water, and while cooking combine egg, garlic, butter, cheese and basil in a blender. When spaghetti is cooked al dente and drained, place in large bowl and spoon over the cheese-garlic mixture. Add parsley and pepper and toss. Serve with red pepper flakes and grated Parmesan cheese. Makes 2 to 4 servings, either as an entrée or a side dish. Inspired by the Dairy Hollow House.

CURRIED FRUIT COMPOTE

1/3 cup butter	1 (16-ounce) can of pears, drained
3/4 cup packed light brown sugar	1 (16-ounce) can of sliced peaches, drained
4 teaspoons curry	1 (17-ounce) can of apricot halves, drained
1 teaspoon cinnamon	1 (13-ounce) can of pineapple chunks, drained
1/2 teaspoon nutmeg	Maraschino cherries, as desired (optional)
1/4 cup honey	1 (2 3/4-ounce) package slivered almonds, toasted (optional)

Fruit dishes to also consider as side dishes are found in the salad chapter (pp. 58-60) as well as fruits with dessert sauces (pp. 58 and 267).

Preheat oven to 325°F. Melt butter with brown sugar and curry. Add cinnamon, nutmeg, and honey. Drain fruit and arrange in a 9 x 13-inch pan, dotting with maraschino cherries if desired. Drizzle sauce over arranged fruit. Top with almonds, if desired, and bake for 1 hour. Serve hot. Makes 8 servings.

SPICED PEACHES

1 (29-ounce) can peach halves	2 cinnamon sticks
1/2 cup packed brown sugar	1 teaspoon whole cloves
1/2 cup white wine vinegar	1 teaspoon ground allspice

Drain peaches and reserve syrup. In a medium sized pan, combine syrup, brown sugar, vinegar, cinnamon, cloves and allspice, and heat over medium-high heat to bring to a boil. Add peaches and simmer for 5 minutes. Refrigerate overnight in syrup, along with the cinnamon sticks. For less "bite," use less vinegar. Serve in a compote cup, or on the side of a main entrée with peach on a lettuce leaf.

FROZEN PEACHES

A dry sugar pack is an easy way to put up peaches in small quantities. Prepare 8 to 10 ripe peaches at a time. Wash and pit, and peel by quickly dipping in boiling water to loosen skin. Add ascorbic acid (such as "Fruit Fresh") as directed on product label, to 3 cups of sugar. Slice peaches directly into pint freezer containers, alternating fruit and sugar mixture. Add sugar lightly at first, increasing near top. Shake container to distribute sugar, making sure that top slices are coated. Try a scant 1/4 cup of sugar for each pint of fruit, but adjust to individual taste. Seal, date and freeze. Keeps well for up to one year. Thaw in refrigerator and serve cold or even a little slushy. One pint makes 6 servings.

HOT CHEESY PINEAPPLE

This very retro and hot pineapple dish sounds strange, but has been a hit since the '60s.

8 ounces grated Cheddar cheese	1 (20-ounce) can pineapple chunks (2 1/2 cups)
1/2 cup flour	and reserved juice
1/3 cup sugar	

Preheat oven to 300°F. Combine cheese, flour and sugar. In a 1 1/2 quart casserole dish (8 x 8-inch), alternate layers of pineapple and cheese mixture. Pour 3 tablespoons of reserved juice over layers. Bake for 45 minutes. Serve hot. Makes 4 servings; doubles easily. May also increase heat of oven to 350°F and bake for just 20 minutes if the timing and oven temperature works better for your meal plan.

RUTH'S SWEET DILL PICKLES

2 (1-quart) jars whole dill pickles	4 cups sugar
2 cups vinegar	1 1/2 tablespoons pickling spices
1 cup water	

This no-cook method, also described by M.F.K. Fisher, makes crisp "candied" pickles because sugar draws out juice from the dills. "Zesty-type" dills make especially flavorful ones. Some add a few drops of green food coloring.

Pour off all the brine from the pickles. Remove pickles from the jar; wash and slice 1/4-inch thick. Return to jars. Combine vinegar, water, sugar, and spices and bring to boil. Pour hot liquid over pickles and seal jar. Put into refrigerator immediately. Ready to serve in 4 hours. If you desire, when jars are empty you may save the liquid and add a little more vinegar for the next batch. From Shirley Beggs.

Mastering Muffins

Vigorous batter stirring creates tough muffins with pointed tops. Stir only until dry ingredients are moistened. Lumps will disappear during baking.

Grease muffin pans with shortening or nonstick cooking spray, not butter.

Never grease muffin cups that won't be used. Place an ice cube or several tablespoons of water in unused cups to prevent warping the pan.

Use a large spoon sprayed with nonstick cooking spray, or a cookie scoop, to transfer the batter in even amounts into the cups of the muffin tins.

Muffins are done when tops are domed and dry to the touch, or when a toothpick comes out clean.

MORNING GLORY MUFFINS

Previous page:

Benjamin Kopman
Flowers, 1937, oil on canvas, WAM, gift of Mr. and Mrs. Kurt A. Olden, 1983.23

These little carrot cake muffins, plumped up with apples, coconut and pecans, are always popular. The recipe originally came from the Morning Glory Café in Nantucket, and the recipe spread quickly. Variations have even been published in many places, including the New York Times, and Gourmet magazine even named it one of the "50 Baking Favorites" in 1991. I had to laugh though when I saw it served now at Starbuck's cafés. This recipe doubles well. [Editor's note: In recalling how popular these muffins were at church gatherings, Dr. Meyers, Carlene's minister called these "Carlenes".]

2 cups unbleached flour
1 1/4 cups sugar, plus additional for sprinkling
2 teaspoons baking soda
2 teaspoons cinnamon
1/2 teaspoon salt
2 cups peeled and grated carrots (about 5 carrots)

1 apple, peeled, cored, and shredded (prefer Granny Smith apple)
1/2 cup raisins or currants
1/2 cup sweetened shredded coconut
1/2 cup chopped pecans (or walnuts)
3 eggs, lightly beaten
1 cup vegetable oil
2 teaspoons vanilla extract

Preheat oven to 400°F. Grease 18 muffin cups or line with paper or foil baking cups. In a large bowl, stir together flour, sugar, baking soda, cinnamon and salt. Stir in carrots, apples, raisins, coconut and nuts. In a medium-sized bowl whisk together eggs, oil and vanilla. Add to the dry ingredients and stir just until the dry ingredients are moistened. Spoon into the muffin cups and sprinkle sugar on tops before baking. Bake for 20 minutes or until the tops are golden and spring back when touched. Cool in pan for 5 minutes then turn out onto a wire rack to cool. Eat immediately, or even better, wait 24 hours and savor. Keeps for 2 to 3 days. Makes 18 muffins or 7 dozen mini-muffins.

Variation: add 1 cup canned crushed pineapple, drained, to the batter along with the carrots and apples.

LEMON GLAZED BLUEBERRY MUFFINS

This sour cream batter makes for a great blueberry muffin and the lemon glaze and topping take it to perfection.

2 cups unbleached flour
1 tablespoon baking powder
1/2 teaspoon salt
1 egg
1 cup sugar
4 tablespoons butter, melted

1 1/4 cups sour cream
1 1/2 cups frozen or fresh blueberries
1/4 cup fresh lemon juice
1/4 cup sugar
For lemon sugar topping: 1 teaspoon grated
    lemon rind added to 1/2 cup sugar

Tossing berries or nuts into flour before adding to the muffin batter keeps them from sinking to the bottom of the muffin.

Preheat oven to 350°F. Grease a 12 cup muffin tin. Combine flour, baking powder and salt in a bowl. Whisk the egg in a separate bowl for about 30 seconds, add the sugar and continue to whisk vigorously for another 30 seconds; slowly add the butter (melted but slightly cooled), whisking between each addition. Add sour cream in 2 steps, and whisk to combine. Combine berries with the flour mixture and toss to coat. Fold in to the sour cream egg mixture just until the batter comes together. Do not over stir; small spots of flour are fine. Divide the batter into the muffin cups. Bake for 25 to 30 minutes, transfer muffins to a wire rack and cool 5 minutes before glazing.

To prepare the glaze, combine the lemon juice and 1/4 cup sugar in a small saucepan, bring to a simmer, stirring to dissolve the sugar and simmering until mixture is thick and reduced to about 1/4 cup. Brush tops with glaze, then dip each top in lemon sugar. Set upright on a wire rack to cool. Makes 2 dozen.

LINGONBERRY MUFFINS

1/2 cup plus 2 teaspoons butter,
    room temperature
3/4 cup sugar
2 eggs
1 1/4 cups flour

1 teaspoon baking powder
1 teaspoon vanilla extract
1/4 cup water
1/2 cup canned lingonberries
Powdered sugar

Lingonberries are tart red berries that grow wild in the mountainous regions of northern Europe, Canada, and Maine in the U.S. They can be purchased packed in jars with syrup.

Preheat oven to 400°F. Grease a 12 cup muffin tin. Beat butter and sugar until creamy. Add eggs, one at a time. Add flour and baking powder, blending well. Add vanilla and pour in water, just mixing until incorporated. Divide batter into muffin cups and top with berries. Bake 15 minutes, remove from oven and sprinkle with powdered sugar. Makes 1 dozen.

PEACH MUFFINS

1 1/2 cups flour
1 cup sugar
3/4 teaspoon salt
1/2 teaspoon baking soda
2 eggs
1/2 cup vegetable oil

1/2 teaspoon vanilla extract
1/4 teaspoon almond extract
1 1/4 cups peeled, chopped peaches (or 1
    [16-ounce] can chopped peaches, drained)
1/2 cup chopped toasted almonds

Preheat oven to 375°F. Grease a 12 cup muffin tin. Whisk together flour, sugar, salt and baking soda in a large bowl. In a separate bowl, beat together the eggs, oil, vanilla and almond extract; add to the flour mixture and stir just until moistened. Fold in the peaches and almonds. Divide into muffin cups and bake for 20 minutes. Remove to a wire rack to cool. Makes 1 dozen.

Henry Varnum Poor
Family Tea Set, 1940,
tin-glazed earthenware,
WAM, Burneta Adair
Endowment, Fund,
2006.15,
(detail opposite page)

Photo by Ric Wolford

SIX-WEEK BRAN MUFFINS

This is an old standby; so handy to have in the refrigerator, ready for great morning muffins.

5 cups flour
3 cups sugar
1 (12-ounce) package bran flakes cereal
   with raisins
5 teaspoons baking soda
2 teaspoons salt

1 teaspoon cinnamon
1/2 teaspoon ground allspice
4 eggs, beaten
4 cups (1 quart) buttermilk
1 cup vegetable oil
1 (14-ounce) can crushed pineapple

Preheat oven to 400°F. Grease muffin cups. In a large bowl combine the flour, sugar, cereal, baking soda, salt, cinnamon, and allspice. Add eggs, buttermilk, oil and pineapple. (Batter keeps for up to 6 weeks in a covered container in the refrigerator.) Pour batter into muffin tins. Bake for 15 to 20 minutes. Remove to a wire rack to cool. Makes 5 dozen muffins. From Karen Root.

BRAN MUFFINS

1 cup raisins
1 tablespoon baking soda
1 cup boiling water
1 cup sugar
1/2 cup butter
2 eggs
2 cups flour
1/2 teaspoon salt

1 cup All Bran cereal
2 cups Raisin Bran cereal
3/4 cup coarsely chopped walnuts
2 tablespoons sugar
1 teaspoon cinnamon
2 cups buttermilk
Grape Nuts cereal

Generously butter large muffin tins or line with paper or foil baking cups. In a small bowl combine the raisins, baking soda and boiling water. Let cool. In a large mixing bowl cream together 1 cup of sugar, butter and eggs. Add the flour and salt. Stir until blended. Stir in the cooled raisin mixture just until combined. Pour the cereals, walnuts, 2 tablespoons of sugar and cinnamon over the mixture. Do not stir. Cover and refrigerate for up to 2 weeks, if desired. When ready to serve, add the buttermilk and stir just until blended. Fill each muffin cup two-thirds full. Sprinkle with 1/2 teaspoon of Grape Nuts cereal. Bake in 375°F oven for 20 minutes. Make about 3 dozen.

CARAMEL APPLE MUFFINS

Tart apples and caramel: a classic combination enjoyed in these attractive and tasty muffins. An inexpensive apple corer is the secret to perfectly shaped apples rings. This moist batter may be baked in muffin pans, loaf pans or an 8-inch round pan. Adapted from a community recipe which also appeared in Southern Living *magazine.*

1 (3 pounds) bag small tart apples, 12 to
    14 apples
2 cups sugar
1 cup vegetable oil
3 eggs, lightly beaten
2 teaspoons vanilla extract
3 cups flour
2 teaspoons cinnamon
1 teaspoon baking soda

1/2 teaspoon salt
2 1/2 cups chopped pecans, toasted and divided

Quick Caramel Frosting
2 (14-ounce) cans sweetened condensed milk
1/2 cup firmly packed light brown sugar
1/2 cup butter
1 teaspoon vanilla extract

Peel, core and cut 4 apples into 24 (1/4-inch thick) rings. Preheat oven to 350°F. Sauté apple rings, in batches, in a lightly greased skillet over medium heat, 1 to 2 minutes on each side or until lightly browned. Remove from skillet, and place 1 apple ring in the bottom of each of 24 lightly greased muffin pan cups. Peel and finely chop enough remaining apples to equal 3 cups. Set aside. Stir sugar, oil, eggs and vanilla together in a large bowl. In another large bowl stir together flour, cinnamon, baking soda and salt; add sugar mixture, stirring just until blended (batter will be stiff). Fold in finely chopped apples and 1 cup pecans. Spoon batter evenly over apple rings in muffin pan cups, filling cups three quarters full. Bake for 25 minutes or until wooden pick inserted in center comes out clean. Remove muffins from pan, and cool, apple ring up, on a wire rack. Press the handle of a wooden spoon gently into the center of each apple ring, forming a 1-inch deep indentation in the muffins. While muffins are cooking, prepare frosting by mixing ingredients in saucepan, cooking over medium-low heat, stirring constantly for 3 to 5 minutes, until it has a pudding-like consistency. Spoon warm Quick Caramel Frosting evenly over muffins, filling indentations. Sprinkle evenly with remaining 1 1/2 cup chopped pecans. Makes 2 dozen muffins.

Variations:
Caramel-Apple Coffee Cakes   Omit apple rings and prepare apple muffin batter as directed. Divide batter evenly between 2 greased and floured 8-inch round baking pans. Bake at 350°F for 45 to 50 minutes or until a wooden pick inserted in center comes out clean. Remove from pans, and cool on wire racks. Spoon warm Quick Caramel Frosting evenly over coffee cakes; sprinkle tops with remaining 1 1/2 cups chopped pecans. Makes 16 servings.

Apple Bread   Omit apple rings and prepare apple muffin batter as directed. Divide batter evenly between 2 greased and floured 9 x 5 inch loaf pans. Bake at 350°F for 1 hour or until wooden pick inserted in center comes out clean. Remove from pans after 5 minutes and cool on wire racks. Spoon Quick Caramel Frosting over top and sprinkle with 1 1/2 cups pecans. Makes two 9-inch loaves.

Henry Varnum Poor, born in Chapman in 1887, is one of the most successful artists to hail from Kansas (See self portrait on p. 247).

He was a Renaissance man and an artist-craftsman. On picturesque land off the Hudson River outside of New York City he built Crow House, an Arts and Crafts house and studio. Poor was one of the first American fine artists to produce functional ceramics. From the 1920s his pots were exhibited in New York galleries otherwise devoted solely to painting and sculpture. In the 1950s Mrs. Navas purchased three of his ceramics for the Art Museum collection.

In 1940 he produced a masterpiece of modern craft: a tea set in which each piece was uniquely decorated with events from the life of the family. The two teapots commemorate two novels written by his wife Bessie Breuer Poor. A saucer shows daughter Annie playing the piano. Another commemorates the birth of son Peter (p. 135). It is inscribed, "Earth I am it is most true; disdain me not for so are you," a truism of both ceramics and children. - SG

PECAN PIE MUFFINS

These delicious little bites are more like a crustless pecan pie than a muffin. Making them in a miniature muffin tin is my favorite way; nice to serve perched on the side of a plate or a great tidbit for a holiday or dessert buffet. Use a liner (foil looks great) as the middles are a bit gooey.

1 cup chopped pecans
1 cup packed light brown sugar
$^1/_2$ cup flour

2 eggs
$^1/_2$ cup butter, melted
Garnish: 36 pecan halves

Preheat oven to 350°F. Mix all ingredients together in a bowl with a wooden spoon. Place foil baking papers in muffin tin and coat with cooking spray. Spoon batter into cups, filling two-thirds full. Garnish each with a pecan half. If using large muffin tin, bake for 20 to 25 minutes or until done; for a mini-muffin tin, bake for 12 to 15 minutes. Remove from pans immediately, cool on wire racks or serve warm. Makes $2^1/_2$ dozen mini-muffins or 9 large muffins.

PECAN SWEET POTATO MUFFINS

A moist muffin sweetened with dates; eat for breakfast or serve with an entrée like grilled pork.

$1^3/_4$ cups all-purpose flour
1 teaspoon baking soda
$^1/_2$ teaspoon cinnamon
$^1/_4$ teaspoon salt
2 eggs
1 cup sugar
$^1/_2$ cup packed brown sugar
$^1/_2$ cup vegetable oil
1 (17–ounce) can sweet potatoes, drained
 and mashed

$^1/_2$ chopped pecans
1 cup chopped dates (or currants)
$^1/_4$ cup flour

Topping
$^1/_4$ cup pecans, chopped
$^1/_4$ teaspoon cinnamon
$^1/_4$ teaspoon ginger

Preheat oven to 350°F. Combine flour, baking soda, cinnamon and salt in a large bowl; make a well in center of mixture. Combine eggs, sugars, oil and sweet potatoes in a bowl; beat at medium speed with an electric mixer until blended. Add sweet potato mixture to flour mixture; stir until moist. Dredge pecans and dates in $^1/_4$ cup flour; fold into batter. (May also add $^1/_2$ cup of flaked coconut if desired.) Spoon into greased muffin pans, filling three-fourths full. Mix together topping ingredients; sprinkle over top of batter in pan. Bake for 27 to 30 minutes. Remove from pans immediately. Makes 18 muffins. If baking in mini-muffin pans, cook at 350°F for 12 to 14 minutes. Makes 48 mini-muffins.

QUICK PRAIRIE CORN MUFFINS

The secret to cornbread with real corn taste is to simply add corn, not just corn meal. Briefly purée $^3/_4$ cup of thawed frozen corn in blender. Using corn muffin mix (suggest Betty Crocker brand), make according to package directions, adding $^3/_4$ cup of the puréed corn. Bake according to mix instructions in medium size muffin pan. Makes 11 muffins.

Other nice additions to corn muffin mix include chopped canned jalapenos (seeded) or chopped red peppers (which add some great color), chopped green onions and cheddar cheese.

"The sun shines, the rain falls, and the dry kernel becomes plump and sends forth a sprout, and lo, the first green leaf.

The scent of a field of corn is honey-sweet, a trifle musky. You can hear the cornstalks grow. On a warm summer night the corn talks. It cracks its knuckles and seems to chuckle to itself."

- Elizabeth Landeweer

CORN MUFFINS with RASPBERRIES

These excellent corn muffins are very moist, and great with or without the raspberries. However, the raspberry preserves nicely complement the cornbread and make for an attractive muffin with this technique popularized by the "Barefoot Contessa". The batter may be made the day before and refrigerated to be breakfast-ready.

3 cups flour
1 cup sugar
1 cup yellow cornmeal
2 tablespoons baking powder
1 1/2 teaspoons salt

1 1/2 cups whole milk
1 cup unsalted butter, melted and cooled
2 extra large eggs
Sanding or granulated sugar for topping
3/4 cup good raspberry preserves

Preheat oven to 350°F. Line 12 large muffin cups with paper liners. Mix flour, sugar, cornmeal, baking powder and salt together in a large bowl. In a separate bowl, combine milk, melted butter and eggs. With the mixer on the low speed, pour the milk mixture into the flour mixture and stir until they are just blended. Spoon the batter into paper liners, filling each one to the top. Bake for 30 minutes, or until the tops are crisp and a toothpick comes out clean. As they come out of the oven sprinkle with sanding or coarse granulated sugar. Cool slightly and remove from the pan. After the muffins cool, place raspberry preserves into a pastry bag fitted with a large round tip. Poke the pastry bag tip through the top of the muffin and pipe 1 to 2 tablespoons of preserves into the middle. Repeat for each muffin. Makes 12 large muffins.

Grant Wood
Fertility, 1937, lithograph, WAM, gift of the Friends of the Wichita Art Museum, Inc., 1987.37, ©Estate of Grant Wood/ Licensed by VAGA, New York, NY

SCONES

Many scones turn out like hockey pucks, but not these. These are all light, moist and delicious. The secret to a flaky scone is to not overblend the butter. A time saver tip is that you may cut out scones ahead of time, store covered in the refrigerator for two or three days, and bake just before serving.

Scones orginated in Scotland. Their name came from the stone which was in front of where Scottish kings were crowned. The stone was called a scone, in the shape of its food counterpart.

CRANBERRY-ORANGE SCONES

These are so good that English women asked for the recipe when Cindy and family were living in London.

2 cups flour
1 tablespoon baking powder
1/2 teaspoon baking soda
1/4 teaspoon salt
3 tablespoons sugar (divided use)
1 tablespoon grated orange rind

1/2 cup butter, chilled
2/3 cup buttermilk
1 cup dried cranberries
1 tablespoon milk

Preheat oven to 425°F. Combine flour, baking powder, baking soda, salt, 2 tablespoons sugar, and grated orange rind. Cut butter into 1/2-inch cubes and add to the flour mixture with a pastry blender, until mixture is crumbly (or use a food processor and pulse about 15 times). Add buttermilk and dried cranberries, stirring just until moistened. Turn dough out onto a lightly floured surface, knead 5 or 6 times. Pat into an 8-inch circle. Cut into 8 wedges, and place 1 inch apart on a lightly greased baking sheet. Brush with milk, and sprinkle with 1 tablespoon sugar. Bake for 15 minutes or until golden brown. Makes 8 scones. From Cindy Banks.

PEACHY KEEN SCONES

6 cups flour
1 1/4 cups sugar (divided use)
1/4 cup baking powder
1/4 teaspoon salt
1 1/2 cups butter, chilled

1 1/2 to 2 cups buttermilk
1/2 cup peach jam
1 (8-ounce) package frozen peaches, thawed and drained

Preheat oven to 425°F. Combine flour, sugar, baking powder and salt. Cut butter into 1/2-inch cubes and add to the flour mixture with a pastry blender, until mixture is crumbly. (Alternatively use a food processor and pulse about 15 times). Slowly pour in buttermilk, adding enough until dough begins to form a ball. Place dough ball on lightly floured surface and pat it into a rectangle about 12 inches x 10 inches (should be about 1/4-inch thick). Spread a layer of jam over half of the dough (lengthwise) and arrange the peach slices in a layer on top of the jam. Fold the plain half of the dough over the jam half to make a 12 x 5-inch rectangle with jam and peaches all folded inside. Cut dough into 10 triangles and sprinkle the tops with remaining 1/4 cup of sugar. Bake on ungreased heavy baking sheet for 10 to 15 minutes until light golden brown. Makes 10 large scones.

BACON AND CHEDDAR SCONES

3 cups flour
1 tablespoon baking powder
1 teaspoon salt
2 teaspoons freshly ground black pepper
1/2 cup chilled, unsalted butter
1 1/2 cups grated Cheddar cheese
4 green onions, thinly sliced

10 slices bacon, cooked and chopped into
    1-inch pieces (prefer applewood
    smoked bacon)
1 to 1 1/2 cups buttermilk
1 large egg
2 tablespoons water

Preheat oven to 400°F. Combine flour, baking powder, salt and black pepper in a large bowl. Cut butter into 1/2-inch cubes and gradually add to the flour mixture with a pastry blender, until mixture is crumbly. Add grated cheese and blend by hand. Stir in green onions, bacon and 1 cup of the buttermilk, mix until just incorporated and dough forms a ball. Add additional buttermilk if needed, but avoid over-stirring in order to keep these light. Place dough on a lightly floured surface and pat into an 8-inch circle. Cut the dough into 8 wedges. Whisk egg and water together, brush this on each wedge. Place 1 inch apart on an ungreased baking sheet and bake for 18 to 20 minutes until golden brown. Makes 8 scones.

AUSTRIAN KUCHEN

Dr. Stephen Gleissner shares the signature pastry of his grandmother, Josephine Gleissner. "Like many exceptional cooks of her day, she never wrote out her recipes and steadfastly refused to do so. I obtained the recipe by making the kuchen with her over the course of a summer month spent at the family farm. The scone will never rise again!"

2/3 cup milk
1/2 cup sugar
1 1/4 teaspoons salt
6 tablespoons shortening
2/3 cup tepid water
3 teaspoons sugar
3 packets yeast (7 1/2 teaspoons)
3 beaten eggs

6 cups sifted flour (divided use)

Topping
3/4 cup sugar
1/4 cup flour
2 tablespoons plus 2 teaspoons butter

Filling (see suggestions below)

In a small saucepan, scald milk over medium-high heat. Add sugar, salt and shortening and stir. In a bowl combine water, sugar, and yeast and let this stand until properly dissolved, then add milk mixture to it. Add eggs and 3 cups flour and beat all together until smooth. Beat in another 3 cups of flour gradually. Be careful not to let the dough get too dry, for water added after this stage will result in a hard dough and the tops of your kuchen will crack. You may not need all of the flour.

Turn the dough onto a floured board and knead vigorously, without turning or folding the dough over itself. Place the dough in a greased bowl and coat the top with shortening; cover with a towel and let double in size (about one hour, depending on the room temperature). Punch down and let rise again.

Preheat oven to 400°F. In a small bowl, combine the topping ingredients. Pull tablespoon amounts of dough from the ball and form into flat rounds. Add a heaping teaspoon of your filling of choice (see below), close up, and place on greased cookie sheet. Let them double in size (15 to 30 minutes), brush with melted butter, and cover with the topping. Bake for about 15 minutes or until browned.

Fillings: Many work beautifully: sweetened cherries were the favorite of most. Grandmother's favorite (and mine) was the following: poppyseed, currants, scant sugar, lemon zest, and a dash of vanilla. From Stephen Gleissner.

CRANBERRY SOUR CREAM COFFEE CAKE with STREUSEL TOPPING

Streusel Topping

$^1/_2$ cup cold butter, cut into 8 pieces
$^1/_4$ cup sugar
$^3/_4$ cup plus 2 tablespoons flour

Cake

$1^1/_4$ cups sour cream
$1^1/_4$ teaspoon baking soda
$^1/_8$ teaspoon salt

$^1/_2$ cup butter, room temperature
$1^1/_4$ cups sugar
2 eggs, lightly beaten
$1^3/_4$ cups flour
$1^3/_4$ teaspoons baking powder
$^1/_2$ cup semisweet chocolate chips
$^1/_2$ cups dried cranberries, soaked in warm water
    for 15 minutes, drained

To make the streusel topping, combine butter, sugar and flour in a chilled bowl. Using a pastry blender or two knives, cut the butter into the dry ingredients until it is the consistency of fine, moist bread crumbs. Work the mixture with your hands until it will hold together, then compress into several firm pieces. Cover and refrigerate until the cake is ready to go into the oven.

Preheat oven to 350°F. Grease a 9 x 13-inch baking dish with butter. Place sour cream in a bowl and sift baking soda and salt into it; stir to blend and set aside. In a large bowl, using an electric mixer on medium speed, beat together the butter, sugar and eggs until fluffy, about 3 minutes. Sift flour and baking powder over the top and mix in, then stir in the sour cream mixture. Scatter the chocolate chips and drained cranberries (may need to pat dry) over the top and just barely mix in with a spatula. Scoop batter into baking dish and smooth. Scatter the streusel evenly over the top, breaking it up into large $^3/_4$-inch pieces. Bake until a toothpick inserted into the center comes out clean but not completely dry, about 40 to 45 minutes. Transfer to a wire rack to cool. Serve warm or at room temperature, cut into squares. Makes 10 servings.

LAYERED PECAN SOUR CREAM COFFEE CAKE with CHOCOLATE GLAZE

This is a great coffee cake to serve for a special brunch along with a breakfast casserole (p. 182) and curried fruit (p.163). Baked in a bundt pan, the cake is attractive when inverted with visible layers of nuts and topped with a subtle chocolate glaze.

Cake
1 cup butter or margarine, softened
2 cups sugar
2 eggs
2 cups flour
1 1/2 teaspoons baking powder
1/2 teaspoon salt
1 cup sour cream
1/2 teaspoon vanilla extract

Pecan Streusel Layer
1 cup chopped pecans
2 tablespoons granulated sugar
1 teaspoon cinnamon

Chocolate Glaze
1/2 cup semisweet chocolate chips
1/4 cup butter or margarine

Preheat oven to 350°F. For the cake, cream butter and sugar in a large bowl until fluffy. Add eggs, beating until smooth. In a medium bowl, combine flour, baking powder, and salt. Gradually add dry ingredients to creamed mixture, blending well. Gently fold in sour cream and vanilla. For the streusel layer, combine pecans, sugar, and cinnamon in a small bowl. To make the chocolate glaze, melt chocolate chips and butter in a small saucepan over low heat, stirring until smooth.

To assemble, sprinkle 2 tablespoons of streusel layer in bottom of greased and floured 9-inch bundt pan. Spoon half of cake batter into pan. Sprinkle 4 tablespoons streusel over batter and drizzle half of glaze over it. Spoon in remainder of batter, sprinkle remainder of streusel. Reserve remaining glaze. Bake 1 to 1 1/4 hours or until toothpick inserted in center of cake comes out clean. Cool in pan. Invert and transfer to a serving plate. Reheat remaining glaze and drizzle over cake. Makes about 16 servings.

NIGHT BEFORE COFFEE CAKE

This excellent yet simple coffee cake may be prepared one day in advance, or baked immediately. It is nice to try different ingredients (raisins, nuts, dates or combinations of them) in the topping.

Cake
2/3 cup butter, softened
1 cup sugar
1/2 cup brown sugar, packed
2 eggs
2 cups flour
1 teaspoon baking powder
1 teaspoon baking soda
1 teaspoon cinnamon

1/4 teaspoon salt
1 cup buttermilk (or sour milk)
1/2 cup raisins, pecans, walnuts or dates (all 3 can be used in various combinations to make up 1/2 cup)

Topping
1/2 cup brown sugar
1 teaspoon cinnamon

In a large bowl, cream butter and sugars with mixer. Add eggs, one at a time, beating slightly after each addition. Whisk dry ingredients together in a separate bowl. Alternately add flour mixture and buttermilk to butter-egg mixture. Add raisins, nuts or dates. Pour batter into a greased 9 x 13-inch pan. Combine cinnamon and brown sugar, sprinkle topping on cake and cover tightly with foil until next morning. Uncover and let stand about 30 minutes at room temperature before baking. Bake in a 350°F preheated oven for 35 to 40 minutes. It's best served warm. Try drizzling coffee cake with a thin powdered sugar frosting before serving. Makes 10 to 12 servings.

Variation: add 1 cup of apples, peeled, cored and chopped to batter.

FRENCH TOAST BRULEE

When you invert the French toast onto plates it has a great golden-brown caramel topping and you won't need syrup. Variations of this dish have been made popular by Bed and Breakfast establishments, where hosts seek great, make-ahead recipes. Your guests will be delighted too.

$^1/_2$ cup butter, melted
1 cup packed brown sugar
2 tablespoons light corn syrup
1 loaf French bread, crust removed and cut into
   1-inch slices
5 eggs

1 $^1/_2$ cups half-and-half (or milk works fine)
1 teaspoon vanilla extract
2 teaspoons Grand Marnier (or other orange
   flavored liqueur) (optional)
$^1/_4$ teaspoon salt
Powdered sugar

Combine butter, brown sugar and syrup. Pour into bottom of 9 x 13-inch baking dish. Arrange bread slices in single layer in baking dish, packing tightly. Place eggs in a bowl; whisk to blend. Whisk in half-and-half, vanilla, Grand Marnier and salt. Pour evenly over bread. Cover and refrigerate 8 to 24 hours.

Preheat oven to 350°F. Bake, uncovered, in middle of oven until puffed and edges are golden, 35 to 40 minutes. Dust with powdered sugar before serving. Makes 8 to 10 servings. From Bonnie Aeschilman.

COLORADO GRANOLA

Jeanne Gordon received this yummy granola recipe from her daughter Genevieve after she worked in Colorado one summer, and it became a standard in their kitchen. She likes to add golden raisins to this recipe too, and if so, may reduce some of the dried fruit. Other good additions are sesame, pumpkin and sunflower seeds.

Granola became popularized in the late 1970s as a "health food", bursting onto the food scene along with yogurt at a time when we only had cereals like frosted cornflakes.

10 cups old-fashioned rolled oats
1 cup nuts (any kind except peanuts)
3 cups wheat germ
1 cup shredded coconut, unsweetened
1 cup canola oil

1 $^1/_2$ cups honey
2 cups brown sugar
3 cups dried fruits (apricots, cherries, figs, etc)
1 $^1/_4$ cup raisins

Granola long ago moved to the main grocery aisle, but it is nice to make your own, adjusting to taste and having an especially good fresh flavor from roasting.

Mix oats, nuts, wheat germ and coconut together on a sheet pan. Toast in 350°F oven until coconut is browned, stirring often to toast evenly. Put in a large bowl and reserve. Bring oil, honey, and brown sugar to a full rolling boil; stir until all sugar is dissolved. Pour hot syrup mixture over mix and stir until well coated. Add dried fruits and mix well. Pack into sheet pans and cool thoroughly. Break up cooled granola and store in an airtight container in the refrigerator. Some people prefer to bake the granola again on sheet pans after it has been combined wih the hot syrup. From Jeanne Gordon.

Vary fruit, nuts and seeds to taste. Some good additions include pumpkin seeds, chopped walnuts or raisins.

CRANBERRY APRICOT GRANOLA

Kept in a countertop glass jar it makes a good breakfast cereal or a snack mix.

$^3/_4$ cup canola oil
$^1/_2$ cup honey
1 cup packed golden brown sugar
1 tablespoon vanilla extract
$^1/_2$ teaspoon salt
8 cups old-fashioned rolled oats

$^1/_2$ cup unsalted sunflower seeds (hulled)
$^1/_2$ cup sweetened flaked coconut
1 cup sliced almonds (or coarsely chopped)
1 cup chopped dried apricots
1 cup dried cranberries

Preheat oven to 325°F. Combine oil, honey, brown sugar, vanilla and salt in a saucepan and stir over medium heat until sugar dissolves, remove from heat. Combine oats, sunflower seeds, coconut and almonds in a large bowl, stir and then add warm oil mixture, stirring carefully to combine. Spread evenly on two baking sheets, and bake for 20 minutes, stirring twice. Cool completely and add apricots and cranberries. Store in an airtight container. Makes 14 cups of granola.

FARMHOUSE YEAST WAFFLES

This recipe, from the 1896 edition of the "Fannie Farmer Cookbook", has won many accolades and was a farmhouse favorite. While it uses yeast, you simply leave it in a warm place overnight (no kneading required), and it is ready to use in the morning. It is a good standard waffle recipe that always brings compliments, and fills the kitchen with the wonderful aroma of baking bread.

MENU:
*BREAKFAST
FOR SUPPER*

*Farmhouse Yeast
Waffles 177*

Applewood Smoked Bacon

*Broiled Grapefruit with
Vanilla Sugar*

$^1/_2$ cup warm water
$2^1/_2$ teaspoons (1 package) active dry yeast,
   or 2 teaspoons instant yeast
2 cups milk, warmed
$^1/_2$ cup butter, melted

1 teaspoon salt
1 teaspoon sugar
2 cups flour
2 eggs
$^1/_4$ teaspoon baking soda

Use a rather large mixing bowl, as the batter will rise to double in size. The night before you intend to make the waffles, put the water in the mixing bowl and sprinkle in the yeast. Let stand for 5 minutes to dissolve. Add the milk, melted butter, salt, sugar and flour to the yeast mixture and beat until smooth and well blended (a hand mixer works well, beat just enough to get rid of the lumps). Cover with plastic wrap and let stand overnight at room temperature. The batter will rise an inch or two and bubble on the surface.

Just before cooking, beat in the eggs, add the baking soda and stir until well mixed (the batter will be very thin). Pour about $^1/_2$ to $^3/_4$ cup batter onto a very hot waffle iron. Bake until golden and crisp. Batter will keep for several days in the refrigerator. Makes 8 waffles.

BUTTERMILK WAFFLES

3 cups flour
3 teaspoons baking powder
1 teaspoon salt
1 teaspoon soda

1 tablespoon sugar
3 eggs, beaten
3 cups buttermilk (divided use)
6 to 8 tablespoons butter, melted

Sift together (or whisk together) the flour, baking powder, salt, soda and sugar. Beat eggs until fluffy. Add 2 cups buttermilk. Add liquids to dry ingredients and add the rest of the buttermilk and butter. Add more buttermilk if thinner batter is desired. Pour onto hot waffle iron. Super served with hot buttered syrup with rum flavoring. Makes 10 to 12.

BELGIAN WAFFLES

4 cups flour
$^1/_2$ teaspoon salt
$^1/_2$ cup powdered sugar
2 cups water

3 eggs, separated
$^1/_2$ cup butter. softened
2 cups milk

Whisk together flour, salt, sugar, water and egg yolks in a medium bowl. Add butter and beat until smooth; add milk and beat until smooth. In another bowl, beat egg whites to stiff peaks. With a spatula, carefully fold whites into batter just until incorporated. Preheat Belgian waffle maker and cook waffles according to manufacturer's instructions. Top waffles with syrup, fresh whipped cream and/or fresh berries. Makes 12 waffles.

ANDY'S FAVORITE SMOOTHIE

Grandson Andy has become a smoothie expert, burning out several "Magic Bullet" machines while keeping us all nicely served. It's great to see what he will invent in the kitchen and we like this one very much.

1 cup frozen strawberries
1 medium banana, peeled and sliced

1 cup yogurt (any kind)
$^1/_4$ cup fruit juice or milk

Place all ingredients into a blender, purée until smooth (about 1 minute). Serve! Makes 1 serving.

PERFECT PANCAKES

- It is important to have a very hot griddle. To test, sprinkle surface with water. The griddle is ready if the water "dances".
- Cook the first side until bubbles break all over the surface. Flip and cook second side until just golden brown.
- Never press down on a pancake with a spatula, as it will compress it and make it heavy.
- Best to serve immediately, but if not, keep warm by placing in a single layer on a dishtowel-covered baking sheet in a 200°F oven.

HAPPY DAY PANCAKES

These fluffy, hearty pancakes handle additions well; try adding bananas, blueberries or a toss of granola on one side. If you like thick pancakes, use the smaller amount of buttermilk. Powdered buttermilk is an easy way to keep it available for baking; just mix up the amount you need. Keep batter a bit lumpy; over beating makes tough pancakes.

2 eggs	1 teaspoon salt
3 1/2 to 4 cups buttermilk	2 teaspoons sugar
1 teaspoon baking soda	1/4 cup butter, melted
3 cups flour	1 teaspoon vanilla extract
2 teaspoons baking powder	Butter for frying

Whisk eggs and buttermilk together in a large bowl; add baking soda and combine. Add flour, baking powder, salt and sugar and whisk just enough to combine. Add butter and vanilla. For ease of use at griddle, pour batter into a large glass measuring cup with a spout, or a pitcher. (May be kept in refrigerator for up to 3 days). Heat griddle or frying pan over medium heat. Add tablespoon of butter to griddle and when it begins to foam, pour batter to make pancakes. When bubbles break on surface, flip and cook until bottom is golden. Recoat griddle by scribbling with butter as needed. Makes 16 pancakes.

SWEDISH PANCAKES

This is a grandkid favorite and often requested, with contests ensuing between Grandpa, parents and children as to who could eat the most. Great fun to stand at the griddle, flipping out pancakes until all were ready to burst. Lots of good memories with this recipe, and I think your family will enjoy these light and delicious pancakes too. Best just fresh off the griddle, but you can also make in batches and keep warm in the oven.

2 tablespoons butter	1/2 teaspoon salt
1 1/4 cups milk	1/4 teaspoon baking powder
3 eggs, beaten	2 tablespoons sugar
1/2 cup flour	

Put butter and milk in microwaveable pitcher or bowl and cook on medium until butter is melted and milk is lukewarm. Add beaten eggs and beat. Add flour, salt, baking powder and sugar and stir until lumps dissolve. Use a wire whisk or place in a glass jar with a lid, and shake or mix until smooth. Batter may be prepared 8 hours ahead. Cover tightly and refrigerate.

Preheat oven to 200°F. Place ovenproof platter in oven. Heat large griddle to medium-high heat. Scribble on griddle with stick of butter. Working in batches, add batter to skillet, about a tablespoon for each pancake. Turn after a minute or less and brown on other side. Transfer to platter to keep warm or serve immediately. Recoat griddle by scribbling with butter as needed. Delicious served with syrup and melted butter, dusted with powdered sugar or try the classic Swedish lingonberry topping (purchased). Enjoy.

Paul Sample
Maple Syrup Time,
ca. 1950, oil on panel,
The John W. and Mildred
L. Graves Collection,
1998.40

GERMAN PANCAKE with LEMON BUTTER GLAZE

This is a cross between an omelet and a soufflé. It puffs during baking and falls when served. Great with coffee and crisp bacon. While we name them differently here in the Midwest, in the Pacific Northwest they refer to these as "Seattle Dutch Babies" and are often served with the blackberries that grow wild in and around Seattle. Whatever you call them, they are fantastic for a special breakfast or even dinner.

¹/₃ cup butter	1¹/₄ cups flour
5 eggs	1¹/₄ cups milk

Heat oven to 425°F. Place butter in a heavy 10-inch skillet; place in oven to melt, and roll when removing to paint the sides and bottom of the skillet with the melted butter. In a medium bowl, beat eggs with mixer or rotary beater. Add flour and milk and beat just until smooth (do not over beat). Pour batter in hot buttered pan and return to oven. Do not open oven while baking. Bake for 20 to 25 minutes or until puffed and golden. Loosen pancake with knife; cut into wedges. Top with Lemon Butter Glaze, and toasted almonds if desired.

Lemon Butter Glaze

Juice of ¹/₂ lemon	Powdered sugar
2 tablespoons butter, melted	¹/₂ cup almonds, toasted

Mix the lemon juice with the melted butter. Pour over the cooked batter and sprinkle with powdered sugar and toasted almonds.

Variation: Omit the Lemon Butter Glaze and top with shredded cheese, crumbled bacon or ham.

NO FAIL QUICHE LORRAINE

This is indeed a "no fail" quiche. With the use of sour cream instead of milk, it always sets up well and handles additions of about anything you add to it. Great to just see what is in your refrigerator that might be tasty in a quiche and make your own combination! This was served at the Wichita Symphony Showhouse Tea Room, 2001. Most of the quiche-of-the-day entrées for the Tea Room were made from this basic recipe. Daughter in law Cindy made 36 quiches when a caterer was not able to supply such at the last minute, and this recipe was really put to work. You'll like it too. Thanks to the Victorian Sampler Tea Room (Eureka Springs, Arkansas) for sharing this gem.

5 or 6 slices bacon, fried crisp and crumbled
1/2 small onion, chopped
3 tablespoons diced green pepper
1 cup sliced mushrooms
2 or 3 tablespoons butter, melted
3 eggs, slightly beaten
1 1/4 cups sour cream
Dash of salt

Dash of garlic powder
Dash of white pepper
Dash of hot pepper sauce
1 1/2 cups Swiss cheese, grated
1 cup mild Cheddar cheese (like longhorn)

1 (9-inch) pastry shell, baked to light brown

Preheat oven to 350°F. Lightly sauté onion, green pepper and mushrooms in melted butter. (This can be accomplished in the microwave oven: slice butter over onions and green pepper and sliced mushrooms, cook for 2 or 3 minutes on high setting in microwave and drain off liquid.) Combine eggs, sour cream and seasonings and thoroughly mix with whisk, or at low speed with electric mixer. Stir in vegetables, cheeses and bacon and pour into pastry shell. Bake for 35 to 40 minutes until set and lightly browned on top. Cool on wire rack for 15 minutes. Makes 6 to 8 servings.

Variations: For vegetable quiche, eliminate bacon, onion, green pepper and mushrooms and substitute as follows: equal quantities for a total of approximately 2 cups per quiche of onion, cauliflower, broccoli, zucchini, and carrots, chopped or sliced or sautéed or cooked in microwave oven with butter until crisp-tender. Season as desired.

CRAB QUICHE

Dry pie crust mixes are not recommended, nor are frozen pie crusts. A decent timesaver however is to use refrigerated pie crusts. Try Pillsbury's 'Just Unroll.'

1 pound King crab leg, thawed if frozen, or
1/2 pound lump crabmeat
4 eggs
2 cups heavy cream
2 tablespoons finely chopped fresh chives
2 tablespoons finely chopped fresh parsley
2 tablespoons finely chopped fresh cilantro
1/2 teaspoon seafood seasoning (such as
Paul Prudhomme's)

1/2 teaspoon salt
1/4 teaspoon black pepper
1/8 teaspoon nutmeg
1/2 cup (2 ounces) coarsely grated Monterey
Jack cheese
1/2 cup (2 ounces) coarsely grated Swiss cheese
1 (9-inch) pastry shell, baked to light brown

If using crab leg, hack through shell with a large heavy knife and cut meat into 1/2-inch pieces. Discard shell. Whisk together eggs, cream, herbs, seafood seasoning, salt, pepper and nutmeg, then stir in cheeses and crabmeat. Pour into pre-baked crust and bake until filling puffs and is no longer wobbly in center when quiche is gently shaken, 40 to 50 minutes. Cool in pie plate on rack for 15 minutes. Makes 6 to 8 servings.

CHICKEN DIJON QUICHE

1 (9-inch) pastry shell
2 tablespoons butter
1/2 cup sliced mushrooms
1/4 cup chopped onion
2 tablespoons minced garlic
3/4 cup diced cooked chicken
1 teaspoon dried Italian seasoning

1/4 cup white wine
1/4 cup shredded fresh Parmesan cheese
1/4 cup shredded Swiss cheese
1 cup whipping cream
1 tablespoon Dijon mustard
3 eggs

Heat oven to 400°F. Prepare pie crust and bake for 9 to 13 minutes or until crust appears dry and golden brown. Meanwhile, in medium skillet, melt butter over medium heat. Add mushrooms, onion and garlic. Cook and stir until tender. Stir in chicken, Italian seasoning and wine; cook over medium heat until liquid evaporates, stirring occasionally. Spread chicken mixture over bottom of partially baked pie shell. Sprinkle with 2 tablespoons of each of the cheeses. In medium bowl, combine cream, mustard and eggs; beat well. Pour over cheese mixture; sprinkle with remaining cheeses. Bake at 400° F for 23 to 28 minutes or until quiche is golden brown and knife inserted near center comes out clean. Let stand for 5 minutes before serving. Makes 6 to 8 servings.

HASH BROWN QUICHE

This is a great flavor combination, substituting hash browns for the standard crust. Add chopped jalapenos and salsa on the side to take the flavors another great direction.

1 (24-ounce) package frozen uncooked hash browns, thawed
3 tablespoons unsalted butter, melted
2 eggs, beaten
1/2 cup half-and-half
1/2 teaspoon seasoned salt

4 ounces Monterey Jack cheese with peppers, shredded (1 cup)
4 ounces Swiss cheese, shredded (1 cup)
1 cup diced ham
Garnish: fresh chopped parsley

Preheat oven to 425°F. Press hash browns into bottom and sides of deep pie plate; blot with paper towel to remove all moisture from potatoes. Brush with melted butter or spray with cooking spray; bake 25 minutes. Remove from oven to cool. Reduce oven to 350°F. Combine eggs, half-and-half, and salt. Place cheeses and ham in hash brown shell. Pour egg mixture over top. Bake 40 to 50 minutes until eggs are set and top is slightly browned. Garnish with parsley. Makes 8 servings.

Variation: add 1/4 cup chopped jalapenos (seeded, drained) to egg mixture. Serve with salsa on the side.

GREEN CHILI SQUARES

This recipe is adapted from Joyce Haynes' favorite "Cheese Fudge" from Joyce Mader. It is like a quiche without the crust, can be served as an appetizer, cut into small squares, or included on your buffet table for brunch.

1 (4-ounce) can diced green chilis, drained
16 ounces sharp Cheddar cheese, shredded (divided use)
6 eggs, beaten

1/2 cup chopped roasted red peppers
2 tablespoons chopped jalapenos
2 tablespoons chopped fresh parsley (or cilantro)

Preheat oven to 325°F. Coat a 9 x 13-inch casserole with cooking spray. Spread out green chilis on bottom of the dish. Sprinkle cheese evenly over chilis. In a large bowl, combine the eggs, red peppers, jalapenos and parsley. Pour into the prepared casserole and bake for 30 minutes until just set. Do not over cook. Cut into squares and serve warm or at room temperature.

GROWING *up on a farm with fresh eggs,*

I like them simply sunny-side up but enjoy all manner of egg dishes. Occasionally I will also put them on a piece of toast to serve like an open-faced sandwich, or cut a hole in the middle of the bread and break the egg into the cutout and fry (called a "Toad in the Hole" by the English).

SCRUMPTIOUS EGGS

1 1/2 pounds Monterey Jack cheese, shredded
3/4 pound fresh mushrooms, sliced
1/2 large onion, chopped
1/2 cup diced red pepper
1/4 cup butter, melted
1 cup diced ham or bacon
7 eggs, beaten

1 3/4 cups milk
1/2 cup flour
1 tablespoon minced parsley
1 tablespoon seasoned salt
1 teaspoon freshly ground black pepper
Tomato slices for top

Preheat oven to 350°F. Coat a 9 x 13-inch baking dish with butter or cooking spray. Arrange half the cheese in the dish. Sauté mushrooms, onion and red pepper in butter until soft, but not browned, pour over cheese. Arrange diced ham or bacon evenly. Add remaining cheese. If desired, cover and refrigerate until time to bake. About one hour before serving, beat eggs, milk, flour, parsley, salt and pepper together. Pour evenly over top. Arrange tomato slices centered on each serving. Bake for 45 minutes or until golden brown. Let stand 5 minutes before serving. Makes 10 to 12 servings.

CHEESY POTATO BREAKFAST CASSEROLE

This breakfast casserole is perfect for weekend guests. Serve with cinnamon rolls and fresh fruit.

1 pound mild sausage, browned and drained
   (prefer Rice's brand)
1 cup diced cooked potatoes (frozen hash
   browns work well)
10 medium fresh mushrooms, sliced and sautéed
1 cup cubed processed American
   cheese (Velveeta)

1 (10 3/4-ounce) can condensed cream of
   celery soup
2/3 cup milk
3 eggs
1/2 cup grated Cheddar cheese
Croutons as desired

Preheat oven to 350°F. Stir together sausage, hash browns, mushrooms and cheese. Pour into a 9 x 13-inch casserole (buttered or coated with cooking spray). Whisk together soup, milk and eggs; pour evenly over potato mixture. Sprinkle with Cheddar cheese and croutons. Bake for 30 to 40 minutes. Keeps well in warm oven for delayed serving. Makes 8 servings. From Cindy Banks.

CLASSIC BREAKFAST CASSEROLE

1 1/2 pounds pork sausage
3 to 4 bread slices, cubed
1 1/2 cups (6 ounces) shredded Cheddar cheese
9 eggs

3 cups milk
1 1/2 teaspoons dry mustard
1 teaspoon salt
1/8 teaspoon pepper

Preheat oven to 350°F. Cook sausage in a skillet, stirring until it crumbles and is no longer pink; drain well. Arrange bread cubes in bottom of a lightly greased 9 x 13-inch baking dish. Top with sausage and cheese. Whisk together eggs, milk, dry mustard, salt and pepper; pour evenly over cheese. Cover and chill 8 hours. Let stand at room temperature for 30 minutes after removing from refrigerator. Bake at for 45 minutes or until set. Let stand 5 minutes before serving. Makes 8 to 10 servings.

ITALIAN SAUSAGE BREAKFAST STRATA

5 cups cubed day-old bread

4 links Italian turkey sausage, casings removed, browned and crumbled

1/4 cup chopped sun-dried tomatoes packed in oil, oil reserved

1/2 cup chopped onion

1 tablespoon chopped fresh rosemary

6 ounces Monterey Jack cheese, shredded

6 eggs

1 1/2 cups milk

1 teaspoon salt

1/4 teaspoon freshly ground black pepper

1 teaspoon dry mustard

1/4 teaspoon ground nutmeg (optional)

Spray a 9-inch square baking dish with nonstick cooking spray. Sprinkle bread cubes in casserole. Sprinkle sausage evenly over bread cubes. Pour 1 tablespoon reserved sun-dried tomato oil into skillet. Add onions and sauté until tender. Add tomatoes and rosemary, stirring until blended. Sprinkle onion mixture over sausage. Cover with cheese. In a medium bowl, whisk together the eggs, milk, salt, pepper, dry mustard, and nutmeg until well blended. Pour egg mixture over casserole. Cover and refrigerate at least 8 hours or overnight. Bring to room temperature before baking. Preheat oven to 350°F and bake 30 to 40 minutes, or until set. Makes 6 servings. From Marlene Phillips.

SAUSAGE AND EGG CASSEROLE with SUN-DRIED TOMATOES

This is a very adaptable recipe; choose whatever sausage or cheese your family likes best. Good for brunch served with fresh fruit, or as a dinner entrée served with a green salad and bread. Adapted from recipe published in Bon Appétit.

1 pound hot sausage (or Italian sweet sausage, casings removed)

1/2 cup chopped shallots

2 cloves garlic, minced

1/2 cup oil-packed sun-dried tomatoes, rinsed, drained and chopped

4 tablespoons chopped fresh parsley (divided use)

8 eggs (or 5 eggs plus 3 yolks)

2 cups half-and-half

2 cups grated Monterey Jack/Cheddar cheese (or mozzarella), divided use

1/2 teaspoon salt

Preheat oven to 375°F. Butter a 9 x 13-inch baking dish. Brown sausage in medium nonstick skillet over medium heat, breaking up with back of fork into small pieces, about 10 minutes. Add shallots and garlic and sauté 3 minutes; drain. Add sun-dried tomatoes and 2 tablespoons parsley; stir 1 minute. Spread sausage mixture in baking dish (Can be made 1 day ahead to this point; cover and refrigerate). Whisk eggs, egg yolks, half and half, 1 1/2 cups cheese and salt in large bowl to blend well. Pour egg mixture over sausage in dish. Sprinkle remaining 1/2 cup cheese and 2 tablespoons parsley over top. Bake until casserole is golden brown and knife inserted into center comes out clean, about 30 to 40 minutes. Let stand 5 minutes before serving. Makes 8 to 10 servings.

SOUTHWEST BRUNCH CASSEROLE

10 eggs

2 cups (8 ounces) grated Monterey Jack cheese with peppers

2 cups (8 ounces) grated sharp Cheddar cheese

2 cups small-curd cottage cheese

2 (4 1/2-ounce) cans chopped green chilies, drained

1/2 cup butter, melted

1/2 cup flour

1 teaspoon baking powder

1/2 teaspoon salt

Salsa

Preheat oven to 350°F. Butter a 9 x 13-inch baking dish. Beat eggs in a large bowl. Stir in cheeses, add remaining ingredients and mix well. Pour into prepared dish. Bake uncovered for 35 to 45 minutes, until thoroughly heated. Cool for 10 minutes before serving. Serve with salsa on the side. Casserole may be prepared the night before baking and refrigerated. Makes 8 to 10 servings.

Timing is very important when serving a late-morning meal for overnight guests. Make it easy on yourself by choosing an entrée which can be made the night before and also set the table the night before so you don't have to get up at the crack of dawn.

Have juice and coffee ready to serve as soon as guests appear.

SCRAMBLED EGGS WITH GOAT CHEESE AND CHIVES

If you want to scramble eggs to make 4 servings, try this:

Beat 10 eggs together in a medium bowl; season with salt and pepper. In a medium nonstick skillet, melt 1 tablespoon of butter. Add eggs and cook over low heat, stirring with a rubber spatula. When they begin to set up, add 3 ounces of soft goat cheese and stir. Top with chives, thinly sliced on the diagonal. Serve immediately.

OMELET TIPS

*Get a great but inexpensive
nonstick omelet pan; throw
it out if it gets scratched
as the nonstick surface is
necessary to a good omelet.*

*If an omelet sticks and
turns out messy, just add
some cheese to it and call
it scrambled eggs!*

OMELETS FOR A GROUP

*The classic omelet is both simple and elegant. To create an omelet party for twelve, first assemble the ingredients.
Then provide a generous choice of garnishes and please your guests with made-to-order omelets in just 1 minute each.*

24 eggs
¼ cup cold water
½ teaspoon hot pepper sauce
1 teaspoon salt
12 tablespoons butter

Suggested garnishes:
½ cup mixed finely chopped fresh, chives,
   parsley, tarragon or basil
1 pound bacon, crisp-cooked, crumbled
2 cups shredded Swiss or Cheddar cheese or
   grated Parmesan cheese
1 pound mushrooms, chopped, sautéed

Beat the eggs, water, hot pepper sauce and salt with a wire whisk until they look "stringy" and make threads
when you lift up the whisk. Heat a skillet over medium heat until several drops of water flicked into the pan
"dance" on the hot surface. Add the butter. Use 1 tablespoon butter and ½ cup of the egg mixture for each
omelet and cook the omelets 1 at a time. To cook, hold the skillet in the left hand. Pour the eggs into the
skillet; stir with the flat side of a fork in a fast circular motion, shaking the skillet in a rocking motion to keep
the eggs from sticking. Spread the eggs evenly to cover any breaks and allow eggs to set. Tilt the skillet and
fold the outer edge of the omelet over; slide onto a warm plate. Have each guest finish their own omelet by
choosing from the garnishes. Makes 12 omelets.

SEAFOOD STRATA

2 tablespoons butter
1 cup chopped onion
4 (8-inch) flour or spinach tortillas
4 ounces cooked, peeled shrimp
4 ounces cooked flaked crabmeat
¾ cup shredded Swiss cheese
½ cup shredded mozzarella cheese

1 tablespoon chopped fresh dill (or ¾ teaspoon
   dried dill weed)
3 eggs
1½ cups milk
1 tablespoon flour
¼ teaspoon freshly ground black pepper

Preheat oven to 350°F. Spray a 2-quart baking dish with nonstick coating. In a medium skillet, melt butter
and cook onion until tender. Tear tortillas into bite-size pieces. In the baking dish layer half of the tortilla
pieces, half of the onions, half of the shrimp and crab, half of the cheese and half of the dill. Repeat layers.
Beat together the eggs, milk, flour and pepper until smooth. Pour egg mixture over strata, cover and
refrigerate overnight. Bake for 45 to 50 minutes or until a knife inserted near the center comes out clean
and top is golden brown. Let stand for 5 minutes. Cut into squares and serve. Makes 6 servings. From
Debbie Deuser.

BATCH OF BACON

My family likes bacon and when we have large gatherings it is difficult to fry the quantity needed in a skillet. Microwave bacon is a convenience, but with a large quantity it can be time consuming and not have a good crisp. Oven frying is quick and consistent; you will like this technique too and wonder why you hadn't done it before.

12 slices of bacon (prefer Farmland Hickory Smoked or Hormel Original Black Label)

Preheat oven to 400°F. Place bacon on a large rimmed baking sheet (should be at least $^3/_4$ inch deep, but shallow enough for browning). Bake for 5 to 6 minutes and then rotate pan to promote even browning, but no need to turn the bacon strips over. Continue to cook for another 5 to 6 minutes, or longer depending on thickness of the bacon (you may wish to brush with maple syrup right before removing from the oven). Remove from oven and prop up one end of the pan on a pot holder so that the grease drains to one end. Remove bacon from pan with tongs and drain on paper towels. More than one tray of bacon may be cooked in the oven at the same time, just rotate the positions of the trays during cooking.

SWEET SPICY BACON

This could be called "That Bacon" as that is often the name given to it by those requesting it. It is rather decadent but your guests will name it too and ask for it again and again.

1 pound thick-cut bacon (12 slices)
1 $^1/_2$ tablespoons packed brown sugar

$^1/_4$ teaspoon cayenne pepper
$^1/_4$ teaspoon black pepper

Preheat oven to 350°F. Arrange bacon slices in 1 layer on a wire rack on a large foil lined pan and bake in middle of oven for 20 minutes. Meanwhile, mix brown sugar, cayenne, and black pepper together in a small bowl. Turn slices over and sprinkle evenly with spiced sugar (rub it in as you would a dry rub on meat before barbecue). Continue baking until bacon is crisp and brown, 15 to 20 minutes more, and then transfer to paper towels to drain or cool on foil.

FARM HOME FRIES

Fried potatoes were a favorite on the farm, using potatoes freshly dug from the garden. Cooking them first briefly in water is the trick to having them done just right. Any variety of potato will cook well, but Yukon Gold or Red Bliss have good flavor and texture.

1 pound (2 small-medium) potatoes, scrubbed
   and diced
Salt, preferably kosher
1 medium onion, finely chopped

2 $^1/_2$ tablespoons corn or peanut oil (divided use)
1 tablespoon unsalted butter
1 teaspoon paprika (optional)
Salt and pepper to taste

Placed the diced potatoes (best with skins left on) in a large saucepan, cover with $^1/_2$ inch of water and sprinkle with salt. Turn on high heat and as soon as water begins to boil, drain the potatoes in a colander. While potatoes are reaching this stage, place onion and 1 tablespoon of oil in a heavy skillet (cast iron works best) over medium-high heat. Stir frequently until browned, about 8 minutes. Transfer onions to a small plate and reserve.

On medium-high heat melt the butter and 1 $^1/_2$ tablespoon of oil in the heavy skillet used to brown the onions. Add potatoes and shake to spread out them out evenly in a single layer. Cook, without stirring, until one side of the potato is browned and then turn with spatula. Repeat the process until all potatoes are tender and brown. May take another 10 minutes and three turns. Add onion, paprika, salt and pepper and stir. Serve immediately. Note: this recipe may be doubled by placing the first batch on a large baking sheet to keep it warm (300°F oven), while the second batch is made.

Cookies & Bars

COOKIE SUCCESS

Good cookie sheets are very important to cookie quality. My favorite one is a commercial grade made by Vollrath (see "A Few Favorite Things" near the Index). It performs better than more expensive ones, gives consistent results and has handles on the short side. You will find others reviewed by periodicals such as *Cook's Illustrated*. Spend the money and get a good one.

Measure the batter so cookies will be all of the same size and therefore bake at the same rate. Spring-loaded ice cream scoops will nicely portion cookie dough and muffin batter. They come sized according to how many scoops yield a quart. For large cookies, use a #16 scoop, which will portion out a $^1/_4$ cup of dough. For standard sized cookies, which use about a heaping tablespoon of dough, use a #30 scoop.

To get even results, reverse the top and bottom baking sheets (and also rotate them front to back) halfway through the baking.

The most common mistake is to over bake cookies. They cook in a short time, usually at 350° to 375°F. A few degrees and a few extra minutes can make a big difference. Watch for browning on the edges to indicate that cookies are baked. Often they look undercooked when they are actually perfectly done.

BEST EVER SNICKERDOODLES

Ummm, the best with a cold glass of milk! While simple to make, technique is important to achieve perfection. The small amount of corn syrup is an important ingredient for great texture, but can be made without it if necessary.

Previous page:

John Francis
Still Life: Apples and Biscuits, 1862, oil on wood panel, WAM, gift of George E. Vollmer in memory of Lillian M. George, 1999.1

2$^1/_4$ cups flour
2 teaspoons cream of tartar
1 teaspoon baking soda
$^1/_2$ teaspoon salt
12 tablespoons (1$^1/_2$ sticks) butter, slightly softened

$^1/_4$ cup shortening
1$^1/_2$ cups sugar
1 tablespoon light corn syrup
2 eggs
For topping: 3 tablespoons sugar, combined with 1 tablespoon of cinnamon

Preheat the oven to 400°F. Prepare several baking sheets with nonstick spray, parchment paper or silicone liners. In a large bowl, whisk together the flour, cream of tartar, baking soda, and salt; set aside. In another large bowl, with an electric mixer on medium speed, beat together the butter, shortening, sugar, and corn syrup until well blended and fluffy, about 2 minutes. Add the eggs and beat for 30 seconds more, scraping down sides. Beat in half of the flour mixture until evenly incorporated (about 30 seconds). Stir in the remaining flour mixture until evenly incorporated (about another 30 seconds). Let the dough stand for 5 to 10 minutes, or until slightly firm. Mix the cinnamon sugar topping in a shallow bowl.

With lightly greased hands, roll portions of the dough into generous 1$^1/_2$-inch balls (dough will be soft). Roll each ball in the cinnamon-sugar. Place on the baking sheets, spacing about 2$^1/_2$ inches apart. Slightly pat down the balls with your hand.

Bake the cookies, one sheet at a time, in the upper third of the oven for 8 to 11 minutes, or until just light golden brown at the edges. Reverse the sheet from front to back halfway through baking to ensure even browning. Transfer the sheet to a wire rack and let stand until the cookies firm up slightly, 1 to 2 minutes, and then transfer cookies to wire racks. Let stand until completely cooled. Let the baking sheets cool between batches to keep the cookies from spreading too much. Store in an airtight container for up to 10 days or freeze for up to 2 months. Makes 2$^1/_2$ dozen.

Boston and Sandwich
Glass Company
Sugar Bowl with Cover,
ca. 1840-50, pressed glass,
WAM, gift of George E.
Vollmer, the Lillian George
American Glass Collection,
1990.96.10

JOY'S SNICKERDOODLES

This is a crisper version, very simple and straightforward, made by my mother Joy Olson for a farmhouse lifetime and lots of harvest crews.

1 cup butter, softened
1¹/₂ cups sugar
2 eggs
3 cups flour
2 teaspoons cream of tartar

1 teaspoon soda
1¹/₂ teaspoons salt
For topping: 2 tablespoons sugar combined with
    2 teaspoons of cinnamon

Preheat oven to 375°F. Cream butter and sugar together with mixer; add eggs one at a time. Combine dry ingredients in a separate bowl; gradually add to the butter mixture. Chill dough for 45 minutes, then divide into 1¹/₂-inch balls, roll in cinnamon sugar. Space cookies 2 inches apart on a greased cookie sheet and bake until edges just begin to turn golden, about 10 minutes. Cool on wire rack. Makes 3 dozen.

FIRST PRIZE SUGAR COOKIES

This recipe is from my good friend, and excellent cook, Joan Schulz. I think they are aptly named!

1 cup sugar
1 cup powdered sugar
1 cup shortening
1 cup vegetable oil

2 eggs
4¹/₂ cups sifted flour
1 teaspoon cream of tartar
1 teaspoon vanilla extract

Preheat oven to 350°F. Cream sugars and shortening. Add remaining ingredients and mix. Drop by tablespoon onto cookie sheet. Flatten with bottom of a glass dipped in sugar. Bake for 12 minutes.

DELICIOUS COOKIES

3¹/₂ cups flour
1 teaspoon salt
1 teaspoon cream of tartar
1 teaspoon baking soda
1 cup butter
1 cup vegetable oil
1 cup brown sugar
1 cup sugar

1 large egg
1 teaspoon vanilla extract
1 cup old-fashioned oatmeal
1 cup crispy rice cereal
1 cup shredded coconut
12 ounces white chocolate chips
Small can macadamia nuts, halved (about
    1¹/₂ cups)

Preheat oven to 375°F. Sift and blend flour, salt, cream of tartar and baking soda. In a mixer bowl, cream butter, oil, sugars, egg and vanilla. Slowly mix in dry ingredients. Stir in oatmeal, cereal, coconut, white chocolate chips and nuts. Roll into walnut-sized balls and place on cookie sheet coated with cooking spray, parchment paper or silicone liner. Bake for 12 minutes. Makes about 6 dozen.

Variations: may also substitute other types of nuts, or top with colored or clear sugar sprinkles before baking.

SUGAR COOKIE TIP

Roll a piece of dough between your palms into a ball, and then roll the ball of dough in a bowl filled with granulated sugar. Place on baking sheet. Butter the bottom of a drinking glass (about 2 inches across the bottom) and dip it into a bowl of sugar. Use the glass to flatten the dough balls, dipping the glass back into the sugar after shaping every other cookie.

This technique is an easy way to lightly coat the cookie with sugar, but also makes for uniform thickness.

The life of Herschel C.
Logan is a great American
success story. He was born
in Missouri in 1901, the
year before his mother died,
after which his father moved
to a farm near Winfield, KS,
where Herschel was reared.
There the Kansas landscape
made an impression on him
so strong that it was never
to leave his sensibility or
his art. After high school
graduation in 1920 he left
the farm for a year of study
at the Chicago Academy of
Fine Arts. On his return
to Kansas, he was hired
as an apprentice artist
at Wichita's McCormick
Armstrong. At the time,
there were two truly
outstanding figures at the
press. The director was
Robert T. Aitchison (p. 106)
--a rare combination of
businessman and humanist,
whose magnificent collection
of rare early books form
the core of Wichita State
University's special
collections. The other man,
C. A. Seward (p. 199),
though poor, was rich in
artistic talent and technical
knowledge. Aitchison and
Seward took Logan under
their wing. During his
first year at McCormick-
Armstrong, they taught him
the woodcut process and he
produced seven prints. By
1923 Logan's prints were
so admired that the Beacon
newspaper featured him.
In 1930 the young artist
was among the co-founders,
along with his friend C. A.
Seward and Birger Sandzen,
of the Prairie Print Makers.
Eight years later he was in
Who's Who in America.
His woodblock print
Winter Day was shown
in the 1939 New York
World's Fair.
(continued on p. 226)

SWEDISH SPRITZ COOKIES

Lots of possibilities for beautiful "company cookies" with this lovely buttery dough and a cookie press. Cookie press shapes and a few drops of food coloring make for seasonal shapes too. Fun to make green wreath shaped cookies with the template for a spaghetti like dough to make the circle, and add a few red hot cinnamon candies for decoration. My favorite though is just as a plain butter cookie, in any pretty shape, sprinkled with a little sugar before baking.

1 cup butter or margarine	1 teaspoon almond extract
1/2 cup sugar	2 1/2 cups flour
1 egg yolk	

Preheat oven to 375°F. Beat butter or margarine and sugar in a medium bowl with electric mixer until fluffy. Add egg yolk and almond extract; beat well. Beat or stir in flour. Force the unchilled dough through a cookie press and onto parchment-paper lined cookie sheet. Bake for 8 to 10 minutes or till edges are firm, but not brown. Cool the baked cookies on wire racks. Makes 5 dozen.

Variations: For a nutty cookie, stir in a 1/2 cup finely ground nuts with the flour (toast nuts before grinding, if you like). For a chocolate cookie, reduce the flour to 2 1/4 cups. Add an additional 1/4 cup sugar and 1/4 cup unsweetened cocoa powder (add cocoa powder before adding the flour).

SWEDISH HEIRLOOM COOKIES

1/2 cup shortening	1 tablespoon water
1/2 cup butter, softened	1 tablespoon vanilla extract
1 cup sifted powdered sugar	1 1/4 cups ground almonds
1/2 teaspoon salt	Powdered sugar for rolling
2 cups flour	

Preheat oven to 325°F. Cream shortening and butter with electric mixer until fluffy; add powdered sugar and salt. Add flour, 1 cup at a time; mix after each addition. Add water, vanilla and almonds, stirring until combined. Roll dough, with slightly moistened hands, into 1-inch balls. Place on ungreased cookie sheet and flatten with the bottom of a glass slightly coated with butter. Bake for 12 minutes, cool for 2 minutes on baking sheet. Place warm cookies in dish with powdered sugar and coat. Let cookies cool in sugar. If cookies are too hot the sugar will melt. Makes 4 dozen.

CRACKLE CRUNCH COOKIES

This recipe was clipped from a flour sack in the 1980s. Simple but good.

1 1/2 cups flour	1 1/4 cups packed brown sugar
1/2 teaspoon soda	1 egg
1/2 teaspoon salt	1/4 cup milk
1 cup shortening	2 cups crispy rice cereal

Preheat oven to 375°F. Sift together flour, soda and salt. Set aside. In a large bowl cream shortening and sugar until fluffy. Beat in egg and milk. Blend in flour mixture; fold in cereal. Drop by teaspoonfuls on ungreased cookie sheet. Bake for 12 minutes. Remove and let cool. Makes 3 dozen.

LEMON BUTTER COOKIES

A dainty cookie ideal for a spring tea or shower, these are made with a cookie press.

2 cups butter, softened	1 teaspoon lemon extract
1 cup powdered sugar	1 to 2 teaspoons grated lemon rind (optional)
3 cups flour	

Preheat oven to 325°F. Beat butter until creamy; gradually add powdered sugar, beating well. Add flour, 1 cup at a time, beating well after each addition. Stir in extract and if desired, zest. Use a cookie press to form dough into desired shapes, and place onto parchment paper-lined baking sheets. Bake for 12 to 15 minutes. Cool completely on wire racks. May dust with powdered sugar. Makes 8 dozen.

MOLASSES COOKIES

These are soft and chewy the first day, and then on day two or three a pleasant thin crust envelopes a chewy center. This is the kind of cookie that can set in a cookie tin and even taste better after a few days.

1 cup packed dark brown sugar
1/2 cup shortening
1/2 cup unsulfured molasses
1 egg
2 1/2 cups unbleached flour
2 teaspoons baking soda
1 teaspoon cinnamon

1/2 teaspoon ground cloves
1/2 teaspoon ginger
1/4 teaspoon salt

For rolling
1/2 cup cold water
1/4 cup sugar

Combine brown sugar and shortening in a large bowl and beat with mixer at medium speed until light and fluffy. Add molasses and egg and continue to beat well. In a separate bowl, combine flour, baking soda, cinnamon, cloves, ginger and salt, stirring with a whisk. Add flour mixture to batter and beat at low speed just until blended. Cover and freeze for 1 hour.

Preheat oven to 375°F. Place cold water in a small bowl. Place 1/2 cup granulated sugar for rolling in another small bowl. Lightly coat hands with cooking spray or water. Using a tablespoon measure, scoop a heaping tablespoon of dough and roll between palms into a ball and then shape into 1-inch balls. Dip one side of each ball in water, dip wet side in sugar. Place balls, sugar side up, 1 inch apart, on baking sheets coated with cooking spray or silicone liner. Bake for about 8 minutes, one sheet at a time. Cool on baking sheet for 5 minutes. Remove from cookie sheets and cool on wire racks. Makes 4 dozen.

OLD-FASHIONED GROUND RAISIN COOKIES

My Grandma Harri raised six children in a little stone Kansas farmhouse in the 1880s, without a refrigerator and long before indoor plumbing. She made these cookies, which stay moist for a very long time (but I can't imagine that happening with six children). This recipe has been worth hanging onto, indeed.

1 cup butter
1 1/2 cups sugar
2 eggs, beaten
1/4 cup molasses
2 1/2 cups flour
1 teaspoon salt

1 teaspoon baking soda
1 cup raisins, chopped very fine
1/2 cup nuts, chopped
1/4 teaspoon cinnamon
1/4 teaspoon nutmeg

Preheat oven to 350°F. Mix butter and sugar then add beaten eggs with molasses. Sift together dry ingredients and add a little at a time to first mixture. Roll into balls and flatten with a fork. Bake for 10 to 12 minutes. Makes 4 dozen.

Good flavor comes from fresh spices and dark molasses; milder flavor from light molasses. Be sure to use unsulfured molasses though as the blackstrap and extra-dark molasses are too bitter.

Herschel C. Logan
Barker Homestead, 1930,
block print, WAM, gift of
Samuel H. and Martha F.
Logan 2005.13.55

TOFFEE PEANUT COOKIES

These great cookies freeze well, so don't be scared off by the quantity; they disappear quickly!

You may have to go to a large grocery store to find the toffee chips; they are usually in the baking goods aisle. I like to use "Heath's Bits of Brickle" brand. They keep well, so when I find them I usually buy a couple of bags. You will also find the recipe for a yummy oatmeal toffee cookie on the back of the package, but this toffee peanut cookie is my favorite.

3 cups cake flour (not self-rising)
3 cups flour (all-purpose)
3 teaspoons baking soda
3/4 teaspoon salt
2 1/4 cups butter
1 1/2 cups sugar

1 1/4 cups light brown sugar
3 eggs
1 1/2 teaspoons vanilla extract
4 1/2 cups toffee brickle chips
3 3/4 cups coarsely chopped peanuts

Preheat oven to 350°F. Whisk together flour, baking soda and salt. Cream butter and sugars with an electric mixer until fluffy, about 2 minutes. Add eggs and vanilla, beat until combined. Add flour mixture, beat on low just until combined. In a small bowl, mix a little flour with the toffee chips and peanuts, then hand stir them into the batter. Form dough into 1 1/4-inch balls (dough can be frozen at this point, but thaw before baking). Place balls on baking sheets lined with parchment or silicone liner. Slightly flatten balls with your palm. Bake until golden and set, 10 to 12 minutes. Let cool 5 minutes on sheets before placing cookies on wire rack to cool completely. Freezes well. Makes 7 dozen cookies.

WHITE CHOCOLATE MACADAMIA NUT COOKIES

This is one of my favorite cookies and your family will adopt them quickly. It is worth investing in good quality macadamia nuts and white chocolate for this special cookie.

1 1/2 cups old-fashioned rolled oats
1 1/3 cups flour
3/4 teaspoon baking soda
1 cup minus 2 tablespoons butter, slightly softened
1 cup sugar
1/3 cup packed dark brown sugar

1 egg
1 1/2 tablespoons milk
2 teaspoons vanilla extract
1/4 teaspoon almond extract
1 1/3 cups (8 ounces) white chocolate morsels
1 (6 1/2-ounce) jar of salted macadamia nuts, coarsely chopped (about 1 1/3 cups)

Preheat oven to 375°F. Grease several baking sheets or use parchment paper or silicone liners. Process oats by pulsing in a food processor until ground to a powder. (Alternatively, grind oats to a powder in a blender, stopping and stirring a number of times to redistribute the contents.) In a medium bowl, mix together the ground oats, flour, baking soda; set aside. In a large bowl, with an electric mixer on medium speed, beat the butter and sugars together until lightened, about 1 minute. Add egg, milk and extracts; beat until evenly incorporated. Beat or stir in the flour mixture until mixed; stir in the white chocolate and macadamia nuts until evenly incorporated (Note: if the nuts you use are not salted, add 1/4 teaspoon of salt to the batter).

Using an ice cream scoop or spoons, drop the dough onto the baking sheets in golf-ball-sized portions, spacing about 3 inches apart. Pat the balls down slightly. Bake the cookies one sheet at a time, in the middle of the oven for 12 minutes, or until the tops are barely golden and the edges are just lightly browned; be very careful not to over bake. Let the cookie sheet cool on a wire rack until the cookies firm up slightly, about 2 to 3 minutes. Using a spatula, transfer cookies to wire racks to completely cool. When cool, store in an airtight container for up to 1 week or freeze for up to 1 month. Makes 4 dozen.

SUNFLOWER SEED COOKIES

What better cookie to represent Kansas? These unassuming unique cookies ship well too. If you like them sweeter, try adding a handful of butterscotch chips; or add a handful of sesame seeds if you want them crunchier. I like to use salted sunflower seeds, as the salt adds a nice twang, but unsalted works too.

1 cup sugar
1 cup brown sugar
1/2 cup butter
2 eggs, beaten
1 teaspoon vanilla extract
1 tablespoon water

2 cups flour
1 teaspoon baking powder
1/2 teaspoon baking soda
1 cup coconut
1 cup sunflower seeds, shelled and roasted
1 cup oatmeal (quick oats work fine)

Preheat oven to 350°F. Cream butter and sugars with an electric mixer until fluffy. Add eggs, vanilla and water; mix well. Whisk together flour, baking powder and baking soda. Add flour mixture to sugar mixture. Stir in coconut, sunflower seeds and oatmeal. Drop by teaspoon on ungreased cookie sheet. Bake for 15 minutes or until golden. Makes 4 dozen.

ALMOND BRICKLE COOKIES

This recipe was clipped from a flour sack in the 1980s. Simple but good.

1 cup sugar

1 cup powdered sugar

1 cup oil

1 cup butter, softened

2 eggs

1 teaspoon almond extract

3$\frac{1}{2}$ cups flour

1 cup whole-wheat flour

1 teaspoon salt

1 teaspoon baking soda

1 teaspoon cream of tartar

2 cups chopped almonds

2 (8-ounce) packages toffee brickle chips

Granulated sugar for rolling

Preheat oven to 350°F. Mix sugars, oil and butter until light and fluffy. Add extract and eggs, mix well. Gradually add dry ingredients. With a large spoon, stir in almonds and butter brickle chips. Shape into balls, roll in sugar. Bake for 12 to 15 minutes. Cool 1 minute before transfering to wire rack. Freezes well. Makes 3$\frac{1}{2}$ dozen.

CHOCOLATE CHUNK PEANUT COOKIES

$\frac{1}{2}$ cup butter, softened

$\frac{1}{2}$ cup shortening

1 cup chunky peanut butter

1 cup sugar

1 cup packed brown sugar

2 eggs

2$\frac{1}{2}$ cups flour

1$\frac{1}{2}$ teaspoons baking soda

1 teaspoon baking powder

$\frac{1}{2}$ teaspoon salt

1 teaspoon cinnamon

1 cup unsalted dry-roasted peanuts

1 (11$\frac{1}{2}$-ounce) bag chocolate chunks

Preheat oven to 375°F. Beat butter and shortening at medium speed with electric mixer until creamy; add peanut butter and sugars, beating until fluffy. Add eggs, beating until blended. In a separate bowl, whisk together the flour, baking soda, baking powder, salt and cinnamon. Add to butter mixture, beating well. Stir in peanuts and chocolate chunks by hand.

Shape dough into 2-inch balls (about 2 tablespoons for each cookie). Place on ungreased baking sheets, flatten slightly. Bake for 12 to 15 minutes or until lightly browned. Cool on pan 1 to 2 minutes; remove to wire rack and cool completely. Makes 2 dozen.

CREAM CHEESE WALNUT ROUNDS

These are a nice combination of a creamy, almost shortbread interior with a crunchy nut exterior texture. While I like the nuts added to the batter coarsely chopped, you may find it easier to slice the dough if you finely chop them.

4 cups flour

1$\frac{1}{4}$ teaspoons salt

2 cups butter, softened

6 ounces cream cheese, room temperature

1$\frac{1}{3}$ cups sugar

2 tablespoons plus $\frac{1}{2}$ teaspoon vanilla extract

2$\frac{1}{2}$ cups toasted and chopped walnuts (divided use)

Whisk flour and salt together in a large bowl; set aside. Mix butter and cream cheese together with electric mixer until pale and fluffy, about 2 minutes. Add sugar and vanilla; then add flour mixture and mix until just combined. Add 1$\frac{1}{2}$ cups toasted walnuts and hand stir just enough to combine. Divide dough in half; shape each half into an 8-inch long log (about 2 inches in diameter). Wrap each in parchment or wax paper and freeze for 30 minutes. Preheat oven to 350°F, with racks on upper and lower thirds. Line two baking sheets with parchment or silicone liners. Finely chop the remaining 1 cup of walnuts. Remove dough logs from freezer and roll each in chopped walnuts, coating completely. Slice into $\frac{1}{4}$-inch thick rounds and place on baking sheets. Bake, switching positions of sheets, until cookies are golden around the edges, 16 to 18 minutes. Transfer to wire racks to cool completely. Repeat process with remaining dough using cooled baking sheets, or keep one of the logs in the freezer to bake at another time. Makes 4 dozen.

HAZELNUT CHOCOLATE CRINKLES

3 cups flour
2 teaspoons baking powder
1/2 teaspoon salt
1 (11-ounce) jar chocolate-hazelnut spread
   (prefer Nutella)
1/4 cup butter
1 1/3 cups sugar

1 teaspoon vanilla extract
2 eggs
1/3 cup milk
1/2 cup coarsely chopped, toasted hazelnuts
2 cups finely chopped, toasted hazelnuts
Sifted powdered sugar

Whisk together flour, baking powder and salt; set aside. In a large mixing bowl combine chocolate-hazelnut spread, butter and sugar; beat with an electric mixer on medium to high speed until fluffy. Add vanilla and eggs; beat till combined. Add half of flour mixture and then half of milk to creamed mixture, beating on medium speed just till combined; repeat. Use a spoon to stir in the 1/2 cup chopped hazelnuts. Cover and chill for several hours or till firm.

Preheat oven to 375°F. Shape dough into 1 or 1 1/2 inch balls. Roll the balls in finely chopped hazelnuts, then roll in powdered sugar. Place the balls 2 inches apart on a lightly greased cookie sheet. The cookies will spread and crinkle as they bake. Bake for 8 to 10 minutes or till surface is cracked and cookies are set. Cool cookies on a wire rack. Makes 4 to 6 dozen.

MONSTER COOKIES

A favorite of cookie monsters great and small, this hearty cookie is chock full of treats. Recipe triples easily to make a monster-sized batch for such times as shipping to a college dorm or camp address. These also freeze well.

3 eggs
1 1/4 cup brown sugar
1 cup sugar
1/2 teaspoon salt
1 teaspoon vanilla extract
1 (12-ounce) jar creamy peanut butter

1/2 cup butter
1/2 cup chocolate chips
1/2 cup multi-colored chocolate candies
1/4 cup raisins
2 teaspoons baking soda
4 1/2 cups quick-cooking oatmeal (not instant)

Preheat oven to 350°F. Line cookie sheets with parchment or silicone mat. In a very large bowl, mix in order given. Use ice cream scoop to scoop dough and flatten on cookie sheet, six to a sheet. Bake for 8 to 10 minutes, let stand for about 3 minutes before transferring to wire racks to cool. Makes 2 1/2 dozen.

PEANUT BUTTER COOKIES

1/2 cup butter, room temperature
1/2 cup vegetable shortening, room temperature
1 cup light brown sugar
3/4 cup sugar
2 eggs plus 1 egg yolk
1 teaspoon vanilla extract

1 (12-ounce) jar creamy peanut butter
2 cups flour
2 teaspoons baking soda
1/2 teaspoon kosher salt
1 cup quick-cooking oatmeal (not instant)

Preheat oven to 350°F. Mix butter and shortening together, add sugars and beat until light and fluffy. Beat in eggs, egg yolk and vanilla, then peanut butter. In a separate bowl whisk the flour, baking soda and salt together; add to the batter. Stir in the oatmeal. With moistened hands, roll dough into balls 1 1/2 inches in diameter. Place on ungreased cookie sheet. Place some flour in a small bowl, dip in fork times, tap off excess and press down on the balls to flatten. Dip again in flour and then press down again in the opposite direction, creating a cross-hatch. Sprinkle each cookie with a bit of sugar. Bake for 12 minutes. Cool on sheet for a minute and then transfer to finish cooling on wire rack. Makes 3 dozen.

Peanuts, native to South America, were grown as far north as Mexico by the time the Spanish began their exploration of the New World. By the 1800s they were commercially grown in South Carolina.

During the Civil War (1861–64), soldiers on both sides turned to peanuts for nourishment, and brought the taste for them home. Peanut butter was created in the 1890s by a St. Louis physician as a soft protein substitute for people with poor teeth. It was introduced to the world at the 1904 World's Fair in St. Louis (Smith, 2002).

In 1903, George Washington Carver began his research at the Tuskegee Institute where he developed more than 300 other uses for peanuts and improved peanut horticulture so much that he is considered by many to be the "father of the peanut industry." Prior to his becoming one of the most important scientists of his time, Carver, born of slave parents, spent his formative years with an adoptive family in Ft. Scott, Kansas.

Vincent Price was noted not only as an actor, but as an art lover and epicure as well. He was a celebrity advocate for the Wichita Art Museum who wrote articles in its praise in the Washington Post *and the* Hollywood Citizen News. *Among his many visits to the Museum was his appearance at the Vedere Ball of 1980. Here he is seen being appropriately entertained by his friends Howard Wooden and Bud Beren. Mr. Price's zest for life is also apparent in the luxuriously produced cookbook he co-authored with his wife Mary, A* Treasury of Great Recipes *(1965) a beautiful 460 page copper leather bound book which sold well in the Museum gift shop. It is a wonderful period piece that is fun to revisit. - SG*

OATMEAL LACE COOKIES

Vincent Price, describes this cookie which was served at a dinner honoring him at the Virginia Museum of Fine Arts in 1964: "They have a way with bread, muffins, cookies, and other baked goods in the South. Light, deft hands and a pride in the ladylike accomplishments must be responsible for this regional talent. And then they dote on old family recipes, and the South has countless old families to supply them. Here's the recipe for the delightful cookies that were served with dessert at the Virginia Museum. If you want to be fancy, you can roll them around the handle of a wooden spoon while they're still warm and soft. The rolled cookies can be served plain or filled with whipped cream."

1 cup quick-cooking oatmeal	1 teaspoon vanilla
1 1/2 cups packed dark brown sugar	1/2 teaspoon salt
1 egg, beaten	1 1/2 cups melted butter

Preheat oven to 350°F. Process the oatmeal in a blender or food processor. Add brown sugar, egg, vanilla, salt and butter and mix well until you have a thick dark brown batter. Drop by half teaspoonfuls onto buttered cookie sheet, 2 or 3 inches apart – the cookies spread into large, thin circles while baking. Bake for 12 minutes. Remove cookies with spatula while they are still warm. As soon as they cool, they harden and will stick. If that happens, put them back in warm oven for a few seconds until they are soft enough to remove. Store in airtight container. Makes 4 dozen.

TOASTED OATMEAL COOKIES

Toasting the oats gives these cookies a unique rich flavor that complements the walnuts very well. Quick oats used in place of the old-fashioned rolled oats will yield a slightly less chewy cookie.

2 1/2 cups quick-cooking or old-fashioned oats	1 egg
1 cup chopped walnuts	1 cup flour
1 1/2 cups packed brown sugar (preferably dark)	1 teaspoon baking soda
1 cup butter, softened	1/4 teaspoon salt
1 teaspoon vanilla extract	

Preheat oven to 350°F. Spread oats and walnuts on ungreased jelly roll pan. Bake 15 to 20 minutes, stirring occasionally, until light brown. Cool. Mix brown sugar, butter, vanilla and egg in a large bowl. Stir in cooled oat mixture and remaining ingredients. Drop dough by rounded tablespoonful about 2 inches apart onto ungreased cookie sheet. Bake 8 to 10 minutes or until golden brown. Bake these cookies a minute or two less for soft cookies, a minute or two longer for crisp cookies. Cool slightly; remove from cookie sheet. Makes 3 1/2 dozen.

OATMEAL COOKIES

Excellent! The ideal oatmeal cookie: crisp around the edges and chewy in the middle.

1 cup butter
1 cup sugar
1 cup packed brown sugar (preferably dark)
2 eggs
1 teaspoon vanilla extract
1 1/2 cups flour

1 teaspoon cream of tartar
1 teaspoon baking soda
1 teaspoon salt
3 cups old fashioned rolled oats
1 cup chopped pecans, toasted
1 cup raisins and/or coconut (optional)

Cream butter and sugars together with electric mixer until light and fluffy. Blend in eggs and vanilla. Combine flour, baking soda, salt and cream of tartar in a separate bowl. Add to butter mixture, mixing well. Stir in oats, nuts, raisins and/or coconut if desired. Dough will be stiff. Shape dough into a roll 2 1/2-inches in diameter on wax paper. Roll up in the wax paper and place in freezer for 2 hours or longer.

Preheat oven to 350°F. Slice in 1/4-inch slices, place on ungreased baking sheet. Bake for 12 to 15 minutes, or just until barely beginning to brown. Makes 4 dozen.

Variation: add 3/4 cup chocolate chunks to dough.

CHOCOLATE RAISIN OATMEAL COOKIES

1 1/4 cups butter, softened
3/4 cup packed brown sugar
1/2 cup sugar
1 large egg
1 teaspoon vanilla extract
3 cups quick-cooking oats, uncooked
1 1/2 cups flour

1 teaspoon baking soda
1 teaspoon salt
1 teaspoon cinnamon
1/4 teaspoon nutmeg
2 (7-ounce) packages chocolate-covered raisins (2 cups)

Preheat oven to 350°F. Beat butter at medium speed with an electric mixer until creamy; gradually adding sugars, beating well. Add egg and vanilla, beating until mixture is blended. In a separate bowl, combine oats, flour, baking soda, salt, cinnamon and nutmeg; gradually add to butter mixture, beating at low speed until blended. Stir in chocolate-covered raisins.

Drop cookie dough by rounded teaspoonfuls onto ungreased baking sheets. Bake for 12 minutes or until done to touch. Let cookies cool on baking sheet 10 minutes then remove to finish cooling on rack. Makes 3 dozen.

Goblets in the Roman Key, Ribbed Palm, Harp, Lincoln Drape with Tassel, and Star and Circle patterns, 19th century, American lead glass, WAM, gift of the family of Marjorie Molz, 2007.4.144, 142, 83, 100, 157.

AWESOME OATMEAL CHOCOLATE CHIP COOKIES

These are perfection. I like to make half of the batter with chocolate and half with raisins.

1 1/4 cups flour
1 teaspoon baking powder
1/2 teaspoon salt
14 tablespoons butter, softened
1/2 cup dark brown sugar, firmly packed
1/2 cup granulated sugar

1 large egg, at room temperature
2 teaspoons vanilla extract
2 1/2 cups old-fashioned rolled oats
3/4 cup raisins
3/4 cup chocolate chips
3/4 cup chopped walnuts (optional)

Preheat oven to 375°F. Line baking sheets with parchment paper or silicone mats, or grease generously with butter or cooking spray. Whisk together the flour, baking powder, and salt in a medium bowl. In a large bowl, mix butter and sugars together with an electric mixer until light and fluffy. Add the egg and mix until combined. Stir in vanilla extract. With the mixer on low speed or using a wooden spoon, gradually add the flour mixture until combined. Stir in oats, add nuts if desired. Divide the batter in half. Stir the raisins into one half and the chocolate chips into the other half, so you end up with some of each flavor. Drop the dough by rounded teaspoons onto the baking sheet. Leave about 3 inches between each one for spreading. Flatten each cookie slightly with the back of the spoon, but keep the edges of the dough craggy for the rough borders are a nice earthy texture. Bake 1 or 2 baking sheets at a time for 10 to 13 minutes, until lightly browned around the edges. Place baking sheets on a wire rack to cool completely. Store in an airtight container. Best eaten within two days. Freezes well. Makes 3 dozen.

MY FAVORITE CHOCOLATE CHIP COOKIES

This variation on the classic recipe is dependable and full of chocolate and nuts.

1 1/2 cups walnuts
1 1/2 cups pecans
1 cup butter, room temperature
1 cup packed dark brown sugar
1 cup sugar
2 eggs

1 tablespoon vanilla extract
2 1/3 cups flour
1 1/4 teaspoons baking soda
1 scant teaspoon salt
3 cups chocolate chips

Preheat oven to 350°F. Place nuts on a jelly roll pan to toast for 7 to 9 minutes, until golden brown. Cool and coarsely chop nuts. Line baking sheets with parchment paper or silicone mats. Cream butter and sugars with electric mixer until fluffy. Add eggs and vanilla and beat for 1 minute. In a separate bowl, whisk together the flour, baking soda, and salt. Add flour to batter and mix until just incorporated. Stir in the walnuts, pecans, and chocolate chips. The dough is pretty stiff so do this part by hand.

Drop the dough onto the prepared baking sheets using a #30 scoop (this will make mounds of dough about the size of a golf ball) or a tablespoon. Space the cookies about 1 1/2 inches apart, as they will spread. Bake for 10 to 12 minutes, until the cookies are just browned around the edges. Do not overbake. Makes 3 dozen.

HOME ON THE RANGE CHOCOLATE OATMEAL COOKIES

This chocolate batter cookie is a nice chewy rough hewn oatmeal cookie. One could also daringly label these as "CowPie Cookies".

1 cup butter, softened
1 1/2 cups sugar
1 cup brown sugar (preferably dark)
2 eggs
2 teaspoons vanilla extract
1 1/2 cups flour
3/4 cup unsweetened cocoa

1 teaspoon baking soda
1/2 teaspoon salt
3 cups quick-cooking oatmeal
1/2 cup chopped nuts
12 ounces bittersweet chocolate, chopped into
   small chunks (optional)

Preheat oven to 350°F. In a large mixing bowl, beat butter and sugars until light and fluffy. Add eggs and vanilla. Whisk together flour, cocoa, baking soda and salt; add to butter mixture mixing well. With spoon, mix in oats and nuts (batter will be stiff). Add bittersweet chunks if desired, but also good without. Drop by teaspoonfuls onto ungreased cookie sheet. Bake for 11 to 12 minutes or until set, do not over bake. Cool 1 minute, remove cookies from cookie sheet and finish cooling on wire rack. Cool completely before removing from rack or they will crumble. Makes 2 dozen.

C.A. Seward
On a Kansas Farm, 1931,
lithograph, WAM, gift
of George E. Vollmer,
the Clarence E. Vollmer
Collection, 1991.18
(See curator note on p.190
for information on the artist.)

CHEWY CHOCOLATE GINGERBREAD COOKIES

7 ounces best-quality semisweet chocolate
1 1/2 cups plus 1 tablespoon flour
1 1/4 teaspoons ground ginger
1 teaspoon cinnamon
1/4 teaspoon ground cloves
1/4 teaspoon nutmeg
1 tablespoon cocoa powder

1/2 cup unsalted butter
1 tablespoon freshly grated ginger
1/2 cup packed dark brown sugar
1/4 cup unsulfured molasses
1 teaspoon baking soda
1 1/2 teaspoons boiling water
1/4 cup sugar

Line two baking sheets with parchment paper. Chop chocolate into 1/4-inch chunks; set aside. In a medium bowl, whisk together flour, ground ginger, cinnamon, cloves, nutmeg, and cocoa. In a separate bowl beat butter and grated ginger with electric mixer until whitened, about 4 minutes. Add the brown sugar, and beat until combined. Add molasses, and beat until combined. In a small bowl, dissolve the baking soda in boiling water. Beat half of the flour mixture into the butter mixture. Beat in the baking soda mixture, then the remaining half of the flour mixture. Mix in the chocolate, and turn out onto a piece of plastic wrap. Pat the dough out to about 1 inch thick; seal with plastic wrap and refrigerate until firm. Chill for 2 hours or more.

Preheat oven to 325°F. Roll the dough into 1 1/2-inch balls and place 2 inches apart on baking sheets. Refrigerate 20 minutes. Roll the balls in granulated sugar. Bake until the surface crack slightly, 13 to 15 minutes; let cool 5 minutes; transfer to a wire rack to cool completely. Makes 2 1/2 dozen.

CHOCOLATE GINGER BALLS

1 cup sugar
3/4 cup butter
1 egg, beaten
2 teaspoons molasses
2 cups flour
2 teaspoons baking soda

1/2 teaspoon salt
1 teaspoon cinnamon
1/2 teaspoon ground cloves
1 teaspoon ginger
2 (1-ounce) squares unsweetened
    chocolate, melted

Preheat oven to 325°F. Prepare parchment-lined cookie sheets. Beat sugar and butter together with electric mixer until light and fluffy. Mix in remaining ingredients, adding chocolate last. Roll into small balls and roll in sugar. Bake for 6 to 10 minutes until done. Dip tops in sugar again before cooled. Makes 1 1/2 dozen.

DEATH BY CHOCOLATE COOKIES

A great treat for dunking in a glass of milk or for sharing, this recipe was orginally on the package of Baker's chocolate. Yes, it really is two cups of nuts and just 1/2 cup of flour! Nice you only have to use one bowl: easy.

Another great chocolate cookie, Chocolate Chewies, is in the "Chocolate Finishes" chapter, p. 255

2 packages (16 squares) semi-sweet baking
    chocolate (prefer Baker's) (divided use)
3/4 cup packed brown sugar
1/4 cup butter
2 eggs

1 teaspoon vanilla extract
1/2 cup flour
1/4 teaspoon baking powder
2 cups chopped nuts

Preheat oven to 350°F. Prepare cookie sheet by greasing or lining with parchment paper. Coarsely chop 8 squares (1 package) of the chocolate; set aside. Microwave remaining 8 squares chocolate in a large bowl on high 1 to 2 minutes. Stir until chocolate is melted and smooth. Stir in sugar, butter, eggs and vanilla. Stir in flour and baking powder. Stir in reserved chopped chocolate and nuts. Drop dough by teaspoonfuls onto the cookie sheets and bake 12 to 13 minutes or until firm to touch. Cool on sheet for one minute before transferring to wire rack. Makes 3 dozen.

BROWNIE CRACKLE COOKIES

This is a nice cookie for a bake sale or gift box as it is really pretty. Soft on the inside and just barely crunchy on the outside, it is nicely named. If you want to add pecans, walnuts or even peanuts, they all work nicely, just finely chop.

1 1/2 cups unbleached flour
1 tablespoon good quality cocoa powder
   (like Valhrona)
1 1/2 teaspoons baking powder
1/2 teaspoon salt
6 tablespoons vegetable oil
1 1/2 cups sugar

3 ounces unsweetened chocolate, melted
   and cooled
2 teaspoons vanilla extract
3 eggs, room temperature
1 cup minature semi-sweet chocolate morsels
2 cups powdered sugar for coating cookies

Whisk together the flour, cocoa powder, baking powder and salt in a medium bowl. Mix oil, sugar, melted chocolate, vanilla and eggs with an electric mixer in a large bowl until well blended. Add flour mixture slowly, while running mixer on low, beating just until flour is incorporated. Blend in the chocolate morsels. Batter will be more like cake batter than cookie dough at this point. Cover and refrigerate for at least 6 hours, or overnight, until firm enough to handle.

Preheat oven to 350°F. Line cookie sheets with parchment paper or silicone liner. Put powdered sugar in a bowl. Roll dough into 2 tablespoon-sized balls; roll in powdered sugar to coat. Place on baking sheet 2 1/2 inches apart. Bake for 12 to 14 minutes (insides will be moist and fudgy). Cool on baking sheet for 2 minutes then transfer to wire rack. Store in covered container after cool. Makes 2 1/2 dozen.

ROLLED COOKIES

Dough handling is a major part of the success with cut out cookies. After mixing the batter divide the dough into half. Place each half onto a piece of plastic wrap, overlap it and pat into a 1-inch thick circle and refrigerate for 30 minutes. Remove one half at a time from the refrigerator; roll out on top of a piece of plastic wrap on top of a lightly floured surface. To finish the process, place another piece of plastic wrap on top and smooth it over the top of a lightly floured surface of dough. This will give you an even texture. Roll the dough to $1/4$-inch thickness; remove the top layer of plastic and flip it over, remove remaining plastic and use rolling pin to finish smoothing. Cut out cookies and place on cookie sheet with parchment paper.

BUTTERSCOTCH ROLL-OUT DOUGH

This butterscotch roll-out cookie dough has a nice flavor. Directions given here for how to frost into shapes of basketball players and basketballs, but of course use the dough for any fun shape.

1 cup butterscotch chips	**Frosting**
1 cup butter, softened	$3/4$ cup butter
$1/2$ cup sugar	$1/4$ cup water
$1/2$ cup packed brown sugar	2 tablespoons flour
1 egg	$1 1/2$ teaspoons vanilla extract
2 tablespoons milk	4 cups powdered sugar
2 teaspoons vanilla extract	Paste food coloring
3 cups flour	

Preheat oven to 375°F. In a microwave using low setting, melt butterscotch chips; cool for 10 minutes. In a mixing bowl, cream butter and sugars. Add egg, milk, and vanilla; mix well. Beat in melted chips. Gradually add flour; mix well. Handle dough as describe above. Cut with a floured $4 1/2$-inch gingerbread man cookie cutter ("basketball players") and a 3 inch round cutter ("basketballs"). Place 2 inches apart on cookie sheet. Bake for 5 to 8 minutes or until edges are lightly browned. Cool for 1 minute; remove to wire racks to cool completely.

For frosting, combine shortening, water, flour and vanilla in a mixing bowl, gradually beat in sugar. Place a cup of frosting in a pastry bag with an icing tip or in plastic bag with a small hole cut in corner of bag. Pipe shirt and shorts on players. Fill in outline and smooth with a metal spatula. Tint $1/4$ cup of frosting black; place in a plastic bag. Pipe lines on round cookies to create basketballs; pipe hair, eyes and noses on players. Tint $1/4$ cup frosting red; pipe a mouth on each player. Tint remaining frosting to match team colors; pipe around shirts and shorts and a letter on shirts if desired. Makes about 2 dozen.

WHITE BUFFALO ROLL-OUT DOUGH

This is a good sugar cookie dough for cut out cookies. Fun as White Buffalos, with Chocolate Buffalos on next page.

See "Favorite Things" for sources to purchase great buffalo cookie cutters, as well as other Kansas shapes from the Kansas Heritage Center.

1 cup butter	**Frosting**
$2/3$ cup sugar	$3/4$ cup powdered sugar, sifted
1 egg	1 tablespoon butter
1 teaspoon vanilla extract	1 tablespoon milk
$1/2$ teaspoon salt	$1/2$ teaspoon vanilla extract
$2 1/2$ cups sifted flour	$1/4$ teaspoon lemon juice

Mix dough ingredients until all are well blended. Chill dough 3 to 4 hours before rolling. Preheat oven to 350°F. Roll out and cut, handling dough as described at top of page. Bake cookies on parchment paper for about 8 to 10 minutes or until barely colored. For frosting, melt butter, combine all ingredients and beat until smooth. Makes 2 dozen.

CHOCOLATE BUFFALO ROLL-OUT DOUGH

4 1/4 cups flour

1/4 teaspoon cream of tartar

1/4 teaspoon salt

1 teaspoon baking soda

5 (1-ounce) squares unsweetened chocolate

1 1/2 cups sugar

1/4 cup butter

1/4 cup vegetable shortening (butter-flavored)

1 extra large egg

1 1/2 teaspoons vanilla extract

1/2 cup evaporated milk

Fudgy Chocolate Frosting (see below)

Mix flour, cream of tartar, salt, and soda together with a wire whisk and set aside. Melt the chocolate squares on medium heat in a microwave. Cream together the sugar, butter and shortening with an electric mixer until light and fluffy. Add the egg and mix well. Stir in vanilla and evaporated milk and mix until incorporated. Add flour mixture in three batches, stirring well after each time. This will form a stiff dough. Let it set for 5 minutes and divide in half. Roll out and cut, handling dough as described on previous page. Bake on parchment paper lined baking sheet at 350°F for 8 minutes. Remove from sheet with wide spatula and place on wax paper on cool counter immediately. Allow cookies to cool before frosting. Makes 3 dozen.

Fudgy Chocolate Frosting

This frosting is like a heavy glaze, but gives a good even coating and just after it is spread you can decorate the cookie further with sprinkles.

1/2 cup butter

6 (1-ounce) squares of unsweetened chocolate

7 cups powdered sugar, sifted

3/4 cup coffee, hot

2 teaspoons vanilla

Melt butter and chocolate together over medium heat in a saucepan; stir until blended, remove from heat and transfer to mixing bowl. Add remaining ingredients and beat on high until well blended and smooth. May add additional hot coffee if needed until good spreading consistency is achieved. This will be a relatively thin frosting. Transfer into a shallow bowl with a surface large enough which will allow you to dip the entire top of your cookie. Dip top of cookie, holding carefully on the edges. As you raise it out of the frosting, angle down wards and smooth excess frosting from the surface with unserrated dinner knife, letting extra frosting fall back into bowl. Run knife around edge of cookie to remove excess and place cookie on wax paper for frosting to setup.

Charles M. Russell
Indian Buffalo Hunt, 1897, oil on canvas, WAM, The M.C. Naftzger Collection, 1937.4

BITE SIZE JAM SWIRLS

3 cups flour
Dash of salt
1 (8-ounce) package cream cheese
1 cup butter, softened

1/2 cup raspberry or apricot jam
1 cup finely chopped nuts
Coarse sugar for coating cookies

In a medium-mixing bowl, combine the flour and the salt. Using a pastry blender cut in the cream cheese and the butter until the mixture resembles fine crumbs and begins to cling together. Divide the dough in half. Cover and chill the dough for 1 hour. On a lightly floured surface, roll each half of dough to 1/4-inch thickness. Fold dough into thirds. Wrap in clear plastic wrap and chill for 2 hours.

Preheat oven to 375°F. Roll each half of the dough in a 12 x 14-inch rectangle. Spread each with jam to within 1/2 inch of the edge of dough; sprinkle with nuts. Beginning with the long side, roll up, jellyroll style; seal the seam. Cut into 1/2-inch slices. Roll one side of each slice in coarse sugar. Place the cookies, sugar side up, 1 inch apart on an ungreased cookie sheet. Bake for about 15 minutes or till lightly browned. Remove from cookie sheet to cool on a wire rack. Makes 3 dozen.

DANISH APRICOT ALMOND RIBBONS

This buttery cookie is very pretty and delicious. Can also be made with raspberry jam, and a nice way is to make them half apricot and half raspberry.

1 cup butter, room temperature
1/2 cup sugar
1 egg yolk
1 teaspoon vanilla extract
1/2 teaspoon grated lemon rind
2 1/2 cups flour

1/4 teaspoon salt
About 6 tablespoons apricot jam
1/2 cup powdered sugar
1 tablespoon cream or orange juice
Toasted sliced almonds

Preheat oven to 375°F. Beat butter and sugar until creamy with an electric mixer; beat in egg yolk and vanilla. Combine flour, salt and lemon zest; add to butter mixture, stirring completely. Shape dough into ropes about 3/4-inch in diameter and as long as the baking sheets. Place about 2 inches apart on baking sheets. With the side of your clean little finger, press a long groove down the center of each rope (but don't press all the way to the bottom of the baking sheet). Bake cookies for 10 minutes.

Remove cookies from oven and spoon jam into the grooves. Return to oven for 5 to 10 minutes or until cookies are firm to the touch and light golden. Meanwhile combine powdered sugar and cream (or juice). When cookies are done but while still hot, drizzle them with powdered sugar mixture. Sprinkle with almonds. Slice at 45-degree angle into 1-inch thick slices. Let cool briefly on baking sheets, then cool completely on wire rack. Store airtight. Makes 4 dozen. From Bonnie Aeschliman.

DUSEN CONFECTO

This simple and delicious cookie, appearing in the US during World War I, was popularized due to wartime economics and rationing of shortening and sugar. The results always bring compliments, looking and tasting much more sophisticated than one would expect.

2 cups flour
1/2 cup sugar
1/4 teaspoon salt
1 cup butter

1/4 pound (3/4 cup) unblanched almonds, grated
1 1/2 teaspoons vanilla extract
1/2 cup raspberry jelly or jam
Granulated sugar for coating cookies

In a small bowl, sift together the flour, sugar and salt. Cut in butter with pastry blender until mixture resembles a coarse meal. Blend in almonds, and vanilla and work the mixture with your fingers until a ball is formed. Cover and chill at least 3 hours.

Preheat oven to 350°F. Roll thin on floured work area and cut into desired shapes with donut hole cutter, or a flower shaped cookie cutter. Bake for 7 to 10 minutes on a parchment lined or greased baking sheet. While cookies are hot, spread 1/4 teaspoon of raspberry jam on bottom half, and press 2 cookies together to make a sandwich. Coat cookies with granulated sugar. Makes 7 dozen.

CHOCOLATE ALMOND THUMBPRINT BUTTER COOKIES

I have made these cookies for over 40 years, with fond memories of how my children always looked forward to having them cool enough to eat. They are nice anytime a special cookie is needed.

1 cup butter
3 tablespoons sugar
1 tablespoon almond extract
1/4 teaspoon salt
2 cups flour

Frosting
1 cup sifted powdered sugar
2 tablespoons cocoa
2 tablespoons hot water
1/2 teaspoon vanilla extract

The best thumbprints are deep and round to hold the chocolate securely. Your thumb can be used, but for perfectly round indentations press the backside of a melon baller into dough balls before baking.

Preheat oven to 400°F. Cream butter and sugar until soft and fluffy; add extract and flour mixed with salt. Roll into 1-inch balls. With the end of wooden spoon (or your thumb) make a well in the middle of each cookie for frosting. Bake 10 to 12 minutes. In a small bowl stir together the powdered sugar, cocoa, water and vanilla extract. Frost while still warm, filling the well in cookie.

ALMOND HORNS

These are delicious and the shape curves nicely around a cup of coffee.

1 pound almond paste, crumbled
1 cup sugar
2/3 cup powdered sugar, sifted

5 egg whites (divided use)
2 1/2 cups sliced almonds
Dipping chocolate

Preheat oven to 350°F. Line cookie sheets with parchment paper. Beat almond paste and sugars together at medium speed with electric mixer. Add 3 whites and beat 2 minutes. The dough will be very sticky; refrigerate for 1 hour. Roll tablespoons of dough into balls and place on sheets. Roll balls between palms to form 3-inch long logs, keeping the center slightly thicker. Dip the logs into 2 whites, slightly beated, then roll in almonds. After completing for all, shape them into a curve, a slight crescent, and refrigerate for 15 minutes. Bake 15 to 18 minutes or just until golden brown. Slide the parchment paper off the sheets and cool on counter. Dip one end of the horn in dipping chocolate (1 cup of chocolate bark, melted in microwave), place on sheet and chill 10 minutes until chocolate is set. Makes 3 dozen.

CHEWY PECAN DIAMONDS

Crust
1 ¾ cups flour
⅓ cup powdered sugar
¼ cup cornstarch
½ teaspoon salt
¾ cup unsalted, chilled butter, cut into ½-inch pieces (if using salted butter, omit salt)

Topping
1 ¼ cup packed golden brown sugar
½ cup light corn syrup
¼ cup unsalted butter
3 cups coarsely chopped pecans
½ cup heavy cream
2 teaspoons vanilla extract
Garnish: ½ to ¾ cup chocolate chips, melted (can be either semi-sweet or milk chocolate)

To prepare the crust, preheat oven to 350°F. Line a 9 x 13-inch baking pan with foil, leaving 1 inch overhang on each side. Butter foil. Blend flour, powdered sugar, cornstarch and salt in food processor. Add butter and pulse (quick on and off) until mixture begins to clump together. Press dough evenly onto bottom of foil-lined pan. Bake crust until set and golden, about 25 minutes. Remove from oven and let stand while preparing topping. Reduce oven temperature to 325°F.

To prepare the topping, stir brown sugar, corn syrup and butter in heavy saucepan over medium high heat until sugar dissolves; boil 1 minute. Add pecans and cream. Boil until mixture thickens slightly, about 3 minutes. Stir in vanilla. Pour hot topping over warm crust. Bake until caramel is darker and bubbles thickly, about 20 minutes. Transfer pan to rack; let cool completely in pan and the top will harden. When cool, lift foil sling and cookies from pan onto cutting board. Using heavy sharp knife, cut into 1-inch diamonds. Drizzle tops with a thin stream of chocolate that has been melted in microwave oven. May be made a week ahead. Store between sheets of waxed paper in airtight container. Makes 2½ dozen.

OPERA BARS
Both Opera Bars and Vienna Bars were served at the Wichita-Sedgwick County Historical Museum Wreath Festival.

Crust
1 cup butter
½ cup powdered sugar
½ cup cornstarch
2 cups flour
Pinch of salt

Filling
4 eggs
2½ cups brown sugar
½ teaspoon baking powder
Pinch of salt
2 cups chopped nuts
1 cup coconut
2 teaspoons vanilla extract

Cream Cheese Frosting
½ cup butter
1 package powdered sugar (3½ cups)
1 (8-ounce) package cream cheese
1 teaspoon vanilla extract

Preheat oven to 325°F. For crust, mix crust ingredients together and press in 11 x 17-inch pan and bake 15 minutes. For filling, stir eggs and brown sugar together; beat until light. Add baking powder, salt, nuts, coconut and vanilla, and stir. Pour over crust and bake for 30 minutes. For frosting, stir ingredients until creamy. When cool, ice with Cream Cheese Frosting and cut into bars. Makes 2 dozen. From Wanda Spencer.

VIENNA BARS

1 cup butter
1½ cups sugar (divided use)
¼ teaspoon salt
¼ teaspoon nutmeg
2 egg yolks

2½ cups flour
1 (13-ounce) jar raspberry preserves
4 egg whites
2 cups finely chopped walnuts (or almonds)

Preheat oven to 350°F. In a large bowl, cream butter with ½ cup sugar. Beat in salt, nutmeg and 2 egg yolks. Gradually add flour. Mix until hard to work, then knead on a lightly floured surface until dough is smooth. Pat dough into a greased 12 x 17-inch jellyroll pan. Bake for 15 to 20 minutes or until lightly browned. Remove from oven and spread with jar of raspberry preserves. In a deep bowl, beat egg whites with a beater until stiff peaks form. Fold 1 cup of sugar and nuts into egg whites. Gently spread mixture over the jelly. Bake for 25 minutes. Remove from oven, cool 5 minutes and cut into 50 pieces.

GOLDEN GLAZED ALMOND BARS

1 1/2 cups butter
3/4 cup sugar
1 egg
1/2 teaspoon baking powder
3/4 teaspoon almond extract (divided use)
1/4 teaspoon salt

1 3/4 cups flour
Milk, as needed
1/2 cup sliced almonds
1/2 cup powdered sugar
2 to 3 teaspoons milk

Winslow Homer
In the Mowing, 1874,
oil on canvas, WAM,
The Roland P. Murdock
Collection, M127.54

Beat butter with electric mixer on medium speed for 30 seconds. Add sugar; beat well. Beat in egg, baking powder, 1/2 teaspoon almond extract and salt. Stir in flour just until incorporated. Cover and chill dough until easy to handle, about 1 to 3 hours.

Preheat oven to 375°F. On lightly floured surface, roll dough, half at a time, to a 6 x 12-inch rectangle. Cut each strip of dough crosswise into 1-inch bars. Brush with milk. Sprinkle with almonds, gently pressing almonds into the dough. Transfer to a cookie sheet, placing the cookies 1 inch apart. Repeat with remaining dough. Bake for 8 to 10 minutes or till edges are firm and bottoms are very lightly browned. Remove bars from cookie sheet; cool on wire racks. Make glaze, combining powdered sugar, 1/4 teaspoon almond extract and enough milk to make a drizzle consistency. Drizzle over bars. Makes 4 dozen.

LAYERED TRIPLE CHOCOLATE OAT BARS

1/2 cup butter
1 cup quick-cooking oatmeal
1 cup graham cracker crumbs (or vanilla
    wafer crumbs)
1 (14-ounce) can sweetened condensed milk

1 cup milk chocolate chips
1 cup bittersweet chocolate chips
1 cup white chocolate chips
1 1/3 cups sweetened flaked coconut
1 cup chopped walnuts

Preheat oven to 350°F. Place butter in a 9 x 13-inch baking pan and place in oven for 5 to 7 minutes, to melt butter. In a medium bowl, stir together oats and graham cracker crumbs and sprinkle mixture evenly over melted butter. Pour condensed milk evenly over crumbs. Sprinkle surface evenly with the three types of chocolate chips, then the coconut and walnuts. Press down firmly. Bake for 25 to 30 minutes or until lightly browned. Remove pan to a wire rack and cool completely. Cut into bars. Store cooled bars in an airtight container. Makes 2 1/2 dozen.

MIRACLE SQUARES

1 cup packed brown sugar
1 cup butter, softened
1 teaspoon vanilla extract
1 egg
1 cup flour (all-purpose)
1/2 cup whole wheat flour
1 cup chopped walnuts or pecans

1 (10-ounce) jar orange marmalade or
    apricot preserves

Glaze
1/2 cup powdered sugar
2 to 3 teaspoons milk

Preheat oven to 350°F. Lightly grease a 9 x 13-inch pan. In a medium bowl, cream brown sugar and butter until light and fluffy. Add vanilla and egg, beating well. Add flours and nuts to the sugar mixture, blending well. Press half of the dough into the prepared pan and spread with the marmalade. Drop the remaining dough by teaspoonfuls over the marmalade. Bake for 25 to 30 minutes. In a small bowl combine the powdered sugar and enough milk to make a glaze. Drizzle the glaze over top of bars. When glaze is set, cut into squares. Makes 2 1/2 dozen.

LUSCIOUS APRICOT BARS
Many happy memories with this recipe from Barbara Rensner.

2/3 cup dried apricots
1/2 cup butter, softened
1/4 cup sugar
1 1/3 cups flour (divided use)
1/2 teaspoon baking powder
1/4 teaspoon salt

1 cup dark brown sugar
2 eggs, well beaten
1/2 teaspoon vanilla extract
1/2 cup chopped nuts
Powdered sugar for coating

Rinse dried apricots, cover with water and boil for 10 minutes, cool and chop. Preheat oven to 350°F. Mix butter, sugar and 1 cup flour together until crumbly. Pack this mixture into a 9 x 12-inch pan and bake for about 25 minutes or until lightly browned. Sift together 1/3 cup flour, baking powder and salt. Gradually beat brown sugar into eggs. Add flour mixture to the egg mixture and mix well. Stir in vanilla, nuts and apricots. Spread this over baked layer and bake for another 30 minutes or until done. Cool in pan, cut into bars; roll in powdered sugar.

BLONDE BOMBSHELL BROWNIES

Combining white chocolate chips and chunks, as well as the coconut, makes this a very pretty "blondie".

¹/₂ cup plus 2 tablespoons cake flour
¹/₂ cup flour
¹/₄ teaspoon baking powder
¹/₈ teaspoon salt
¹/₂ cup butter, melted and briefly cooled
¹/₂ cup plus 3 tablespoons light brown sugar

1 egg
1 egg yolk
1¹/₂ teaspoons vanilla extract
6 ounces white chocolate, cut into small chunks
1 cup white chocolate chips (divided use)
³/₄ cup sweetened flaked coconut

Preheat oven to 350°F. Coat a square 8-inch square baking pan with cooking spray. Whisk flours, baking powder and salt together in a small bowl. Whisk butter and sugar together in a medium bowl; stir in flour mixture and blend until just combined. Add white chocolate chunks, ²/₃ cup of white chocolate chips and coconut. The batter will be stiff and very dense. Scrape batter into pan and smooth. Sprinkle the remaining ¹/₃ cup of white chocolate chips over the top. Bake for 30 minutes or until set and a light golden color around the edges. Cut into 16 squares, and carefully remove from pan. Store in an airtight tin. Makes 16 brownies.

Choose "white chips" with the highest fat content for their softer texture. I like Guittard's Choc-Au-Lait White Chips.

Morris Kantor
Still Life of Flowers, 1929,
oil on canvas, WAM,
Art Fund, Friends of the
Wichita Art Museum, Inc.,
1986.90

While some purchased ones can be tough enough to crack a tooth, these aren't. Butter in two of these recipes helps to keep the biscotti just soft enough.

HAZELNUT BISCOTTI

Don't be scared off by the size of this recipe; the biscotti keep well, so freeze or give away whatever you don't eat right away.

QUICK COOK TIP

If you are running short on time, you can try a shortcut for the second baking interval which dries the biscotti. Instead of flipping the cut slices halfway through the drying time, place the biscotti on a wire cooling rack set on a cookie sheet when baking. The rack elevates the slices, allowing air to circulate all around them and drying both sides at once.

1 1/4 cups unsalted butter, room temperature	1 teaspoon vanilla extract
4 cups sugar	7 cups flour
2/3 cup honey	1 tablespoon plus 2 teaspoons baking powder
3 eggs	1/4 teaspoon salt
3 tablespoons Frangelico liqueur	2 cups hazelnuts, coarsely chopped

Preheat oven to 450°F. Line a 12 x 17-inch baking sheet with parchment paper or silicone mats, or grease generously with butter or cooking spray. Beat butter and sugar together in a large bowl with an electric mixer for 2 to 3 minutes, until light. Add honey, eggs, Frangelico and vanilla extract; beat until combined. Add flour, baking powder, and salt; mix until just combined. The dough will be very stiff, but not sticky. Add the hazelnuts and use your hands to incorporate them evenly.

Spread a large piece of parchment paper or waxed paper over a flat work surface. Divide the dough in half. Shape each half into a roll about 16 inches long, about 4 inches wide. Use the waxed paper to roll and work the dough into shape. Place dough rolls on a prepared baking sheet, leaving about 2 inches between them. Bake for 10 minutes, until the edges are golden brown and the insides are a light golden brown. The dough will flatten and have vertical cracks down the middle. Cool the baked dough completely on the baking sheet, about 1 hour at room temperature or 20 to 25 minutes in the refrigerator. (It breaks apart if handled when hot.)

Lower the oven temperature to 350°F. Cut each roll diagonally into 1/4-inch-thick slices using a heavy knife with a 10-inch blade (a good clean chop works best). Place the slices on the baking sheet. The biscotti do not spread as they bake the second time, so they can be placed close enough to touch. Bake for about 20 to 25 minutes. The biscotti are done when they are golden brown. Initially, the biscotti will be slightly soft; they harden and become crisp as they cool. Let them rest for about 10 minutes before removing them from the baking sheet. Biscotti keep for 2 weeks in an airtight container, or 1 month if wrapped and frozen. Makes 6 dozen.

Variations: try adding 2 cups of dried cranberries, dried cherries, or chocolate chips (add along with the hazelnuts.) Or to get four flavors from one batch, divide the dough into quarters before adding the hazelnuts, combine 1 cup of the hazelnuts with 1/2 cups of any mix-in to one portion of dough. Another variation is to substitute blanched slivered almonds for the hazelnuts, and if so, substitute an equal amount of almond extract for the Frangelico.

BITTERSWEET CHOCOLATE HAZELNUT BISCOTTI

Use the freshest hazelnuts and the finest cocoa powder you can find.

2 1/4 cups flour (plus more for dusting)
1/4 cup of good cocoa powder (prefer Valhrona)
1 teaspoon baking soda
1 teaspoon salt
2 generous cups of bittersweet (60% cocoa) chocolate chips

1 1/2 cups hazelnuts
4 eggs
1 egg white (lightly beaten)
1 1/4 cups sugar
Sparkly sanding sugar

Preheat oven 350°F. Line baking sheet with parchment or silicone mat. In a food processor briefly pulse flour, cocoa powder, baking soda, salt, 1cup of the chocolate chips and all of the hazelnuts, until you have largish pea-sized chunks. In the bowl of an electric mixer beat eggs and sugar on medium-high speed for several minutes until the mixture is pale yellow and holds a ribbon-like trail on the surface. Turn the mixer to low speed and slowly add the flour mixture and finally the remaining chocolate chips until just combined. Don't over mix!

On lightly floured board turn out the dough and dust enough just not to be sticky. Divide the dough in two. Place dough on baking sheet and shape each piece into 18-inch log (shape to the length of the baking sheet). Brush the tops with egg white and the sprinkle with sparkly sugar. Bake 12 minutes, rotate and bake another 12 minutes. Transfer to cooling rack and cool for about 25 minutes. Place logs on a cutting board and slice 1/4 to 1/2-inch slices on the diagonal. Place wire rack on the baking sheet and then arrange the slices cut side down, on the rack. Bake for another 12 minutes, remove from oven and cool completely. Makes 4 dozen. From Amy Cunningham.

Biscotti may be frosted after cooled. Melt 1 1/2 cups chocolate chips with 2 tablespoons of shortening in microwave on medium-high, stirring after each 3-minute interval, until melted. Frost each cookie with melted chocolate only on bottom. Set on wire rack to dry.

MACADAMIA BISCOTTI

Lee calls these his "dog bones" and comes looking for them when he gets a cup of coffee. They are soft enough however that they do not have to be dunked.

2 cups flour
2 teaspoons baking powder
1/8 teaspoon salt
2/3 cup unsalted butter, softened
2/3 cup sugar

2 eggs, room temperature
1 teaspoon vanilla extract
1/4 teaspoon grated lemon peel (optional)
2/3 cup finely chopped lightly salted macadamia nuts

In a medium bowl, stir together flour, baking powder and salt. In a large bowl, using a wooden spoon, cream together butter and sugar until blended. One at a time, add eggs, stirring well after each. Stir in vanilla and lemon rind. Gradually stir in flour mixture until combined. Stir in nuts. Cover and refrigerate dough for 1 hour, or until firm enough to shape. Shape dough into two 6-inch long rolls, each about 1 3/4 inches in diameter. Wrap rolls in plastic wrap; refrigerate rolls for 3 hours, or until firm.

Preheat oven to 350°F. Lightly butter two large baking sheets or use parchment paper to line sheets. Working with one dough roll at a time, roll dough back and forth on a hard surface to reshape. Place dough rolls on one of the baking sheets leaving 6 inches between them. Bake for 22 to 27 minutes, or until bottoms are lightly browned and tops are dry. Lower oven temperature to 275°F. Remove baking sheet to a wire rack and cool for 5 minutes. Using a wide spatula, transfer rolls to wire rack and cool for 20 minutes. Transfer rolls to a cutting board. Using a large serrated knife and with a sawing motion, slice rolls into 1/2-inch thick slices. The slices may still be slightly doughy. Lay slices on the other large baking sheet, leaving about 1/2 inch between slices. Bake for 20 minutes. Using a small metal spatula, turn cookies over. Bake for 20 to 25 minutes more, or until cookies are lightly browned. Remove baking sheet to a wire rack and cool for about 2 minutes. When cool, store in an airtight container; they keep very well. Makes about 2 dozen. Recipe can be doubled.

Pies & Tarts

PERFECT PIE PASTRY

Nothing makes the appreciation of baked goods easier than a tender and flaky crust. There are, however, varying amounts of time that can be devoted to the process. In a pinch, using a refrigerated dough in lieu of your own recipe will work quite well. You can also consider an elegant touch with frozen puff pastry or phyllo dough available from your grocer.

PIE PASTRY FOR TWO-CRUST PIE
Pâte Brisée
Adapted by niece Linda Ade Brand from the Beyond Parsley *cookbook published by the Junior League of Kansas City. Linda is an excellent cook and she adeptly guides the novice to making a perfect crust. Thank you Linda!*

PASTRY TIPS

Measure flour by dipping the measuring cup into the flour and scraping off excess. Measuring in a different way will change the proportions.

Make sure your butter and shortening are chilled. Tablespoons of shortening chill quickly if dropped into a small bowl of ice water.

Beat your egg in a small glass measuring cup, then add enough ice water to reach ³/₄ cup. You will only use about half of this mixture in the dough. Reserve the rest for an egg wash to be used later in assembling the pie.

1 ³/₄ cups flour
1 teaspoon salt
¹/₂ cup chilled unsalted butter, cut into
    small pieces

3 tablespoons shortening, chilled
1 egg plus enough ice water to equal ³/₄ cup)
    (divided use)

Assemble ingredients. Measure flour and salt into the bowl of food processor and process briefly to combine. Add chilled butter pieces and shortening. Pulse the mixture until the butter and shortening are no bigger than small peas. With the processor running, gradually add approximately HALF the egg and water mixture in small increments, processing just until the dough comes together into a ball. Do not over-process. Remove the dough from the processor and place it on a lightly floured board (a marble slab is recommended here). Divide dough in half and form each half into a disc. Wrap each disc in plastic wrap and refrigerate for at least 30 minutes. (May be frozen for later use; just soften the dough in the refrigerator before proceeding.) Refrigerate the remaining egg and water mixture to use as an egg wash later on the rolled-out crust. Meanwhile, prepare desired filling. Preheat oven according to recipe for the pie you wish to make.

When ready to proceed, remove dough from the refrigerator. Place one disc on a lightly floured board or marble slab. Beat the dough with a rolling pin to soften it if it is too firm to immediately roll out. Roll one portion out for a 9-inch crust, adding flour if necessary to keep dough from sticking. Fold the dough gently in half and then fold in half again to form a triangle. Place the point of the folded pastry at the center of pie pan and unfold, gently pressing the pastry into the bottom of the pan with the edges of the pastry hanging a bit over the sides of the pan. Fill pie with desired filling.

Roll out second disc of dough for top crust, or slice it into strips for a lattice crust if desired. Brush the edge of the bottom crust with the reserved egg wash before placing the top crust in place. Trim excess dough and crimp edges in a decorative manner. Brush entire top crust with egg wash and sprinkle lightly with sugar to obtain a nicely browned crust. If using a solid top crust, cut air vents into top before baking. Bake according to recipe for the desired filling.

NEVER FAIL PIE CRUST

Previous page:

William Merritt Chase
(attributed to),
Still Life with Cherries,
no date, oil on canvas,
WAM, gift of Mrs.
Hortense Kirkwood,
1986.57

4 cups flour
1 ¹/₂ teaspoons salt
1 tablespoon sugar
1 ¹/₂ cups shortening (butter flavored)

1 egg, beaten
¹/₂ cup cold water
1 teaspoon vinegar

Stir flour and salt together. Cut in shortening. Mix beaten egg, 6 tablespoons water and vinegar and stir into flour. Add more water if needed. Chill several hours or overnight. Roll out (as above). Makes 4 crusts.

PUFF PASTRY DOUGH FOR TARTS

Anything is fabulous in a puff pastry crust. Here is how to use the thawed frozen dough.

Line a 10-inch tart pan with puff pastry dough, overlapping if necessary to cover the bottom and sides. Press foil inside and fill with raw rice or beans (termed "baking blind"). Bake at 350°F for 10 minutes. Carefully remove foil and beans. Then return to oven and continue baking until golden. Cool and fill with custard and top with fresh fruits. Or paint with melted chocolate chips and sprinkle with chopped nuts, then fill with whipped cream and fresh sliced strawberries.

PHYLLO PASTRY FOR TARTS or TARTLETS

Another favorite pastry trick is the very versatile and delicious phyllo dough. Phyllo can be used to wrap almost anything, turning the most simple of foods into great treats, from small individual pastries to larger tarts with sweet or savory fillings. Buy phyllo dough frozen and defrost overnight in the refrigerator or at room temperature for 3 to 4 hours. Here is how to make tartlet shells from phyllo dough.

10 sheets frozen phyllo pastry, thawed
Melted butter, or butter-flavored cooking spray (for a lower fat option)

Place 1 sheet of phyllo on a flat surface (keeping remaining phyllo covered). Lightly brush with melted butter or spray phyllo with butter-flavored cooking spray. Repeat procedure with 3 more sheets of phyllo and butter or cooking spray. Cut phyllo into 24 (3 inch) squares, using kitchen shears or a sharp knife. Coat miniature (1³/₄ inch) muffin pans with cooking spray; place one square layered phyllo in to each muffin cup, pressing gently in center to form a pastry shell. Repeat procedure with remaining 4 sheets of phyllos and butter or butter flavored cooking spray. Bake shells at 350°F for 8 minutes or until golden. Carefully remove from pans; let cool on wire racks. Makes 4 dozen.

QUICK APPLE TART

2 Granny Smith apples, cored and sliced thinly
2 teaspoons fresh lemon juice
2 teaspoons brown sugar
2 teaspoons cinnamon

4 ounces prepared puff pastry, thawed,
    if frozen

Caramel Topping
¹/₂ cup butter
¹/₂ cup dark corn syrup
2 cups sugar
¹/₂ cup heavy cream

Cinnamon ice cream

Preheat oven to 400°F. Toss apple slices with the lemon juice, brown sugar and cinnamon. Place puff pastry on baking sheet. Top with the apples. Bake for about 15 minutes, or until pastry is puffed and golden. Meanwhile, to make the caramel topping, melt the butter in a heavy saucepan over medium heat, add corn syrup and sugar and bring to a boil, stirring constantly. Remove from heat and whisk in the heavy cream. When ready to serve heat the caramel topping and spoon onto 6 plates. Slice pastry into 6 pieces and place one on each plate Top with scoop of cinnamon ice cream and drizzle with a little caramel topping. Makes 6 servings.

Rolling out dough to a uniform thickness can take a little practice. A nifty device to assist is called "Perfection Strips".

They are broad lengths of wood of different widths. You just place these along side of your dough and roll your untapered rolling pin on top of them and you have flawless uniformity! See "A Few Favorite Things" for purchasing.

Herschel C. Logan
Harvest, 1924, block print, WAM, gift of Samuel H. and Martha F. Logan, 2005.13.82

APPLE WALNUT PIE

Any treat with apples is a family favorite, but this is really great. The addition of ground walnuts keep this crust crisp, and the flavor of nuts always pair very nicely with apples.

3/4 cup ground walnuts

2 tablespoons brown sugar

2 tablespoons beaten egg

1 tablespoon milk plus scant for top crust

3 tablespoons butter, softened (divided use)

1/4 teaspoon vanilla extract

1 1/4 teaspoons lemon juice (divided use)

Pastry for 9-inch double crust pie

5 cups sliced peeled tart apples (about 6)

3/4 cup sugar

2 tablespoons flour

1 teaspoon cinnamon

1/4 teaspoon nutmeg

1/4 teaspoon salt

Preheat oven to 375°F. Combine walnuts, brown sugar, egg, milk, 1 tablespoon butter, vanilla and 1/4 teaspoon lemon juice. Line a 9-inch pie plate with bottom pastry and spread nut mixture over it. Combine sugar, flour, cinnamon, nutmeg and salt. Toss the apples with 1 teaspoon lemon juice in a large bowl, sprinkle with sugar mixture, toss and then spread over the nut mixture. Dot with the remaining butter. Make a lattice crust with the other pastry, brush top with milk. Bake for 50 to 60 minutes until golden brown. Makes one 9-inch pie.

BUTTERSCOTCH NUT APPLE PIE

Adapted from recipe in the Eureka Springs newspaper The Echo, *the nuts and butterscotch are brilliant additions.*

1 1/4 cup sugar

1/2 teaspoon cinnamon

1/4 teaspoon nutmeg

1/8 teaspoon salt

3 tablespoons flour

1/3 cup chopped pecans

1/4 cup butterscotch chips

5 cups Granny Smith apples, cored, peeled and sliced

Pastry for 9-inch double crust pie

3 tablespoons butter

Cinnamon sugar

Preheat oven to 350°F. Mix the sugar, cinnamon, nutmeg, salt, and flour together in a large bowl. Add chopped pecans and butterscotch. Add apples to the spice mixture; stir to coat well. Put into 9-inch pie plate lined with pastry. Dot with butter and cover with top crust. Seal and flute edges. Cut slits in top; spray with cooking spray and sprinkle cinnamon-sugar on top (about 2 teaspoons of sugar and 1/2 teaspoon cinnamon). Bake for about one hour or until crust is brown and the filling is bubbling through the slits on top. Makes one 9-inch pie.

BEST EVER FRESH PEACH PIE

1/2 cup sugar

1/2 cup brown sugar

3 tablespoons flour

1/2 teaspoon salt

3/4 teaspoon or less cinnamon

1/2 cup butter

1 tablespoon fresh lemon juice

1 teaspoon almond extract

6 to 7 large fresh peaches, peeled and sliced

Pastry for 9-inch double crust pie

1 egg

Preheat oven to 425°F. Combine sugars, flour, salt, and cinnamon. Cut in butter, lemon juice, and almond extract with pie dough cutter. Mix with peaches. Put in 9-inch pastry lined pie dish and top with crust. Beat together 1 egg with 1 tablespoon water and using pastry brush cover top and crust of pie; sprinkle top with 1 tablespoon sugar and 1/4 teaspoon cinnamon. Bake for 15 minutes; reduce oven to 350°F and continue baking for 30 minutes or until edges are bubbly. Makes one 9-inch pie.

GRANDMA KING'S PIE

This is a great pie for a beginning baker as it can be adapted for any type of fruit and is a good exercise in adding ingredients "to taste." The dough is very forgiving, easy to roll out and tender, even if overworked a little. Grandma's advice is to work quickly when making a pie to ensure a light and tender dough.

Dough
1 ³/₄ cups flour
³/₄ cup butter, melted
¹/₂ cup ice water

Filling
2 ¹/₂ pounds fruit, peeled seeded and chopped
    as needed (see suggestions in margin note)
³/₄ cup sugar
Cinnamon
Ginger
Ground cloves

Preheat oven to 400°F. Grease a 9-inch pie pan. Mix the flour and butter together until evenly mixed. Gradually add the cold water, adding only enough to make a cohesive dough. Working quickly, divide the dough into two balls, wrap in plastic and refrigerate until ready to roll.

Combine the prepared fruit with the sugar. Add a bit of cinnamon, ginger and cloves to suit your taste and stir to combine. Allow to sit while you roll out the dough.

Working with one ball of dough at a time, roll to ¹/₄-inch thickness between two sheets of wax paper. Drape one sheet of dough into the bottom of the pan and fill with the fruit mixture. Cover with the second sheet of dough, trim all but 1-inch of dough from around the edges and fold under. Crimp the edges together in a decorative pattern. Using a fork, neatly poke a few holes into the top crust to let steam escape. Bake 35 to 40 minutes until the pastry is golden brown. Makes one 9-inch pie. From Charles K. (King) Steiner.

Suggested fruit combinations for the filling:
- *Pears combined with fresh or dried cranberries (be sure to use slightly under-ripe pears)*
- *Granny Smith apples combined with dried tart cherries*
- *Peaches, plums or nectarines*
- *A combination of summer berries: blueberries and raspberries*

Marguerite Stix
Flowers, ca. 1953, watercolor, WAM, gift of the Estate of Marguerite Stix, 1978.34.3

MOLASSES PECAN PIE

When the crust is flaky and tender, a good pie becomes a great pie.

PASTRY TIPS:

1) Make sure that the water added is chilled; ice cubes added to the water will achieve this.

2) Do not over knead the dough. In fact, the less you work it, the better.

3) Chill your pie dough at least an hour before rolling out.

Pastry Crust
1 cup flour
1/2 teaspoon salt
1/3 cup shortening (butter flavored)
3 tablespoons cold water

Filling
3 eggs
1/2 cup sugar
1 cup light molasses
1 tablespoon cornmeal
1 teaspoon vinegar
1/4 cup butter, melted
1 cup chopped pecans

Preheat oven to 350°F. Stir flour and salt together. Cut in shortening. Mix in water, adding more water if needed. Let stand 10 minutes (but preferably chill several hours). Roll out as you would for pie crusts. Prepare unbaked pastry shell in a 9-inch pie plate. Beat eggs with an electric mixer at medium speed, add sugar, molasses, cornmeal, vinegar and butter and combine, stir in chopped pecans. Pour mixture into pastry shell. Bake for 35 to 45 minutes. Let cool completely and garnish with whipped cream and a pecan half, if desired. Makes one 9-inch pie.

SOUTHERN PECAN PIE

1 unbaked 9-inch pastry crust (add additional teaspoon of salt to favorite pie crust recipe)
1 1/2 cups pecan halves
3 eggs
1 tablespoon butter

1 cup dark corn syrup
1/2 teaspoon vanilla extract
1 cup sugar
1 tablespoon flour

Preheat oven to 350°F. Arrange pecans in bottom of pie shell. Beat eggs until light. Add butter, corn syrup and vanilla. Stir until blended. Combine sugar and flour and blend with egg mixture. Pour over nuts in pie shell and let stand until nuts rise to surface. Bake for 45 minutes. Makes 8 servings.

KEY LIME PIE with ALMOND CRUMB CRUST

Key Lime pie, made and served the old-fashioned way with uncooked eggs, is considered risky today. This recipe, with full flavor and great texture, addresses those concerns by baking the filling briefly, spreading on the meringue and then baking again for 15 minutes.

1 cup graham cracker crumbs
2/3 cup blanched almonds, toasted lightly, cooled and ground fine in food processor
6 tablespoons butter
1/4 cup sugar
4 teaspoons grated lime zest

4 egg yolks, lightly beaten
1 (14-ounce) can sweetened condensed milk
1/2 cup Key lime juice (fresh, if possible)
4 egg whites
Pinch cream tartar
1/2 cup sugar

Preheat oven to 350°F. Combine graham cracker crumbs, ground almonds, butter and sugar. Press into bottom and side of 10-inch pie plate; bake in oven for 10 minutes and let shell cool, leaving oven on. In a large mixing bowl, combine egg yolks and zest and whisk together condensed milk and key lime juice, stirring for 3 minutes so that the acid in the juice has time to work on the yolks. Pour filling into the crust and bake for 15 minutes. In a very clean metal bowl, beat egg whites and cream of tartar until foamy; add sugar 2 tablespoons at a time and continue beating until peaks are stiff. With a large spatula, transfer to top of warm filling, swirling to make sure that meringue touches crust all the way around. Return pie to oven and bake for 15 minutes more, until meringue is just slightly browned on tips. Cool several hours and serve at room temperature, garnishing each slice, if desired, with sugared lime slice (made by slicing half of a lime paper thin and dipping in sugar). Make 6 to 8 servings.

PARADISE PUMPKIN PIE

This is a delicious way to cheer on autumn. If you are sweet on pumpkin, you must give this pie a try. Also, try the Pumpkin Gooey Butter Cake on p. 238, another Fall favorite.

First Layer
1 (8-ounce) package cream cheese, softened
1/4 cup sugar
1/2 teaspoon vanilla extract
1 slightly beaten egg

1 unbaked 9-inch pastry shell

Second Layer
1 cup canned pumpkin
1 cup evaporated milk
2 beaten eggs

1/4 cup brown sugar, packed
1/4 cup sugar
1 teaspoon cinnamon
1/4 teaspoon ground nutmeg
1/2 teaspoon salt

Topping
1/2 cup chopped pecans
2 tablespoons butter, softened
2 tablespoons flour
2 tablespoons brown sugar

Preheat oven to 350°F. In a small mixing bowl, beat cream cheese, sugar, vanilla and egg until smooth. Chill for 30 minutes. Turn into the unbaked pastry shell. Prepare the second layer by mixing the pumpkin, evaporated milk, eggs, sugars, cinnamon, nutmeg and salt. Carefully pour over cream cheese mixture. Cover the edge of pie with foil. Bake for 25 minutes. Remove foil; bake 25 minutes more.

For the topping, stir together the pecans, butter, flour and brown sugar. Sprinkle mixture over the top of the pie. Bake for 10 to 15 minutes more or until a knife inserted near the center comes out clean. Cool the pie on a wire rack. Makes one 9-inch pie.

CLASSIC CHESS PIE

Chess pie has been popular for generations, originating during difficult economic times as you just need a few eggs from the henhouse, some cornmeal, sugar and butter. But now it is popular for another reason: it is easy! Try using refrigerated pie crusts to make it even easier. Rolling two refrigerated pie crusts together creates a tender flaky pastry which is pretty darn good (see margin note).

1 (15-ounce) package refrigerated pie crust
2 cups sugar
2 tablespoons cornmeal
1 tablespoon flour
1/4 teaspoon salt

1/2 cup butter or margarine, melted
1/4 cup milk
1 tablespoon white vinegar
1/2 teaspoon vanilla extract
4 eggs, lightly beaten

Dry pie crust mixes are not recommended, nor are frozen pie crusts. A decent timesaver, however, is to use refrigerated pie crusts. Try Pillsbury's 'Just Unroll.'

Preheat oven to 425°F. Unroll pie crust, and stack on a lightly floured surface. Roll into 1 (12-inch) circle. Fit pie crust into a 9-inch pie plate according to package directions; fold edges under, and crimp. Line pie crust with aluminum foil, and fill crust with pie weights or dried beans. Bake for 4 to 5 minutes. Remove weights and foil; bake 2 to 3 more minutes or until golden brown. Let cool completely. Lower oven temperature to 350°F. Stir together sugar and next 7 ingredients until blended. Add eggs, stirring well. Pour into pie crust. Bake at 350°F for 50 to 55 minutes shielding edges of pie with aluminum foil after 10 minutes to prevent excessive browning. Cool pie completely on a wire rack. Makes one 9-inch pie.

Variations:
Coconut Chess Pie: Add 1 cup toasted flaked coconut to filling.
Chocolate-Pecan Chess Pie: Add 3 1/2 tablespoons cocoa and 1/2 cup toasted pecans to filling.
Lemon Chess Pie: Add in 1/3 cup lemon juice and 2 teaspoons grated lemon rind to filling.

OH MY! COCONUT CREAM PIE

This has wonderful rich flavor! The popular Mud Street Café coconut cream pie in Eureka Springs, Arkansas will set you back almost $80 if you buy the whole pie, so we have been in search of how to create it. We think this is pretty darn close and actually quite wonderful: the filling is very rich and is a nice switch up from the usual vanilla custard. To take it even further over the top, try the great animal cracker crumb crust variation.

Coconut Milk is different than Cream of Coconut; be sure to use coconut milk (I use Thai Kitchen brand) in this recipe.

Unsweetened shredded coconut rather than the sweetened coconut is more flavorful and best in this recipe.

1/2 (15-ounce) package refrigerated pie crust
1 (14-ounce) can coconut milk
1 cup whole milk
1/2 cup unsweetened shredded coconut
1/2 cup plus 1 tablespoon sugar
3/8 teaspoon salt
5 egg yolks
1/4 cup cornstarch

2 tablespoons unsalted butter, cut into 2 pieces
1 teaspoon vanilla extract

Topping
2 cups cold whipping cream
1/3 cup sugar
1 1/2 teaspoons vanilla extract
Garnish: toasted coconut

Fit one pie crust into a 9-inch pie plate; fold edges under and crimp. Prick bottom and sides of pie crust with a fork. Bake according to package directions for a one-crust pie. Mix coconut milk, milk, coconut, 1/2 cup sugar and salt together in a saucepan, bring to a simmer and remove from heat. In a separate bowl, whisk the egg yolks, cornstarch and 1 tablespoon of sugar together. While continuing to whisk, add in 1 cup of hot milk mixture and whisk until fully combined. Repeat process for three more additions, until all combined. Return all to saucepan and boil until fully thickened, whisking constantly (about 1 minute). Remove from heat, whisk in butter and vanilla, and pour into cooled pie shell. Smooth with spatula; press plastic wrap directly on filling and refrigerate until firm (about 3 hours). Just before serving, beat whipping cream at high speed with an electric mixer until foamy; gradually add sugar and vanilla, beating until soft peaks form (1 to 2 minutes). Spread over pie filling. Toast 1 tablespoon unsweetened shredded coconut in small dry skillet until golden brown, sprinkle on top. Makes 8 to 10 servings.

Variation for crust: Instead of pastry, mix 6 ounces animal cracker crumbs (powdery), 2 tablespoons unsweetened shredded coconut, 1 tablespoon sugar and 4 tablespoons unsalted butter, melted. Press into 9-inch pie plate, use bottom of measuring cup to press evenly. Bake for 15 minutes at 325°F. Cool before filling.

Don Freeman
Automat Aristocrat, 1934, lithograph, WAM, gift of Friends of the Wichita Art Museum, Inc., 1988.13

COCONUT CREAM TART with MACADAMIA NUT CRUST

This is a very good, rich custard, nicely complemented by the sturdy crust. Adapted from a 1997 Southern Living *recipe, this was delicious served at several Christmas dinners. May be baked as a large tart or 12 individual tarts.*

Macadamia Nut Crust

1 1/3 cups salted Macadamia nuts (about 7
  ounces), divided use
1 1/2 cups flour
1/2 cup cold butter, cut into 8 pieces
1/4 cup sugar
2 egg yolks
2 tablespoons cold water

Coconut Cream Filling

1 1/2 tablespoons unflavored gelatin
2 tablespoons dark rum
8 large egg yolks
1/2 cup plus 2 tablespoons sugar
1/4 teaspoon salt
2 cups canned unsweetened coconut milk
1/2 cup heavy cream, chilled
1 1/4 cup flaked coconut (divided use)

Preheat oven to 350°F. Place nuts in a baking pan in a single layer and toast until golden, about 10 minutes; cool. Chop nuts coarsely. Select either an 11-inch tart pan with removable bottom, or individual 3 or 4-inch tart pans (makes 10 to 12).

To make the crust: Pulse flour and cold butter pieces in food processor, just until crumbly. Add 1 tablespoon water and pulse another 30 seconds. Add 2/3 cup chopped nuts. Pulse again just to mix. Add sugar, yolks and 1 tablespoon water; blend until dough just forms a ball. Press in bottom and up sides of an 11-inch tart pan with removable bottom, or else divide dough into 12 parts and press into the individual tart pans and place these on a jellyroll pan. Freeze for 30 minutes. Preheat oven to 375°F. Bake crust in middle of oven until golden, about 20 minutes (or 15 minutes for small tarts). Cool on rack. If making the large tart, leave in pan; if small tarts, remove from pans and cool completely on the wire rack. While oven is hot decrease heat to 325°F, bake 1/2 cup coconut in a shallow pan for about 5 minutes until lightly toasted.

To make the filling: Place rum in a small dish. Sprinkle gelatin over the top. In a bowl, whisk together yolks, sugar and salt. In a large saucepan, bring coconut milk to a boil. Gradually whisk half the coconut milk into yolk mixture and whisk back into pan with remaining coconut milk. Cook custard over moderate heat for about 7 minutes, whisking constantly, until thickened, but do not let custard boil. Remove pan from heat. Add rum-gelatin mixture, whisking until it is dissolved; stir in 1/2 cup of flaked coconut. Transfer custard to a bowl to cool and chill, stirring frequently, until thickened but not set, about 30 minutes. Beat cream until it holds soft peaks and fold gently into custard. Pour filling into crust. Chill tart until filling is set, about 4 hours.

Remove rim of large tart pan and sprinkle with reserved toasted coconut plus 1/4 cup untoasted coconut, and reserved chopped nuts. Makes one 11-inch tart or 12 individual sized tarts. From Bonnie Aeschilman.

SASSY LEMON PIE with BIG HAIR MERINGUE

The lemon filling is rich and flavorful, but what makes this pie a standout is the meringue presentation. It is from a recipe from a 1949 cooking magazine, Homemaker's Digest, *but the technique is a recent one from Texas chef Rebecca Rather* (Pastry Queen, 2004), *who seems to indeed know a thing or two about Big Hair.*

1 1/4 cup sugar
6 tablespoons cornstarch
2 cups water
3 egg yolks
1/3 cup fresh lemon juice
1 1/2 teaspoon lemon extract
3 tablespoons butter
2 tablespoons vinegar

1 baked 9-inch pie shell

Big Hair Meringue
4 egg whites (room temperature)
3/4 cups sugar
Dash salt

Severin Roesen
Nature's Bounty (detail),
ca. 1860, oil on canvas,
WAM, gift of George E.
Vollmer, 1995.15

Opposite page:
Sigmund Menkes
Red Roses (detail),
1941, WAM, oil on
canvas, WAM, The Roland
P. Murdock Collection,
M38.42

In the top of a double boiler, mix sugar, cornstarch and water. Whisk egg yolks together with lemon juice and add to the sugar mixture. Cook over boiling water (water shouldn't touch bottom of the bowl) until thick, about 25 minutes, stirring lightly with a whisk about every 7 minutes. Remove from heat, add lemon extract, butter and vinegar and stir to combine. Pour into deep 9-inch pie shell and let cool.

Preheat oven to 400°F. To make the meringue, place the ingredients in a perfectly clean metal bowl so the eggs will reach their full volume. Beat with hand held electric mixer until thoroughly blended. Place the bowl over boiling water and cook, beating constantly, about one minute. Test to see that there are no visible grains of sugar in the mixture. Remove from hot water and continue beating 2 minutes longer at high speed or until mixture stands in stiff and shiny peaks. Pile meringue on filled, cooled pie, stroking with the back of spoon to form spikes and waves: make it a stylish bouffant! Add a few side curls for sass. Set on the middle rack of the oven and bake for 1 to 2 minutes until slightly browned. Watch carefully, it will brown quickly. Makes one 9-inch pie with "big hair".

LEMON BUTTER PECAN TART with RASPBERRIES

This beauty features a bright lemony filling encased in a buttery pecan crust; a very elegant dessert.

Butter Pecan Crust
1/3 cup finely chopped pecans
3 tablespoons powdered sugar
1/2 cup butter, softened
1 1/4 cups flour
1 egg yolk
1/4 teaspoon salt

Filling
3 eggs, beaten

1 cup sugar
1 tablespoon flour
3 tablespoons fresh lemon juice
Finely grated rind of 1 lemon
Powdered sugar (optional)

Raspberry Topping (optional)
1 1/2 pints fresh raspberries
12 ounces currant jelly

Preheat oven to 350°F. Arrange pecans on a baking sheet and toast in the oven for 7 to 9 minutes. Cool and finely chop the pecans. In a mixer bowl, cream the butter and sugar on medium-high until fluffy, about 3 minutes, then gradually add the flour, egg yolk and salt and combine on low. Add the nuts and stir just until combined. Form dough into a ball, cover and refrigerate for 30 minutes. Press chilled dough evenly into a buttered 9-inch tart pan, bake for 10 minutes. Set aside to cool. To prepare the filling, combine eggs, sugar, flour, lemon juice and rind; stir until smooth. (To keep from picking up a metallic taste, use glass or plastic mixing bowl.) Pour into crust and bake for 20 to 25 minutes, or until set. Place on wire rack to cool.

To serve, dust with powdered sugar or cover with Raspberry Topping. To prepare topping, arrange raspberries on top of cooled tart, starting at outside and working toward center to cover tart completely. Melt jelly over low heat until liquid and then brush jelly on each raspberry with a pastry brush. Jelly must be very hot to glaze well. Let glaze cool to set before cutting. Store, covered, in refrigerator. Makes 8 to 10 servings. From Marlene Phillips.

LEMON CREAM NAPOLEONS with RASPBERRY COULIS

Phyllo Squares
6 frozen phyllo pastry sheets,
   thawed (or 12 half sheets)
3 tablespoons sugar
1/4 cup unsalted butter, melted

Lemon Cream
2 eggs
3 egg yolks
1 cup sugar
2/3 cup fresh lemon juice
2 teaspoons grated lemon rind
1/4 cup unsalted butter, room
   temperature, cut into pieces

Raspberry Coulis
1 (12-ounce) bag
   frozen, unsweetened
   raspberries, thawed
1 teaspoon fresh lemon juice
1/3 cup sugar

Garnish: Powdered sugar,
   whipped cream

Start by making the phyllo squares. Line 2 large baking sheets with parchment paper, or lightly coat with cooking spray. Set aside. Preheat oven to 375°F. Place 1 sheet of phyllo on work surface. Cover remaining sheets with plastic wrap and damp towel. You will be working with one sheet on the work surface. Brush lightly with butter; sprinkle with 2 teaspoons sugar. Top with second phyllo sheet. Brush with butter; sprinkle with sugar. Top with third phyllo sheet. Brush with butter. With pastry cutter or sharp knife, trim and remove ragged edges. Cut phyllo stack into 3-inch squares. Transfer to baking sheet. Repeat process with remaining phyllo. Before baking, cover phyllo with a piece of parchment and top with another baking sheet. This will weight down the phyllo and prevent it from puffing during baking. Bake 8 minutes. Remove the top pan; continue to bake until golden, about 4 to 6 minutes. Cool completely.

To make the Lemon Cream; select a saucepan that will hold the bowl from your mixture to serve as a double boiler. Fill the pan with 2 or 3 inches of water. Bring to a simmer. Combine eggs, egg yolks and sugar in mixing bowl. Beat on high speed until light and creamy. With mixer on low, blend in lemon juice and zest. Place bowl in the saucepan of hot water. With water simmering, cook the lemon mixture, whisking constantly until it becomes very thick and almost reaches a boil. Remove from heat and whisk in butter until it is melted. Transfer to a container and press plastic wrap on the surface. Refrigerate until chilled and set, several hours or overnight. Lemon curd will keep several days in the refrigerator.

To assemble the Napoleons, spread 2 tablespoons lemon cream on each of 6 phyllo squares. Top each with 1 phyllo square and 2 more tablespoons lemon cream (save any remaining lemon cream for another use). Top each with 1 phyllo square (may be prepared 2 hours ahead; cover loosely and refrigerate). To serve, place on plate. Sift powdered sugar over desserts and garnish with whipped cream and Raspberry Coulis. Makes 6 servings. From Bonnie Aeschliman.

To make the Raspberry Coulis, place thawed raspberries, lemon juice and sugar in food processor. Process to blend. Sieve them with a food mill fitted with a fine disc or work through a strainer to remove seeds. Store coulis in a covered container in the refrigerator. Will keep 7 to 10 days.

The Innes Tea Room, on the sixth floor of the Innes Department Store was the place for ladies to lunch downtown Wichita from the 30s to the 70s (men had a separate Grill Room!). "A-listers were often spotted heading for their favorite tables among the hoi polloi" Diane C. Lewis recounts. "I went there as a child with my mother and continued through my early working years in the 60s and 70s. Baking was done in-house at Innes. The fresh rolls and pies and cakes were always a highlight. For a time, there was a carry-out bakery on the first floor, near the woman who repaired scarce silk and nylon stockings during WWII."

Walter Innes built the six-story building in 1927 that Wichitans called "Inneses" at the corner of Broadway and William. He impressed Wichita with his standard for sophistication and elegance with walnut fixtures and large sculptured columns gracing the first floor, and clothing departments carrying the latest fashions from New York and Paris. It boasted the state's first escalators and it was the largest department store in the state. It was converted into the State Office Building in 1994. The store was only part of the legacy of the Innes family, who were known as merchants throughout the city's history (see too their gift to WAM of English Copper Lusterware, p. 103)

RUM CREAM PIE

For decades, Innes dazzled us as we walked through the doors. We could find it all there, from furs to needlework. Innes Tea Room brings recollections of linen napkins and tablecloths, Friday fashion shows, and grace. This pie is a version of a Tea Room favorite, although theirs was layered.

1 9-inch baked pastry shell (or graham cracker crust)
6 egg yolks
7/8 cup sugar

1 tablespoon gelatin
1/2 cup cold water
1/2 cup dark rum
2 cups whipping cream

Beat yolks until light; add sugar gradually. Soak gelatin in cold water; place over low flame and bring to boil. Pour over the egg mixture in a slow stream, beating constantly. Cool. Whip cream until stiff; fold into egg mixture, add rum and pour into the pie shell and refrigerate. When set, top with shaved chocolate, toasted coconut or pistachios. From Diane Lewis.

CHOCOLATE PECAN PIE

1/2 cup butter
1/2 cup chocolate chips
1 cup sugar
2 eggs, beaten

1/2 cup chopped pecans
1/2 cup shredded coconut
1 8-inch unbaked pastry shell (not deep dish)

Preheat oven to 350°F. Combine chocolate chips, butter, sugar, eggs, pecans and coconut in a medium sauce pan. Over medium-low heat, stirring until just melted. Be careful to not scorch. Remove from heat and pour into unbaked pie shell. Place several pecan halves, if desired around perimeter for decoration. Bake for 35 to 40 minutes (will be moist in center). Makes one 8-inch pie.

SPECTACULAR BLACK BOTTOM PIE

This pie was so popular at the Connoisseur Restaurant, circa 1955 in Wichita, that customers would call in the morning to reserve a slice for lunch or dinner!

Crust
1 1/2 cups fine chocolate wafer crumbs
1/4 cup sugar
1/2 cup butter, melted

Filling
1/2 cup (generous) brown sugar
1 1/4 tablespoons cornstarch
1/4 teaspoon (scant) salt
4 eggs, separated, room temperature
1 1/2 cups milk, scalded

5 tablespoons brandy
1 1/2 ounce unsweetened chocolate, melted
3/4 teaspoon vanilla
2 tablespoons cold water
1 tablespoon brandy
1 envelope unflavored gelatin
1/4 teaspoon cream of tartar
1/2 cup sugar

Garnish: Unsweetened whipped cream, chocolate ribbons, powdered sugar

Preheat oven to 325°F. Mix crust ingredients together and press into a well buttered 9-inch pie plate. Bake for about 10 minutes, and cool. Sift brown sugar together with cornstarch and salt. Beat egg yolks in top of double boiler until light, gradually adding brown sugar mixture and slowly add scalded milk and brandy. Cook, stirring constantly, over simmering water until thick and smooth. Remove from the hot water bath, and combine 1 cup of this custard with the chocolate and vanilla. Pour into the pie shell and let cool. Combine the cold water and brandy in a small bowl and sprinkle the gelatin over the top. Let sit one minute then stir to soften. Combine with the remaining custard, stirring. Let the mixture cool slightly but do not let it set. Beat the egg whites until foamy, add cream of tartar and continue to beat, gradually adding sugar, until the whites form stiff, but not dry, peaks. Fold the whites into the slightly warm custard, pour onto the chocolate layer and chill for at least 3 hours. To serve spread the pie generously with unsweetened whipped cream, reserving enough to pipe a border with a pastry tube fitted with a star tip. Decorate the top with shaved ribbons of sweet chocolate and dust lightly with powdered sugar to which has been added (by those of us who leave no lily unpainted), a dash of cinnamon. Makes one 9-inch pie. From Barry Bradley.

CHOCOLATE ICEBOX PIE

²/₃ cup milk

³/₄ cup semisweet chocolate morsels

¹/₄ cup cold water

2 tablespoons cornstarch

1 (14-ounce) can sweetened condensed milk

3 eggs, beaten

1 teaspoon vanilla extract

3 tablespoons butter or margarine

1 (6-ounce) chocolate crumb pie crust

1 cup whipping cream

¹/₄ cup sugar

¹/₂ cup chopped pecans, toasted

1 (1¹/₂-ounce) milk chocolate candy
   bar, chopped

Heat milk until it just begins to bubble in a medium saucepan over medium heat, and whisk in chocolate morsels until melted. Cool slightly. Stir together cold water and cornstarch until dissolved. Whisk cornstarch mixture, sweetened condensed milk, eggs, and vanilla into chocolate mixture. Bring to a boil over medium heat, whisking constantly. Boil 1 minute or until mixture thickens and is smooth (do not overcook). Remove from heat, and whisk in butter. Spoon mixture into pie crust. Cover and chill at least 8 hours. Beat whipping cream at high speed with an electric mixer until foamy; gradually add sugar, beating until soft peaks form. Spread whipped cream evenly over pie filling, and sprinkle with pecans and candy bar pieces. Makes 8 servings.

Trevor Allen (British)
Yellow Couch with Zippo,
1973, color wood block,
WAM, gift of Barry Wayne
Bradley in memory of Patricia
Ann Brace, 2005.14.2

There are two more good chocolate pies in the "Chocolate Finishes" chapter, Pecan Fudge Pie (p. 252) and the Rich Chocolate Tart (p. 256)

(continued from p. 190)
Between 1921 and 1938, Herschel Logan created around 140 different prints, mostly woodcuts, in editions of around 50. His style is characterized by the dramatic juxtaposition of rich black and stark white, robust volume, a sense of the eternal in the frozen moment, and a sharpness of focus that monumentalizes everyday Kansas scenes.

In 1938, the year after creating three of his most compelling prints, Tornado, Threshing, *and* The Dust Storm, *Logan virtually abandoned printmaking. In 1929 he was appointed managing director of Mid-Continent Engraving in Salina and in 1939 his friend and mentor C. A. Seward died. Logan had other artistic and entrepreneurial ideas to pursue. In 1967 he retired to California, where, among many other activities, he made and collected miniature books.*

A delightful example of historical serendipity is that Herschel's son Samuel (and his wife Martha returned from California, where he had been a professor at U. C. Davis, to retire in Winfield, KS. Among their many acts of community dedication was their donation of multiple impressions of almost every print made by Logan through 1930. It is largely due to their generosity that the display of the warm woodblock prints of Herschel C. Logan can appear throughout this book. — SG

WALNUT MOCHA SUNDAE PIE

This recipe was clipped from Grit *magazine in 1967, and has been around the kitchen ever since.*

Crust
1 egg white
¼ teaspoon salt
¼ cup sugar
1½ cups chopped walnuts (or pecans)

Filling
1 pint coffee ice cream
1 pint vanilla ice cream

Preheat oven to 400°F. To make the crust, beat egg white with salt, using an electric mixer on high, and gradually add sugar. Fold in nuts; spread evenly on bottom of a buttered and floured 9-inch pan (but not on the rim). Bake 10 to 12 minutes. Cool and chill. To make the filling, let the ice cream thaw only enough to be able to spread (do each layer separately). Fill crust and freeze, and then repeat with the next flavor of ice cream. Remove from freezer 10 minutes before slicing. Cut pieces with a sharp knife dipped in warm water. Top each slice with Raisin Sauce. Makes one 9-inch pie.

Brown Sugar Raisin Sauce
3 tablespoons butter
1 cup brown sugar
½ cup half-and-half

½ cup golden raisins, chopped
1 teaspoon vanilla extract

Combine butter and sugar in a small saucepan over medium heat. Cook until sugar is lightly brown. Remove and slowly add half-and-half and raisins. Heat 1 minute. Stir in vanilla and serve warm over pie. Makes about 1 cup.

KAHLUA ICE CREAM PIE

This recipe is scaled to make three pies, to provide some efficiency in the time it takes to prepare each layer. If scaling for one pie, use appropriate proportions for crusts, and just one pint of each ice cream flavor.

Crusts
3 cups graham cracker crumbs
1½ cups chopped walnuts
¾ cup butter or margarine, melted

Filling
½ gallon vanilla ice cream, softened
½ cup Kahlua liqueur (divided use)
½ gallon chocolate ice cream, softened

Preheat oven to 375°F. Combine ingredients for crust, stirring well. (Alternatively, use purchased graham cracker crusts.) Firmly press mixture into 3 buttered 9-inch pie plates. Bake 8 minutes; cool.

Mix softened vanilla ice cream and ¼ cup of Kahlua in electric mixer just until spreadable. Layer in bottom of the three crusts. Freeze until firm. Mix chocolate ice cream and ¼ cup of Kahlua in electric mixture until spreadable. Spread over vanilla mixture. Freeze.

Remove from freezer 10 minutes before serving, and slice with knife dipped in hot water. Pipe whipped cream rosettes across the edge. Drizzle purchased fudge chocolate or caramel topping or prepared chocolate sauce (p. 256) across the top, sprinkle with chopped pecans. Makes 3 8-inch pies (each 8 servings).

Variation: serve with a brown sugar sauce, as follows. Melt 3 tablespoons butter in a heavy saucepan over low heat, stir in 1 cup packed brown sugar. Cook for 5 to 6 minutes, stirring constantly. Remove from heat and stir in ½ cup half-and-half, return to heat and cook for 1 minute. Remove from heat again, stir in 1 cup chopped toasted walnuts and 1 teaspoon vanilla extract. Serve warm over pie.

FRESH STRAWBERRY PIE

3 egg whites (room temperature)
½ teaspoon baking soda
1 cup sugar
10 square soda crackers, crumbled to
   fine crumbs

½ cup chopped pecans
1 quart strawberries, halved
½ pint cream
Powdered sugar

Preheat oven to 300°F. Beat egg whites until stiff; add baking soda. Beat in sugar, adding gradually. Fold in soda crackers and pecans. Spread in a well-buttered 9-inch pie pan. Bake 30 minutes. Cool. Prepare strawberries; drain excess juice so crust will not be soaked. Top with sweetened whipped cream. Chill several hours. Makes 6 to 8 servings. From Anita Jones.

PINK LEMONADE PIE

This easy pie has been on our summertime family table for the 30 years since a version appeared in the Sunflower Sampler *cookbook from the Junior League of Wichita. It adapts well to using low-fat versions of frozen whipped topping and sweetened condensed milk.*

1 (9-inch) purchased graham cracker pie shell
1 (6-ounce) can frozen pink lemonade
   concentrate, partially thawed
1 (14-ounce) can sweetened condensed milk

1 (9-ounce) carton frozen whipped
   topping, thawed
Dash red food coloring
Garnish: 1 tablespoon graham cracker or "Lorna
   Doone" cookie crumbs

Mix sweetened condensed milk and undiluted lemonade together. Stir in whipped topping; do not beat. Add several drops of food coloring to tint the filling a nice pink. Pour into pie shell and sprinkle top with crumbs. Refrigerate overnight. Makes 8 servings.

TWISTER PEANUT BUTTER PIE

⅓ cup crunchy peanut butter
1 (3-ounce) package cream cheese, softened
2 tablespoons butter, softened
1 cup powdered sugar
¼ cup milk
1 (8-ounce) carton frozen whipped
   topping, thawed
1 (9-inch) chocolate cookie crumb crust
Garnish: 2 tablespoons chopped peanuts and
   chocolate curls, optional

Beat peanut butter, cream cheese and butter with an electric mixer in a large bowl until smooth. Add sugar and milk; fold in whipped topping. Pour into the crust. Cover and freeze for 4 hours. Remove from freezer just before serving. Garnish with peanuts and chocolate curls if desired, and any other edible "debris" which the twister may have picked up. Makes 8 servings.

Herschel C. Logan *Tornado*, 1938, block print, WAM, gift of Geoege E. Vollmer, The Clarence E Vollmer Collection, 1997.28

Cakes, Crisps & Cobblers

APPLES *make for great cakes, keeping them moist and flavorful.*

...here are three different approaches.

Previous page:

R.S. Dunning
*Still Life with Grapes and
Peaches,* 1881, oil on
canvas, WAM, gift of
the Wichita Art Museum
Member's Foundation,
1968.5

*Birger Sandzen
(1871-1954) was the
great statesman of fine art
in Kansas. His old world
manner, his distinguished
background, and his
commanding presence—
along with the beauty and
force of his art—instilled
the art spirit in many
Kansans. He was a student
of Anders Zorn in Sweden
and of Arman-Jean (a
colleague of George Seurat)
in France.*

*In 1894 Sandzen moved
to Lindsborg, KS, turning
Bethany College into a
midwestern center of art
education. Sandzen's
painting style is defined
by his bright, high-pitched
color and thick, vigorous
brushwork. Most striking
in his work, however, is
his ability to convey the
emotional intensity and
vitality of the landscape of
the American Midwest, West,
and Southwest. Sandzen
had an exceptionally
deep appreciation of the
almost sublime effect of our
landscape. - SG*

APPLE PECAN SPICE CAKE with BUTTERMILK GLAZE

Served at Wichita Art Museum 'Art on a Monday' event featuring crop artist Stan Herd: A Prairie Art Story, this moist, dense cake is like a carrot cake but with apples.

3 cups flour
1 teaspoon baking soda
$^1/_2$ teaspoon salt
2 teaspoons cinnamon
2 cups sugar
3 eggs, slightly beaten
1 $^1/_4$ cups vegetable oil
2 teaspoons vanilla extract
$^1/_4$ cup orange juice

2 $^1/_4$ cups peeled, shredded Granny Smith apples
   (about 3)
1 cup shredded coconut
1 $^1/_2$ cups chopped pecans

Buttermilk Glaze

1 cup sugar
$^1/_2$ cup butter
$^1/_2$ teaspoon baking soda
$^1/_2$ cup buttermilk

Preheat oven to 350°F. Combine flour, baking soda, salt and cinnamon in a medium bowl; set aside. Combine sugar, eggs, oil, vanilla and orange juice in a large bowl; add flour mixture and combine well. Fold in apples, coconut and pecans. Pour batter in prepared large (15 cup) bundt pan or 9 x 13-inch pan. Bake 1 hour and 15 minutes or until wooden pick comes out clean. Cool in pan 10 to 15 minutes; remove from pan. (If using 9 x 13-inch pan leave in pan when adding glaze.)

For glaze, combine ingredients in a small saucepan. Cook over medium heat for 5 minutes or until butter is melted and mixture is bubbly. Makes 1 $^1/_2$ cups. Poke holes in top of cake using long pick. Spoon hot buttermilk glaze over warm cake (cake will absorb most of the glaze). Cool completely before serving. Great served with Hot Buttered Rum Sauce (see below). Makes 16 servings.

FRESH APPLE CAKE with HOT BUTTERED RUM SAUCE

Very rich and special. Served at Wichita-Sedgwick County Historical Museum dinners.

$^1/_2$ cup butter
2 cups sugar
2 eggs
2 cups sifted flour
1 teaspoon baking powder
$^3/_4$ teaspoon baking soda

$^1/_2$ teaspoon salt
$^1/_2$ teaspoon nutmeg
$^1/_2$ teaspoon cinnamon
3 Washington or Delicious apples, peeled,
   cored and chopped
1 $^1/_2$ cups chopped pecans

Preheat oven to 325°F. Cream butter with electric mixer on medium speed, gradually add sugar and beat until light and fluffy. Beat in eggs, one at a time. Sift together flour, baking powder, baking soda, salt, nutmeg and cinnamon. Gradually add to egg mixture. Dough will be fairly stiff. Stir in apples and nuts. Turn into buttered 11-inch square pan (or 9 x 13-inch pan). Bake for 55 to 70 minutes. Test after 55 minutes, time for doneness depends on the juiciness of the apples. Serve with Hot Buttered Rum Sauce drizzled over serving and top with whipped cream. Makes 12 to 16 servings.

Hot Buttered Rum Sauce

1 cup sugar
$^1/_2$ cup butter
$^1/_2$ cup half-and-half

3 tablespoons dark rum or rum extract
$^1/_2$ cup golden or dark raisins (optional)

Combine sugar, butter and cream. Warm over low heat, stirring occasionally. Add rum when hot and drizzle over a slice of Fresh Apple Cake.

230   CAKES, CRISPS AND COBBLERS

CHUNKY APPLE CAKE with CREAM CHEESE FROSTING

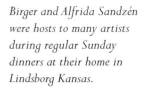

1/2 cup butter
2 cups sugar
2 eggs
1 teaspoon vanilla extract
2 cups flour
1 teaspoon baking soda

1 teaspoon salt
2 teaspoons cinnamon
4 Granny Smith apples, peeled and sliced
1 cup chopped walnuts, toasted
Garnish: chopped walnuts, toasted and crushed

Preheat oven to 350°F. Stir together butter, sugar, eggs and vanilla in a large bowl until blended. Whisk together flour, baking soda, salt and cinnamon; add to butter mixture, stirring until blended. Stir in apples and walnuts. Spread into a greased 9 x 13-inch pan. Bake for 45 minutes or until a wooden pick inserted in center comes out clean. Cool completely in pan on a wire rack. Spread with Cream Cheese Frosting; sprinkle with walnuts. Makes 12 to 15 servings.

Cream Cheese Frosting

1 (8-ounce) package cream cheese, softened
3 tablespoons butter, softened
1 1/2 cups powdered sugar

1/8 teaspoon salt
1 teaspoon vanilla extract

Beat cream cheese and butter at medium speed with an electric mixer until creamy. Gradually add sugar and salt, beating until blended. Stir in vanilla.

Below: Birger Sandzén, *Early Fall, Smoky River,* 1937, oil on canvas, WAM, gift of the Estate of Harry G. Cooney, 1974.4

Birger and Alfrida Sandzén were hosts to many artists during regular Sunday dinners at their home in Lindsborg Kansas.

This recipe speaks to the shortage of sugar during World War I:

Alfrida's War Cake (ca. 1917)
3/4 cup sour milk
1 teaspoon soda
1 egg
1 cup molasses
1 teaspoon baking powder
2 cups flour
Raisins

ITALIAN CREAM CAKE

This is a big beautiful three layer cake and is a real hit whenever served.

1 3/4 cups sugar
2 cups butter
4 eggs, separated
2 cups flour
1 teaspoon baking soda
1 1/4 cups buttermilk
1 teaspoon vanilla
1 1/2 cups sweetened flaked coconut
1 cup chopped pecans

Frosting

1 cup butter, room temperature
2 (8-ounce) packages cream cheese, softened
1 teaspoon vanilla (or almond) extract
3 to 4 cups powdered sugar

Topping

2/3 cup sweetened, flaked coconut
1/2 cup chopped pecans (or walnuts)

Preheat oven to 350°F and lightly butter and flour three 8-inch round cake pans (or one 2 1/2 inch by 8 inch springform pan). Cream sugar and butter; add egg yolks, one at a time and cream well. Mix flour and baking soda together in a small bowl. Add the buttermilk mixture and flour mixture to batter alternately, beginning and ending with flour mixture. Fold in vanilla, coconut and pecans. Beat egg whites in another bowl until they just begin to hold stiff peaks, then fold into the batter gently. Divide batter among pans, smoothing tops, and place in upper two thirds of oven; rotate position of pans halfway through baking. Bake for 30 to 35 minutes (or 60 – 70 minutes for springform pan), or until tester comes out clean. Cool in pans for 10 minutes, then invert on rack to cool. Chill layers before frosting.

To make the frosting, blend butter, cream cheese and vanilla with an electric mixer; add powdered sugar to taste and beat until smooth (If using the springform pan, slice the cake into 3 layers, making 2 cuts carefully). Plate the first layer and frost; add the other two layers with frosting spread on each layer. Sprinkle with coconut (toasting some of it makes for nice color) and nuts. Makes 10 to 12 servings.

CHOCOLATE CARROT CAKE

This is a delicious and moist cake; an inspired combination of two favorites – chocolate and carrot cake!

3 (1-ounce) squares unsweetened chocolate
1 1/2 cups sifted cake flour
2/3 cups (2 ounces) unsweetened cocoa powder
1 1/2 teaspoons baking powder
1 1/2 teaspoons baking soda
1/2 teaspoon salt
1 1/2 teaspoons cinnamon

2 cups sugar
1 cup vegetable oil
3 eggs, beaten
2 teaspoons vanilla extract
Grated rind of 1 lemon
3/4 cup plus 2 tablespoons buttermilk
2 1/2 cups shredded carrots (1 pound)

Heat oven to 350°F. Melt chocolate squares in microwave and set aside to cool. Sift dry ingredients together. Cream sugar and oil; add beaten eggs, vanilla and zest of lemon. Add dry ingredients alternately with buttermilk. Stir in melted chocolate until combined. Add carrots (I like to add a little flour to the carrots to help them combine into the batter without clumping). Pour batter into pan that has been oiled and floured. Bake 1 hour if using bundt pan (must use large bundt pan or will overflow). If using two 9-inch layer cake pans, bake 40 to 50 minutes. If using mini-bundt pans bake about 15 minutes, checking to see if done. May be iced with Chocolate Cream Frosting, or simply dusted with powdered sugar. Makes 12 servings.

Chocolate Cream Frosting

1 1/2 cup heavy cream
16 ounces semisweet chocolate chips

1/4 cup corn syrup
1 teaspoon vanilla extract

Heat cream in saucepan until boiling. Pour over chocolate chips and let stand for 3 minutes. Stir in syrup and vanilla. Put in refrigerator to cool for 1 1/2 hours, stirring every 15 minutes until it is the consistency you desire. For the mini-bundt cupcakes, pour or ladle the frosting letting it run down the sides.

RED VELVET CAKE with MASCARPONE CREAM CHEESE FROSTING

Invented in the 1930s, this economy-minded cake with only 2 eggs and half cup of shortening, became popular and has stayed that way. There are many versions of this cake, but this one is my favorite, using butter instead of shortening, and sour cream in addition to the traditional buttermilk, soda and vinegar. Yes, red food coloring does stain so use glass or ceramic bowls, not plastic. This version makes for an extremely moist dessert and you will absolutely love the rich frosting.

$3\frac{1}{2}$ tablespoons cocoa powder (not Dutch-processed)

2 ounces red food coloring (or 1 teaspoon red food-coloring paste)

1 cup unsalted butter at room temperature

$1\frac{3}{4}$ cups sugar

2 eggs, at room temperature

2 cups cake flour

$1\frac{1}{2}$ cups all purpose flour

1 teaspoon kosher salt

1 teaspoon baking soda

2 teaspoons vanilla extract

1 cup buttermilk

1 cup sour cream

1 tablespoon white vinegar

Preheat oven to 350°F. Grease and flour two 9-inch cake pans. Put cocoa in small glass bowl, and add food coloring, stirring until mixture is smooth and set aside. Using an electric mixer, cream butter and sugar on medium-high speed until fluffy, about 2 minutes. Cream butter and sugar with electric mixer until fluffy, about 4 minutes. Add eggs one at a time, beating each for about 30 seconds. Add cocoa mixture and decrease speed to medium, blending for about 4 minutes. On a sheet of wax paper, sift together the remaining dry ingredients, making sure not to forget both types of flour. Combine vanilla and buttermilk; add buttermilk alternately with the dry ingredients, beginning and ending with the dry ingredients. Mix on medium until ingredients are just incorporated. Add sour cream and vinegar, mixing on low speed until combined. Pour into prepared pans and bake for 25 to 30 minutes. Let layers cool on a rack for 10 minutes before turning out; cool completely before frosting. Frost with Mascarpone Cream Cheese Frosting. Makes 12 servings.

Mascarpone Cream Cheese Frosting

1 cup unsalted butter at room temperature

1 cup (8 ounces) cream cheese at room temperature

2 cups powdered sugar

Pinch kosher salt

1 cup (8 ounces) mascarpone cheese (Italian cream cheese), room temperature

1 teaspoon vanilla extract

Blend butter, cream cheese and powdered sugar with an electric mixer until fluffy. Carefully mix in the mascarpone until just incorporated; vigorous mixing after this point will ensure curdled frosting, so take care. Gently stir in vanilla extract.

BUTTERSCOTCH CAKE

This easy favorite makes regular appearances at our family gatherings.

$1\frac{1}{4}$ cups water

$\frac{2}{3}$ cup butterscotch flavored morsels

1 package (2 layer size) yellow cake mix

3 eggs

$\frac{1}{3}$ cup vegetable oil

$\frac{1}{8}$ teaspoon cinnamon

Preheat oven to 350°F. Heat water and butterscotch in a saucepan over medium heat, just until melted. Cool 10 minutes. Grease two 8 or 9-inch cake pans. Combine cake mix, eggs, oil, cinnamon and butterscotch mixture. Beat as directed on cake mix instructions. Pour into prepared pans. Bake for 25 to 35 minutes or until done. Cool completely before frosting. Makes 12 servings.

Butterscotch Frosting

1 (8-ounce) package softened cream cheese

3 cups sifted powdered sugar

$\frac{1}{3}$ cup butterscotch morsels, melted and cooled

1 tablespoon lemon juice

$\frac{1}{8}$ teaspoon cinnamon

Beat cream cheese, powdered sugar, melted butterscotch, lemon juice, and cinnamon until well blended. Beat in enough of the powdered sugar to make the frosting spreadable.

COCONUT SHEET CAKE

Cream of Coconut is available in the liquor mix sections of most grocery stores.

3 eggs
1 (8-ounce) container sour cream
$^1/_3$ cup water
1 (8$^1/_2$-ounce) can cream of coconut

$^1/_2$ teaspoon vanilla extract
1 (18$^1/_4$-ounce) package white cake mix
Coconut Cream Cheese Frosting (recipe follows)

Preheat oven to 325°F. Beat eggs with an electric mixer (high speed) for 2 minutes. Add sour cream, water, cream of coconut and vanilla, stirring in each addition. Add cake mix, beating at low speed just until blended, then beat at high speed for 2 minutes. Pour batter into a greased and floured 9 x 13- inch baking pan, and bake for 40 to 45 minutes or until a wooden pick comes out clean (or a 10 x 15- inch jellyroll pan for 30 to 32 minutes). Cool cake in pan on wire rack. Cover pan with plastic wrap, and freeze cake 30 minutes. Remove from freezer. Spread Coconut Cream Cheese Frosting on top of chilled cake. Cover and store in refrigerator. Makes 12 servings.

Coconut Cream Cheese Frosting

1 (8-ounce) package cream cheese, softened
$^1/_2$ cup butter or margarine, softened
3 tablespoons milk

1 teaspoon vanilla extract
1 (16-ounce) package powdered sugar, sifted
1 (7-ounce) package sweetened flaked coconut

Beat cream cheese and butter at medium speed with an electric mixer until creamy; add milk and vanilla, beating well. Gradually add sugar, beating until smooth. Stir in coconut. Makes 4 cups. This frosting is very thick.

QUICK COCONUT CAKE

This is a very easy cake, and is a favorite for family birthdays. The cake is great the day you make it, but allowing it to sit in the refrigerator 2 to 3 days makes this the most moist coconut cake you have ever eaten. Even people that don't like coconut love this recipe. This cake should be covered and refrigerated until consumed. May tint coconut green for Easter and decorate with candy eggs.

1 (two layer size) package white cake mix
1 cup sweetened condensed milk
1 cup cream of coconut

1 (8-ounce) carton frozen whipped topping, thawed
1 cup sweetened, shredded coconut

Franklin C. Watkins
Bouquet of White Roses (detail), 1941, oil on canvas, WAM, The Roland P. Murdock Collection, M32.42

Mix and bake white cake mix according to box directions in a 9 x 13-inch pan. Combine sweetened condensed milk and cream of coconut. While cake is hot, poke holes with meat fork and pour and spread cream of coconut mixture on hot cake. If it needs more moisture, add more cream of coconut. Store in refrigerator until cold. Before serving cake, frost with whipped topping and sprinkle with coconut. Makes 12 to 16 servings.

CRAZY FOR COCONUT CUPCAKES

$^3/_4$ pound unsalted butter, room temperature
2 cups sugar
5 extra large eggs, at room temperature
$1^1/_2$ teaspoons vanilla extract
$1^1/_2$ teaspoons almond extract
3 cups flour
1 teaspoon baking powder

$^1/_2$ teaspoon baking soda
$^1/_2$ teaspoon salt
1 cup buttermilk
14 ounces sweetened, shredded coconut
  (divided use)
Cream Cheese Frosting (recipe follows)

Preheat oven to 325°F. Cream butter and sugar with electric mixer until light and fluffy, about 5 minutes. Add the eggs one at a time, with the mixer running on low. Add extracts and mix well. In a separate bowl, sift together the flour, baking powder, baking soda and salt. In three parts, alternately add the dry ingredients and the buttermilk to the batter, beginning and ending with the dry; mix until just combined. Then fold in 7 ounces of coconut with a spatula.

Line a muffin pan with paper liners. Fill each cup to the top with batter. Bake for 25 to 35 minutes, until the tops are brown and a toothpick comes out clean. Allow to cool in the pan for 15 minutes. Remove to a baking rack and cool completely. Frost with cream cheese icing and sprinkle with the remaining coconut. Makes 15 to 18 cupcakes.

Cream Cheese Frosting
1 pound cream cheese, room temperature
$^3/_4$ pound unsalted butter, room temperature
1 teaspoon vanilla extract

$^1/_2$ teaspoon almond extract
$1^1/_2$ pounds powdered sugar, sifted

Blend cream cheese, butter, vanilla and almond extracts together with an electric mixer. Add the powdered sugar and mix until smooth.

CREAM CHEESE POUND CAKE
This moist cake is a knockout served with fresh fruit.

$1^1/_2$ cups butter, softened
1 (8-ounce) package cream cheese, softened
3 cups sugar
6 eggs

$1^1/_2$ teaspoons vanilla extract
3 cups flour
$^1/_8$ teaspoon salt

Preheat oven to 300°F. Beat butter and cream cheese with electric mixer for 2 minutes or until creamy. Gradually add sugar, beating 5 to 7 minutes. Add eggs one at a time, just until yellow disappears. Add vanilla and mix well. Combine flour and salt; gradually add to butter mixture, beating at low speed just until blended after each addition. Pour batter into a greased and floured 10-inch tube pan.

Fill a 2-cup ovenproof measuring cup with water; place in oven with tube pan. Bake for 1 hour and 30 minutes, or until a wooden pick inserted in center of cake comes out clean. Cool in pan on a wire rack 10 to 15 minutes; remove from pan, and cool completely on wire rack. Makes one 10-inch cake.

CUPCAKES!

Served on an attractive platter or stacked to resemble a cake, cupcakes are transformed from a child's delight to a sophisticated personal confection!

THESE ARE "OLD-FASHIONED" *simple cakes which are all very good unfrosted or just topped with whipped cream.*

ASK ME FOR A DATE CAKE

2 cups pitted dates, cut into bite-size pieces
3 tablespoons butter
1 teaspoon baking soda
1 cup boiling water

1 cup sugar
1 egg
1 1/3 cups flour
1/2 cup chopped toasted walnuts (or cashews)

Preheat oven to 350°F. Grease an 8-inch square cake pan and set aside. Place dates, butter, and baking soda in mixing bowl. Add boiling water; stir until butter is melted. Add sugar and egg and stir until mixed. Stir in flour and nuts. Pour into the prepared pan and bake for 40 minutes, or until toothpick inserted in the center comes out clean. Serve warm with whipped cream. Makes 9 servings.

OLD FASHIONED SPICY OAT CAKE

This is tasty and not to be confused with the highly unsuccessful Old Spice Cake!

1 cup rolled oats, quick or regular
1 cup scalded milk
1 1/4 cups sifted flour
1 teaspoon baking powder
1/2 teaspoon baking soda
1 teaspoon salt

1 teaspoon cinnamon
1/4 teaspoon ground cloves
1 1/2 cups brown sugar packed
1/2 cup butter
2 eggs

Preheat oven to 350°F. Add oats to milk; let stand. Sift flour, baking powder, soda, salt, cinnamon and cloves. Cream brown sugar with butter; add eggs one at a time and continue beating until creamy and smooth. Add dry ingredients alternating with oat-milk mixture; blend well after each addition. Pour into 2 greased and floured 8-inch pans. Bake for 35 minutes. Makes 10 servings.

TOSCATARTA (Swedish Almond Cake)

1/3 cup butter or margarine
2/3 cup sugar
1 egg
1/2 cup milk
1/2 teaspoon vanilla (or almond) extract
1 cup flour
1 1/2 teaspoons baking powder

Topping
1/4 cup sugar
1 tablespoon flour
1 tablespoon milk
1/3 cup butter or margarine, cut up
1/2 cup sliced almonds

Preheat oven to 350°F. Beat butter and sugar together with an electric mixer till fluffy. Add the egg, beating well. Blend in milk and the vanilla (or almond) extract. Stir together flour and baking powder. Add to the egg mixture, beating on low speed till just combined. Pour batter into greased 9-inch round cake pan. Bake for 20 minutes (cake won't be done yet).

While cake is baking, prepare topping by combining sugar, flour and milk in a small saucepan over low heat and stir until sugar is dissolved. Add butter and cook, stirring until bubbly, then stir in almonds. Carefully spoon topping evenly over hot cake. Return cake to oven and bake for 10 to 15 minutes more or till cake is done and topping is bubbly and golden. Let cool in pan on wire rack. Makes one layer cake, 6 servings.

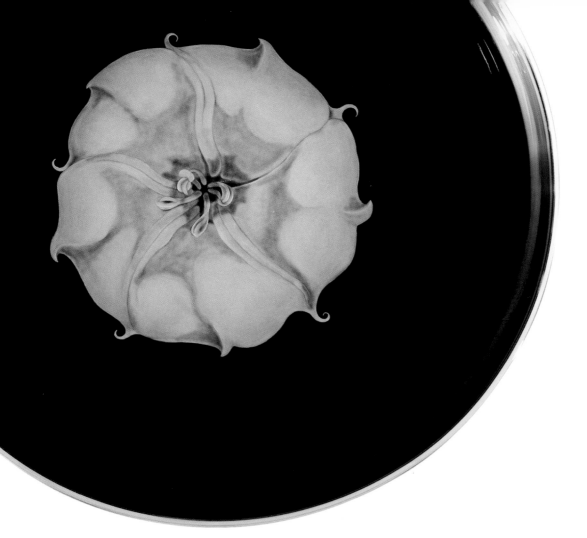

ITALIAN ALMOND CAKE

3 1/2 cups blanched, slivered almonds
   (14 ounces)
1 1/4 cups sugar (divided use)
Pinch salt
3/4 cup cake flour

1/2 teaspoon baking powder
8 tablespoons unsalted butter, room temperature
3 eggs, room temperature
1/2 cup whole milk

Preheat oven to 350°F. Lightly grease a 9-inch springform pan and line bottom with parchment paper. Toast almonds on a baking sheet in oven for 5 to 7 minutes, until lightly browned. Cool and then grind in food processor with 1/2 cup sugar for about 10 seconds or until it looks like flour. Add in flour, salt and baking powder and set aside. Cream butter and 3/4 cup sugar until light and fluffy with an electric mixer. Add eggs, then almond mixture and beat to just incorporate. Add milk and beat briefly. Spoon into prepared pan, smooth batter and bake for 30 to 40 minutes. Cool on wire rack, remove sides of pan and serve. Makes 10 servings.

PECAN "CORNBREAD" CAKE

A sweet, simple, delicious cake; the finely chopped pecans resemble cornmeal when baked, hence the name.

1 cup sugar
1 cup brown sugar
4 eggs, beaten
1 teaspoon vanilla extract

1 cup vegetable oil
1 1/2 cups self-rising flour
2 cups pecans, chopped very fine

Preheat oven to 350°F. Lightly grease and flour a 9 x 13-inch baking dish. Stir together sugar, brown sugar, eggs, vanilla and oil in a medium bowl. Stir in flour. Add pecans and stir until evenly mixed. Spoon into prepared pan, smooth batter and bake for 30 to 35 minutes. Makes 12 servings.

In the late 1930s Steuben Glass commissioned 27 of the most important contemporary artists to produce a design to be engraved on a Steuben form. Among the artists included were Henri Matisse, Isamu Noguchi, John Steuart Curry, and Georgia O'Keeffe. The latter submitted a lovely drawing of a JimsonWeed flower. Each artist received one of the finished pieces--not an inconsiderable gift, given their 1940 retail price of around $500 each. One wonders, however, how much Ms. O'Keeffe valued her plate, as she actually used it. When it was shown in a major Steuben exhibition in 2003 it had to be professionally polished to remove the knife scratches. - SG

FONDEST REGARDS TO THE FAMILY GOOEY BUTTER CAKE

The phenomenon of "gooey butter cake" seems to tag right along after the Southern affection for "chess pie". Lots of easy variations on this recipe; this one is a yummy Pumpkin Gooey Butter Cake.

Cake "crust"
1 (18¼-ounce) package yellow cake mix
1 large egg
8 tablespoons (1 stick) butter, melted

Filling
1 (8-ounce) package cream cheese, softened
1 (15-ounce) can solid pack pumpkin

3 eggs
1 teaspoon vanilla extract
8 tablespoons butter, melted
1 (16-ounce) box powdered sugar (3¾ cups)
1 teaspoon cinnamon
1 teaspoon nutmeg

Preheat oven to 350°F. Combine all of the cake-crust ingredients and mix well with an electric mixer. Pat the mixture into the bottom of a lightly greased 9 x 13-inch baking pan. Prepare filling.

To make the filling, beat the cream cheese and pumpkin together in a large bowl until smooth. Add the eggs, vanilla, and butter; beat together. Add the powdered sugar, cinnamon, nutmeg; mix well. Spread pumpkin mixture over cake batter and bake for 40 to 50 minutes. Make sure not to over bake as the center should be a little gooey. Yummy served warm with fresh whipped cream. Makes 12 to 15 servings. From granddaughter Analee, adapted from a Paula Deen recipe.

Variations:
Pineapple Gooey Cake: Substitute drained 20-ounce can of crushed pineapple for the pumpkin.
Banana Gooey Butter Cake: Substitute 2 ripe bananas instead of the canned pumpkin.
Peanut Butter Gooey Cake: Use a chocolate cake mix instead of yellow. Add 1 cup creamy peanut butter to the cream cheese filling instead of the pumpkin.
Lemon Chess Gooey Butter Cake: Make filling by combining 1 (8-ounce) package of cream cheese, zest of 2 large lemons (about 2 teaspoons), juice from 2 lemons (about 6 tablespoons), 2 eggs, 1 melted stick of butter, and 2 tablespoons of cornmeal; beat with electric mixer for a minute. Gradually add 3¾ cups of sifted powdered sugar and mix just until it is incorporated, about one minute. Pour filling onto cake batter and spread with spatula so filling covers surface and reaches edges. Bake as above. Cool pan on wire rack, cut into squares to serve.

PUMPKIN SHEET CAKE

1 (16-ounce) can solid pack pumpkin
2 cups sugar
1 cup vegetable oil
4 eggs, lightly beaten

2 cups flour
2 teaspoons baking soda
1 teaspoon cinnamon
½ teaspoon salt

Preheat oven to 350°F. Beat pumpkin, sugar and oil together with electric mixer. Add eggs; mix well. Combine flour, baking soda, cinnamon and salt; add to pumpkin mixture and beat until well blended. Pour into a greased 10 x 15-inch jellyroll pan. Bake for 25 to 30 minutes. Cool pan on wire rack and then freeze for 30 minutes before frosting.

Frosting
1 (8-ounce) package cream cheese, softened
5 tablespoons butter
1 teaspoon vanilla extract

1¾ cups powdered sugar
3 to 4 teaspoons milk
Chopped nuts for topping

Beat cream cheese, butter and vanilla in a mixing bowl until smooth. Gradually add sugar; mix well. Add milk until frosting reaches spreading consistency. Frost cake. Sprinkle with nuts. Makes 20 to 24 servings.

HOT BUTTERED RUM CAKE

1 cup butter
2 cups sugar
4 eggs
3 cups all-purpose flour
2 teaspoons baking powder
1 teaspoon salt
1/2 cup dark rum (prefer Myer's)

1/2 cup crushed walnuts

Rum Syrup
1 cup butter
1 cup sugar
1 1/2 cups dark rum
6 tablespoons crushed walnuts

Preheat oven to 325°F. Grease and flour a 10-inch springform pan. Cream butter and sugar with electric mixer until they are fluffy. Add eggs, blending briefly after each one. Add flour, baking powder, salt, rum and nuts and mix until smooth. Pour batter into pan. Bake for 70 minutes until wooden pick inserted into center comes out clean.

In the last few minutes before removing from the oven, prepare the syrup. Melt butter in a saucepan; add sugar and stir until melted. Add rum and boil for a few minutes. Poke cake with wooden pick. Leaving cake in the pan, pour half of hot rum syrup over hot cake and sprinkle with walnuts. When cool, remove from pan. When ready to serve heat remaining syrup to serve drizzled over the slices. After sliced, you may wish to heat in the microwave to serve warm. Delicious with vanilla or rum raisin ice cream. Makes 12 servings.

IRISH WHISKEY CAKE

Cake
1 box yellow cake mix with pudding
3 eggs
1/3 cup oil
1/2 cup water
1/2 cup Irish whiskey
1/2 cup pecan pieces

Glaze
1/2 cup butter
1 cup sugar
1/2 cup water
1/2 cup Irish whiskey

Preheat oven to 325°F. Mix all cake ingredients together with an electric mixer on low speed for 3 minutes. Spray bundt pan with cooking spray. Coat bottom and sides with 3/4 cup finely ground pecans. Pour cake batter into pan, over the pecans. Bake for 1 hour. Cool for 10 minutes, and make glaze by combining ingredients in a small saucepan. Bring glaze to a boil and simmer for 5 minutes, then pour glaze over cake in the pan. Cool and refrigerate. Serve with whipped cream. Makes 12 servings. From Bev Hoover.

May the road rise to meet you. May the wind be always at your back. May the sun shine warm upon your face. And rains fall soft upon your field. And until we meet again, May God hold you in the hollow of His hand.

- Traditional Irish Blessing

Severin Roesen
Nature's Bounty (detail),
ca. 1860, oil on canvas,
WAM, gift of George E.
Vollmer, 1995.15

FRESH BANANA CAKE

If you like a moister cake, use the larger amount of buttermilk suggested. Frost with Coconut Pecan Cream Cheese frosting, or spread the baked layers with whipped cream and top with sliced banana (brush with a bit of lemon juice to keep from turning brown) or fresh strawberries.

2¼ cups sifted cake flour
2½ teaspoons baking powder
½ teaspoon baking soda
½ teaspoon salt
½ cup shortening

1¼ cups sugar
2 eggs
1 teaspoon vanilla extract
1 cup mashed ripe bananas
¼ to ½ cup buttermilk

Preheat oven to 375°F. Sift the flour, baking powder, baking soda and salt together twice and set aside. Combine the shortening and sugar in a mixer bowl, beat until light and fluffy. Add the eggs, one at a time, beating well after each addition; add the vanilla. Combine the bananas and the buttermilk in a bowl; mix well. Add the dry ingredients and the banana mixture to the sugar mixture alternately, beginning and ending with the dry ingredients, beating well after each addition. Pour into 2 greased and floured 8½-inch cake pans. Bake for 30 minutes. Cool in the pans for about 15 minutes; remove to a wire rack to cool completely. Spread Coconut Pecan Cream Cheese frosting between layers and over the top and sides of the cake. This cake also works well in a bundt pan. Makes 10 to 12 servings.

Coconut Pecan Cream Cheese Frosting

1 (8-ounce) package cream cheese,
  room temperature
½ cup butter, room temperature
2½ cups powdered sugar, sifted

1 teaspoon vanilla extract
½ cup unsweetened grated coconut
½ cup finely chopped pecans

Mix cream cheese and butter with electric mixer until combined. Add powdered sugar gradually, until incorporated, about 1 minute. Add vanilla and beat for 1 minute more until fluffy. Stir in pecans and coconut.

ZUCCHINI CAKE

Cake

1 package yellow cake mix with pudding
  (Duncan Hines) or 1 package yellow cake mix
  and 4 ounce package instant pudding mix
4 eggs
½ teaspoon salt
1½ teaspoons cinnamon

4 cups chopped (shredded) zucchini
1 cup chopped nuts

Frosting

1 (9½-ounce) container whipped topping
1 package instant vanilla pudding
1 large can of pineapple and juice

Preheat oven to 350°F. Combine cake ingredients in large bowl and beat with electric mixer for 4 minutes. Grease and flour bundt pan. Bake 50 to 55 minutes, cool briefly and then turn out onto wire rack. To make frosting, combine pudding and pineapple; fold in whipped topping. Slice cake once horizontally and frost. Makes 12 servings. From Darla Farha.

STRAWBERRIES AND CREAM CAKE

This is a big beautiful cake. Some versions end up being a soggy mess, but not this one. The cream cheese added to the whipped cream fortifies the filling. The extra steps in preparing the strawberry filling give it a nice flavor. You will be proud to serve this.

Cake

3 eggs
1 cup milk (divided use)
2 teaspoons vanilla extract
$^1/_2$ teaspoon almond extract
$^1/_2$ teaspoon grated lemon rind
3 cups sifted cake flour
1$^1/_2$ cups sugar
1 tablespoon plus 1 teaspoon baking powder
$^3/_4$ teaspoon salt
$^3/_4$ cup butter, room temperature

Strawberry Filling

1$^1/_2$ quarts (a little less than 2 pounds) strawberries, washed, dried and stemmed
4 tablespoons sugar
2 tablespoons Kirsch liqueur
1 tablespoon strawberry jelly

Whipped Cream Filling

1 (8-ounce) package cream cheese, room temperature
$^1/_2$ cup sugar
1 teaspoon vanilla extract
$^1/_8$ teaspoon salt
2 cups heavy cream

Preheat oven to 350°F. Grease and flour two 9-inch cake pans; set aside. Combine eggs, $^1/_4$ cup milk, vanilla, almond extract and lemon rind in a small bowl. Combine flour, sugar, baking powder and salt in a separate large mixer bowl; mix on low speed just enough to combine ingredients. Add butter and remaining $^3/_4$ cup milk; mix on low to blend, then turn mixer to medium and beat 2 minutes. Gradually add egg mixture in 3 batches, beating well after each addition and scraping down sides as needed. Divide batter between prepared pans and smooth surface. Bake 25 to 35 minutes or until a wooden skewer inserted in the center comes out clean and the cake springs back when lightly pressed near the center. Cool on rack for 10 minutes. Remove cakes from pans; cool completely.

Halve the 14 prettiest strawberries and reserve. Quarter the remaining berries; sprinkle with 4 tablespoons sugar in a medium bowl and let stand at room temperature 30 to 45 minutes for juices to accumulate. Strain juice and reserve (about $^1/_2$ cup). Pulse quartered berries into a food processor a few times. Place reserved juice and Kirsch in a small saucepan and simmer over medium heat until syrupy and reduced to about 3 tablespoons (about 3 minutes). Pour reduced syrup over chopped berries, toss and set aside until cake is cooled.

When the cake has cooled, mix cream cheese, sugar, vanilla and salt in the bowl of a mixer; whisk at medium speed until fluffy (about 2 minutes). Add cream and beat until mixture holds stiff peaks (about 3 minutes).

To assemble the cake, place the bottom layer on a cake plate and arrange ring of 20 strawberry halves, cut sides down and stem ends out, all around the perimeter of the layer. Pour puréed strawberry mixture in center, spread half of the whipped cream over the berry layer, leaving a $^1/_2$-inch border from edge. Place top cake layer on top and press down gently. Spread remaining whipped cream over top and decorate with remaining cut strawberries. Brush berries with melted strawberry jelly if desired. Serve or cover with dome and refrigerate. May be made up to 8 hours ahead of time. Makes 10 to 12 servings.

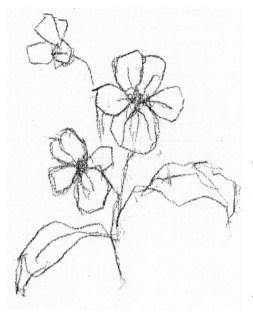

PRETTY PANSY ANGEL CAKE

Perfect for a special tea, luncheon or shower, this beautiful cake is a spring-time show stopper. This unique recipe is a fresh adaptation of one published in "Southern Living."

You will get lots of comments on the edible flowers. I like to use pansies, violas (both taste like sweet nectar) and bee balm (tastes like bergamot) for the garnish, but there are many other edible flowers to use. You may even like lilacs (tastes a little lemony and floral). Just be careful to use pesticide free flowers, and if you wonder if a flower might be edible, research it first as some are not (lilies), and some have a spicy taste (like marigolds) that may be splendid in a salad but not in a cake. Also, pay attention to color when making the confetti. Pink, yellow and orange flowers look great in the confetti, just be careful to avoid nasturtiums as they will turn brown. If you don't have edible flowers in your garden, large grocery stores are now carrying them packaged in the fresh herb section.

DRIED FLOWER CONFETTI:

Spread 3 cups edible flower petals in a single layer on two jellyroll baking pans or cookie sheets. (Nasturtiums tend to darken and brown when dried, so avoid using them.) Let stand 2 to 3 days until completely dry, stirring occasionally to help the drying process. Snip the dried flower petals into small pieces and measure 1/2 cup to use in the cake. Store remaining in an airtight container in a cool, dark place.

1 1/2 cups sifted powdered sugar
1 cup sifted cake flour
1 1/2 cups egg whites (10 to 12 eggs), room temperature
1 1/2 teaspoons cream of tartar
1 teaspoon orange flower water (or orange extract)
1 cup granulated sugar
1 cup chopped edible flowers or 1/2 cup dried flower confetti

Icing

2 tablespoons light corn syrup
1/2 teaspoons orange flower water
2 tablespoons orange juice
4 cups powdered sugar (sifted)
1 to 2 tablespoons hot water

Edible flowers, such as pansies, calendula, dianthus or bee balm. Rosa rugosa petals may also be used but be careful to remove the bitter white portion of the petal

Preheat oven to 350°F. Sift powdered sugar and flour together 3 times; set aside. In a large bowl, combine egg whites, cream of tartar and orange flower water and beat with mixer on medium speed until soft peaks form (tips curl). Add granulated sugar, about 2 tablespoons at a time, beating until stiff peaks form (tips stand straight). Sift about one-fourth of the flour mixture over beaten egg whites; fold in gently. Repeat, folding in remaining flour mixture by fourths, along with chopped edible flowers (for a more colorful effect in the cake, use dried flower confetti). Pour into an ungreased 10-inch tube pan. Gently cut through batter with a narrow metal spatula or knife to remove large air pockets. Bake on the lowest rack of the oven for 40 to 45 minutes or until top of cake springs back when lightly touched. Immediately invert cake (leave in pan); cool thoroughly. Using a narrow metal spatula, loosen sides of cake from pan; remove cake.

Make icing by combining corn syrup and orange flower water. Stir in 2 cups powdered sugar and orange juice, then add remaining powdered sugar and enough hot water to make icing of right consistency to drizzle (about 1 to 2 tablespoons).

To frost cake, lightly brush off any excess crumbs. Place cake on wire rack over a jellyroll pan. Use a spoon or ladle to pour icing over cake to cover the cake completely. Let stand 20 minutes. Repeat with a second layer of icing. Let dry 20 minutes. Repeat with a third layer of icing. If necessary, reuse the icing that has dripped on the pan, straining it to remove crumbs. Let icing dry completely. Place edible flowers in a circle around bottom edge of cake. Place daisies or other flowers in a tiny vase in center hole of cake. Makes 12 servings.

WALNUT TORTE with CARAMEL BUTTERCREAM

1/2 cup (1 stick) butter, room temperature
1/2 cup vegetable oil
2 cups sugar
5 eggs, separated
1 tablespoon grated orange rind, optional
1 teaspoon baking soda
2 cups flour
1 cup buttermilk
1 teaspoon vanilla extract
1 3/4 cups ground walnuts

Caramel Buttercream Icing
1 (8-ounce) package cream cheese
1/2 cup butter
1/2 cup homemade thick caramel sauce, room
   temperature (see recipe)
1 (16-ounce) box powdered sugar
1 teaspoon vanilla extract
2/3 cups chopped walnuts

Garnish: 8 walnuts
   1 cup whipped cream

Preheat oven to 350°F. Butter and flour three 9-inch round cake pans. With electric mixer, cream butter and oil until smooth. Gradually beat in sugar; beating until creamy. Add egg yolks, one at a time, beating well after each addition. On slow speed, add orange zest, baking soda and flour; then add buttermilk, vanilla and walnuts. In a separate bowl, beat egg whites with clean wire whisk until they form a stiff peak but are still moist. Gently fold whites into batter in two separate additions. Divide batter evenly among the prepared pans. Bake cake layers until they are golden and the cake springs bake when touched gently, about 20 to 25 minutes. Remove the pans from the oven. Cool in pan for 5 to 10 minutes, then unmold layers onto rack to cool completely.

Prepare the icing: Place cream cheese and butter in food processor bowl. Pulse until softened and creamy. Add the caramel. Process until smooth. Add the powdered sugar and vanilla; process until just mixed and smooth.

Cake assembly: Place cake layers on a large plate. Spread the layer evenly with 1/2 cup icing. Sprinkle half the chopped walnuts over the icing. Repeat with the second layer. Then top with the final layer flat side down. Spread remaining icing evenly and smoothly over the sides and top of the cake. Place walnut halves evenly around the edge of the cake. Keep refrigerated until ready to serve. The cake can be prepared to this point 1 to 2 days in advance; cover with a cake cover and refrigerate. Decorate with whipped cream rosettes and walnut halves. Makes 12 servings. From Bonnie Aeschliman.

Thick Caramel Sauce
1 1/2 cups sugar
1/2 cup water
1/2 cup cream

Combine sugar and water in heavy skillet. Bring to boil, stirring to dissolve sugar. Once liquid begins to boil, do not stir. Cook over medium-high heat until sugar caramelizes and turns the color of a copper penny. Remove from heat immediately. Carefully add cream (mixture will foam up and splatter). After sputtering subsides, return to medium heat; stir and cook until lumps melt and sauce is smooth. Cool to room temperature before using in icing. Makes 1 cup; you only need half of it for icing so enjoy the rest over ice cream!

Opposite page and below:

Jeanne Harter Gordon
Flowers, 2007, charcoal
on paper, from the artist's
collection

To prevent cracks from forming in the top of your cheesecake, first do not over-beat the batter. Too much air incorporated will cause the cake to rise, then fall (like a soufflé). You can also wrap the springform pan with two layers of heavy duty foil and bake in a water bath to prevent cracks.

Also, avoid extreme temperature fluctuations Cool completely at room temperature before refrigerating.

CLASSIC CHEESECAKE

This recipe is adapted from the 1973 Junior League of Wichita cookbook Sunflower Sampler, *and is a long-time favorite.*

Crust
1 1/2 cups Lorna Doone
    cookie crumbs
2 tablespoons sugar
1 1/2 teaspoons cinnamon
6 tablespoons butter, melted

Filling
3 (8-ounce) packages cream
    cheese, softened
1 cup sugar
3 eggs, at room temperature
2 teaspoons vanilla extract

Topping
2 cups sour cream, at
    room temperature
3 tablespoons sugar
1/2 teaspoon vanilla extract

Preheat oven to 375°F. Mix crust ingredients thoroughly. Depending on presentation you choose, pat evenly into bottom and sides of a well-buttered 9-inch springform pan or an 8-inch square pan.

To prepare the filling, mix the cream cheese and sugar on medium speed for 2 minutes with electric mixer. Add the eggs one at a time and mix until blended. Add the vanilla and stir. Pour the filling into the crust. Bake for 20 minutes. It should still have some jiggle in the center when tapped. Remove from the oven and allow to cool for at least 5 minutes to firm up before adding the topping. Set oven to 500°F.

Prepare the topping by whipping the sour cream, add sugar and vanilla. Pour evenly over the cheesecake, return to the oven for 5 minutes. (If problems with your oven at that temperature may alternatively bake for 10 minutes at 375°F). Let cool to room temperature in a draft-free area. Refrigerate for at least 4 hours before serving. Run a warm sharp knife around the perimeter of the pan to loosen the cake; remove outer ring. Makes 10 to 12 servings.

CHEESECAKE *as a dessert or as an hors d'oeurve*

For passed hors d'oeurves, bake the cheesecake in a 8-inch square pan. Then with a sharp knife that has been wiped down with a hot, damp towel, first trim ¹/₄ inch off of the cake from one side. Then cut the cake into 16 squares, lifting them out with a small spatula. Arrange the squares on a platter with plenty of room between each piece.

For a traditional, classic wedge presentation for a dessert, bake the cheesecake in a springform pan. Again, make very clean cuts with a very sharp knife that is warmed by wrapping in a hot, damp kitchen towel. Wipe knife after each cut.

Garnish is important with cheesecake - try two or three mint leaves; for cheesecake with a chocolate cookie crust, garnish with a sliver of an Oreo cookie; for that made with a fruit coulis, garnish with the featured fruit.

WHITE CHOCOLATE AMARETTO CHEESECAKE with PEACH AMARETTO SAUCE

Chocolate Cookie Crust
18 Oreo cookies
²/₃ cup toasted almonds
3 tablespoons butter,
   room temperature

Filling
4 (8-ounce) packages cream
   cheese, room temperature
1 cup sugar
¹/₄ cup Amaretto liqueur
2 teaspoons vanilla extract
3 ounces white chocolate,
   melted and cooled to
   room temperature
2 eggs
2 egg yolks

Peach Amaretto Sauce
1 pound frozen
   peaches, thawed
1 tablespoon fresh lemon juice
¹/₃ to ¹/₂ cup sugar
1 tablespoon Amaretto liqueur

Garnish: whipped cream and
   toasted almonds

Oppostite page:

Charles Demuth
African Daisies (detail),
1925, watercolor and
graphite on cream woven
paper, WAM, The Roland
P. Murdock Collection,
M92.51

Preheat oven to 350°F. To make the crust, process cookies for coarse crumbs in a food processor or blender. Add almonds; pulse machine on and off until almonds are coarsely chopped. Add butter; process a few times to mix it in. Line bottom of a 9-inch springform pan with parchment paper for easy removal. Spray with nonstick spray. Pour crumbs in bottom of pan, press 1 inch up sides and firmly across bottom of pan. Wrap outside of the pan in a double layer of heavy-duty foil to prevent leaking. Bake for 10 minutes. Set aside.

To make the filling, beat cream cheese on high speed of electric mixer until light and creamy. Add sugar, Amaretto and vanilla. Beat 2 minutes until sugar is dissolved. With mixer running, add chocolate, beat until combined. Reduce speed to low and add eggs and yolks, one at a time, beating just until combined. Pour batter into prepared crust. Set pan in a larger pan. Place cheesecake in oven and pour 1 inch of very hot water in the larger pan. Bake for exactly 45 minutes. Turn off the oven; do not open the oven door. Leave cheesecake in oven for 1 hour. Transfer to rack. Center may be a little wiggly. Cool for 1 hour. Cover with plastic wrap and refrigerate at least 6 hours or overnight.

Prepare the sauce by blending all ingredients in a blender or food processor. Chill until serving time. To serve, pool a little of the Peach Amaretto sauce on bottom of dessert plates. Place a wedge of cheesecake on plate. Decorate with whipped cream and chopped toasted almonds if desired. Makes 8 to 10 servings. From Bonnie Aeschliman.

RHUBARB CRISP

There are two types of rhubarb in the market. Hothouse rhubarb has a pink or pale red stalk and yellow-green leaves; field grown rhubarb has very bright red stalks, deep green leaves, and a stronger flavor.

Select rhubarb with crisp, bright stalks. Refrigerate, tightly wrapped in a plastic bag, for up to 3 days. Remove all leaves and wash stalks just before using.

All fibrous strings should be removed from the field-grown rhubarb.

One pound rhubarb yields 3 cups chopped.

4 cups rhubarb, cut into 1-inch pieces
1 tablespoon lemon juice
$^1/_2$ cup flour
1$^1/_2$ cups sugar
$^1/_4$ teaspoon salt
3 tablespoons butter, melted

Topping
$^1/_2$ cup flour
$^1/_2$ cup brown sugar
$^1/_2$ cup butter
$^1/_2$ cup old-fashioned rolled oats
$^1/_2$ teaspoon cinnamon

Preheat oven to 350°F. Sprinkle lemon juice over rhubarb. Mix flour, sugar and salt and toss with rhubarb until all are coated. Pour melted butter over all. Combine topping ingredients with a fork and sprinkle over rhubarb. Bake for 45 minutes or until topping is lightly browned. Makes 8 servings.

RHUBARB CHERRY CRUNCH

Adapted from the cookbook Really Rhubarb, *this sweet-tart dessert is a pretty red, and a nice standout in taste too with the streusel topping. Served at the 2003 Wichita Symphony Showhouse Tea Room, it was a surprise hit.*

1 cup sugar
3 tablespoons cornstarch
1 cup water
1 (21-ounce) can cherry pie filling
$^1/_2$ teaspoon almond extract
1 cup flour
1 cup old-fashioned rolled oats

1 cup packed brown sugar
$^1/_4$ teaspoon salt
$^1/_2$ cup butter
4 cups chopped rhubarb
$^1/_4$ cup chopped nuts

Ice Cream or Whipped Topping

Preheat oven to 350°F. Stir sugar and cornstarch together in a medium saucepan, and add water. Cook over medium heat and stir till thickened and bubbly; cook and stir 1 minute more. Stir in cherry pie filling and almond extract. Set aside. Mix flour, oats, brown sugar and salt in a large bowl. Cut in butter till mixture resembles coarse crumbs. Press 2 cups of the mixture in bottom of a greased 9 x 13-inch baking dish. Spoon the rhubarb evenly over crust. Spread with cherry mixture. Combine remaining crumbs and nuts; sprinkle over top. Bake for 40 minutes. Serve warm or at room temperature. Add ice cream or whipped topping. Makes 12 servings.

Henry Varnum Poor
Self Portrait with Amaryllis, ca. 1950, oil on canvas, WAM, gift of Peter Poor, 2007.46.1 (detail on opposite page)

RHUBARB CRUMBLE with BOURBON CREAM

1 cup plus $^1/_3$ cup sugar (divided use)
1 tablespoon cinnamon
$^1/_2$ teaspoon nutmeg
4 cups rhubarb, cut into 1-inch pieces
$^2/_3$ cup flour
$^1/_3$ cup old-fashioned rolled oats
1 teaspoon baking powder

$^1/_8$ teaspoon salt
3 tablespoons butter, at room temperature

Bourbon Cream
2 cups vanilla yogurt, chilled
2 tablespoons bourbon

Preheat oven to 400°F. Grease a 9-inch square glass baking dish. Combine 1 cup sugar, cinnamon, and nutmeg in a large bowl; gently toss rhubarb into sugar mixture. Spread rhubarb mixture evenly in prepared baking dish. Combine flour, oats, baking powder, salt, and remaining $^1/_3$ cup sugar. Cut in butter until mixture resembles coarse meal. Spread evenly over top of rhubarb. Bake 20 to 25 minutes, set on wire rack to slightly cool. Prepare Bourbon Cream by beating yogurt until very thick; stir in bourbon. Serve crumble warm, topped with Bourbon Cream. Makes 9 servings.

EASY PEACH PANDOWDY

This pandowdy, cousin to a cobbler, looks a bit messy before it goes into the oven, but while it bakes the batter rises above the peaches to form a crisp, golden topping. Other fruit, such as blueberries or raspberries, are also good in this.

1 1/4 pounds firm, ripe peaches (5 to 6 medium, about 3 cups sliced)
1 tablespoon fresh lemon juice
1 2/3 cups sugar (divided use)
1/2 cup butter, melted
1 cup flour

1 tablespoon baking power
1/4 teaspoon salt
1 cup whole milk
Cinnamon or nutmeg for sprinkling (optional)

Preheat oven to 375°F (oven rack in middle position). Cut an X in bottom of each peach and blanch in 2 batches in a kettle of boiling water for just about 7 seconds. Transfer peaches with a slotted spoon to a bowl of ice and cold water. Peel off skin, beginning from scored end. Halve peaches, then pit and cut lengthwise into 1/4-inch slices. Place peach slices (and bits) in a 3-quart heavy saucepan and add lemon juice and 2/3 cup sugar. Bring to a boil over high heat, stirring constantly, then boil, stirring occasionally, 4 minutes. Remove from heat.

Pour butter into a 9 x 13-inch baking dish. Whisk together flour, baking powder, salt, and remaining cup sugar in a bowl, then whisk in milk just until combined. Pour batter over butter (do not stir). Pour peaches over batter, but do not stir as the batter will migrate while cooking to partially cover the peaches. Sprinkle lightly with cinnamon if desired and bake until pandowdy is bubbling and top is golden brown, 40 to 45 minutes. Cool in pan on a rack until warm, about 25 minutes. Serve with a dollop of sweetened whipped cream or a scoop of vanilla or cinnamon ice cream. Makes 8 servings.

BLUEBERRY PECAN COBBLER

4 pints fresh or frozen blueberries
1¹/₂ cups sugar
¹/₂ cup flour
¹/₂ teaspoon cinnamon
¹/₃ cup water
2 tablespoons lemon juice

1 teaspoon vanilla extract
1 (15-ounce) package prepared pie crusts
¹/₂ cup chopped pecans, toasted
Vanilla ice cream
Garnish: fresh mint sprigs

Preheat oven to 475°F. Bring blueberries, sugar, flour, cinnamon, water, lemon juice and vanilla to a boil in a saucepan over medium heat, stirring until sugar melts. Reduce heat to low; cook, stirring occasionally, for 10 minutes. Spoon half of blueberry mixture into a lightly greased 8-inch square pan. Roll 1 pie crust to ¹/₈-inch thickness on a lightly floured surface; cut into an 8-inch square. Place over blueberry mixture; sprinkle with pecans. Bake for 10 minutes. Spoon remaining blueberry mixture over baked crust. Roll remaining pie crust to ¹/₈-inch thickness; cut into 1-inch strips. Arrange in lattice design over blueberry mixture. Bake for 10 minutes or until golden brown. Serve with vanilla ice cream, and garnish, if desired. Makes 4 servings.

APPLE CRANBERRY CRISP with ALMOND STREUSEL TOPPING

1 cup cranberries, fresh or frozen
¹/₄ cup plus ³/₄ cup sugar
¹/₄ cup currants
¹/₄ cup dark rum
6 to 7 medium Granny Smith apples, cored, peeled, and sliced ¹/₄-inch thick, (6 cups)
1 tablespoon fresh lemon juice
1 teaspoon grated orange rind
¹/₂ teaspoon cinnamon
3 tablespoons flour

Topping
4 tablespoons butter, at room temperature
¹/₄ cup flour
¹/₄ cup brown sugar, firmly packed
¹/₂ cup blanched slivered almonds
¹/₄ cup old-fashioned rolled oats

Preheat oven to 350°F. Toss cranberries with ¹/₄ cup sugar in a small bowl. Set aside. Combine currants and rum in a separate small bowl. Set aside. Toss apples with lemon juice in a large bowl. Stir in remaining ³/₄ cup sugar, orange zest, and cinnamon. Fold in cranberries and currants. Stir in flour until mixture is combined. Set aside. Mix butter, flour, and brown sugar in a large bowl until mixture resembles course meal. Stir in almonds and oats. Spoon apple mixture into a 2-quart soufflé dish and top with topping. Bake 45 minutes. Cool at least 20 minutes before serving. Make 6 to 8 servings.

APPLE CRUNCH
Excellent, easy.

Crust
1 cup flour
1 cup light brown sugar
1 cup old-fashioned rolled oats
¹/₂ cup butter
¹/₂ teaspoon cinnamon
¹/₄ teaspoon nutmeg

Filling
6 to 8 tart apples, cored, peeled and thinly sliced
¹/₂ cup light brown sugar
¹/₂ cup sugar

Vanilla ice cream or whipped cream

Preheat oven to 350°F. Blend crust ingredients. Arrange apples in the bottom of a 9-inch square glass baking dish. Sprinkle apples with the sugars and top with a layer of crust. Repeat layers, ending with a heavy ¹/₄-inch crust. Press layers gently. Bake 50 to 60 minutes. Serve with whipped cream or vanilla ice cream. Makes 9 servings.

Chocolate Finishes

COME HITHER FUDGE PIE with RASPBERRY SAUCE

I think the name speaks for itself! Highly irresistible!

If chocolate is melted near a burner that is too hot, it will "seize", which is a greasy curdled appearance. If this happens, start over.

1/2 cup butter
2 (1-ounce) unsweetened chocolate squares
2 eggs
1 cup sugar
1/2 cup flour
1 teaspoon vanilla extract
1/4 teaspoon salt
2/3 cup chopped pecans, toasted (optional)

Raspberry Sauce
3 tablespoons pure maple syrup
2 tablespoons sugar
1 (16-ounce) package frozen raspberries (do not thaw)

Toppings: powdered sugar, fresh raspberries

Preheat oven to 350°F. Melt butter and chocolate in a small saucepan over low heat, stirring constantly; remove from heat. Beat eggs at medium speed with an electric mixer for 2 minutes. Gradually add sugar, flour, vanilla and salt, beating until blended; stir in pecans, if desired. Pour mixture into a lightly greased 9-inch pie plate. Bake for 20 to 25 minutes, or until center is firm. While pie is baking prepare raspberry sauce. Cook syrup and sugar in a saucepan over medium heat, stirring constantly, until sugar dissolves. Add raspberries and cook, stirring constantly, 10 minutes or until thickened. Pour mixture through fine wire-mesh strainer; press with back of spoon against sides of strainer to squeeze out sauce and discard solids (makes 1 cup). Serve pie warm with Raspberry Sauce, whipped cream or other desired toppings. Makes 8 to 10 servings.

PICNIC CHOCOLATE SHEET CAKE

This classic cake is often called a "Texas Sheet Cake" because of its size. Baked and served in a jellyroll pan, the cake is sturdy and easy to transport too (particularly nice if you have a jellyroll pan that also has a lid).

2 cups flour
2 cups sugar
4 tablespoons unsweetened cocoa
1/2 cup vegetable oil
1/2 cup butter
1 cup water

2 eggs, beaten
1 cup buttermilk
1 teaspoon baking soda
1 teaspoon vanilla extract
1 teaspoon cinnamon (optional)

Heat oven to 350°F. Coat a jellyroll pan (10 x 15-inch or 11 x 17-inch) pan with cooking spray, and dust with flour. Mix flour and sugar together. Combine cocoa, oil, butter, and water in a small saucepan and bring to a boil, stirring frequently. Remove cocoa mixture from heat and pour over flour and sugar. Mix well. Add remaining ingredients. Pour batter into prepared pan. Bake for 25 to 30 minutes, until wooden pick inserted in center comes out clean. Frost immediately. Makes 24 servings.

Icing
6 tablespoons milk
4 tablespoons unsweetened cocoa
1/2 cup butter

1 box (3 cups) powdered sugar
1 cup chopped pecans, toasted
1 teaspoon vanilla extract

Combine milk, cocoa and butter in a small saucepan and bring to a boil, stirring constantly. Remove from heat and gradually stir in powdered sugar, pecans and vanilla. Spread over hot cake and cool completely before serving.

DECADENT GLAZED CHOCOLATE TORTE

Elegant and easy. After the glaze has set, try out some of the garnishes on page 256 and it will be beautiful too. This was served for several years at the Wichita Festival luncheons at the Wichita-Sedgwick County Historical Museum.

¹/₂ cup butter
¹/₂ cup light corn syrup
1 cup semi-sweet chocolate chips
¹/₂ cup sugar
3 eggs
1 cup flour
1 cup chopped walnuts
1 teaspoon vanilla extract

Glaze
¹/₂ cup chocolate chips
2 tablespoons butter
1 tablespoon corn syrup
1 teaspoon vanilla extract

Preheat oven to 350°F. Melt butter and corn syrup in a saucepan over medium heat; stir in chocolate until melted. Add sugar and eggs and stir until well blended. Stir in flour, nuts, and vanilla. Bake in a 9-inch buttered and floured cake pan for 35 to 40 minutes or until center springs back to touch. Cool in pan for 10 minutes, then turn out on wire rack. Prepare the glaze by melting all ingredients in a saucepan over medium heat. Place a piece of wax paper under the wire rack. Pour the warm glaze over the cake and spread with a spatula. Chill about one hour before transferring to serving dish. Torte freezes well glazed. Makes 8 to 10 servings.

CHOCOLATE ROULADE with MOCHA CRÈME

This delightful roulade (a soufflé-type mixture baked in a jellyroll pan until firm but still moist, then spread with a filling and rolled up) is a beautiful finish to make any meal special. Your guests will happily linger long after dinner. Barbara Kieffer thankfully shares this recipe and describes the tradition, "It took me years to attempt this recipe before discovering how easy it actually is to make. It has been our Christmas dessert now for over 15 years. Although the main course may vary from year to year, my sons travel home, in part (perhaps in large part) for this light-as-a-feather chocolate roulade."

Mocha Crème
1¹/₂ cups heavy cream
¹/₂ cup powdered sugar
¹/₄ cup cocoa
2 teaspoons instant coffee or expresso
  powder (optional)
1 teaspoon vanilla

Roulade
6 eggs, separated, room temperature
³/₄ cup sugar
¹/₃ cup unsweetened cocoa
1¹/₂ teaspoons vanilla
Dash salt
Powdered sugar

To make the filling, in a large mixing bowl, beat the cream until very soft peaks form. Sprinkle in the powdered sugar, cocoa, coffee granules (if desired) and vanilla and continue beating until stiff peaks form. Cover with plastic wrap and refrigerate until ready to use.

Adjust oven rack to upper-middle position and preheat oven to 375°F. Grease bottom of 15¹/₂" x 10¹/₂-inch jellyroll pan. Line pan with wax or parchment paper. Grease lightly. To make the roulade, beat egg whites in large mixer bowl at high speed until soft peaks form. Add ¹/₄ cup sugar, 2 tablespoons at a time, beating until peaks are stiff. Set aside. In separate bowl, with same beaters, beat yolks at high speed adding remaining sugar, 2 tablespoons at a time, until mixture is very thick (about 4 minutes). At low speed, beat in cocoa, vanilla and salt with egg yolk mixture until smooth. Fold cocoa mixture into egg white mixture just until blended. Spread in pan. Bake for 15 minutes. Cool in the pan for 5 to 10 minutes or until cool enough to handle, but not yet cold.

Sift powdered sugar onto a linen towel. Run paring knife around perimeter of baking sheet to loosen cake. Turn cake upside down onto the towel and peel off wax paper very carefully. Starting at the long side, roll cake and towel together into jelly roll shape. Let sit on rack 30 minutes. Carefully unroll cake and spread filling over top leaving ¹/₂-inch margin on either end. Gently roll up again, snugly around filling. Trim ends. Place on serving dish seam side down. Dust with powdered sugar. Enjoy! May be refrigerated for up to 24 hours, but best served at room temperature. Makes 10 servings. From Barbara Kieffer.

*German sweet chocolate was
first introduced in 1852 by
Baker's Chocolate Company.
German sweet chocolate, a
dark chocolate formulated
especially for baking
purposes, is sweeter than
semi-sweet chocolate due to
the addition of sugar.*

HOT CHOCOLATE SOUFFLÉ

7 ounces German sweet chocolate
3 teaspoons instant coffee granules
5 tablespoons water
1/3 cup flour
Pinch of salt

2 cups cold milk
1/2 teaspoon vanilla extract
4 eggs separated, plus 2 extra whites
1/2 cup sugar
Powdered sugar

Preheat oven to 375°F. Combine chocolate, coffee granules and water in top of double boiler over medium heat. Stir until smooth. Set aside over hot water to keep warm. Mix flour and salt in a non-reactive saucepan over medium heat. Gradually, add cold milk then add vanilla and stir until free of lumps. Continue stirring while blending in chocolate mixture and remove from heat. Stir in egg yolks one at a time (can be made ahead of time to this point, re-warming over low heat). Beat egg whites with salt. Slowly add sugar, beating to meringue consistency. Stir 2 large spoonfuls into warm chocolate mixture to lighten. Fold in remainder. Place a 2-inch collar on soufflé dish, spray with cooking spray or grease and sprinkle powdered sugar on bottom and sides. Bake for 25 to 30 minutes (if instead you decide to use individual dishes, bake 20 minutes). Serve with whipped cream and strong coffee. Makes 4 to 6 servings. From June Peugh.

SOUTHERN SWEET CHOCOLATE with VANILLA SAUCE

4 ounces German sweet chocolate
1/4 cup butter
1 (12-ounce) can evaporated milk
1 1/2 cups sugar
3 tablespoons cornstarch
1/4 teaspoon salt

2 eggs
1 teaspoon vanilla extract
1 cup flaked coconut
3/4 cup chopped pecans

Whipped cream or Vanilla Sauce

Preheat oven to 375°F. Melt chocolate and butter in microwave on low until soft. Stir to combine. Add evaporated milk. Mix sugar, cornstarch and salt in bowl. Beat in eggs and vanilla and add to chocolate mixture. Mix coconut and pecans in separate bowl. Pour chocolate mixture into 8-inch square pan. Sprinkle with coconut/pecan mixture. Cover with foil and bake for 55 minutes. Cool. When ready to serve, top with whipped cream or vanilla sauce. Makes 9 servings. Can add fresh berries or kiwi slice to top for garnish or sprig of mint on the side if using whipped cream. Nice to serve piled high in egg cups.

Vanilla Sauce

4 egg yolks
1 cup powdered sugar
1 tablespoon vanilla extract

1/4 cup dry sherry
1 cup heavy cream, whipped

Beat yolks in double boiler; add sugar, and sherry. Cook over hot water 10 minutes or until thick. Beat until smooth, refrigerate and fold in with whipped cream right before serving.

BAKED FUDGE DESSERT

Served for many Wichita Art Museum special banquets and in the museum restaurant during the 80s and 90s, this continues to be a favorite, great scaled either for home cooking or larger events. From Susan Wilhite and Karen Root.

1 cup butter
4 eggs, beaten
2 cups sugar
1/2 cup flour
1/2 teaspoon salt

1/2 cup cocoa
2 teaspoons vanilla extract
1 cup chopped pecans or walnuts
Vanilla ice cream or whipped cream topping

Preheat oven to 350°F. Melt butter, set aside to cool. Combine eggs and sugar, then stir in cooled butter and remaining ingredients and blend well. Pour into a buttered 9-inch square pan which has been set into larger pan. Pour hot water to a depth of 1 inch in larger pan. Bake for 1 hour. Cool slightly, cut into squares. Serve warm, topped with ice cream or cool to room temperature and top with sweetened whipped cream. Makes 9 to 12 servings.

FUDGE CUPCAKES

Served at Wichita Center for the Arts event, Holiday Tables *lunchroom for several years, this is a great standard.*

5 ounces semi-sweet chocolate
1 cup butter
1 3/4 cups sugar
1 cup flour

3 cups chopped pecans
4 eggs, lightly beaten
1 teaspoon vanilla extract

Preheat oven to 325°F. Line muffin tins with foil or paper baking cups. Melt chocolate and butter in microwave on low. In a large mixing bowl combine sugar, flour, nuts and add eggs and vanilla. Stir into chocolate mixture until dry ingredients are barely incorporated, do not beat. Fill muffin papers full. Bake for 18 minutes (full sized cupcakes need to bake 25 minutes or less). These do not test dry. Centers will be fudgy. Makes approximately 28 mid-sized or 18 full sized cupcakes.

CHOCOLATE CHEWIES

Oohh la la. See "Cookie" chapter of this book for other chocolate cookies, but this one is probably my favorite little chewy bite of chocolate. I discovered them at a bakery in Houston one hot summer day with granddaughter Analee, and then came home and made my own version after they haunted my tastebuds.

2 cups pecans
2 1/2 cups powdered sugar
1/2 cup good quality unsweetened cocoa powder
   (like Valrhona)

2 tablespoons flour
Pinch of salt
3 large egg whites
1 teaspoon vanilla extract

Preheat oven to 350°F. Line two cookie sheets with parchment paper. Toast pecans in oven, stirring until slightly brown, for about 5 to 10 minutes; let cool, then coarsely chop. Mix sugar, cocoa, flour and salt with electric mixer on medium speed until well blended. Beat in the egg whites, one at a time. Add vanilla and beat at high speed for one minute. Fold in pecans with spoon and mix until just blended. Drop tablespoons onto cookie sheets, about 2 inches apart. Bake for 15 minutes, rotating sheet halfway though baking. They should appear dry in the center when done. Cool on parchment paper and then peel off. Store in airtight container. Makes 3 dozen.

CHOCOLATINI

Mix 2 ounces Godiva chocolate liqueur, 2 ounces of vodka and splash of raspberry liqueur together in a cocktail shaker. Add crushed ice and shake. Strain into 2 chilled martini glasses.

For an extra special touch, melt 1/2 cup of chocolate and dip the rim of the martini glass into the melted chocolate, making a scalloped pattern by dipping only 2-inch sections of the rim at a time.

RICH CHOCOLATE TARTS with STRAWBERRY RHUBARB COMPOTE

Follow instructions very carefully and you will be rewarded with two very rich chocolate tarts.

22 ounces 67% bittersweet chocolate (prefer
   Valrhona chocolate), chopped very fine
2 vanilla beans
3 1/3 cups whipping cream (not heavy cream,
   it has too much fat)
1 1/2 cups whole milk

3/4 cup super fine sugar
6 large egg yolks
Pastry for 2 (9-inch) tarts, baked until
   golden brown
Garnish: lightly sweetened whipped cream,
   strawberry rhubarb compote with blackberries

Preheat oven to 225°F. Split the vanilla beans and scrape out the seeds from the insides and add the beans and the seeds to the cream and milk. Scald the cream and milk over high heat, just below the boiling point, then set aside to cool. Once cool, remove and discard the vanilla beans. Cook the sugar to a dark caramel, almost burnt. Slowly add the scalded cream to the caramel, making sure to dissolve all the sugar off the bottom of the pan. Be careful, the caramel will sputter and then harden, but keep stirring-the sugar will melt again. Cool the caramel cream down to 140°F then pour over the chocolate. Stir constantly with a spatula trying not to add any air to the mix. Once chocolate is completely melted and you have a perfectly smooth mix (it will appear broken at this point!) cool it to 90°F then add the eggs. Divide the filling among the two tart shells, place on rimmed baking sheets and bake about 45 minutes, then check the consistency. It is done when the filling looks set on the outside, but the center one-third to one-quarter of the tart will still wobble a little bit. Cool at least 6 hours at room temperature. Do not refrigerate. Serve within 24 hours, garnished with whipped cream and strawberry rhubarb compote with blackberries. Makes two 9-inch tarts, with 8 servings each. From Chef Stephen Giunta.

Strawberry Rhubarb Compote with Blackberries

1 pound strawberries, rinsed and hulled
1/2 pound blackberries, rinsed
1 pound rhubarb, trimmed

1 teaspoon finely grated lemon zest
1 tablespoon fresh lemon juice
3/4 cup sugar

Select about 4 ounces of the smallest strawberries and cut lengthwise into quarters. Cut blackberries in half. Set aside the quartered strawberries and blackberries as they will be added raw to the cooked compote. Cut the remaining larger berries in halves or quarters so that the pieces are about the same size (you should have about 2 1/2 cups). Place in a medium saucepan. With a paring knife, pull away and discard the strings that run the length of the rhubarb stalks. Cut the stalks into 3/4-inch pieces (you should have about 3 cups) and add to the saucepan. Add the rhubarb, lemon zest and juice, and sugar to the pan. Cook over medium-high heat, stirring often to dissolve the sugar. By the time the sugar has dissolved, the fruit will have released a lot of juice. Boil for about 4 minutes to reduce the liquid somewhat, then reduce the heat and simmer for another 2 minutes, or until the rhubarb is soft. Don't worry if some of the rhubarb falls apart. Remove from the heat and stir in the reserved strawberries and blackberries. Cool to room temperature, then refrigerate in a covered container until cold. Makes about 4 cups of compote, but the extra will keep for a couple of weeks and is delicious for breakfast, especially with crème fraîche. From Chef Stephen Giunta.

CHOCOLATE GARNISHES *are an easy way to enhance a dessert.*

CHOCOLATE FLOURISHES Melt chocolate in the microwave (time depends upon the quantity). Pour the melted chocolate into a plastic bag and seal. Snip a small corner of the bag to allow the chocolate to squiggle out in a small stream. Drizzle the chocolate over the entire dessert, over each individual serving, or on the individual serving plates before placing the dessert. The chocolate may even be drizzled onto wax paper into desired shapes. When hardened, remove from the wax paper and place on the dessert.

CHOCOLATE LEAVES Brush melted chocolate onto the back of a clean, non-poisonous leaf, such as a rose or lemon leaf. Peel the leaf away when the chocolate has hardened.

SIMPLE SPRINKLE Grate chocolate and sprinkle over the dessert.

CHOCOLATE CURLS To make small chocolate curls, run a vegetable peeler down the side of a block of chocolate. To make large, showy chocolate curls, spread a length of melted chocolate on a baking sheet to a thickness of 1/4 inch. When hardened, scrape across the chocolate in a long, slow motion using a knife or metal spatula held at a 45-degree angle.

NANCY KASSEBAUM BAKER'S CHOCOLATE ICE CREAM PIE CRUST

Former US Senator Nancy Landon Kassebaum Baker notes that her children and grandchildren have loved this for years. Favorite ice cream fillings are coffee or chocolate chip, or mint ice cream at Christmas.

3 ounces semi-sweet chocolate
2½ tablespoons butter

2 cups crispy rice cereal
1 quart ice cream

In a small saucepan over medium heat, melt chocolate with butter. Add rice crispies and mix. Butter a 9 or 10-inch pie pan and press the mixture into the plate. Fill remaining plate with the ice cream of your choice (let it slightly soften first). Freeze. Remove from freezer 30 minutes before serving. Top with fudge or chocolate sauce (see below), whipped cream, nuts or chocolate curls.

CHOCOLATE SAUCE

This is a chocolate ganache with a two to one ratio of cream to chocolate; the corn syrup is added mostly for consistency. Take care to use good chocolate and you will have something grand to top anything.

8 ounces semisweet chocolate, finely chopped
1 cup heavy cream
½ cup light corn syrup

Place the chocolate in a metal bowl. Combine the cream and corn syrup in a small heavy saucepan and bring to a simmer. Pour the liquid over the chocolate and allow it to sit for 3 to 4 minutes, or until the chocolate has melted. Whisk to combine. Allow the sauce to cool slightly, then pour into a bowl or other container. (Stored in the refrigerator, tightly covered, the sauce will keep up to 2 weeks.) To serve, warm the sauce gently in the top of a double boiler or microwave. Makes about 2 cups.

DARK CHOCOLATE FILLING FOR TARTS

Can be made 2 days ahead of time, then stored in a glass jar in the refrigerator. Spoon into a pastry or chocolate tart shell, or bake squares of phyllo dough in a muffin tin to create phyllo cups.

2 ounces bittersweet chocolate (Baker's is fine)
1½ cups sugar
4 tablespoons flour
2 tablespoons cornstarch
2 cups milk (divided use)
2 egg yolks, lightly beaten
2 tablespoons butter
1 teaspoon vanilla extract

Melt chocolate in microwave oven in well-greased pyrex cup. Combine sugar, flour and cornstarch, add ½ cup milk and stir until smooth. Scald 1½ cups milk and place in top of double boiler; cook until it begins to thicken; carefully add egg yolks. Stir in melted chocolate. Continue to cook until thick, stirring frequently. Remove from heat and whisk together with the butter and vanilla. Cool.

CRÈME de MENTHE TEA BROWNIES

These have been a dependable favorite at Wichita-Sedgwick County Historical Museum teas. Cut these into small pieces as they are very rich. Very attractive served on a silver platter.

1 cup sugar
$^1/_2$ cup butter
4 eggs, beaten
1 cup flour
$^1/_2$ teaspoon salt
1 (16-ounce) can chocolate syrup
1 teaspoon vanilla extract

Filling
2 cups powdered sugar
$^1/_2$ cup butter
4 tablespoons crème de menthe (green) or
    3 tablespoons grenadine (pink)

Icing
6 ounces semisweet chocolate chips
4 tablespoons butter

Preheat oven to 350°F. Spray a 9 x 13-inch pan with vegetable oil cooking spray. Cream sugar and butter, stir in eggs. Mix in flour, salt, chocolate syrup and vanilla. Bake for 25 to 30 minutes. Cool in pan. Make the filling by combining the ingredients with an electric mixer and spread evenly over cooled brownies. Prepare icing by melting chocolate in microwave, add butter. Spread over mint layer. Let stand to set, then cut into squares. May be refrigerated but must be cut first. Makes 18 large brownies or 6 dozen bite-sized brownies.

BIG YUMMY BROWNIES

These are dense, unfrosted brownies. Flouring the chips and nuts keeps them from sinking to the bottom. It is important to allow the batter to cool before adding the chocolate chips, or the chips will melt and ruin the batter. This recipe can be baked up to a week in advance and stored wrapped in plastic in the refrigerator.

2 cups unsalted butter
1 pound plus 12 ounces semisweet chocolate
    morsels (divided use)
6 ounces unsweetened chocolate
6 extra-large eggs
3 tablespoons instant coffee granules

2 tablespoons vanilla extract
$2^1/_4$ cups sugar
$1^1/_4$ cups flour (divided use)
1 tablespoon baking powder
1 teaspoon salt
3 cups chopped walnuts or pecans

Preheat oven to 350°F. Butter and flour a 12 x 18-inch jellyroll pan. Melt together the butter, 1 pound of chocolate chips and the unsweetened chocolate in a medium bowl over simmering water. Allow to cool slightly. In a large bowl, stir (do not beat) together the eggs, coffee granules, vanilla, and sugar. Stir the warm chocolate mixture into the egg mixture and cool to room temperature. In a medium bowl, sift together 1 cup of flour, baking powder, and salt; add to the cooled chocolate mixture. Toss the nuts and 12 ounces of chocolate chips in a medium bowl with $^1/_4$ cup of the flour, then add them to the chocolate batter. Pour into the baking pan. Bake for 30 to 35 minutes, until a toothpick comes out clean. Do not overbake! Allow to cool thoroughly, refrigerate, and cut into 24 large squares. Makes 2 dozen.

DOUBLY DECADENT BROWNIE PIE

During the ice storm of 2005 we were without power for several days, so Lee and I stayed with our son Scott and his family. After a long hard day, it was such a treat to have daughter-in-law Michele deliver hot brownies to our room. She says they are quick and easy, and a favorite in their neighborhood: they are with me! She says that the honey is the secret ingredient to this frosting.

1/2 cup butter
1 cup sugar (baking sugar is best)
2 extra-large eggs
1 teaspoon vanilla extract
1/3 cup unsweetened cocoa powder
1/2 cup flour (may use cake flour)
1/4 teaspoon salt
1/4 teaspoon baking powder

Frosting
3 tablespoons butter, softened
3 tablespoons unsweetened cocoa powder
1 tablespoon honey
1 teaspoon vanilla extract
1 cup powdered sugar

Preheat oven to 350°F. Grease and flour a shallow 9-inch pie pan. In a saucepan, melt the butter. Remove from heat, stir in sugar, eggs and vanilla. Beat in cocoa, flour, salt, and baking powder. Do not overbeat. Spread into prepared pan. Bake in preheated oven for 25 to 30 minutes, being careful not to overcook. Just before they come out of the oven, prepare the frosting by combining ingredients with an electric mixer. Frost brownies while they are still warm. Recipe adapted from "All Recipes Dinner Tonight", from Michele Banks. Makes 10 to 12 brownies.

WATKINS BROWNIES

Adapted from a recipe in a 1930s Watkins Spice pamphlet, these have stood the test of time and pleased hungry harvest crews as well as ladies at teas. No need for a mix when these are so easy. The variation of the mint crème frosting, by Barbara Rensner, makes these a holiday treat.

1/2 cup butter
2 squares unsweetened chocolate
1 cup sugar
2 eggs
3/4 cup flour

1/2 teaspoon salt
1/2 cup nuts
1 teaspoon vanilla extract
Powdered sugar

Preheat oven to 325°F. Melt butter and chocolate. Stir in sugar, add eggs one at a time and beat each one about 30 seconds. Add flour and salt, then stir in nuts and vanilla. Pour into greased 9 x 9- inch pan and bake for 30 minutes. Sprinkle powdered sugar over top or ice with chocolate frosting and pecan pieces. Makes 12 to 15 servings.

Variation: Barbara's Mint Creme Frosting: combine 1 cup powdered sugar, 2 tablespoons softened butter and 1 tablespoon of light cream. Add 1/2 teaspoon peppermint extract and 2 drops of green food coloring. Spread on cooled brownies and then refrigerate to let frosting harden. Melt 1 ounce of semisweet chocolate with 1 tablespoon of butter, and while this is warm, drizzle with a spoon over the Mint Creme frosting. Let frosted brownies come to room temperature before serving.

CHEESECAKE BROWNIES

Brownies topped with a yummy cheesecake layer, are pure decadence. The layer works well as an addition to either of the brownie recipes above or with a boxed mix. Recipe here is scaled for brownies to be baked in a 9 x 13-inch pan.

2 (8-ounce) packages cream cheese,
   room temperature
1 egg, beaten

1 egg yolk
1/2 cup sugar
1 1/2 teaspoons lemon juice

Mix brownie batter, transfer into a lightly greased 9 x 13-inch pan and place in freezer while preparing cheesecake batter. Preheat oven to 275°F. Combine ingredients with electric mixer until well blended. Spread over uncooked brownie batter. Bake for 45 to 60 minutes, until tests dry with a wooden pick. Cool on wire rack; refrigerate until chilled before serving.

MACADAMIA NUT FUDGE

1/2 cup butter, cut up

1 cup semisweet chocolate chips (about 6 ounces)

1 cup (4 ounces) coarsely chopped macadamia nuts

1 ounce unsweetened chocolate, finely chopped

1 teaspoon vanilla extract

2 1/4 cups sugar

5 ounces evaporated milk

12 large marshmallows (about 3 ounces)

Butter an 8-inch square baking pan. Line the bottom of the pan with foil. In a large bowl, combine the butter, chocolate chips, macadamia nuts, unsweetened chocolate and vanilla; set aside. Attach a candy thermometer to a medium saucepan. Add the sugar, evaporated milk and marshmallows. Bring to a boil over medium heat, stirring constantly to prevent burning. Cook, stirring constantly, until the mixture reaches 238°F. Pour the hot mixture into the bowl with the chocolate and nuts and let stand for 30 minutes. Stir until the mixture begins to thicken, about 1 minute. Spread evenly in the prepared pan. Wait until completely cooled, then cover with foil and let stand overnight to allow the flavors to mellow. Invert the fudge and remove the foil. Re-invert and cut into 1-inch squares. Store, stacking layers on waxed paper, in a tightly sealed container. Makes about 2 pounds.

FANTASTIC FUDGE

An easy confection are CHOCOLATE PEANUT CLUSTERS

1 package of chocolate almond bark
1 tablespoon of vanilla extract
2 cans of honey roasted peanuts

Microwave the chocolate until melted, about 2 to 3 minutes. Stir in the vanilla and then the peanuts. Spoon onto wax paper and cool. Makes about 5 dozen. From Julie Balay.

5 cups sugar

1 1/2 cups evaporated milk

1 (18-ounce) package chocolate morsels

1 (6-ounce) package butterscotch morsels

2/3 cup light or dark corn syrup

1/4 cup butter

2 teaspoons vanilla extract

1 1/2 cups chopped pecan or walnuts

Lightly butter two 8-inch square baking pans. Combine sugar and evaporated milk in a heavy saucepan and cook over medium heat, stirring constantly, until mixture boils. Reduce heat to low and simmer for 10 minutes, stirring constantly, and scraping down crystallization on sides of pan. Remove from heat and quickly stir in chocolate and butterscotch morsels, corn syrup, butter and vanilla. Stir well until smooth and creamy. Use a wooden spoon for this, as the mixture gets stiff rapidly. Add nuts and mix until just blended. Spread quickly into pans with a rubber spatula. Chill for 1 to 2 hours and then cut into 1-inch squares. You may need to make a small cut 1/4 inch from the sides and lift out this sliver in order to be able to remove the other pieces cleanly. Store, stacking layers on waxed paper, in a tightly sealed container. Makes 4 dozen pieces.

MARY CASSATT'S CARAMELS AU CHOCOLAT

American born and educated, Mary Cassatt (1844 – 1926), whose painting Mother with Child *(p. 45) ranks as one of the most popular of the WAM Murdock Collection, maintained a home in Paris and enjoyed entertaining. Curried chicken was a specialty of chez Cassatt, as well as chocolate caramels. Translated from French, her recipe appeared in* Miss Mary Cassatt: Impressionist from Pennsylvania *(1966), adapted here for the modern kitchen.*

1 1/2 cups powdered sugar

1 cup honey

6 ounces bittersweet chocolate, coarsely grated or finely chopped

6 tablespoons unsalted butter

1 cup heavy cream

1/4 cup cocoa powder (for dusting)

Combine ingredients (except for the cocoa powder) in a heavy saucepan; stir with a large metal kitchen spoon. Bring to a boil over moderately-high heat, cooking and stirring until mixture is thick. When mixture reaches 248° F (or tests "firm ball" by dropping drizzle into a cup of cold water), remove from heat, pour onto a greased cookie sheet or marble surface; allow to cool and don't spread. Gather into a ball with a pastry scraper and dust with cocoa powder; roll into a log, dust again with cocoa powder, cover and refrigerate overnight or until firm and ready to serve. Unwrap caramel log, lightly oil blade of a large heavy knife and cut into 1-inch pieces. Place in individual candy papers or foil cups, dust again with cocoa powder. (Instead of rolling into a log when cooling, you can pour into candy molds. Also, instead of purchased candy papers you can wrap with 4-inch squares of wax paper and twist ends to close.) Makes 4 dozen.

CHOCOLATE MICE

These are a little bit cheesy (pun intended), but you may have seen them on a buffet table where they usually bring a smile. This is more a construction direction than a recipe. They can be fun to put on top of a chocolate cake, or to scatter on a wide ribbon that winds through your buffet table. Fun for kids to help with.

Package chocolate kisses candy
Medium jar of maraschino cherries, drained
Sliced almonds

2 cups milk chocolate morsels
2 tablespoons vegetable shortening
Red gel frosting

Unwrap package of Hershey's chocolate kisses. Rinse and drain jar of maraschino cherries with stems until no liquid comes out, then lay on paper towels. Select sliced almonds that would be suitable for ears, two per cherry. Trim if needed.

Melt 2 cups milk chocolate chips with vegetable shortening in microwave on medium for 2 minutes. Stir and turn for 2 more minutes until chips are melted and smooth when stirred. Check and stir every minute until melted. The chips may not look like they are melted, but when you stir them they are.

When chocolate mixture is smooth, hold cherry by the stem and dip in chocolate, completely coating cherry but not stem, as that is the mouse's tail. Immediately stick on a chocolate kiss to form the mouse's nose. Set on wax paper or parchment paper and slide two slices of almond between cherry and kiss for ears. Sometimes a pair of tweezers is handy for placing the ears. Let harden; may be put in refrigerator.

When hard enough to handle use red gel frosting to make his eyes (just a dot) above the point of the kiss. Can be made a week ahead and kept in refrigerator or cool place. You will have to repeat the chocolate-shortening mixture several times depending on the number of mice needed. Put in cupcake papers for serving if you wish. You have made a *Chocolate Mouse!*

TRUFFLE LOVE

While in graduate school and on a tight budget, newlywed granddaughter Analee made all of her Christmas presents: delightful boxes of truffles. (Testing truffle recipes had been a nice activity for newlyweds not able to afford cable TV.) I was happy to receive her recipes too. These are great to set on the side of a cup of coffee, to mound on a tray, or to serve in the lacey chocolate basket described below.

Chocolate Raspberry Truffles

3 cups semi-sweet chocolate morsels (divided use)

2 tablespoons heavy cream

1 tablespoon butter

2 tablespoons seedless raspberry jam

Powdered sugar to taste

Combine $1^1/_3$ cups of the chocolate morsels, cream and butter in top part of a double boiler. Cook over hot water until smooth, stirring constantly. Stir in the jam. Allow the mixture to cool, then freeze, covered with plastic wrap, for 20 minutes. Shape into balls, placing on a cookie sheet lined with parchment paper. Freeze until firm. Melt the remaining $1^1/_3$ cups of chocolate morsels in a double boiler over hot water, stirring occasionally. Using a wooden pick, dip the candy balls one at a time in the chocolate. Place on a cookie sheet lined with parchment paper. Chill until set. Dust with powdered sugar. Makes 5 dozen.

Tia Maria Truffles

$^1/_2$ cup sugar

1 cup whipping cream

8 ounces semi-sweet chocolate morsels

2 tablespoons Tia Maria liqueur

$^1/_2$ cup chopped toasted almonds

$^1/_2$ cup powdered sugar

Heat sugar and whipping cream in a small saucepan over medium heat. Remove from heat, stir in chocolate until melted, and then add liqueur. Cover and freeze for 3 to 4 hours or overnight. Spoon out mixture and form into small balls. Roll half in almonds and half in sugar. Place in a covered container and refrigerate or freeze until ready to serve. Makes 5 to 6 dozen.

Mayan Truffles

1 cup whipping cream

12 ounces semi-sweet chocolate morsels

1 teaspoon instant coffee granules

$^1/_8$ cup coffee liqueur

6 ounces semi-sweet chocolate morsels

$^1/_4$ cup cocoa

Bring cream to boiling point in a medium saucepan and remove from heat. Add 12 ounces chocolate chips and instant coffee and cover. Allow to set for 10 minutes, then remove lid and stir and add coffee liqueur. Allow mixture to cool 2 hours in the refrigerator. Shape into small balls on wax paper lined trays and place in freezer. Melt remaining chocolate and allow to cool slightly. Dip balls in the chocolate and roll in cocoa. Store in refrigerator. Makes 6 dozen.

Milk Chocolate Orange Truffles

1/2 cup whipping cream
24 ounces milk chocolate, finely chopped, (divided use)
2 tablespoons unsalted butter

1 1/2 teaspoons grated orange rind
Unsweetened cocoa powder for dusting
2 teaspoons shortening

Line a cookie sheet with foil. Bring cream to simmer in heavy saucepan. Reduce heat to low. Add half the chocolate and whisk until melted. Whisk in butter and orange peel. Let cool and then freeze until chocolate mixture is firm enough to mound on spoon, about 40 minutes. Drop mixture by rounded spoonfuls onto foil-lined sheet, spacing apart. Freeze until almost firm but still pliable, about 30 minutes. Roll each mound in cocoa powder. Then roll between palms of hand into ball. Place on same sheet. Freeze until firm, about 1 hour.

Melt remaining half of chocolate with shortening in top of double boiler over simmering water, stirring until smooth. Remove mixture from over water. Grasp 1 truffle between thumb and index finger; roll truffle in melted chocolate, coating completely. Shake to remove excess chocolate. Place truffle on same foil-lined sheet. Repeat with remaining truffles. Refrigerate until coating is firm, about 1 hour. Dust truffles with cocoa powder, brush off excess. (Can be prepared 2 weeks ahead. Store in refrigerator in an airtight container.) Let stand at room temperature 10 minutes and serve. Makes 3 dozen.

Chocolate Lace Basket

6 ounces chocolate-flavored confectioner's coating, finely chopped

Using chocolate-flavored confectioner's coating will ensure that your basket holds it shape. You can substitute 6 ounces (1 cup) semisweet chocolate morsels melted with 1 teaspoon vegetable shortening for the confectioner's coating. However, if you use the chocolate chips to make your basket, refrigerate it until serving time and place it in a cool place during the party, or it will melt.

Invert a round or oval shallow 1 1/2 -quart dish. Cover the outside of the bowl smoothly with aluminum foil. Freeze the covered bowl for 15 minutes. Meanwhile, melt the coating in a heatproof bowl over hot, but not simmering, water. Pour into the corner of a small, heavy-duty plastic food bag. Let cool until slightly thickened, about 15 minutes. Snip a 1/8-inch opening from the corner of the bag. Reach up underneath inside an inverted bowl with one hand so you can turn it easily while piping. Holding the bag a couple of inches above the bowl, and using small, tight spiral wrist movements, pipe a lacey pattern all over the foil-covered bowl. If the coating is the right temperature, it should flow from the bag without squeezing. Return the bowl to the freezer and let it chill until firm, about 15 minutes. Carefully lift the foil from the bowl and place, right side up, onto a serving platter. Carefully peel off the foil.

A fun, edible serving dish, for your truffles or other chocolate treat! Fun at easter to make these as "nests" to fill with plastic easter grass, Peeps marshmallow chicks and chocolate eggs. Or make them as a container for strawberries.

Morris Kantor
Still Life of Flowers (detail),
1929,
oil on canvas, WAM,
Art Fund, Friends of the
Wichita Art Museum, Inc.,
1986.90

Other Desserts & Holiday Treats

*Food historian Virginia
Jenkins states that prior
to 1880 most Americans
had never seen a banana,
but by 1910 they were
so common that streets
were littered with their
peels. Developments
in international
transportation enabled
banana shipments (and
education on how to eat
and store the bizarre fruit)
from the Caribbean to reach
even the most rural towns by
the 1920s. This widespread
availability gave rise to the
acclaim that bananas enjoy
today; the most popular and
least expensive fruit in the
USA today, with Americans
eat an average of 75 per
year. (Jenkins, 2002)*

BANANA'S DELIGHT

This is a version of "Bananas Foster" created by Chef Paul Blange at the famed Brennan's Restaurant in New Orleans. Simple, fun and easy, it is one of those old recipes that shouldn't be lost. To make serving easy, pre-scoop ice cream into a large bowl and store in freezer.

4 small ripe bananas
1/4 cup butter
1 cup brown sugar
1/4 cup banana liqueur

1/2 teaspoon cinnamon
1/4 cup dark rum
Vanilla or cinnamon ice cream

Peel bananas and cut them in half, slice each half lengthwise again (you will have 16 pieces). Set aside. Melt butter in a 12-inch nonstick skillet over medium heat. Add brown sugar, banana liqueur and cinnamon. Cook for a few minutes. Add bananas and cook until sauce begins to thicken, stirring constantly (about two minutes). Remove skillet from heat, pour rum over mixture evenly. Ignite with a long match (may bring to the table to ignite, but dim lights). When the flames disappear, serve over ice cream. Garnish, if desired, with crushed Almond Biscotti. Makes 8 servings.

SHERMAN STRIKES AGAIN

4 large peaches, peeled and sliced
1/2 cup white wine
2 ounces peach or apricot brandy
1 quart peach ice cream

Place peaches in a 12-inch nonstick skillet (an attractive one is good), add wine; heat over medium heat right before serving, just long enough to heat the peaches through. Add brandy and heat just enough to warm the brandy. Bring tableside, dim the lights, ignite with a long match and serve flaming over ice cream. Makes 8 servings.

WAR EAGLE BAKED APPLES

War Eagle is close to our vacation home in the Ozarks. A trip to the Bean Palace Restaurant provides a nice meal of beans, cornbread and slaw, with this delicious finish.

1/2 cup sugar
1/4 teaspoon cinnamon
Dash of nutmeg (freshly grated is great)
2 cups apple juice
6 large Rome apples

1/4 cup coarsely chopped walnuts
1/4 cup cake crumbs (yellow, white, spice) or
    cookie crumbs (gingersnaps, vanilla wafers)
1/4 cup chopped dates or currants or raisins
1/2 cup heavy cream

Preheat oven to 400°F. Combine the sugar, cinnamon, nutmeg and apple juice in a small saucepan. Bring to a boil, and then reduce the heat and simmer only until the sugar dissolves. Set this aside.

Start at the stem end of the apple and peel one-third of each apple. Core the apple, very carefully, leaving 1/2 inch at the bottom (the blossom end). In a bowl, mix the nuts, crumbs and dates, then stuff into the apples.

Arrange the apples in a shallow 8 x 11-inch baking dish and pour the hot apple syrup over the top. Bake, basting often with the pan juices, for 45 minutes or until the apples are shiny, sticky and soft. Transfer to dessert plates. Strain the juices into a saucepan. If necessary, boil over high heat until the liquid is reduced to about 1/2 cup, but do not allow juices to caramelize. Stir in the cream and pass separately as a sauce. Makes 6 servings.

ZABAGLIONE with FRESH STRAWBERRIES

Makes an excellent presentation. Nice also to use a variety of summer fruits, like a mixture of peaches, nectarines and berries for example, or add just a few blueberries to the strawberries.

8 large egg yolks
1/2 cup sugar
Pinch salt
1/2 cup Marsala
1/4 cup sherry
1 1/2 cups heavy cream, whipped

1 quart strawberries, washed, capped and
    sliced vertically
1/2 cup sugar
Optional garnish: crushed Amaretti cookies (or
    crushed almond macaroons or biscotti)

Combine egg yolks, sugar and salt in a large stainless steel bowl. Whisk in Marsala and sherry. Place over a pot of boiling water (the water level should be about 2 inches below the bottom of the bowl) and whisk vigorously for about 4 minutes or until it is thick and tripled in volume. It should mound slightly when dropped from the whisk. Immediately place bowl in an ice-water bath and whisk until cold. Fold whipped cream into chilled Zabaglione (mixture may be covered and chilled, it will hold well for up to 24 hours). Place strawberries in a bowl with sugar. Stir and let set for 30 minutes. To serve, spoon berries into stemmed glass and top with Zabaglione. Garnish with crushed cookie crumbs if desired. Makes 8 servings.

CRÈME ANGLAISE

This wonderful vanilla custard sauce, served cold, enhances a variety of desserts or can be served over berries.

4 egg yolks
Pinch salt
3 tablespoons sugar

1 cup half-and-half
1 teaspoon vanilla extract
Optional: 2 to 3 tablespoons liqueur

Stir yolks, salt and sugar together in a smally heavy saucepan until blended. Microwave half-and-half in a glass measure for 1 minute on high power until scalded. Stir a few tablespoons into the yolks, then gradually add the rest. Cook the mixture, stirring constantly, on medium heat just before the boiling point. Mixture will thicken and will coat the back of a wooden spoon. When a finger run across the back of wooden spoon leaves a path, remove from heat. Strain into a small bowl, stir in vanilla and chill. Stir in optional liqueur, variety of choice, to compliment the dessert if desired, before serving. Makes 1 1/4 cups.

FRESH PEACH ICE CREAM

1 1/2 pounds pitted and sliced peaches (about
    large 4 peaches), preferably Alberta
2 tablespoons fresh lemon juice, divided use
1 1/2 cups sugar

3 cups cream
1/4 teaspoon salt
2 teaspoons vanilla extract
1/2 teaspoon cardamom

In a food processor or with a food mill, grind the peaches with 1 tablespoon lemon juice. Pour into a saucepan and add the sugar. Bring to a boil, then reduce the heat and simmer 10 minutes until it is thick and syrupy. Chill at least 4 hours or until very cold. Stir in the cream, salt, vanilla and cardamom. Taste and add more lemon juice, if needed, to bring out the flavor of the peaches. Churn in an ice cream freezer according to manufacturers directions. Store in airtight containers in the freezer. Makes about 1 quart. From Jayne Milburn.

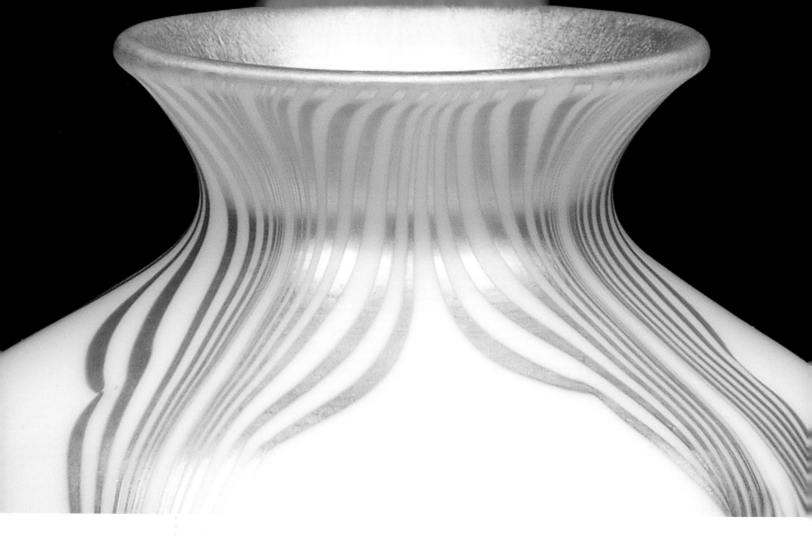

CREAM PUFFS

Cream puffs have a reputation for being daunting to make and persnickety to perfect. This recipe, written by Granddaughter Analee in the infancy of her cooking career, really takes the process down to brass tacks. I enjoyed the candor and simplicity of this recipe, and I think you will too.

1 cup flour
1 cup water

$^1/_3$ cup butter
4 eggs

Preheat oven to 400°F. Add butter to water and melt over high heat; boil. Turn off heat. Add flour all at once. Blend, blend, blend. Cool slightly and add eggs one at a time and stir constantly until smooth. Fill the biggest pastry bag you can find and squeeze dollops onto buttered sheet pan, or into buttered tins. Try to make the puffs pretty. Bake until golden, about 10 minutes, but watch them like a hawk. Remove from oven and make a small slit to allow air to escape. Maybe give the slit a little twist. Return the beauties to the oven to allow them to dry. Just a few minutes — now let them cool before you fill them with a crème custard or the secret filling. Makes about 24.

The "secret filling"

1 package vanilla pudding
2 cups milk

Hazelnut liqueur
Some whipped cream

Mix this and squirt this stuff into the pastries.

Variation: make this into a dazzling Croque-en-Bouche

Make the cream puffs. Burn some sugar and dip the tops of the puffs in the sugar. Be careful; remember you got burned last time. Stack these guys in a pyramid. Spin the sugar to top the masterpiece. Serve immediately to avoid sogginess.

PAVLOVA

A Pavlova is something ethereal, and while your guests may think you worked hard on this magical stunning thing, it is really quite simple. It is a giant crater-like meringue filled with sweetened whipped cream and fresh fruit.

1 cup super-fine sugar (divided use)	1/4 teaspoon salt
1 tablespoon cornstarch	1 teaspoon white vinegar
4 large egg whites, room temperature	1 teaspoon vanilla extract
1/4 teaspoon cream of tartar	1 tablespoon cornstarch

Topping
1 cup whipping cream
1/3 cup powdered sugar
2 cups sliced, chopped or whole fresh fruit (a mixture of strawberries, blueberries, raspberries are pretty)

Preheat oven to 275°F. Line a baking sheet with foil or parchment paper. Using a 10-inch round cake pan or plate as a guide, trace a circle (toothpick for foil, pencil for parchment). Lightly butter the circle, or use cooking spray. Set aside. Mix 1/4 cup of the sugar with the cornstarch in a small bowl and set aside.

With electric mixer on high speed, beat the egg whites to a foam and add the salt and cream of tartar, continuing to beat until soft peaks form, then add 3/4 cup of sugar, 2 tablespoons at a time while constantly beating until peaks stiffen. Beat in the cornstarch mixture until just blended. Add the vanilla and vinegar, continuing to mix until just blended. Mound the mixture onto the prepared baking sheet, using a spoon with an upward motion to curve up the edges of the "nest". The center should be shallow and the edges about 1 1/2 or 2-inches high. Bake for 1 hour and 15 minutes. Turn off the heat and leave the meringue nest in the oven for another hour to dry completely. Remove and cool completely on a wire rack.

Peel the paper from the bottom of the meringue and place meringue on a serving dish. Just before serving, beat the cream until soft peaks form. Gradually add the sugar until stiff peaks are formed. Spoon into the center of the meringue. Top with the fruit and serve immediately. Makes 10 to 12 servings.

CRÈME CARAMEL

Excellent! The secret to this wonderful version of a classic is the long slow cooking. From Azita, a Boston restaurant.

1 1/2 cups sugar (divided use)	1 vanilla bean, split lengthwise
2 cups milk	1 small strip of lemon peel
2 cups heavy cream	5 egg yolks
1/2 cup water	

Preheat oven to 300°F and prepare 8 one-half cup custard cups by buttering them. Mix 1/2 cup sugar, milk, cream, vanilla bean and lemon peel together in a saucepan; bring to a simmer and remove from heat. Cool for 10 minutes, then remove vanilla bean and lemon peel. Whisk egg yolks in a large bowl and then add milk mixture into yolks. Mix 1 cup sugar and water together in a small saucepan and bring to a boil over low heat; do not stir, cover and boil until mixture turns light brown and thickens, about 15 minutes. Pour equal portions of this sugar syrup into each of the custard cups; chill for 15 minutes. Pour equal portions of custard mixture into each custard cup. Bake until knife inserted in center comes out clean, about 80 minutes.

To serve, briefly dip each cup into warm water, cover with a small plate and invert. Leave the cup in place to allow the caramel to drip down the custard. Serve warm. Makes 8 servings.

CROISSANT BREAD PUDDING

Served at Wichita Symphony Showhouse Tea Room, 2003.

3 jumbo whole eggs
8 jumbo egg yolks
5 cups half-and-half
1 1/2 cups sugar

1 1/2 teaspoons vanilla extract
6 stale croissants
1 cup golden raisins

In mixer bowl, stir together the whole eggs, yolks, half-and-half, sugar and vanilla; set aside. Slice the croissants in half, horizontally. In a 9 x 13-inch baking dish, line with the bottom half of the croissants, then add raisins, then the tops of the croissants (brown side up), being sure the raisins are between the layers of croissants or they will float to top and burn during baking. Pour custard over the croissants and allow to soak for 10 minutes or more, pressing down to help distribute the custard. (The pudding can be refrigerated at this point and baked up to 8 hours later.)

Preheat oven to 350°F. Place the baking pan in a larger one. Put into hot oven and add water to the larger pan to a depth of 1 inch. Cover the larger pan with foil, tenting the foil so that it does not touch the pudding. Cut a few holes in the foil to allow steam to escape. Bake for 45 minutes. Uncover and bake for 40 to 45 more minutes or until pudding is puffed up and custard is set. Remove from oven and cool slightly. Serve with vanilla sauce (p. 254) or rum-flavored whipped topping. Makes 10 to 12 servings.

WHITE CHOCOLATE CINNAMON BREAD PUDDING with PRALINE SAUCE

2 cups milk
1 cup heavy whipping cream
3 tablespoons butter
1 cup white chocolate morsels
5 slices white bread, cut into 1/2 inch cubes
3 eggs

1/2 cup sugar
1/2 teaspoon salt
2 tablespoons cinnamon
1 teaspoon vanilla extract
Praline Sauce

Preheat oven to 350°F. Combine milk, cream, butter and white chocolate morsels in a medium saucepan, over medium heat, stirrng often until morsels are melted. Remove from heat; add bread cubes, and let stand 2 minutes. Whisk together eggs, sugar, salt, cinnamon and vanilla in a large bowl. Add bread mixture and stir just to incorporate. Pour into a lightly greased 11 x 7 inch baking dish. Bake uncovered for 1 hour or until set and crust is golden. Let stand 5 minutes. Serve with warm Praline Sauce. Makes 8 servings.

Praline Sauce

1/2 cup butter
2 cups chopped pecans
1 cup heavy cream
1 cup sugar

1 tablespoon cornstarch
2 tablespoons pure maple syrup
1 cup white chocolate morsels
1 teaspoon vanilla extract

Melt butter in a medium saucepan over medium heat; add pecans and cook 5 minutes. Whisk together cream, sugar, cornstarch, and syrup in a small bowl. Add to pecan mixture. Stir in white chocolate morsels. Bring to a boil, and cook, stirring constantly, 1 minute or until mixture begins to thicken. Remove from heat; stir in vanilla. Serve over pudding. Makes about 4 cups.

RICE PUDDING

Rice Pudding is a Swedish and Danish tradition, made with added walnuts and raisins. This version, attributed to a firehouse cook in New York City, became a favorite after 9-11-01 and does well with the traditional additions stirred in before refrigerating, if you wish to add them. It is grand served just with whipped cream.

8 cups (2 quarts) whole milk
1 cup long-grain white rice
1 cup sugar
2 tablespoons unsalted butter
1 teaspoon vanilla

$^1/_4$ teaspoon salt
2 eggs
1 cup heavy cream
$^1/_2$ teaspoon cinnamon

Mix milk, rice, sugar, butter, vanilla and salt in a large saucepan, bring to a boil over medium-high heat. Reduce heat and simmer, uncovered, until rice is very tender, about one hour. Stir frequently. As the rice finishes cooking, whisk the eggs in a medium bowl. Remove rice from heat; add 1 cup of the rice to the eggs and whisk to combine. Stir egg mixture into remaining rice mixture, then stir in cream. Pour into a 9 x 13-inch ceramic dish, sprinkle with cinnamon, cover and refrigerate for at least 3 hours.

WALNUT DATE DELIGHT IN CHOCOLATE COOKIE CRUST

12 Oreo cookies, crushed in pie plate
8 ounces chopped dates
$^3/_4$ cup water
$^1/_4$ teaspoon salt (optional)

2 cups miniature marshmallows
1 cup toasted and chopped walnuts
Garnish: Sweetened whipped cream and
    crumbled Oreos

Press Oreo crumbs into a 9-inch pie plate. Combine the dates, water, and salt and bring to a boil. Lower the heat and simmer for 3 minutes. Remove from heat and stir in the marshmallows until completely melted and smooth. Stir in the nuts then pour into the prepared crust. Refrigerate until well chilled and firm. Serve in very small slices (it is quite rich) topped with whipped cream and crumbled Oreos. Makes one 9-inch pie. From Mary Ellen Joyner.

TIRAMISÙ

Tiramisù hit the American food scene with a tidal wave of acceptance in the early '80s, appearing on almost every restaurant menu with many of us buzzing about the rich mocha Italian dessert. It suffered from overexposure however as well as improper technique and by the '90s, waned in popularity. Properly made it is a lovely dessert, and I think this recipe is as good as it gets, a classic still worth swooning over.

6 egg yolks
1$^1/_4$ cups sugar
1$^1/_4$ cups mascarpone cheese
1$^3/_4$ cups heavy cream (whipping)
2 (3 ounces each) packages ladyfingers

$^1/_3$ cup coffee liqueur or brandied espresso
    (I use crème de cocoa)

Garnish: whipped cream, cocoa and
    chocolate curls

Combine egg yolks and sugar and whip until thick and lemon colored. Place in top of double boiler over boiling water. Reduce heat to low and cook 8 to 10 minutes, stirring constantly. Remove from heat. Add mascarpone cheese, beating well. Whip heavy cream until stiff peaks form. Fold into egg yolk mixture; set aside. Line bottom and sides of 3-quart bowl with ladyfingers that have been brushed with coffee liqueur or quickly dipped into espresso (with a little added brandy) in a 2-cup measure. Ladyfingers should not be soggy. Spoon half of egg yolk mixture in bowl. Repeat ladyfingers, liqueur and cream layers. Can be frozen at this point, but should be refrigerated overnight. Garnish with sweetened whipped cream (I use canned whipped cream), cocoa or chocolate curls. Makes 10 to 12 servings.

The word "tiramisù" means "pick me up", a nice name to refer to this dish's combination of sugar, coffee and alcohol.

HUGUENOT TORTE

Apple Pudding

¹/₄ cup flour
2¹/₂ teaspoons baking powder
¹/₄ teaspoon salt
2 eggs
1 cup plus 3 tablespoons sugar
1 teaspoon vanilla

1 cup peeled and chopped apples
1 cup finely chopped pecans

Garnish: Whipped cream, Crème Anglaise
(p. 267) or vanilla ice cream with a sprinkle
of toasted chopped pecans

Preheat oven to 325°F. Grease a 9-inch pie plate or a 9 x 13-inch pyrex baking dish. In a small bowl, whisk together the flour, baking powder and salt. In another bowl, beat eggs until lemon colored. Beat in sugar until thick, add vanilla then beat in the flour mixture. Stir in the apples and pecans. Pour into the prepared pan and bake for 40 minutes or until top is crusty and brown. The bottom layer will be soft, and top will be crunchy. Spoon into dessert dishes and garnish with the toppings of your choice. Makes 4 to 6 servings. From Marlene Phillips.

Steuben Glass (Frederick
Carder, designer)
*Decorated Gold Aurene
Vase*, ca. 1912, glass,
WAM, F. Price Cossman
Memorial Trust, Intrust Bank,
Trustee, 2006.17

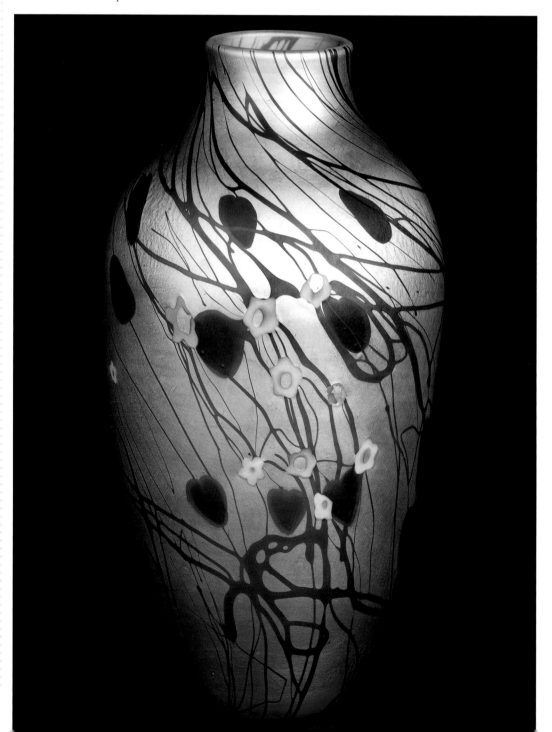

AUTUMN GLORY ACCENTS

Colorful painted pastry leaves in autumn colors make beautiful fall garnishes for any pastry, or even savory foods. You can use refrigerated pie crust and a leaf shaped cookie cutter to turn anything into a special dish, even a store-bought pie! Can be made up to one month ahead and frozen between layers of wax paper.

Leaves: Unfold pie crust on a lightly floured surface. Cut leaves from pie crust using leaf-shaped cutters. Mark leaf veins using the tip of a small paring knife. One (15-ounce) package of refrigerated pie crust will make about 24 (2- to 3-inch) leaves.

Make an egg wash by whisking together 3 eggs and 3 tablespoons water. Pour mixture evenly into small cups, tinting each with a few drops of liquid food coloring to create different colors. (For easy cleanup and to prevent the excess egg wash from burning on the baking sheet, paint leaves on pieces of parchment or wax paper.) Brush leaves evenly with egg wash, beginning with lighter colors first, and overlaying with areas of darker color. Use a small paintbrush to add accents of bolder color with undiluted liquid food coloring. Crumple 2 (14-inch long) pieces of aluminum foil into 1-inch wide strips. Coat with vegetable cooking spray, and place on a baking sheet lined with parchment paper. Gently drape pastry leaves over the strips of aluminum foil to give them some shape; also place several leaves flat on the baking sheet. Bake at 400°F for 6 to 8 minutes or until golden. Cool on the baking sheet on a wire rack. Repeat with remaining leaves. Arrange on baked pastries.

Candy acorns: Sandwich a thin layer of melted chocolate between the flat sides of two pecan halves. To create the texture caps, dip the upper third of each "acorn" into melted chocolate, and roll in finely chopped pecans. Arrange on baked pastry, along with "leaves".

TRIPLE-NUT THANKSGIVING PIE

Another traditional Thanksgiving favorite is the Paradise Pumpkin Pie (p. 219).

Pastry for a single crust pie	1 1/2 teaspoons fresh lemon juice
3/4 cup packed dark brown sugar	1 teaspoon vanilla extract
3 eggs	1/2 teaspoon salt
6 tablespoons unsalted butter, melted	1/2 cup halved pecans
2/3 cup dark corn syrup	1/2 cup halved or broken walnuts
1 tablespoon molasses (prefer "Grandma's")	1/2 cup macadamia nuts

Prepare unbaked pie crust for single crust recipe. Preheat oven to 350°F. In large bowl, combine brown sugar and eggs; beat at medium speed until well mixed. Add all remaining filling ingredients except nuts; beat until combined. Pour filling into pie crust. Sprinkle pecans, walnuts and macadamia nuts on top.

Bake on rack in lower third of oven. Check pie after first 20 minutes of baking, and add foil on crimped edge if needed. Bake for a total of 40 to 45 minutes or until crust and filling are light golden brown. Filling will set as pie cools. Cool on wire rack. Serve at room temperature, store in refrigerator.

ROASTING CHESTNUTS

*Preheat the oven to 475°F.
Cut an "x" in the shell of
each chestnut with a sharp
paring knife. Arrange the
chestnuts on a baking sheet.
Roast for 20 minutes, until
the outer shell has pulled
slightly away from the
chestnut and the shell and
the inner skin peel away
easily. Remove the outer
shell and inner skin of each
chestnut. Work quickly
while they are still hot
(hold with a kitchen towel
if too hot to touch). Or
they may be cooked in the
microwave: slit the shell of
the chestnuts with a sharp
paring knife and cook in
batches of ten on high
power for two minutes
each; process as above.*

ROASTED CHESTNUT SOUP

*Chestnuts are absolutely delicious roasted and eaten as a snack, or puréed into a rich, velvety soup. This is a
wonderful holiday dish, and jars of pre-roasted, vacuum packed chestnuts are available at Williams Sonoma or other
gourmet grocery stores every year around November. It is also fun to roast your own, just be sure to cut into the shell
before placing them in the oven or you will have exploding chestnuts instead.*

1 pound (about 2$^{1}/_{4}$ cups) roasted, shelled
 and peeled chestnuts
6 cups veal stock
$^{1}/_{3}$ to $^{1}/_{2}$ cup rice (uncooked)

$^{1}/_{3}$ cup cream
3 tablespoons butter
$^{1}/_{3}$ cup cognac or brandy
Salt and pepper

Simmer the chestnuts in stock for 20 minutes in a covered casserole; add the rice and cook very low for
30 more minutes. Let cool off the flame for 40 minutes, then run through a food processor or mill.
Return soup to casserole, rewarm, and stir in cream, butter, and brandy. Season with salt and pepper.
From Stephen Gleissner.

PUFF PASTRY ANGELS

The puffy little angels add a nice touch to the Christmas table, and are a delicious pastry with the caramelized sugar.

1 (17³/₄—ounce) package frozen, all-butter puff pastry, defrosted
³/₄ cup sugar (divided use)

Prepare work surface by lightly sprinkling it with sugar. Unfold the puff pastry dough and sprinkle with ¹/₄ cup sugar. Gently press in the sugar with a rolling pin, but don't compress the dough. Flip the dough over and repeat for the other side. Working from a corner, use a sharp knife to cut out a rectangle about 6 x 8 inches, then cut it in half the short length, and then cut each of those halves into 10 rectangles. This will result in rectangles about 4 x 1¹/₂ inches. These will become the angel wings. Place in the refrigerator for about 30 minutes until they become firm.

Meanwhile line 2 heavy baking sheets with parchment paper. Use a 5-inch cookie cutter in the shape of a gingerbread girl (will become your angel instead) and stamp out 9 cookies. Be sure to press hard and evenly. To not waste dough you will need to reverse the cutter each time and cut close together. Arrange on the baking sheet, leaving as much space as possible between them.

Remove the rectangles from the refrigerator and use a sharp knife to slice each horizontally into 6 or 7 thin little strips. Gather the strips in the center and pinch gently. Place this bunch of strips under the upper body of each dough girl, with just a little pressure to adhere. Then arrange these strips upward and trim the edges. Place tray of prepared "angels" in the refrigerator while the oven is preheating to 425°F. Sprinkle sugar over the dough. Bake for 15 minutes or until golden brown. Cooling before lifting off the baking sheet.

BRANDIED CRANBERRIES

1¹/₂ cups sugar
1 cup brandy (or Cabernet Sauvignon wine)
1 (12-ounce) package fresh cranberries

2 teaspoons grated tangerine rind
1 (3-inch) cinnamon stick

In a medium saucepan, bring sugar and wine to a boil over medium-high heat. Add remaining ingredients and return to a boil, stirring constantly. Reduce heat and simmer, partially covered, 10 to 15 minutes or until cranberry skins pop. Remove and discard cinnamon stick. Cool slightly; serve warm or chill 2 hours, if desired. May be stored in refrigerator up to 2 months. Makes 10 servings.

Herschel C. Logan
Snow, 1930, block print,
WAM, gift of Samuel
H. and Martha F. Logan,
2005.13.54

BRANDY BALLS

The brandy needs to mellow before serving, so plan to make these delicious bits at least a day ahead.

If you are making a holiday platter, also consider those listed elsewhere in this book, such as Macadamia Nut Fudge, Fantastic Fudge, Chocolate Almond Thumbprint Butter cookies, Swedish Spritz cookies.

2 1/2 cups finely crushed vanilla wafers (or chocolate-flavored graham crackers)
1 cup powdered sugar (sifted)
2 tablespoons cocoa powder
1/2 to 1 cup finely chopped walnuts

1/4 to 1/2 cup brandy (or bourbon)
2 tablespoons light corn syrup
1/2 cup granulated or powdered sugar, for dipping

Combine cookie crumbs, powdered sugar, cocoa powder and nuts. Stir in brandy and corn syrup. Add a little water (1 1/4 teaspoon or so) if necessary to form mixture into 3/4-inch balls. Roll in granulated or powdered sugar. Store in tightly covered container. Best after 2 or 3 days. Makes 4 dozen.

Variations: Substitutions in making these into rum balls include pecan shortbread cookies for the vanilla wafers, pecans for the walnuts, and dark rum for the brandy.

HOLLY BERRY COOKIES

2 cups flour
1 cup sugar
1 teaspoon cinnamon
3/4 teaspoon baking powder
1/4 teaspoon salt
1/2 cup cold butter (no substitutes)
1 egg
1/4 cup milk
2/3 cup seedless raspberry jam

Glaze
2 cups powdered sugar
2 tablespoons milk
1/2 teaspoon vanilla extract
Red-hot candies
Green food coloring as needed

Whisk together the flour, sugar, cinnamon, baking powder and salt in a large bowl. Cut in butter until mixture resembles coarse crumbs. In a small bowl, beat egg and milk. Add to crumb mixture just until moistened. Cover and refrigerate for 1 hour or until dough is easy to handle.

Preheat oven to 375°F. On a lightly floured surface, roll out dough. Cut with a 2-inch round cookie cutter. Place on ungreased baking sheets. Bake for 8 to 10 minutes or until edges are lightly browned. Cool on wire racks. Spread jam on half of the cookies; top each with another cookie. In a small mixing bowl, combine sugar, milk and vanilla until smooth; spread over cookies. Decorate with red-hots using three candies to resemble holly berries; before glaze is set. Let dry. Using a small new paintbrush and green food coloring, paint holly leaves on cookies. Makes 2 dozen.

CRESCENT COOKIES

1 cup butter
1/4 cup sugar (heaping)
2 1/2 cups flour

2 teaspoons vanilla
1 cup toasted, evenly chopped walnuts
Powdered sugar

Preheat oven to 325°F. In a large bowl or the bowl of an electric stand mixer, cream the butter on high speed 10 to 15 minutes, until very light and fluffy. Add the sugar and beat until combined then add the vanilla. Lower the speed and gently stir in the flour and nuts until just combined. Divide the dough into walnut size pieces, roll between your palms and shape into crescents OR roll the dough to 3/8-inch thickness and cut into desired shapes. Bake for approximately 20-25 minutes. Do not brown. After cookies cool, put on wax paper sprinkled with powered sugar, then dust tops with powered sugar. Just before serving, give the cookies another light dusting of powdered sugar. Makes about 2 dozen. From Mary Ellen Joyner.

SNOWBALL COOKIES

These very rich little cookies coated in powdered sugars are known by a variety of names including Mexican Wedding cookies, Mexican or Russian Tea Cakes. They are a favorite holiday treat for many families, but also good in the summer with fresh berries. Will keep in an airtight container for up to 3 weeks.

1 cup pecans
1 cup butter, room temperature
2 cups powdered sugar (divided use)
2 cups flour

2 teaspoons vanilla extract
$^1/_8$ teaspoon salt

Process pecans by pulsing in food processor until ground, but not pasty. In a medium bowl, use an electric mixer to beat butter and $^1/_2$ cup powdered sugar until fluffy; gradually add 1 cup flour, vanilla and salt. Beat until blended. Add 1 cup flour and pecans, and stir by hand. Shape into large ball, cover with plastic wrap and refrigerate at least one hour, or overnight.

Preheat oven to 350°F. Prepare heavy baking sheets with parchment paper or silicone liners. Roll dough into 1-inch balls. Bake for 12 to 15 minutes, cool 2 minutes on baking sheet. Place hot cookies in 9 x 12-inch dish with powdered sugar and coat. Let cookies cool in sugar; roll additionally if needed to fully coat. If the cookies are too hot, the sugar will melt. Makes 5 dozen.

SWEDISH ROSETTES

These fried cookies are made by dipping a rosette iron (sometimes called a timbale iron) into the batter. These are crunchy, pretty melt-in-your-mouth goodies are best if eaten within 2 days. Store in an airtight container.

2 eggs
1 teaspoon sugar
$^1/_2$ teaspoon salt

1 cup milk
1 cup flour
Powdered sugar for dipping

Beat eggs, then add sugar, salt, milk and flour in this order. Whisk with a fork until there are no bubbles in mixture. Heat cooking oil to 400°F. Dip rosette iron into batter until two-thirds is covered. Immerse in hot oil. Fry until cookie leaves sides of iron and is golden, but not brown. Remove rosette to paper towel to dry. Dip into sugar, either granulated or powdered. Wipe excess grease from iron each time with clean towel. If rosettes do not come off iron, fry a little longer; if not crisp, lower temperature of oil. Makes $2^1/_2$ dozen.

HOLIDAY DATE BALLS

An unbaked version of this delicious cookie that we used for years was called "Chinese Chews" and included crackled rice cereal. There was nothing "Chinese" about them, guess we just thought in the '50s and '60s that it sounded exotic! I like this version because it is not as sweet, but more like a delicious shortbread cookie with lots of dates and nuts. You may use a package of pressed dates, just cut them up with scissors or break into small bits with a cool hand.

$^3/_4$ cup butter
$^1/_4$ cup sugar
$2^1/_4$ cups brown sugar
3 eggs, beaten
$1^1/_2$ cups sifted flour

$^1/_2$ teaspoon salt
1 cup toasted pecans, chopped coarsely
1 cup chopped dates
Powdered sugar

Preheat oven to 375°F. With an electric mixer, cream butter and sugars together until fluffy. Add eggs, one at a time, beating after each. Mix flour and salt together, add to mixture, beat just until incorporated. Stir in pecans and dates, folding in gently so to not smear in the dates, just evenly distribute. Portion into 1½-inch balls, place on ungreased cookie sheet and bake for 25 minutes. While slightly warm, roll in powdered sugar and cool on wire rack. Makes 3 to 4 dozen.

Herschel C. Logan
Church in Winter (detail), early-mid 20th century, block print, WAM, gift of Samuel H. and Martha F. Logan, 2005.13.7

COOKIE CUTTER SUGAR COOKIES

This is an easy dough to prepare a day ahead, bake the cookies the next day, then frost the next. See tips on p. 202 for working with roll-out cookie dough.

3 cups flour
1 teaspoon baking powder
1 teaspoon baking soda
1/4 teaspoon salt
1 cup butter, chilled and cubed

2 eggs, room temperature
1 1/2 cups sugar
1 teaspoon vanilla extract
1/2 teaspoon almond extract

Combine flour, baking powder, baking soda and salt in a medium sized bowl, mixing well with a pastry blender. Cut in butter until the mixture is crumbly. In a separate bowl, slightly beat the eggs, add the sugar slowly and then the extracts. Continue to beat until it is light and fluffy. Add the egg mixture to the flour mixture, and stir by hand until well mixed and the dough forms. Wrap the dough in waxed paper or plastic wrap and refrigerate overnight, or for at least 1 hour.

Preheat oven to 375°F and prepare two heavy bottomed baking sheets with parchment paper or silicone liners. Work with only one-quarter of the dough at a time, and roll out with rolling pin on a lightly floured surface. Cut out shapes using cookie cutters, preferably large ones as the small ones result in a dried out cookie. Place cookies on the baking sheets, 1 inch apart. Bake one sheet at a time, placing on the middle rack of the oven, for 7 to 11 minutes or just until the edges begin to turn golden. Let set on sheet for 1 minute and remove to wire rack to cool. When cool, frost or decorate as desired … preferably with lots of little hands to help make good memories. Makes 2 to 3 dozen cookies.

SANTA CLAUS COOKIES

An old-fashioned favorite from the farmhouse kitchen of my mother, Joy Olson. First make the Cookie Cutter Sugar Cookie dough recipe above, then make them into Santa Claus cookies, with sweet little bellies.

1/2 cup raisins
1/2 cup dates
3/4 sugar

1/2 cup water
1 tablespoon flour
1/2 cup nuts

Begin by making the dough for the cookie cutter sugar cookies (see above). Cover and refrigerate for 1 hour or until dough is easy to handle. Prepare the filling by coarsely chopping the raisins and dates in a food processor or blender and then place in a small saucepan. Cover with water and sugar and simmer for 10 minutes, add flour and cook until thick. Remove from heat then stir in the nuts.

Preheat oven to 375°F. Roll out dough to 1/8-inch thickness, cut Santa Claus shapes with cookie cutter. Use a teaspoon filling for each stomach and cover with round piece of dough. Press sides with wet finger to seal. Bake on greased cookie sheet for 8 to 10 minutes. Cool and frost. Makes about 2 dozen potbellied Santas.

CROWN JEWELS

What fun it is to make these with the junior chefs in your home.

1 (12-ounce) package white chocolate chips
1 1/4 cups oat cereal (prefer Cheerios)
1/2 cup cashews, coarsely chopped

1/2 cup dried fruit pieces (prefer Sunmade Triple Trio)
1/2 cup dried cranberries

Heat white chocolate in top of double boiler over medium heat, stir until melted. Add cereal, cashews and fruit. Drop by heaping teaspoons onto wax paper or into mini-muffin cups. Cool. Makes 24.

EASY PRALINES

This recipe is unique because even people who think they cannot make candy have success with this recipe. Made in the microwave, these pralines are very good and easy, but if in doubt use a candy thermometer to ensure that mixture reaches a softball stage of 234° to 240°F.

1 cup whipping cream
1 (16-ounce) package light brown sugar
Pinch cream of tartar
Pinch salt

2 cups pecans
1/4 cup butter
1 teaspoon vanilla extract

Toast pecans in a 350°F oven for about 10 minutes, turning frequently so they do not burn, but enough to lightly toast. Combine cream and brown sugar in a large microwave-safe mixing bowl and mix well; add cream of tartar and salt. Microwave on high power for 7 minutes, stir. Add butter to cream mixture, stir quickly until butter is melted and microwave on high for 7 minutes longer. Stir vigorously and add vanilla and pecans. Quickly turn out by teaspoonfuls onto baking sheet lined with waxed paper. Let stand until set. Makes 12 pralines.

MICROWAVE PEANUT BRITTLE

1 cup sugar
1/2 cup light corn syrup
1/8 teaspoon salt
1 cup raw peanuts

1 teaspoon butter
1 teaspoon vanilla extract
1 teaspoon baking soda

Combine sugar, corn syrup, salt and peanuts in a medium sized glass bowl, and cook in the microwave for 2 minutes on 100% power (high). Stir, and then cook on high for 8 minutes more, until the mixture turns a light golden color. Add butter and vanilla, and cook 1 more minute on high. Stir in baking soda, and pour mixture onto a greased baking sheet. Spread to desired thickness, working quickly. Cool and break into pieces. Store in a tightly sealed container. Makes about 2 dozen pieces.

CARAMEL POPPYCORN CRUNCH

2 quarts popped popcorn
1 1/3 cups pecans
2/3 cup almonds
1/2 to 1/4 cup shredded coconut

1 1/3 cups sugar
1 cup butter or margarine
2 cups light syrup
1 teaspoon vanilla extract

Mix popcorn, nuts and coconut on cookie sheet. Combine sugar, butter, and syrup in medium saucepan; bring to a boil over medium heat, stir constantly for 10 to 15 minutes until mixture turns a light caramel color. Remove from heat, stir in vanilla and pour over popcorn mixture. Mix to coat well. Spread to dry. Break apart and store in airtight containers.

Over the years Lee has become accustomed to snack mixes I would make up for road trips. A family legend is the time I put some dry dog treats in a paper bag in front of the truck when Todd and Lee were taking our dog along to a horse show. Didn't think I needed to label it, and only after several handfuls did Lee mention that it was a little dry and chewy! So I close with this popcorn mix which could have been in that bag, and dedicate this book with gratitude to my family and friends who have weathered my many explorations in the kitchen, intentional or not. Here's to many good memories and more wonderful times around your tables.

With love and joy in the kitchen, Carlene

And Lee ... be careful what you eat out of paper bags.

A FEW FAVORITE THINGS

Appetizers

Commercially made frozen hors d'oeuvres; The Perfect Bite company's *Pastry Kiss* line, particularly the Caramelized Onion & Feta. 12-pack for $11.95 www.theperfectbiteco.com

Sumac and Za'atar (both .95 cents/ounce) available at The Spice Merchant, 1308 E. Douglas, Wichita, KS (316.263.4121) or *Penzeys Spices* online at www.penzeys.com

Breads and Rolls

Sourdough Bread Starter Culture, $9.50 from *Southern Things Inc.* Online at www.amazon.com

Vegetables and Sides

Stone-ground traditional grits are hard to find on supermarket shelves, but here are some mills that will ship. *Adams Milling Co*, Dothan, Ala. (800.239.4233); old-fashioned whole heart white and yellow grits. *Anson Mills*, Columbia and Charleston, S.C. www.ansonmills.com or (803.467.4122); white and yellow quick and Antebellum-style coarse grits. *Lakeside Mills*, Spindale, N.C., www.lakesidemills.com or (828.286.4866); country-style white grits. *Nora Mill Granary*, Helen, Ga., www.noramill.com or (800.927.2375); "Georgia ice cream" white speckled grits or "Dixie ice cream" yellow speckled grits.

Cookies, Bars and Brownies

Vollrath Cookie Sheet (14 x 17), $19.95, item #895200, *Broadway Panhandler* (800.266.5927) www.broadwaypanhandler.com

Buffalo cookie cutter ($1.25) and other Kansas shapes in a set ($8.95) available at the *Kansas Heritage Center shop* (620.227.1616) PO Box 1207, Dodge City KS 67801-1207, www.ksheritagestore.org

Pies and Tarts

Perfection Strips ($8 for three), Country Kitchen SweetArt (800.497.3927) www.countrykitchensa.com

BIBLIOGRAPHY

Angier, Natalie (2002, May 28). "Cooking and How It Slew the Beast ..." *New York Times*.

Beard, James (1972). *American Cookery*. Boston, MA: Little Brown and Company.

Cunningham, Marion (2003). *Lost Recipes: Meals to Share with Friends and Family*. New York City: Alfred Knopf.

Davis, Mitchell (2006). *Kitchen Sense*. New York: Clarkson Potter.

Editors of Cook's Illustrated (2004). *The New Best Recipe*. Brookline, MA: America's Test Kitchen.

Editors of Cook's Illustrated (2006). *The Best Light Recipe*. Brookline, MA: America's Test Kitchen.

Guthrie, Jane (1994). *A Kansas City Christmas Cookbook*. Kansas City, MO: Two Lane Press.

Jenkins, Virginia S. (2000). *Bananas: An American History*. Washington DC: Smithsonian Institution Press.

The Junior League of Wichita (1973). *Sunflower Sampler*. Wichita, KS: Author.

The Junior League of Kansas City, Missouri (1984). *Beyond Parsley, 2nd ed.* Kansas City, MO: Author.

The Junior League of Little Rock (1983). *Traditions: A Taste of the Good Life*. Little Rock, AR: Author.

Pope, Julie A. (2005, Summer). "The White House Called Red Rocks." *Kansas Heritage*, p. 16 – 22.

Rather, Rebecca (2004). *The Pastry Queen*. Berkley, CA: Ten Speed Press.

Rosso, Julle and Lukins, Shelia (1979). *The Silver Palate Cookbook*. New York City: Workman Publishing Company.

Smith, Andrew F. (2002). *Peanuts: The Illustrious History of the Goober Pea*. Chicago: University of Illinois Press.

Spears, Ruth (1986). *The Victorian Sampler Tea Room Cookbook*. Olathe, KS: Cookbook Publishers.

Stumpe, Joe (2003, June 4). "Wichita's Signature Salad." *The Wichita Eagle*, p. 1C.

Sweet, Frederick. (1966). *Miss Mary Cassatt: Impressionist from Pennsylvania*. Norman, OK; University of Oklahoma Press.

A Word of Thanks

Thank you for purchasing this book, and in doing so, supporting the Wichita Art Museum. Throughout the years, The Friends have sponsored luncheons, lectures, travel, receptions and holiday events. *Artfully Done: Across Generations* is an outgrowth of the many entertaining times Carlene and her friends had in preparing food for some of the Friends activities. This is a book to savor with its fascinating recipes, art, and anecdotes. It tastefully represents the Wichita metropolitan community.

To those of you who gave recipes, art, encouragement, enthusiasm, and whatever else was needed, the Friends thank you with their collective hearts knowing that the whole is greater than the parts. When Carlene blessed us with her talents and gave her blessing to Paula Varner's cookbook idea, RoxAnn had the vision and courage to see the potential for the museum and the community. To this was joined the creative energies of Stephen Gleissner and Kirk Eck. Gathering family and friends, many worked with RoxAnn to complete the book. To each of you we are grateful for your contribution in the company of so many friends.

All proceeds from the sale of *Artfully Done* support The Friends' Endowment and benefits the crown jewel of Wichita - the Wichita Art Museum. So to all who contributed, to the Banks family and all who purchased, thank you. We hope that you find ideas for good food and hospitality for those in your life.

Bon appetite, bon art!
Mary Ellen Joyner, Chairperson
Friends of the Wichita Art Museum, Inc. (FWAM)

ACKNOWLEDGMENTS

Honorary Project Chairman:
Paula Varner

Recipe Editing:
Chef Anne-marie Ramo

Cookbook Marketing Co-chairs:
Patty Bennett
Joan Seaton

Cookbook Production:
RoxAnn Dicker

2008-2009 FWAM Cookbook Committee:

Joy Archer
Susan Arnold
Mary Ellen Barrier
Alta Brock
Nancy Conover
Brian Cunningham
Karla Fazio
Charla Felt
Marie Gillespie
Joyce Haynes
Sharon Heiman
Carol Jones
Mary Ellen Joyner
Connie Kendall

Susan Koslowsky
Eleanor Lucas
Anita Lysell
Libbey Merritt
Dee Miller
Kathie Molamphy
LuAnne Neely
Pam Porvaznik
Adriene Rathbun
Barbara Rensner
Joan Schulz
Carolyn Skaer
Vicki Skaer
Jean Trumpp
Paula Varner
Susan Wilhite
Leslie Wilson

Proofreading:
Joy Archer
Susan Arnold
Gary Barnhart
Alta Brock
Marie Gillespie
Carol Jones
Mary Ellen Joyner
Anita Lysell
Kathie Molamphy
Pam Porvaznik
Barbara Rensner
Joan Seaton
Joan Schulz
Paula Varner
Leslie Wilson

The Friends of the Wichita Art Museum, Inc. is a non-profit organization supporting the Museum by raising funds for art acquisitions, exhibitions, and education. During an almost 50-year history, the Friends established and supported the Docent Program, organized and operated a Gift Shop, a Sales-Rental Gallery, a Restaurant, and the Friend's Library. Also, the Friends initiated the Mobile Gallery traveling in a nine-country area and originated a major source of funding, the Annual Art, Book and Craft Fair.

As part of the Museum's 50th Anniversary celebration the Friends established an Endowment Fund to support art acquisition, the Howard Wooden Lecture Series, and the Library. The Murdock Society, a committee of the Friends, is a generous supporter of this endowment. This fund has becocme vital to the well-being of the museum. More than 339 works of art have been acquired with funds contributed by the Friends.

Michele Banks
Carlene's Kitchen, 2007,
from the artist's collection

Art Index THE WICHITA ART MUSEUM

RECIPES FROM CARLENE BANKS AND FRIENDS

Bonnie Aeschliman
Anna Anderson
Cindy Banks
Michele Banks
Todd Banks
Sen. Nancy Landon
    Kassebaum Baker
Mary Ellen Barrier
Shirley Beggs
Beth Boerger
Linda Boerger
Barry Bradley
Linda Ade Brand
Robert Brand
Amy Cunningham
Alta DeVore
RoxAnn Banks Dicker

Eisenhower Library Archives
Valerie Edwards
Analee Etheredge
Debbie Deuser
Darla Farha
Ann Garvey
Jean Gaunt
Stephen Giunta
Stephen Gleissner
Kathyrn Gleissner
Genevieve Gordon
Jeanne Harter Gordon
Teresa Covacevich Grana
Linda Hager
Joyce Haynes
Bev Hoover
Anita Jones

Carol Jones
Mary Ellen Joyner
Judy Just
Barbara Kieffer
Pamela D. Kingsbury
Diane C. Lewis
Becky Middleton
Jayne Milburn
Betty Minkler
Louise Murdock
Tom Otterness
Barbara Pearce
June Peugh
Marlene Phillips
Vincent Price
Anne-marie Ramo
Barbara Rensner

Becky Ritchey
Karen Root
Alfrieda Sandzen
Katherine Walker Schlageck
Gov. Kathleen Sebelius
Joan Schulz
Charles K. Steiner
Joe Stumpe
Pat Thiessen
Vicky Tiahrt
Joumana Toubia
Randa Toubia
Dora Timmerman
Marni & Rich Vliet
Martie Walker
Melva Webster
Susan Wilhite

TO ORDER ADDITIONAL BOOKS,

Artfully Done Cookbook
Friends of the Wichita Art Museum, Inc (FWAM)
1400 W. Museum Blvd.; Wichita, KS 67203
316.268.4936
Make checks payable to the Friends of the Wichita Art Museum.
For credit card orders please fax 316.268.4980 or visit the website at
www.artfullydonecookbook.com